Northern Ireland a generation after Good Friday

Manchester University Press

Northern Ireland a generation after Good Friday

Lost futures and new horizons in the 'long peace'

Colin Coulter, Niall Gilmartin,
Katy Hayward and Peter Shirlow

MANCHESTER UNIVERSITY PRESS

Copyright © Colin Coulter, Niall Gilmartin,
Katy Hayward and Peter Shirlow 2021

The right of Colin Coulter, Niall Gilmartin,
Katy Hayward, Peter Shirlow to be identified as the authors
of this work has been asserted by them in accordance
with the Copyright, Designs and Patents Act 1988.

Published by Manchester University Press
Oxford Road, Manchester M13 9PL

www.manchesteruniversitypress.co.uk

British Library Cataloguing-in-Publication Data
A catalogue record for this book is available from
the British Library

ISBN 978 1 5261 3926 9 hardback
ISBN 978 1 5261 3928 3 paperback

First published 2021

The publisher has no responsibility for the persistence
or accuracy of URLs for any external or third-party internet
websites referred to in this book, and does not guarantee
that any content on such websites is, or will remain,
accurate or appropriate.

Typeset by
Servis Filmsetting Ltd, Stockport, Cheshire

Contents

List of figures	vi
Acknowledgments	viii
Northern Ireland a generation after Good Friday: an introduction	1
1 From the 'long war' to the 'long peace': Northern Ireland since the Good Friday Agreement	32
2 Fragmented, staggered and inept: addressing the legacy of the Troubles	70
3 Conflict-related prisoners: the perpetual trap of criminalisation	104
4 Ghosts of our lives: spectres of the past in recent Northern Irish cinema and television	129
5 More than two communities: those who are both, neither, other, and next	164
6 Rethinking the post-conflict narrative: women and the promise of peace in the 'new' Northern Ireland	204
7 The political economy of peace in Northern Ireland: social class in an age of boom and bust	245
8 Changed utterly? Northern Ireland's paralysis in a world of uncertainty	275
Index	297

Figures

Figure 5.1	Religious identification by age group. Source: *Labour Force Survey* (2019)	170
Figure 5.2	Regular church attendance (% attending 2+ times per month). Source: *Northern Ireland Life and Times Survey*	170
Figure 5.3	National identity and religion (%). Source: *NI Life and Times Survey* (2019)	172
Figure 5.4	Intention to vote in a referendum on Irish unification, by religion. Source: *Northern Ireland Life and Times Survey* (2019)	172
Figure 5.5	Political identity and religious identity. Source: *Northern Ireland Life and Times Survey* (2019)	174
Figure 5.6	Do you see yourself as British or Irish? (%). Source: *Northern Ireland Life and Times Survey* (2019)	177
Figure 5.7	National identity by religion (2007, 2012, 2019). Source: *Northern Ireland Life and Times Survey*	178
Figure 5.8	National identity and political identity. Source: *Northern Ireland Life and Times Survey* (2018)	178
Figure 5.9	Summary of census data (2011) comparison of Northern Ireland, rest of UK and Ireland	183
Figure 5.10	Levels of net migration in Northern Ireland, July 2000–June 2001 to July 2018–June 2019. Source: *NI Statistics and Research Agency* (2019)	184
Figure 5.11	'Migrant workers are generally good for Northern Ireland's economy', by age. Source: *NI Life and Times Survey* (2017)	185
Figure 5.12	Racist incidents and crimes recorded by the PSNI, July 2004–July 2020. Source: *Police Service of Northern Ireland*	187

Figure 5.13 What would you prefer Northern Ireland's long-term future to be? (% of total respondents) *Source: Northern Ireland Life and Times Survey*   191

Figure 5.14 Those defining themselves as neither unionist nor nationalist (% of total respondents). *Source: Northern Ireland Life and Times Survey*   192

Acknowledgments

The authors wish to acknowledge the generous support offered by both Maynooth University and the National University of Ireland in the form of grants to facilitate the publication of this book. We would also like to thank Tony Mason, Jonathan de Peyer, Rob Byron, Karen Nash and Lucy Burns at MUP for their help in bringing this project to completion.

Northern Ireland a generation after Good Friday: an introduction

Peace in the plural

In the period since the end of the Cold War, there have been multiple attempts to introduce the institutions of 'consociational' governance in various settings where ethno-cultural divisions have given rise to sustained political violence. The context in which this experiment in cross-communal power-sharing is most frequently identified as having worked best is, of course, Northern Ireland.[1] The status of the Good Friday Agreement (hereafter GFA) as 'the brightest star in the new consociational universe'[2] was underlined at a gathering of the great and the good in Queen's University Belfast held on 10 April 2018 to mark the twentieth anniversary of the deal. Flanked by the former British and Irish premiers Tony Blair and Bertie Ahern, as well as former American Senator George Mitchell, who had chaired the talks process, Bill Clinton told a receptive audience in the Whitla Hall that the design of the Northern Irish peace settlement had been crafted with sufficient skill to withstand the human error of those politicians entrusted with putting it into practice. The GFA, the former US President insisted, should be acknowledged as no less than

> the work of genius that's applicable if you care at all about preserving democracy. It called for real democracy, majority rule [sic],[3] minority rights, individual rights, the rule of law, the end of violence, shared political decision-making, shared economic benefits. Shared special relations.[4]

The lavish praise, often shading into hyperbole, that has perennially characterised international commentary on the Northern Irish peace process has, it should be said, no little basis in fact. Since the advent of the GFA, after all, those incidents of politically motivated violence that were once an everyday reality of life in Northern Ireland have, thankfully, become more and more rare. According to one estimate, at the time of its twentieth anniversary there were approximately 2,400 Northern Irish people alive and well who would have been long since cold in the grave had the peace deal never materialised.[5] It is important to mark at the very outset, then, that the single greatest achievement of the GFA has been the (almost complete) 'removal of the gun from Irish politics'.[6]

While the praise that international commentators have frequently heaped on the Northern Irish political settlement has some grounding in fact, it is also a product of the flattering distortions that can arise when viewing events from the safety of a comfortable distance. What sometimes appears to people living elsewhere as an essentially seamless transition to peace has in reality been a remarkably arduous process that has entailed seemingly endless rounds of renegotiation and that has seen the political institutions at Stormont suspended on no fewer than five occasions. The most recent of these suspensions occurred in January 2017, when a visibly ailing Martin McGuinness announced that Sinn Féin was withdrawing from the power-sharing executive. It would take three years, and several fruitless rounds of talks, before the Stormont institutions would begin to function again. The decision of republicans to collapse the Executive meant that when the twentieth anniversary of the GFA came around, the devolved institutions that were supposed to be its principal achievement remained in cold storage. It was hardly surprising, then, that an event such as that hosted in Queen's University Belfast – originally conceived no doubt as a star-studded celebration of two decades of the peace deal – would in the end have a distinctly elegiac tone.

The somewhat deflated mood that marked proceedings in the Whitla Hall invites us to acknowledge that the political settlement in Northern Ireland is in fact rather more complex and contradictory than international commentators are often willing to allow. While convenience dictates that we often speak of the Northern Irish 'peace *process*', there is perhaps a case for talking in other, more plural terms instead. There are, at the very least, two distinct 'peace *processes*' in Northern Ireland that are connected in all manner of ways but have, nonetheless, never quite synchronised. There is, on the one hand, the peace process that has been nurtured at a local level which often draws upon various forms of public money, from multiple jurisdictions, but which exists largely in spaces beyond, or on the margins of, formal politics and the state. As we document in Chapter 3, the last generation has seen the creation of literally thousands of grassroots projects that have been initiated and sustained by, among others, former combatants, women's organisations, faith groups, artists of various stripes, loyalist and republican bands, and so forth. These initiatives have constituted invaluable resources that have promoted inter-community reconciliation, restorative justice and new models of social economy.[7] They have also highlighted and challenged the sectarianism, racism and misogyny that remain doleful features of contemporary Northern Irish society. While the multiple successes that have occurred in the realm of what we might term the 'vernacular peace process' have been genuinely transformative, they have nonetheless been all but overlooked in mainstream commentary. Influential figures operating within the charmed circle that connects politics, the media and academia often seem loath to acknowledge the positive leadership and agency that have facilitated so much important peace-building at ground level. In particular, a seemingly endless preoccupation with the nefarious activities of the 'men of violence', past and present, has served to airbrush out of the picture the often critical contribution to conflict resolution made by men and women who have long since left their former lives as paramilitaries behind.

There is also, and on the other hand, that more familiar version of the peace process that operates rather more clearly in the public eye and which tends to draw most of the attention, and almost all the plaudits. This modality exists at the level of 'high politics', and has been shaped by those public events most likely to spark interest among commentators both at home and abroad. As elsewhere, media coverage of Northern Irish political life tends to operate within a familiar circuit of negotiations, elections and summits, enlivened by the occasional salacious instance of personal or financial scandal. The course of what we might choose to term the 'official peace process' has, as we document in detail in the next chapter, proved to be somewhat less than smooth. Those endless political squabbles and frequent parliamentary suspensions that have defined the era of restored devolution seem to have had little impact, however, on the disposition of those influential opinion makers who often frame international commentary on Northern Ireland. This myopia has ensured that the predominantly glowing appraisals of the political progress assumed to have been made in the six counties provided by global political players often diverge dramatically from everyday realities on the ground. Indeed, as Siobhán Fenton has observed, there are few ordinary people who actually live in the region who would even begin to recognise the 'rosy image' of the Northern Irish peace process that often appears in the international media.[8] The propensity to overstate the progress made in Northern Ireland stems in part from the influence of a specific constellation of perspectives on conflict resolution, drawn from several schools of international relations,[9] that has gained currency in elite circles over recent decades and which was clearly inscribed in the principles and provisions of the GFA. That those powerful political figures in Washington, London, Brussels and Dublin who routinely pass judgement on Northern Irish political life so often prove blind to its many reversals and dysfunctions owes a great deal to their adherence to certain understandings of the nature of war and peace that have almost assumed the status of orthodoxies in recent times. In the discussion that follows, we will draw out three of these pervasive ideological assumptions for closer examination.

A time of war, a time of peace[10]

One of the axioms common to both the 'realist' and 'liberal' schools of international relations is a particular temporal understanding of the nature of war and peace.[11] From both influential perspectives, periods of conflict are regarded as aberrations that are foreclosed by the political settlements that bring hostilities to an end. In plain terms, wars come to an end and are replaced by peace; the two play out in passages of time that are deemed, by definition, to be essentially mutually exclusive. This intuitively reasonable temporalisation of conflict and its resolution would find expression in the terms of the GFA. The text of the deal opens with an explicit acknowledgement that the Troubles entailed many 'tragedies' that have 'left a deep and profoundly regrettable legacy of suffering'.[12] It soon becomes apparent, however, that those who signed the GFA were unwilling or unable to deal with the multiple traumas arising from a quarter-century of political violence. The myriad atrocities and fatalities that marked the Troubles are consigned in the document to 'the past', a discrete historical period evidently assumed to be separated by a firewall from that under construction in a society intent on making 'a fresh start'.[13]

The ambition that the GFA would allow Northern Ireland to 'move on' would, of course, be frustrated with some regularity by the complex practicalities associated with 'real-world' peace-building. While mainstream models of conflict resolution tend to construct war and peace as distinct historical periods, those sentiments, grievances and actors that initiate and sustain hostilities often prove deeply reluctant to respect such neat temporalisations. By their very nature, political conflicts tend to have complex afterlives, and that has certainly proved true in the case of Northern Ireland. The formal ending of the Troubles served little, inevitably, to alleviate the widespread suffering of those who were the victims of violence, or indeed its agents. Even more than two decades after the signing of the GFA, Northern Ireland clearly bears the scars of a conflict often presumed to be 'over'. It is estimated that two in five people in the region experienced some direct form of trauma during the Troubles, that one in seven currently suffer from mental illness as a direct result, and that one in eleven display the symptoms of post-traumatic stress disorder.[14] The legacy of the conflict has had an impact not merely on the generation who lived through it but also on the one that came of age after it had ostensibly come to an end. Perhaps as many as one in five young people in Northern

Ireland have grown up in households where at least one parent has been a victim or agent of violence.[15] This has led to considerable speculation that there exist forms of intergenerational trauma[16] that may go some way to explain the relatively high incidence of suicide, especially among young people, in the six counties. Indeed, more people have died at their own hand since the GFA – in excess of 5,000 in total – than lost their lives during the Troubles.[17] This sobering statistic might prompt the suspicion, to which we return later, that the advent of the Northern Irish peace process has not meant that violence has ended but rather that it has come to assume other, and more varied, forms.

It is worth remembering, though, that those modes of violence that were the hallmark of a past that often felt like war have persisted into a present that even now does not entirely feel like peace. The structures of paramilitary organisations mostly remain intact and some continue to represent a not insignificant threat to the political equilibrium of Northern Ireland. That recalcitrant minority that split from the mainstream republican movement in the early years of the peace process continue to claim the moral right to wage 'armed struggle' against the British state. Indeed, in the period since the latest restoration of the Stormont institutions, in January 2020, dissident republicans have sought to widen their field of operation, directing threats both verbal and physical towards a Sinn Féin leadership that has recently joined the public drive to draw more recruits, especially from the nationalist community, into a local police force that has been substantially reformed during the peace process.[18] In addition, more than a quarter-century after they called their ceasefires, there are some within loyalist groupings intent on using their muscle to exercise influence and maintain substantial criminal empires, creating yet more pressures in working-class Protestant communities that are among the poorest in Northern Ireland.[19]

While most forms of paramilitary violence have declined dramatically during the peace process, the modes of vigilante 'justice' that were prevalent during the Troubles remain a baleful facet of contemporary Northern Irish society. Since the signing of the GFA, there have been more than 4,000 punishment attacks carried out by paramilitaries, almost exclusively in those poor neighbourhoods that were previously at the epicentre of the conflict.[20] These assaults have increased sharply in the last few years and many have been targeted at youngsters involved, as suppliers or customers, in the burgeoning illegal drugs trade that has emerged since the Troubles drew finally to a close.[21] While those modes of paramilitarism that have survived the end of the conflict have often impacted with especial gravity on younger people, they have at the same time exercised a tangible appeal for at least some members of the 'peace generation'. At times, there appears to be a discernible thread of 'Troubles nostalgia' running through

Northern Irish society.²² In the main, this tends to assume entirely innocent forms of expression. The gentle longing for the utopian possibilities that accompanied the paramilitary ceasefires dramatised poignantly in the hit television series *Derry Girls* represents – as we explain in Chapter 4 – an especially prominent and charming case in point. The siren call of Northern Ireland's troubled recent past tends also, however, to assume rather more sinister guises. This allure is captured vividly in *The Firestarters*, Jan Carson's superb magic realist evocation of a Belfast still simmering in the febrile atmosphere summoned by the 'flags protests'.²³ Many of the younger characters in the novel seem resentful at having 'missed out' on the Troubles, and 'they talk of the loud violence their parents knew, as if it is a kind of birthright denied to them'.²⁴

These dark forms of nostalgia are not, alas, restricted to the world of literary fiction. The ongoing appeal of forms of paramilitarism presumed to have been consigned to Northern Ireland's tortured recent past was illustrated clearly in two deaths that occurred within a few weeks of one another in early 2019. In January that year, Ian Ogle was beaten and stabbed eleven times near his home in east Belfast by a gang of loyalists seeking revenge for his association with a fairly commonplace bar-room altercation. Two of the first men arrested for that brutal murder were aged 21 and 22, respectively, and hence would have been born around the time of the signing of the GFA.²⁵ A similar narrative detail would feature in a rather more high-profile killing that occurred in Derry three months later. On 18 April 2019, Lyra McKee was shot dead as she observed rioting in the Creggan district sparked by police raids in advance of a controversial dissident republican Easter commemoration. The author and journalist had written powerfully about the plight of those, like herself, who had come of age after the GFA but had yet to reap the rewards promised by the peace process. In a perverted twist of fate, it would emerge that the dissident republican allegedly responsible for her death was only 18 years old at the time,²⁶ and hence a fellow member of a generation that McKee had christened the 'ceasefire babies'.²⁷

That some of those not even born when the pivotal paramilitary cessations were called in the mid-1990s may have come to commit acts of violence reminiscent of the dark days of the Troubles underlines that conflicts tend to cast long shadows indeed.²⁸ Those who designed the GFA evidently shared the assumption familiar from orthodox approaches to conflict resolution that Northern Ireland's violent recent past could be subject to a moment of 'cauterisation'²⁹ taken to signal the advent of peace in the region. This blinkered commitment to making a 'fresh start' would, unfortunately, ensure that the political settlement would time and again prove entirely unable to deal adequately with the legacies of a quarter-century of low-intensity warfare. There have, admittedly, been a series of major tribunals that have scrutinised key atrocities during the Troubles – most notably, the Saville Inquiry into the deaths of fourteen civilians in Derry at the hands of British paratroopers in January 1972 – and two specialist police bodies have been established to investigate unsolved murders from the period, although with pitifully poor success rates in both cases.[30] However, as we explore in Chapter 2, the absence of a genuinely comprehensive 'truth and reconciliation' process has meant that there remain many people in Northern Ireland who still do not know how, and at whose hand, their loved ones came to be killed, even after all this time. The plight of those who lost friends and relatives during the Troubles has been worsened further by the long-running disagreements among the Northern Irish political parties as to how to make amends to victims. As far back as January 2009, an official commission of inquiry published its recommendations, which included the payment of compensation to close relatives of people who died in the conflict. Ongoing wrangles over who qualifies as a 'victim' of the Troubles would ensure that the proposals contained in the Eames–Bradley Report[31] were never implemented. A comparable scheme would, however, come close on the heels of the *New Decade, New Approach* agreement that facilitated the restoration of the Stormont institutions. In late January 2020, the then Northern Ireland Minister, Julian Smith, announced that there was to be annual financial assistance for those who had suffered serious injuries during the Troubles, although in this instance it would be restricted to those 'injured through no fault of their own'.[32] The introduction of the new scheme would, however, be delayed by ongoing rows between the governments in London and Belfast over who was to foot the bill, and within the Stormont Executive over who precisely was to be considered a 'victim'. In August 2020, the High Court in Belfast ruled that the Stormont Executive was acting unlawfully in its failure to move to the provision of pensions for victims of the Troubles.[33] While Justice McAlinden's ruling has been seen widely as removing the final barrier to financial support for those injured during the conflict, it remains unclear when precisely the scheme might come, finally, to fruition.

The version of peace that has evolved in Northern Ireland also seems unable to deal with the various issues associated with paramilitaries both past and present. As we document in Chapter 3, those political prisoners that were released under the terms of the GFA have often been barred from taking certain forms of paid employment, an exclusion that has compounded the economic and emotional challenges facing former combatants and that has encouraged some to pursue criminal careers. The questionable handling of the prisoners issue has, then, contributed to the conditions that have allowed the vestiges of paramilitarism to survive the putative end of the conflict. In late 2015, the local political parties reached a revised political agreement that once again promised 'a fresh start' for Northern Irish society. While this political deal made ambitious promises about rooting out once and for all the paramilitary influence that remains in many working-class communities, these pledges show little sign of materialising. In particular, certain unionist politicians have at times seemed rather too relaxed about the large sums of public money that continue to be channelled towards civil society organisations with links to loyalist paramilitary groupings, some of which remain engaged in various forms of criminality, and all of which were presumed to have agreed to leave the stage more than a quarter-century ago.[34]

The particular understanding of the nature of conflict resolution that was inscribed in the GFA has, therefore, served to frustrate the progress made during the Northern Irish peace process. In particular, the assumption that conflicts have definitive ends has ensured that attempts to deal with the manifold legacies of the Troubles have often proved pitifully inadequate. It makes little sense to attempt to demarcate neatly the 'past' in a society where the violence of yesteryear continues to define and deform what passes for the 'present'.[35] That Northern Ireland continues to be haunted by a conflict that was supposedly 'over' a generation ago is readily apparent in the mental illness of those bereaved, the inherited trauma of many of their children, and the persistence of a certain undercurrent of desire to return to the days when the region was synonymous with politically motivated violence. The political settlement that obtains in the six counties is, then, in the terminology of political theorists like Johan Galtung[36] and John-Paul Lederach,[37] an essentially 'negative' one. In other words, while Northern Ireland is certainly no longer at war, it does not even now seem to be a society that is entirely at peace with itself.

Hierarchies of victims

A further commonality between the influential 'realist' and 'liberal' schools of international relations is that both tend to advance a distinctly narrow understanding of what constitutes war and peace.[38] In essence, conflicts are understood to centre upon the armed struggles between states and those unofficial agencies that strive to buttress their power or, rather more commonly, to challenge their authority or perhaps even question their very existence. The persistence of war is documented in the death toll among combatants and civilians arising from these specific moments of political violence, while the advent of peace is signalled when the number of fatalities falls towards what is understood as an 'acceptable level'.[39] There is, once again, a certain logic in this familiar understanding of what constitutes the boundaries between war and peace. As we noted earlier, the most convincing evidence routinely produced to establish the credentials of Northern Ireland as a genuinely 'post-conflict' society is the sharp decline in the death toll arising from the activities of state and non-state combatants over the last generation. There remain, nonetheless, certain problems with the particular, influential model of war and peace that has tended to frame the political evolution that has occurred since the end of the Troubles.[40] Most importantly, the preoccupation with the military campaigns maintained by competing and, at times, colluding state and paramilitary forces of various stripes has served to obscure the existence of other forms of violence that were widespread during the years of conflict in Northern Ireland and which have, if anything, become even more prevalent since that dark period ostensibly drew to a close.

As Susan McKay has observed, the narrow definition of 'political violence' prevalent during the Troubles meant that those forms directed against women that were widespread throughout the period were almost entirely overlooked.[41] Indeed, it is telling that while a vast literature would emerge to document the Northern Irish conflict, the first major study of 'domestic abuse' in the six counties would not appear until 1993, the year it became public knowledge that peace might, finally, be at hand. In their pathbreaking study, Monica McWilliams and Joan McKiernan[42] noted that although violence against women was considered a 'rare occurrence' at the time, all available evidence suggested otherwise. In a twelve-month period between 1991 and 1992, for instance, the Royal Ulster Constabulary (RUC) recorded some 2,800 incidents where women were assaulted by their male partners. These figures will undoubtedly have understated vastly the true level of 'domestic violence' in Northern Ireland, not least because women in republican districts were especially reticent about reporting such incidents to the authorities. While police statistics remain far from entirely reliable, the trends mapped out in recent official reports are so dramatic that it seems reasonable to assume that the era of purported peace has in fact seen a sharp rise in the number of attacks directed against women. In the period between 2004/05 and 2019/20, for example, the annual number of incidents of 'domestic abuse' in Northern Ireland rose from 20,959 to 32,127.[43] By way of comparison, the highest level of assaults with a 'sectarian' motivation in any given year during that time frame was 1,840 and by the end of the period the number of such attacks had fallen to 879.[44] At present, there are, therefore, around 37 acts of violence committed by men against women in Northern Ireland for every one that entails unionists or nationalists assaulting one another. This remarkable disparity suggests that those who exercise political influence in the region, both from within and without, have rather skewed priorities. While politicians at home and abroad have remained very clearly, and entirely understandably, concerned with those vastly diminished forms of sectarian conflict that have persisted in the era of the peace process, there seems to be much less urgency in combating what is now evidently the rather more serious political problem of the seemingly ever-escalating levels of violence against women that have come to blight Northern Irish society since the formal end of the Troubles.

The preoccupation with the ethno-national tensions that are closely associated with Northern Ireland has at times overshadowed another form of violence that has become a lamentable feature of everyday life since the signing of the GFA. Over the last generation, the region has seen an influx of people from beyond 'these islands', with the 2004 enlargement of the EU signalling the arrival of a substantial number of eastern Europeans in particular. As we note in Chapter 5, the transition towards a more multicultural society in Northern Ireland has, as elsewhere, not been without its problems. In particular, those migrants who have moved predominantly into working-class unionist neighbourhoods in Belfast[45] have often been subjected to verbal and physical abuse, leading some commentators to claim that the city is the 'race hate capital of Europe'.[46] The data released by the Police Service of Northern Ireland (PSNI) indicate that there was a surge in racist attacks over recent years – dating, apparently, from the 'flags protests' that reached their peak in 2013 – which may now, hopefully, have abated. The most recent twelve-month period for which data are available, 2019/20, reveals that there were 890 recorded incidents of racially motivated violence in Northern Ireland, down from 1,096 in the previous statistical year.[47] While this figure is likely to underestimate seriously the true level of racist violence in a society that still has a relatively small immigrant population, it remains alarming nonetheless. It also suggests that the volume of racially motivated attacks in Northern Ireland currently outstrips those categorised by the authorities as 'sectarian' in motivation. Once again, this bleak development in the era of the peace process seems to have had little impact on the thinking of those who would celebrate the progress that the region has made during the peace process. Indeed, not only have political figures failed in many instances to take seriously the rise of racial prejudice in Northern Ireland, some have even opted to add petrol to the flames. Perhaps the most sinister case in point came in 2014, when the then First Minister Peter Robinson appeared to lend his support to an evangelical Protestant preacher who had expressed explicitly Islamophobic sentiment during a recent sermon captured on film. Reflecting on the controversy surrounding Pastor James McConnell, the senior unionist politician informed journalists that the only way that he personally would be prepared to trust Muslims would be by allowing them to 'go to the shops' for him.[48] These crass and inflammatory comments would prove instrumental in persuading the only member of the Northern Ireland Assembly from a minority racial background, Anna Lo of the Alliance Party, to bow out of public life for good.[49]

In their almost exclusive focus on the armed contests between state and non-state actors deemed to be at the heart of war, those perspectives that have come to exercise most influence over the field of international relations often appear blind to the significance of at least one further critical mode of violence always guaranteed to survive the transition to peacetime. Theorists such as Johan Galtung[50] and Iris Young[51] have noted that mainstream models of conflict resolution cannot accommodate those forms of structural violence and injustice, both material and symbolic, so ingrained in capitalist societies that they are almost taken for granted. In the language of Antonio Gramsci, those vast economic inequalities that exist during war and peace alike come to assume a certain 'common-sense' quality.[52] It is worth marking that what sparked the Northern Irish conflict was not the ambition of nationalists to live in a united Ireland but rather their understandable alienation at being required to live on the ledge of a UK where they were condemned to the status of perpetual second-class citizens when it came to, *inter alia*, the allocation of crucial resources such as jobs and houses.[53] Across the last half-century, the once enormous differences in the 'life chances' enjoyed, or endured, by members of the two principal communities in the six counties have largely evaporated. While nationalist communities remain over-represented among those with the highest incidence of multiple deprivation, the circumstances of Catholic and Protestant workers have over time moved towards 'equality of misery'.[54] This critical transformation of Northern Irish society was driven in part by rigorous fair-employment legislation and has come to be signified by the emergence of an enlarged and culturally confident nationalist middle class in the region. To take just one critical illustration, the majority of high-court judges in Northern Ireland now come from nationalist backgrounds, something that would have been unthinkable during the Troubles, when the involvement of (typically unionist) members of the judiciary in the strategy of 'criminalisation' rendered them 'legitimate targets' in the eyes of the republican movement.[55]

The evidence would, therefore, indicate that those historic economic disadvantages faced by the nationalist community that ignited the conflict in Northern Ireland have been mainly eliminated over time. Indeed, one estimate suggests that the distinction between 'Catholic' and 'Protestant' constitutes a variable that explains less than two per cent of the income inequalities that currently exist in the six counties.[56] While the economic disparities that once marked the sectarian divide in Northern Ireland have been all but ameliorated, those associated with social class have, if anything, become ever more pronounced over the course of the peace process. From the outset, a range of powerful players underlined that a permanent end to political violence would see a dramatic upturn in the Northern Irish economy.[57] As we explain in Chapter 7, these frequent promises of a 'peace dividend' would, however, simply fail to materialise. Northern Ireland has remained the site of a low-wage, low-output economy and those poor neighbourhoods that bore the brunt of the Troubles remain economically deprived to this day. That the vast inequalities associated with social class that existed during the Troubles would survive the end of the conflict owes much to certain predictable policy choices made over the last quarter-century. As Roger MacGinty[58] has noted, those models of peacemaking that have held sway over recent times have tended to be *liberal* when it comes to politics but *neoliberal* when it comes to economics. The relentless pursuit of free-market strategies during the peace process by devolved and direct-rule administrations alike has merely served to widen the already stark material inequalities that mark Northern Irish society. As with many other societies emerging from prolonged periods of conflict,[59] the experience of the 'neoliberal peace' introduced in Northern Ireland has been that those communities most in need of an improvement in their material circumstances have in fact fallen even further behind. One especially stark index of the enduring poverty that exists in the region is that in a twelve-month period in 2019/20, charitable organisations distributed some 45,008 food parcels, almost half of which went to children.[60] The increasingly manifest material inequalities that have attended the Northern Irish peace process have, predictably, had little bearing on the outlook of the local political elite. While the main political parties operating in the region are forever squabbling over the often minor, immaterial distinctions between the 'two communities' in Northern Ireland, they have been rather less exercised by the rather more substantial, material inequities that separate rich and poor in the six counties.

Those perspectives on international relations that have proved most persuasive in elite circles over recent decades tend, therefore, to advance a very particular understanding of war and peace that serves to obfuscate the multiple forms of violence that continue, and often proliferate, in societies that have, in principle, moved beyond conflict.[61] Contemporary Northern Irish society is blighted by escalating levels of structural and personal violence in the guise of attacks on women, assaults against migrants, and the food poverty that marks a disturbing recent addition to the already multiple forms of deprivation that scar the region. In the commentary of its many celebrants, there is of course scant mention of these new or renewed modes of conflict that have become a defining feature of the Northern Irish peace process. This ideological blind spot ensures that the paeans to the 'new Northern Ireland'[62] frequently provided by global political figures often bear only a passing resemblance to the realities of everyday life in the six counties.

'A dual ethnocracy'

A further ideological assumption that has guided international approaches to peace-building in recent times discloses itself clearly in the very specific design of the agreement at the heart of the Northern Irish political settlement. In several of the most pivotal conflict-resolution projects initiated since the end of the Cold War, the transition towards peace is often deemed to entail political elites striking deals that promise to protect the rights and identities of the communities they are presumed to represent. The substance of any stable political settlement requires, *inter alia*, the implementation of power-sharing at executive level, the introduction of weighed voting protocols in the legislature to preclude the return of majority rule, and the reform of the public sector to accommodate those previously excluded, as well as various instances of rights protection designed to defend the interests of minority groups in particular. The figure who originally devised this particular 'consociational' model of governance, Arend Lijphart,[63] counselled that it was not suited to societies like Northern Ireland that were mired in armed conflict. It would, nonetheless, be adopted as the broad template for the political deal widely assumed to have marked the end of the Troubles.[64]

While the GFA sought to forge ties across the Irish border and the Irish Sea, its principal concern, not unreasonably, was to heal the historically fraught relations between the two main ethno-national traditions that coexist within the bounds of the six counties. As Liam O'Dowd[65] has observed, the political deal signed on 10 April 1998 was designed to create a 'bi-communal or bi-national symmetry that recognised the integrity of two communities, two traditions or two identities, embedded in aspirations of parity of esteem and parity of treatment'. At the heart of the new arrangements were a power-sharing executive whose composition would be determined by the D'Hondt mechanism designed to ensure that the new government would be representative of both ethno-national collectivities, as well as a legislature that would require weighted majorities to guarantee that certain unspecified 'key decisions' would be reached on a 'cross-community basis'.[66]

The many influential admirers of the peace deal struck in Northern Ireland typically contest that the consocational arrangements at its centre simply reflect the brute realities of a society in which ethno-national affiliation represents the principal source of political aspiration and practice. In the words of perhaps the most prominent academic advocate of the GFA, Brendan O'Leary, the particular power-sharing form of government that the deal requires merely acknowledges that Northern Irish political culture is one in which 'voters typically make their party "choices" based on who they are, rather than what they think'.[67] The pragmatic model of conflict resolution that necessarily flows from such sardonic, some might say condescending, readings of what animates the plain folk of Northern Ireland may well of course have made sense at the moment when the GFA was signed. That does not necessarily mean, however, that the same remains true a generation down the line. At various points in the last couple of decades, those consociational arrangements at the centre of Northern Ireland's fêted peace deal have appeared less the solution to the long-standing political problems afflicting the region than the source of a whole series of new ones. While the structures of governance introduced under the GFA were often depicted as pragmatic recognition of the 'realities' of Northern Irish political life, over time they have come increasingly to represent fetters that frustrate the emergence of another set of rather more progressive political possibilities.[68]

While there are, as we noted earlier, at least some who came of age during the peace process who harbour a certain curious form of 'Troubles nostalgia', it is clear that the vast majority of their peers fail to share that enthusiasm. As we illustrate in Chapter 5, the evidence garnered from surveys of political opinion in Northern Ireland reveals the existence of a 'peace generation' whose members often have interests and identities – though not necessarily constitutional preferences – that are rather different to those of their parents. Growing up in an increasingly secular environment, the majority of Northern Irish youngsters express liberal attitudes on matters such as abortion and gay marriage that were taboo in the not-so-distant past. Those fortunate enough not to remember the Troubles also frequently seem rather less animated by constitutional concerns that have traditionally mapped the 'narrow ground' of political life in the six counties. Their outlook on the world often appears to be shaped largely by a range of altogether more universal concerns shared with their contemporaries elsewhere: imminent ecological catastrophe, ever-spiralling rents, the precarities of a deregulated labour market, university fees, the ever more fluid and, at times, fraught terrain of contemporary gender identities, and so forth.[69] This rather more global outlook may well be nurtured further by the onset of a COVID-19 pandemic that has at times brought Northern Ireland to a standstill eerily reminiscent of certain critical moments in the early stages of the Troubles. Over the course of 2020, the death toll in the six counties arising from the global health pandemic has continued to mount and has long since overtaken even the worst year of the Northern Irish conflict. The advent and impact of the coronavirus crisis is likely to have underlined something that many members of the 'peace generation' clearly know already, namely that some of the most significant dangers that face us all are increasingly likely to be global rather than local in origin. The broader cultural fields of vision possessed by many younger Northern Irish people are reflected in their growing aversion to the established ethno-national designations that define public discourse in the region. In recent years, a rising proportion of those living in the six counties have informed opinion pollsters that they do not define themselves as 'unionists' or 'nationalists', and this ontological turn has been especially marked among the 'peace generation'. The 2019 General Election Survey conducted at the University of Liverpool, for instance, reveals that 56 per cent of 18–29-year-olds consider that neither of these familiar ethnic categories adequately describes who they feel themselves to be.[70]

One of the many challenges that face people growing up in Northern Ireland is that their particular interests and identities are rarely reflected in mainstream political culture. Under the terms of the GFA, Members of the Legislative Assembly (MLAs) are required to identify themselves as 'unionist', 'nationalist' or 'other'.[71] While these three designations are in principle equally valid, in practice only the first two carry any real weight. When it comes to 'key decisions', for instance, it is solely the balance between the votes cast by 'unionist' and 'nationalist' politicians that matters when it comes to appraising whether decisions have been made on a 'cross-community basis'. This narrow preoccupation with the two traditional ethno-national affiliations in Northern Ireland has ensured that the proceedings at Stormont often have little relevance for those many youngsters who claim to subscribe to neither. Failing to see themselves represented by the parties that appear destined to govern Northern Ireland in perpetuity, most young people have expressed their alienation by simply ignoring the seemingly endless stream of elections that punctuate public life in the region. In the 2015 General Election, for instance, three-quarters of voters aged 18–29 decided simply not to bother casting a ballot.[72] The subsequent polls that have taken place in the heated atmosphere created by the Brexit referendum would, however, seem to have drawn some younger people into the electoral process. While most young people have continued to abstain from voting – 53 per cent of 18–29-year-olds in the case of 2019 General Election[73] – those who have chosen to mark a ballot paper, many for the first time, may have been responsible for a small but potentially significant shift in Northern Irish political life. The sequence of elections held in 2019 saw one in five of those who went to the polls lend their support to parties other than the main four that have become custodians of the twin ethno-national traditions in the six counties. While some commentators have seen this as evidence of 'new political thinking',[74] it is important to note that most of those who opted for parties that are neither unionist nor nationalist in recent elections voted for Alliance, a party that seeks to straddle traditional ethno-national distinctions and hence presupposes their continued existence. If we were to restrict our criteria to those parties that seek to occupy not the space between the polar attractions of unionism and nationalism but rather the spaces that exist beyond them, the evidence of a major shift in Northern Irish political culture becomes rather less persuasive. In the 2019 local government elections, for instance, candidates who stood on platforms seeking to address the damage being done to the planet or to redress the poverty arising out of changes to the welfare system drew support that might in time be seen as the beginning of a progressive political turn. In the meantime, however, it is worth remembering that the Greens and the People Before Profit Alliance polled only around 24,000 votes between them, a level of support absolutely dwarfed by that enjoyed by the main parties that continue to serve the traditional fare of Northern Irish political life.

Although the progressive disposition apparently shared by many of those who have come of age since the GFA may find little expression in the mainstream political culture of Northern Ireland, it has, nonetheless, begun to germinate elsewhere. One of the more heartening trends of recent years has been the growth of a diverse and often genuinely radical civil society that stands in stark contrast to the more established forms of cultural practice that have traditionally dominated public life in the six counties. The annual Pride parade that was once small and routinely abused by those wishing to 'Save Ulster From Sodomy'[75] has, as elsewhere, flourished over time into an extended festival celebrating gay identities in particular and the desire for greater cultural diversity more generally. Furthermore, the Extinction Rebellion movement highlighting the damage that more than two centuries of capitalism have done to the natural world has clearly had a resonance for Northern Irish schoolchildren comparable to that of their contemporaries who live in other, more 'mature' political cultures. And it should be added that many of those who came of age after the Troubles were drawing to a close have nurtured artistic talents that are certainly comparable to those of previous generations in a region with a long and rich cultural pedigree. Recent years have seen the emergence of a whole stream of younger figures who have distinguished themselves across the arts, creating spaces in civic society whose vitality stands in stark contrast to the invariably 'torpid' realities of mainstream Northern Irish political life.[76]

Reflecting on the remarkable degree of change that has accompanied the peace process, it often seems that there have emerged in Northern Irish society certain cultural impulses that are progressive but frustrated at every turn by the nature of the political settlement in the region. This should scarcely come as a surprise, of course. From early on, many commentators warned that the consociational modes of governance prescribed in the GFA had the potential to consign Northern Ireland to a form of suspended animation in which the only versions of political ambition afforded room to breathe would be those competing communal affiliations that helped produce a quarter-century of conflict in the first place.[77] Writing shortly after the political settlement was struck, for example, Rupert Taylor[78] observed archly that 'it is neither obvious nor logical that ethno-nationalism can be cured by prescribing more of it through constitutional engineering'. More than two decades on, the counsel of those who feared that the consociational model of peacemaking inscribed in the GFA would condemn Northern Irish political life to the limbo of perennial sectarian stasis has come to appear ever more convincing. When the deal was struck, there was some optimism that the new political dispensation might see the emergence over time of a more diverse and inclusive public realm in Northern Ireland. The manner in which the GFA was constructed and implemented would conspire, however, to frustrate the possibility of a progressive turn in Northern Irish political life. The Civic Forum envisaged in the terms of the peace deal, for instance, had the potential to represent a critical space in which alternative perspectives on public life may well have blossomed. That body would, however, operate for only two years before being mothballed in 2002, and although a successor was established in 2016 this current incarnation, the Civic Advisory Panel, represents a rather less ambitious undertaking that has yet to make any real impression on the public life of the region. The abiding sclerosis of Northern Irish political life derives rather more substantially, of course, from the specific structures of governance prescribed within the GFA. In seeking to square the circle of the competing demands of the two principal ethno-national communities in the region, the peace deal introduced parliamentary procedures that have suffocated alternative political identities and issues. Given that the only voices at Stormont that really matter are, as we noted earlier, those of 'unionists' and 'nationalists', it should come as no surprise that debates in the Assembly have descended so often into sectarian squabbling. As members of the new political elite in Northern Ireland have engaged in endless bickering over issues – flags, parades, language rights, public health strategies in an age of pandemic – that have transfigured the former conflict into new, and often not so new, forms, many of the citizens they claim to represent have simply lost interest, a disenchantment captured clearly in a long-running decline in electoral turnout that even the constitutional tsunami of Brexit may not be able to arrest indefinitely.

While the GFA raised the prospect of bi-communal democracy for Northern Ireland, more than two decades on the political settlement in the six counties appears rather closer to what Liam O'Dowd has termed 'a dual ethnocracy'.[79] In view of its particular consociational provisions, it was always entirely predictable that the historic peace deal would act to underwrite the sectarian specificities of Northern Irish political life. What was perhaps a little more difficult to foresee was that the architecture of the GFA would facilitate certain other problems of an altogether more universal nature in relation to the governance of the six counties. While those elected to serve in the Northern Ireland Assembly often claim to represent everyone living in the region, political life at Stormont has more often resembled what John Nagle has described, aptly, as a 'sectarian carve-up'.[80] In the pursuit of their own narrow ethno-national interests, the two main parties in the Executive have colluded in practices wildly at variance with the most fundamental standards of democratic governance. Although the questionable conduct of Sinn Féin and DUP ministers during their initial decade in power together would remain shrouded in secrecy for much of their time in office, it would come dramatically to light once the Renewable Heat Incentive (RHI) scheme became a matter of public controversy. Since 2016, the workings of the notorious green energy scheme which gave financial incentives for businesses and individuals to convert to alternative fuel sources – hence the nickname 'cash for ash' – have come under intense scrutiny from journalists and, subsequently, a major public inquiry. As we explore in the following chapter, these investigations have revealed that during their initial decade at the helm of devolved government Sinn Féin and DUP instigated a mode of governance that was profoundly undemocratic and unaccountable. Ministerial meetings went undocumented as a matter of routine, special advisers often exercised more influence than those figures on the Executive who were formally in power, expert advice from within and without frequently went unread and unheeded.[81] The revelations that have emerged from the RHI scandal have, therefore, suggested that the political institutions in Northern Ireland operate in ways defined not only by ingrained sectarianism but by endemic incompetence as well. That public life in the region has proved so profoundly dysfunctional, perhaps even corrupt, means of course that it mimics the modes of governance in many other, more 'developed' democracies in the neoliberal age. While many in Northern Ireland have long wished that the region might converge towards the political practices and mores of other Western societies, it was anticipated that any such brush with 'normality' would, however, assume rather more progressive forms.

It would appear reasonable, therefore, to suggest that the legacies the GFA has bestowed on Northern Ireland have proved to be problematic in a great many regards. The political structures and protocols initiated by the seemingly historic accord have led to modes of governance that are both profoundly sectarian and deeply dysfunctional. Furthermore, as we will observe many times over the course of this book, the deal that was struck on 10 April 1998 often now seems profoundly out of joint with a society that has changed dramatically, and largely for the better, in the interim. While the multiple weaknesses of the Northern Irish peace settlement have become ever more apparent, that seems to have little impact on the outlook of a range influential political figures at home and abroad. Throughout the often fraught Brexit talks, for instance, the chief EU negotiator Michel Barnier spoke frequently of the need for any final deal to respect the terms of the GFA, a view that was roundly echoed by then Tánaiste Simon Coveney when stressing the need to avoid a 'hard' border on the island of Ireland. The political imperative identified by key figures in Brussels and Dublin was evidently shared by most shades of political opinion within Northern Ireland. As the parties who had been its most committed advocates from the outset, the Social Democratic and Labour Party (SDLP) and Alliance were quick to underscore that any solution to the apparent Brexit impasse would have to respect the parameters of the GFA. Even Sinn Féin, which had from the outset sought to cast the 1998 peace accord as a mere 'staging post' on the way to a united Ireland, were at pains to suggest that it needed to be protected in perpetuity. If it were not for the unfortunate Thatcherite connotations of the phrase, it might well have been the case that the Brexit debate would have seen Northern Irish politicians of various shades insisting time and again that 'there is no alternative' to the GFA.

This air of consensus was disturbed momentarily in October 2018 when Arlene Foster insisted that a successful resolution of the Brexit negotiations might require that all interested parties cease approaching the GFA as though it were 'sacrosanct'. As the leader of the only major Northern Irish party that had initially rejected the 1998 accord, the then former First Minister was deemed a less than faithful narrator on the matter and her assertion was summarily dismissed by a range of political opinion both within and without the six counties. While the ease with which Foster's views were disregarded certainly reflects the poor esteem in which the leadership of unionism is held, it also tells us something else rather more significant, and perhaps troubling, about the prevailing political conjuncture in Northern Ireland. With the passage of time, it has become ever more apparent that the GFA holds an essentially hegemonic status for almost all of those political figures and forces that exercise any real influence over the region. Even the fact that it has had to be revised and amended on five separate occasions[82] seems to have been unable to persuade most politicians and commentators to regard the peace accord as something other than a sacred text that brooks no alteration. The further we have moved away from the signing of the GFA, the more problematic this propensity to fetishise its principles and practices has become. Perhaps the time has arrived, then, when we need to puncture the hegemony that surrounds Northern Ireland's celebrated political settlement and to subject it to the kinds of radical scrutiny that it so clearly deserves. More specifically, the moment may well now be opportune to reflect even more critically than before on that very specific sequence of ideological assumptions that has exerted such an influence over the Northern Irish peace process and that was inscribed in the terms of the political accord often assumed to represent its crowning achievement, and, indeed, its final destination. It is hoped that this book might serve to kindle these crucial debates in what is, to return to the vocabulary of Antonio Gramsci once more, a remarkable period of 'interregnum' in Northern Ireland, one in which the old world appears not quite ready to die and the new world is still struggling to be born.[83]

'Nothing like as good as it could have been …'

The very specific ideological frames that have plotted its course have, therefore, meant that the political settlement in Northern Ireland has been constructed and narrated in ways that are often deeply problematic. In more specific terms, the particular approaches to conflict resolution familiar from many other settings around the world that have defined the Northern Irish peace process have proved to have at least three principal shortcomings. First, the temporalisation of war and peace tendered by these perspectives has ensured that there has never been a genuinely comprehensive strategy for dealing with the multiple traumatic legacies of the Troubles. The assumption that there are certain watershed moments when conflicts essentially come to an end has, for instance, ensured that those citizens who lost loved ones are often left to deal with their grief with little support, and that those combatants who were in many cases responsible for that loss are often left on the margins of a society whose peace process required their thorough reintegration. Second, the focus of orthodox models of war and peace on the state and those who would seek to challenge, or uphold, its authority through force of arms has tended to obscure the multiple other forms of conflict that afflict Northern Irish society. While the occasional moments of ethno-national violence that still occur in the region typically draw swift condemnation from political figures at home and abroad, there tends to be rather less concern for, most significantly, the chilling number of assaults on women that have become an ever more commonplace feature of a society that is supposedly 'post-conflict'. Third, the particular forms of governance that are routinely prescribed by mainstream approaches to peace-building have acted to freeze Northern Irish political life in an increasingly dysfunctional mode of perpetual ethno-national competition. In a society where perhaps half the population seems to eschew the tags of 'unionist' and 'nationalist' it has become ever more problematic that the parliamentary institutions in the six counties continue to operate on the basis that those are the only forms of political affiliation that really matter, or, indeed, even exist.

Against this backdrop, the rationale for this particular book is to provide an account of contemporary Northern Ireland that is both critical and comprehensive and that challenges the many questionable ideological assumptions that have so often shaped how powerful political figures, both at home and abroad, have chosen to talk about the region. In the chapters that follow, we will underline that the neat boundaries that are often drawn around war and peace are frequently confounded by the inevitably complex realities of a society emerging from a quarter-century of political upheaval. Our ambition here is to provide a series of critical readings that render familiar those various emerging and ongoing forms of violence that are clearly unfamiliar to powerful political players who seem capable only of speaking of such matters in the past tense. More specifically, we will explore the varied and complicated afterlives of the Northern Irish conflict by examining the plight both of those who were victims of the violence (Chapter 2) and those who were its agents (Chapter 3), and by reflecting on how scriptwriters for cinema and television have come increasingly to summon the spectres of the region's troubled past (Chapter 4). We will set out to illustrate also that there exist within Northern Irish society various forms of conflict other than the ethno-national version that has invariably consumed almost all of the attention of the political elite both within and without the six counties. In the discussion that follows, we will document the escalating assaults against women and racial minorities that have attended the 'post-conflict' era (Chapters 5 and 6) and will cast light on the ingrained structural violence of a society in which the differences between rich and poor have rarely seemed starker (Chapter 7). Finally, we will explore how political structures and cultures that flowed from the GFA have acted increasingly to circumscribe and retard the course of Northern Irish public life. At various stages in the text, we will suggest, in particular, that while the preoccupation with balancing the imperatives of competing ethno-national affiliations at the core of Northern Ireland's celebrated peace deal may well have made sense a generation ago, it has left it poorly equipped to accommodate the changes that have taken place since in a society where a great many people would clearly prefer to see themselves in a host of other ways.

Above all, perhaps, our intention here is to shed light on one of the central paradoxes that defines Northern Ireland a generation into the peace process. In so many respects, Northern Irish society today bears little resemblance to that previous iteration that became famous around the globe for its seemingly intractable political ills. Incidents of what is conventionally understood as 'political violence' are now rare and the deaths that were once an almost daily reality have become all the more shocking for their infrequency. Anyone who remembers, as two of the authors here most certainly do, the miniature crosses that once mushroomed on the lawn of Belfast City Hall to quantify the fatalities in the Troubles – or indeed, the morbid scoreboard that served the same purpose outside a church located at the flank of that ornate building – will attest that the significance of that turn of events simply cannot be overstated. The changes that have attended the peace process have also assumed a range of other forms that are less dramatic, but perhaps no less significant. In the main, Northern Ireland now resembles a modern, secular society that is rather more multicultural than would have been imaginable not so long ago. Most significantly perhaps, there are many among the generation that has grown up since the end of the Troubles that have discarded many of the political and cultural prejudices of their parents and are more than willing to explore the dizzying fluidity of contemporary gender identities and to contemplate the prospect of romantic relations across the sectarian divide.[84]

In so many other respects, however, Northern Ireland often appears frustratingly unchanged by the unfolding of its widely lauded peace process. Those insidious forms of sectarian prejudice that initiated and sustained the Troubles may have receded, but they remain a sinister subtext in what appears, on the surface at least, a predominantly secular society.[85] Mainstream political discourse in the region continues to be characterised by the eternal recurrence of the same intractable, competing ethno-national demands. Many of the multiple forms of cultural and physical segregation that existed during the conflict remain obstinately intact all this time later. Of the 320,000 children who attend Northern Ireland's schools, for example, a mere 22,000 attend institutions that were established specifically to 'integrate' youngsters from different communal backgrounds.[86] And the proliferation of 'peace lines' that has, ironically, occurred in what is supposedly a 'post-conflict' society means that many residents of working-class neighbourhoods endure lives close to being as segregated as they were during the Troubles.[87]

A century into its widely admired peace process, therefore, Northern Irish society appears to be continuing to leave its violent past behind and yet, at the same time, unable quite to escape its gravitational pull. One of the principal ambitions of *Northern Ireland a generation after Good Friday* will be to capture the myriad complexities of what Declan Long characterises well as 'this disconcerting, backwards-and-forwards post-Troubles reality'.[88]

In the chapters that follow, we will underline time and again the intricate interplay of continuity and change that defines a society still emerging from the shadow of its own turbulent recent history. The essentially dialectical, possibly even bipolar, nature of contemporary Northern Ireland is perhaps both symptom and cause of the many setbacks that have defined the era of the peace process. For all the praise that has been heaped on the GFA, it is worth remembering that this is a political settlement that has proved anything but. The terms of the deal would, after all, require serious alteration on no fewer than five occasions within the space of just fourteen years, and the power-sharing bodies at its centre now hold the unenviable status of being the democratic legislature that was suspended for the longest period ever in peacetime.[89]

That there is something amiss with the Northern Irish political settlement is mirrored also in the vocabulary that continues to surround it. The success of a 'peace process' might be said to be confirmed when people cease to feel the need to speak in such terms. In the context of Northern Ireland, we remain very far from that critical moment of letting go. That people still refer habitually to the Northern Irish 'peace process' leads us to mark a certain important irony. In the midst of the Troubles, commentators would often refer to that dark period – and, in particular, the commitment of republicans to sustaining their campaign of violence – as 'the long war'. The lifespan of the conflict has now been overtaken, however, by that of the period of comparative stability that succeeded it.[90] When reflecting on all that has happened since the end of the Troubles we might, therefore, choose to speak of 'the long peace'. There is, after all, something in that phrase that captures the quintessential duality of the Northern Irish 'peace process', expressing as it does both the relief that we have never returned to full-blown conflict and the disquiet that even now, more than a quarter-century down the line, we still feel obliged to speak in terms that implicitly disclose that the gains of the last generation may prove to be merely provisional in the end.

As the shortcomings of the political settlement in Northern Ireland have become ever more apparent, many people have inevitably become frustrated at the direction the region appears to be taking. This palpable sense of disillusionment was captured well by Glenn Patterson in *Backstop Land*, his entertaining polemic dealing with the seismic repercussions for Northern Ireland of the Brexit referendum outcome, a theme to which we return in Chapter 8. Over the course of the book, the Belfast novelist arrives at an appraisal of the peace process that comes close to our own. While Northern Ireland is certainly much 'better than it was', Patterson observes, it is still 'nothing like as good as it could have been, or we thought it was going to be'.[91] There was, of course, a time when the prospects of the Northern Irish peace process looked rather less complicated and rather more favourable. On that sun-kissed late summer's day in 1994 when the Provisional IRA declared its campaign of 'armed struggle' to be at an end, a popular mood that married jubilation and relief in more or less equal measure was captured memorably by the best-selling regional paper in Northern Ireland. Across its front page, the *Belfast Telegraph* proclaimed in enormous font: 'It's Over'.[92] The infringements of paramilitary ceasefires and tortuous political negotiations that marked the following four years would ensure that by the time the GFA was signed some of that initial optimism had already dissipated. Nonetheless, when it was announced on 23 May 1998 that the deal had been endorsed by 71 per cent of those who voted in the required referendum, the ecstatic scenes in the King's Hall in Belfast offered a vivid reminder that there remained a broad, if perhaps now more muted, faith that Northern Ireland was, at last, on the path to a brighter political future. The story of how that mood of qualified optimism would, in many quarters and on many occasions, become one of unqualified scepticism is of course a notoriously complicated one. While some readers will remember its every turn, there will be many others unfamiliar with the byzantine narrative that is the Northern Irish peace process. It would make sense, therefore, to begin with an historical overview setting out the key events and processes that have conspired to shape *Northern Ireland a generation after Good Friday*.

Notes

1 Siobhán Fenton, *The Good Friday Agreement* (London: Biteback Publishing, 2018), p. 3.
2 Rupert Taylor (2009), 'Introduction: the promise of consociational theory', in Rupert Taylor (ed.), *Consociational Theory: McGarry and O'Leary and the Northern Ireland Conflict* (London: Routledge, 2009) pp. 1–12, p. 7.
3 The provisions of the Northern Irish peace accord were very specifically designed to prevent 'majority rule' in a region where there has not in fact been an ethnonational majority for quite some time.
4 Fiach Kelly, 'Clinton Describes Belfast Agreement as "a Work of Genius"', *Irish Times*, 10 April 2018. Available at: www.irishtimes.com/news/politics/clinton-describes-belfast-agreement-as-a-work-of-genius-1.3457441. Accessed 2 September 2020.
5 Steven McCaffery, 'Key legacy of the Good Friday Agreement: Lives saved', *The Detail*, 10 April 2018. Available at: www.thedetail.tv/articles/the-legacy-of-the-good-friday-agreement-how-the-peace-dividend-has-saved-lives. Accessed 7 September 2020.
6 Peter Shirlow, 'Twenty Years after the Belfast Agreement', *Parliamentary Affairs*, 71(2) (2018), 392–4, p. 392.

7 Peter Shirlow, Brian Graham, Kieran McEvoy, Féilim Ó hAdhmaill and Dawn Purvis, *Politically Motivated Former Prisoner Groups: Community Activism and Conflict Transformation* (Belfast: Northern Ireland Community Relations Council, 2005); Peter Shirlow and Ciaran Hughes, *Tar Isteach: A Survey of Conflict-Related Prisoners' Needs* (Belfast: Tar Isteach, 2015).

8 Fenton, *Good Friday Agreement*, p. 3.

9 The political settlement in Northern Ireland might be seen as a hybrid of several different schools of conflict resolution and international relations. It has, for example, been shaped by the commitment to free-market economics central to the 'liberal' peace models, the pragmatic and state-centric reading of the field of political possibility characteristic of the 'realist' school, and, most famously perhaps, the faith in the utility of intercommunal power-sharing expressed by the 'consociational' approach. For a discussion of these distinct, but often interconnected, perspectives, see: Arend Lijphart, *Democracy in Plural Societies* (New Haven, CT: Yale University Press, 1977); John McGarry (ed.), *Northern Ireland in a Divided World* (Oxford: Oxford University Press, 2001); John McGarry, 'Iraq: liberal consociation and conflict management', in Ben Roswell, David Malone and Markus Bouillon (eds), *Iraq: Preventing Another Generation of Conflict* (Boulder, CO: Lynne Rienner, 2007), pp. 169–88, p. 172; Roger Mac Ginty, *No War, No Peace: Rejuvenating Stalled Peace Processes and Peace Accords* (Basingstoke: Palgrave Macmillan, 2006); Roger Mac Ginty, 'Indigenous Peace-Making Versus the Liberal Peace', *Cooperation and Conflict*, 43(2) (2008), 139–63; Roger Mac Ginty, 'The Liberal Peace at Home and Abroad: Northern Ireland and Liberal Internationalism', *British Journal of Politics and International Relations*, 11 (2009), 690–70; Roger Mac Ginty and Andrew Williams, *Conflict and Development* (London: Routledge, 2009); Roland Paris, 'Saving Liberal Peacebuilding', *Review of International Studies*, 36 (2010), 337–65.

10 The reader will notice that in the discussion that follows we use the terms 'war' and 'conflict' interchangeably. There are two reasons for doing so. First, in the sphere of international relations it has long been conventional to use 'war' to describe those forms of political violence that occur between states and are assumed to observe certain legal protocols and 'conflict' to designate those that occur at intra-state level and are assumed to observe few such juridical niceties. Implicit in this distinction is the understanding that 'wars' are both more legitimate and more consequential than 'conflicts'. Neither of these assumptions are necessarily true. There is no inherent reason that the violence that states direct towards one another should be any more morally or legally defensible than that which conjoins competing sub-state forces. And the presumption that violence between states is more substantial than that within them makes little sense, given that almost all the major political upheavals that have occurred in the last forty years have taken place at sub-state level. The distinction between 'war' and 'conflict' seems an increasingly arbitrary and ideologically driven one and hence we have chosen to dispense with it and use the two terms interchangeably. Second, the familiar distinction between 'war'

and 'conflict' has a particular political charge in the specific context we are discussing here. Mindful of the legitimacy that flows from such terminology, the Provisional IRA insisted that it was involved in a 'war' and that it constituted an 'army'. Those various forces ranged against them countered that the republican movement were in fact engaged instead in a campaign of 'terrorism' that was the root cause of a 'conflict'. Both of these arguments have their own inner logic and we have no wish to come down on one side or the other. Accordingly, we have chosen to use both the terms 'war' and 'conflict' to describe that period of political violence that claimed more than 3,700 lives in Northern Ireland.

11 Jolle Demmers, *Theories of Violent Conflict* (London: Routledge, 2012).
12 *Agreement reached in the multi-party negotiations*, 'Declaration of support, paragraph 2' (Belfast, 1998).
13 Ibid.
14 Glenn Patterson, *Backstop Land* (London: Head of Zeus, 2019), p. 89.
15 Mike Tomlinson, 'Risking peace in the "war against the poor"? Social exclusion and the legacies of the Northern Ireland conflict', *Critical Social Policy*, 36(1) (2016), 104–23, p. 118.
16 Fenton, *Good Friday Agreement*, pp. 147–52.
17 Siobhan O'Neill, Cherie Armour, David Bolton, Brendan Bunting, Collette Cory, Barney Devine, Edel Ennis and Finola Ferry, *Towards a Better Future: The Transgenerational Impact of the Troubles on Mental Health* (Belfast: Commission for Victims and Survivors for Northern Ireland, 2015).
18 Rory Carroll, 'Sinn Féin pair tell of police warning over dissident attack plan', *Guardian*, 11 February 2020. Available at: www.theguardian.com/uk-news/2020/feb/11/sinn-fein-pair-tell-of-police-warning-over-dissident-attack-plan-northern-ireland. Accessed 25 March 2020.
19 Peter Shirlow, *The End of Ulster Loyalism?* (Manchester: Manchester University Press, 2012).
20 Patterson, *Backstop Land*, p. 122.
21 Théo Leschevin, 'Conflictuality and the collective definition of a public issue in North Belfast: the case of mental health', paper delivered at the annual postgraduate conference of the Sociological Association of Ireland, Technological University of Dublin, 23 February 2019.
22 Patterson, *Backstop Land*, pp. 85–8.
23 In December 2012, local councillors voted to restrict the number of days on which the Union flag would fly above Belfast City Hall. The decision led to widespread protests and violence, typically involving young working-class Protestant males and often orchestrated by loyalist paramilitary figures. For further discussion, see Chapter 1.
24 Jan Carson, *The Firestarters* (Dublin: Doubleday, 2019), p. 133.
25 *Belfast Telegraph*, 'Second man arrested on suspicion of murder of Ian Ogle', 31 January 2019. Available at: www.belfasttelegraph.co.uk/news/northern-ireland/second-man-arrested-on-suspicion-of-murder-of-ian-ogle-37770795.html. Accessed 5 September 2020.

26 Ciaran Barnes, 'Lyra McKee killer is dad for the first time', *Sunday Life*, 2 February 2020. Available at: www.belfasttelegraph.co.uk/sunday-life/news/lyra-mckee-killer-is-dad-for-first-time-38917653.html. Accessed 5 September 2020.
27 Lyra McKee, 'Suicide of the ceasefire babies', *Mosaic*, 19 January 2016. Available at: https://mosaicscience.com/story/conflict-suicide-northern-ireland/. Accessed 5 September 2020.
28 Donna Halliday and Neil Ferguson, 'The Legacy of Conflict: Memory and Northern Ireland's Post-Conflict Generation', *Culture and Psychology* (forthcoming).
29 Colin Graham, '"Every Passer-by a Culprit?" Archive Fever, Photography and the Peace in Belfast', *Third Text*, 19(5) (2005), 567–80, p. 568.
30 The Historical Enquiries Team (HET) was established in 2005 as a specialist police unit to examine 'cold cases' from the Troubles. After widespread criticism that it had failed to bring many of these investigations to a successful conclusion, and that it had been less stringent in its pursuit of killers who were members of the security forces, the HET was abolished. The body was replaced by another with a similar brief, the Historical Investigations Unit created under the terms of the 2014 Stormont House Agreement. The latter body has not proved any more capable than its predecessor in terms of solving 'legacy killings' from the Troubles period. For further detail, see Chapter 2.
31 The Consultative Group on the Past was chaired by the Episcopalian Archbishop Robin Eames and the former Catholic priest Denis Bradley, and hence its report is often designated in shorthand by their conjoined surnames.
32 Julian Smith, 'Northern Ireland Troubles-related incident victims payments scheme', 31 January 2020. Available at: www.gov.uk/government/news/northern-ireland-troubles-related-incident-victims-payments-scheme. Accessed 12 August 2020.
33 Suzanne Breen, 'Victims see light at end of tunnel as judge to rule on Troubles pension logjam', *Belfast Telegraph*, 20 August 2020. Available at: www.belfasttelegraph.co.uk/news/northern-ireland/victims-see-light-at-end-of-tunnel-as-judge-to-rule-on-troubles-pension-logjam-39466636.html. Accessed 4 September 2020.
34 Allison Morris, 'Calls for Charter NI funding freeze as leading loyalist refuses to resign', *Irish News*, 3 November 2016. Available at: www.irishnews.com/news/northernirelandnews/2016/11/03/news/calls-for-charter-ni-funding-freeze-as-leading-loyalist-refuses-to-resign-767579/. Accessed 5 September 2020.
35 Susan McKay, *Bear in Mind These Dead* (London: Faber & Faber, 2008) p. 303.
36 Johan Galtung, 'Violence, Peace and Peace Research', *Journal of Peace Research*, 6 (1969), 167–91.
37 John Paul Lederach, *Building Peace: Sustainable Reconciliation in Divided Societies* (Washington, DC: United States Institute of Peace, 1997).
38 Ilan Zvi Baron, Jonathan Havercroft, Isaac Kamola, Jonneke Koomen, Justin Murphy and Alex Prichar, 'Liberal Pacification and the Phenomenology of Violence', *International Studies Quarterly*, 63 (2019), 199–212; Niall Gilmartin,

Female Combatants After Armed Struggle: Lost In Transition? (London: Routledge, 2019).

39 This phrase was coined by the British Home Secretary Reginald Maudling after his first visit to Northern Ireland in 1970, as the Troubles were beginning to gather pace. Maudling candidly informed journalists that the limits of his ambition were to reduce the violence in the region to an 'acceptable level'.

40 Baron et al., 'Liberal Pacification and the Phenomenology of Violence'.

41 McKay, *Bear in Mind These Dead*, p. 4.

42 Monica McWilliams and Joan McKiernan, *Bringing it Out in the Open: Domestic Violence in Northern Ireland* (Belfast: Department of Health and Social Services, 1993).

43 Police Service of Northern Ireland, *Trends in Domestic Abuse Incidents and Crimes Recorded by the Police in Northern Ireland, 2004/05 to 2018/19* (Belfast: PSNI, 2019), p. 5; Police Service of Northern Ireland, *Domestic Abuse Incidents and Crimes Recorded by the Police in Northern Ireland: Update to 30 June 2020* (Belfast: PSNI, 2020).

44 Police Service of Northern Ireland, *Trends in Hate Motivated Incidents and Crimes Recorded by the Police in Northern Ireland 2004/05 to 2018/19* (Belfast: PSNI, 2019), p. 6: Police Service of Northern Ireland, *Incidents and Crimes with a Hate Motivation Recorded by the Police in Northern Ireland Update to 30 June 2020* (Belfast: PSNI, 2020), p. 4.

45 Marta Kempny, 'Polish spaces in a divided society', in Bryan Fanning and Lucy Michael (eds), *Immigrants as Outsiders in the Two Irelands* (Manchester: Manchester University Press, 2019), p. 100.

46 Chris Gilligan, 'Northern Ireland and the Limits of the Race Relations Framework', *Capital & Class*, 43(1) (2019), 105–21, p. 107.

47 Police Service of Northern Ireland, *Incidents and Crimes with a Hate Motivation 2020*, p. 4.

48 BBC News, 'Peter Robinson under fire for backing Pastor James McConnell's Islamic remarks', 28 May 2014. Available at: www.bbc.com/news/uk-northern-ireland-27604841. Accessed 25 August 2020.

49 Bethany Waterhouse-Bradley, 'Sectarian legacies and the marginalisation of migrants', in Fanning and Michael (eds), *Immigrants as Outsiders in the Two Irelands*, p. 43.

50 Johan Galtung, 'Violence, Peace and Peace Research', p. 8.

51 Iris Marion Young, *Responsibility for Justice* (Oxford: Oxford University Press, 2011).

52 Antonio Gramsci, *Selections from the Prison Notebooks* (London: Lawrence & Wishart, 1971), p. 626.

53 Daniel Finn, *One Man's Terrorist: A Political History of the IRA* (London: Verso, 2019), pp. 39–48.

54 Goretti Horgan, '"Equality of misery"? Poverty and political violence in Northern Ireland', *CrisisJam*, 12 July 2011. Available at: https://magill.ie/archive/equality-misery-poverty-and-political-violence-northern-ireland. Accessed 30 August 2020.

55 Brendan O'Leary, 'The Twilight of the United Kingdom & *Tiocfaidh ár lá*: Twenty Years after the Good Friday Agreement', *Ethnopolitics*, 17(3) (2018), 223–42, p. 226.
56 Robin Wilson, *Northern Ireland peace monitoring report, number four* (Belfast: Community Relations Council, 2016), p. 83.
57 Colin Coulter, '"Under Which Constitutional Arrangement Would You Still Prefer to be Unemployed?" Neoliberalism, the Peace Process, and the Politics of Class in Northern Ireland', *Studies in Conflict & Terrorism*, 37(9) (2014), 763–76; Matthew Whiting, *Sinn Féin and the IRA: From Revolution to Moderation* (Edinburgh: Edinburgh University Press, 2019), p. 101.
58 Examples of countries where ostensible political progress has not been accompanied by economic improvements for the mass of the population include Bosnia, Timor-Leste, El Salvador, Botswana, South Africa and Zimbabwe. Roger MacGinty, 'Indigenous Peace-Making Versus the Liberal Peace', *Cooperation and Conflict*, 43(2) (2008), 139–63.
59 Roger Mac Ginty, *No War, No Peace: Rejuvenating Stalled Peace Processes and Peace Accords* (Basingstoke: Palgrave Macmillan, 2006), p. 180; Roland Paris, 'Saving Liberal Peacebuilding', *Review of International Studies*, 36 (2010), 337–65.
60 Trussell Trust, *Food Bank Statistics for Previous Financial Years with Regional Breakdown* (2020). Available at: www.trusselltrust.org/news-and-blog/latest-stats/end-year-stats. Accessed 30 August 2020.
61 Cynthia Enloe, *Bananas, Beaches and Bases: Making Feminist Sense of International Politics* (Berkeley: University of California Press, 2014); Ann Tickner, *Gender In International Relations: Feminist Perspectives on Achieving Global Security* (New York: Columbia University Press, 1992).
62 Phil Ramsey, Stephen Baker and Robert Porter, 'Screen production on the "biggest set in the world": Northern Ireland Screen and the case of *Game of Thrones*', *Media, Culture & Society*, 41(6) (2019), 845–62, p. 855.
63 Arend Lijphart, *Democracy in Plural Societies* (New Haven, CT: Yale University Press, 1977).
64 The body of literature pertaining to both consociation in general, and its application in Northern Ireland in particular, is substantial and extensive, and hence well beyond the scope of the current discussion. For a wide range of perspectives on these important debates, see: Bernadette Hayes and Ian McAllister, 'Gender and Consociational Powersharing in Northern Ireland', *International Political Science Review*, 34(2) (2013), 123–39; John McGarry and Brendan O'Leary, *The Northern Ireland Conflict: Consociational Engagements* (Oxford: Oxford University Press, 2004); John McGarry and Brendan O'Leary, 'Consociational Theory, Northern Ireland's Conflict, and its Agreement 2: What Critics of Consociation Can Learn from Northern Ireland', *Government and Opposition*, 41(2) (2006), 249–77; John Nagle and Mary-Alice Clancy, *Shared Society or Benign Apartheid? Understanding Peace-Building in Divided Societies* (Basingstoke: Palgrave Macmillan, 2010); Ronan Kennedy, Claire Pierson and Jennifer Thomson, 'Challenging Identity Hierarchies: Gender and Consociational

Power-sharing', *British Journal of Politics and International Relations*, 18(3) (2016), 618–33; Rupert Taylor, *Consociational Theory: McGarry and O'Leary and the Northern Ireland Conflict* (London: Routledge, 2009).

65 Liam O'Dowd, 'Symmetrical Solutions, Asymmetrical Realities: Beyond the Politics of Paralysis?', *Studies in Conflict and Terrorism*, 37(9) (2014), 806–14.

66 *Agreement reached in the multi-party negotiations*, 'Strand one: Safeguards, section (d)'.

67 O'Leary, 'Twilight of the United Kingdom', p. 236.

68 Katy Hayward and Cathal McManus, 'Neither/Nor: The rejection of Unionist and Nationalist identities in post-Agreement Northern Ireland', *Capital & Class*, 43(1) (2019), 139–55.

69 Nathalie Olah, *Steal As Much As You Can: How to Win the Culture Wars in an Age of Austerity* (London: Repeater Books, 2019).

70 University of Liverpool, *NI General Election Survey 2019* (Liverpool: University of Liverpool, March 2020). Available at: www.liverpool.ac.uk/humanities-and-social-sciences/research/research-themes/transforming-conflict/ni-election-survey-19/. Accessed 30 August 2020.

71 *Agreement reached in the multi-party talks*, 'Strand One: Paragraph 6'.

72 Shirlow, 'Twenty Years after the Belfast Agreement', p. 392.

73 Ibid., p. 6.

74 Patterson, *Backstop Land*, p. 166.

75 Fintan Walsh, 'Saving Ulster from Sodomy and Hysteria: Sex, Politics and Performance', *Contemporary Theatre Review*, 23(3) (2013), 291–301.

76 George Legg, *Northern Ireland and the Politics of Boredom: Conflict, Capital and Culture* (Manchester: Manchester University Press, 2018), p. 64.

77 Colin Coulter, *Contemporary Northern Irish Society: An Introduction* (London: Pluto, 1999).

78 Rupert Taylor, 'Northern Ireland: consociation or social transformation?', in John McGarry (ed.), *Northern Ireland in a Divided World* (Oxford: Oxford University Press, 2001), pp. 37–52, p. 39.

79 O'Dowd, 'Symmetrical Solutions, Asymmetrical Realities', p. 807.

80 John Nagle, 'Between Conflict and Peace: An Analysis of the Complex Consequences of the Good Friday Agreement', *Parliamentary Affairs*, 71(2) (2018), 395–416, p. 403.

81 Sam McBride, *Burned: The Inside Story of the 'Cash-for-Ash' Scandal and Northern Ireland's Secretive New Elite* (Newbridge, Kildare: Merrion Press, 2019).

82 The relevant moments signposting the perilous journey of Northern Ireland's peace deal are the St Andrews Agreement (2006), the Hillsborough Agreement (2010), the Stormont House Agreement (2014), the Fresh Start Agreement (2015) and *New Decade, New Approach* (2020).

83 Gramsci, *Selections from the Prison Notebooks*, p. 556.

84 The 2019 General Election Survey conducted at the University of Liverpool, for example, reveals that 23 per cent of 18-25 year-olds report having partners who are of another religion or none.

85 Fenton, *Good Friday Agreement*, p. 99.
86 Tony Gallagher, *Education, Equality and the Economy* (Belfast: Queen's University, 2019), p. 6.
87 Brendan Murtagh, 'Contested Space, Peacebuilding and the Post-conflict City', *Parliamentary Affairs*, 71(2) (2018), 438–60, pp. 444–5.
88 Declan Long, *Ghost-Haunted Land: Contemporary Art and Post-Troubles Northern Ireland* (Manchester: Manchester University Press, 2017), p. x.
89 Glenn Patterson, *Backstop Land*, p. 33.
90 As with much else in Northern Ireland, there is some confusion over when the conflict ended, or indeed when it began. If we assume that the Troubles began with the widespread 'civil unrest' of August 1969 and came, more or less, to an end with the 1994 paramilitary ceasefires, then it may be said that the 'long war' has already lasted a shorter period of time than the relative peace that followed it.
91 Ibid., p. 148.
92 Colin Coulter and Michael Murray, 'Introduction', in Colin Coulter and Michael Murray (eds), *Northern Ireland after the Troubles: A Society in Transition* (Manchester: Manchester University Press, 2008), p. 1.

1

From the 'long war' to the 'long peace': Northern Ireland since the Good Friday Agreement

Introduction

In the midst of the Troubles, it would certainly have been hard to imagine that one day Northern Ireland would become a globally renowned tourist destination. Back in those bleak times when it seemed that the conflict might never end, the Europa in the centre of Belfast would attain the unenviable accolade of being the most frequently bombed hotel in the entire world. A generation into the peace process, in contrast, some 2.2 million 'hotel room nights' are reserved by visitors to Northern Ireland every year.[1] Drawn by traditional sights such as the Giant's Causeway and attractions of more recent vintage such as the Titanic Visitors' Centre and the locations that feature in the hugely popular television series *Game of Thrones*, the volume of tourists coming to Northern Ireland now surpasses the number of people living there.[2] It is entirely possible that on the afternoon of 11 January 2020, some of those visiting the region might have returned to their hotel rooms after a hearty lunch to pass a little time flicking through the television channels and happened upon live coverage of a rare Saturday sitting of the Northern Ireland Assembly.[3] The scenes in the Stormont chamber doubtless would have confirmed the positive stories that those momentarily detained tourists may well have read in their travel guides or in-flight magazines. On this occasion at least, the politicians of various hues present in the Assembly were on their very best behaviour, airing tributes to their party colleagues and sharing pleasantries across the floor. Even the habitually cantankerous independent unionist Jim Allister appeared to have read the script, engaging in a moment of good humour with Alex Maskey, the republican politician newly appointed as Speaker of the House. Any unwitting tourist straying upon the live broadcast from Stormont might have been forgiven for thinking that Northern Ireland really is just as they had been told beforehand: a society that has left its violent past behind and is now at peace with itself. The truth, as ever, is a little more complicated.

When the Good Friday Agreement (hereafter GFA) was ratified by simultaneous referenda either side of the Irish border in May 1998, there was a widespread, though far from universal, sense that Northern Ireland was now, finally, facing a peaceful, perhaps even prosperous, future. While no one expected that the political path ahead would be easy, there were few who could have anticipated just how difficult that course would transpire to be. As Eamonn O'Kane[4] notes with admirable brevity, 'one of the most notable features of the peace process has been how "messy" it has been'. For all the crucial successes that have flowed from the GFA, there have been a great many disappointments and disruptions as well. Most crucially perhaps, those institutions that were central to the political settlement were meant to bring stable and equitable government to Northern Ireland but have signally failed to do so. Recurrent disagreements between the region's coalition partners have ensured that since their establishment in 1998, the Assembly and Executive have spent in total more than seven and a half years in cold storage.[5] The most recent suspension of the Stormont institutions lasted a world record of more than three years and, as we shall see, only ended when mounting public anger at rapidly deteriorating public services forced the local parties into yet another new deal. Those seemingly amicable members of the legislative assembly (MLAs) who were getting on so well with one another during that rare Saturday sitting sketched above were in fact chastened politicians forced back into the chamber by the threat of further electoral reprisals from an ever more disenchanted general public.

The story of the Northern Irish peace process is, then, rather more complicated than it might appear from the distance maintained by speech writers in the hire of globetrotting politicians or features writers in the pay of the international media. In this chapter, we will seek to provide a more nuanced and balanced account of the frequently tortuous political path that Northern Ireland has followed over the last generation. It is hoped that the narrative that follows will have sufficient breadth to accommodate those who may know little about recent Northern Irish history and sufficient depth to engage those who feel they are already all too familiar with the many twists in that most byzantine of plots. While the story that follows is necessarily dense, it is intended that it will provide the reader with an accessible account of how Northern Ireland managed to move beyond its 'long war' but even now does not quite seem able to move beyond its 'long peace'.

The limits of 'constructive ambiguity'

While the GFA sought to deal with the 'totality of relationships' between the peoples of Ireland and Great Britain, its principal concern was, not unreasonably, to mend the historically troubled relations between the 'two traditions' often said to coexist in Northern Ireland.[6] The peace deal made provision for institutions of government that would require unionists and nationalists to share power and responsibility with one another. At the heart of these 'consociational' structures was an executive which met finally for the first time on 2 December 1999, some eighteen months after the GFA was signed and provided, therefore, an early indication of the thrombosis that would often pass for governance in the region. Northern Ireland's new government was headed by the Ulster Unionist Party (UUP) and the Social Democratic and Labour Party (SDLP), with their electoral competitors the Democratic Unionist Party (DUP) and Sinn Féin in supporting roles. While the Democratic Unionists were nominated to positions within the Executive, they refused to attend meetings. Party leader the Revd Ian Paisley had denounced the GFA as a 'prelude to genocide' and insisted that were his colleagues to assume their positions in government that would require them to sit down with 'the men of blood'.[7]

The hostility of the Democratic Unionists would prove to be only one of several pressures that would face the new power-sharing arrangements. Although the principle of consociationalism found favour among all other shades of political opinion in Northern Ireland from the outset, it would nonetheless take almost a decade for the institutions envisaged in the GFA to begin operating in a manner that even appeared to be sustainable. The main initial obstacle to the formation of a stable power-sharing government illustrated the facility of the peace deal to mean often radically different things to different people.[8] In order to square the circle of at times mutually exclusive ethno-national demands, those who framed the GFA engaged in a certain 'constructive ambiguity'.[9] This particular attribute – and, it would soon become clear, shortcoming – of the document was especially apparent in its provisions for the disposal of illegally held arms, or 'decommissioning'.

While unionist politicians took the view that the GFA required republican (as well as loyalist) paramilitaries to dispose of their armouries, Sinn Féin tended to counter, entirely accurately as it happens, that the text of the deal merely required them to 'use any influence they may have' to persuade the Provisional IRA to give up its arms. These radically divergent readings of one of the principal ambiguities at the heart of the peace settlement would haunt all of the initial attempts to establish cross-community government in Northern Ireland. On each occasion, the choreography of political failure would unfold in the same predictable manner: the UUP would agree to enter government on the proviso that republicans would in the near future decommission their weapons;[10] Sinn Féin would also agree to form a government but insist that the Provisional IRA was under no obligation to put its arms beyond use and that unionist demands that it do so were in fact prompted by a repugnance at the thought of sharing power with nationalists;[11] finally, after a short interlude marked by intense squabbling, the Ulster Unionists, under pressure from the very vocal fundamentalist Ian Paisley, would note that republicans had failed to decommission and then refuse to continue in government, precipitating its collapse. In the initial phase of the peace process, this sequence of mutual recrimination and political stalemate would be repeated on no fewer than four separate occasions.[12] By the time that allegations of republican intelligence gathering at Stormont[13] accelerated the last of these parliamentary suspensions in October 2002, much of the initial enthusiasm for the peace process had dissipated and a palpable sense of political disillusionment had descended on Northern Ireland.[14]

The dismal failure of initial attempts to form sustainable power-sharing government in Northern Ireland would instigate a process of polarisation between the 'two communities' that would in time, ironically, facilitate the cause of political progress in the region. The refusal of unionists to remain in power with republicans in the absence of 'decommissioning' served to alienate members of the nationalist community who came increasingly to see Sinn Féin as the party best equipped to defend their interests. At the same time, the refusal of the republican movement to dispose of their arms became a growing source of disquiet among unionists already sceptical about the peace process, and led them to see the DUP as the most effective bulwark against further concessions to nationalists.[15] The symbiotic interplay between these radicalising forces would become ever more apparent in electoral terms. In the early days of the peace process, Sinn Féin and the DUP were only the secondary political voices within their respective ethnopolitical communities. As each attempt to establish stable devolved government in Northern Ireland ran aground, however, these parties that had been previously dismissed as 'extremists' began to attract larger and more diverse bodies of support.[16] By the time of the 2003 elections to an assembly that was no longer sitting, Sinn Féin and the DUP had clearly established themselves as the principal political forces within their respective communities, and the years since have merely confirmed their electoral pre-eminence.[17]

Although the rise of these radically opposed parties often seemed to imperil the cause of political progress in Northern Ireland, it would in time prove to be its prerequisite. One of the problems that face 'moderate' political parties seeking to reach agreement in all divided societies is the prospect of being outflanked by more radical voices emanating from within their own communities. And that is precisely the fate that befell the UUP and SDLP in the course of the Northern Irish peace process. These parties were once the principal voices within the unionist and nationalist traditions, but they were eclipsed as the wrangles over 'guns and government' rumbled on and the ongoing erosion of their electorate has at times even raised the possibility of their political extinction. The pressures that sent the UUP and SDLP into long-term electoral decline were ones to which the parties that overtook them would remain largely immune. While both Sinn Féin and the DUP continue to face criticism from dissenting voices within their own communities, those political forces adopting more fundamentalist positions have never been able to garner sufficient support to mount a meaningful challenge. The immunity of both parties to 'ethnic outbidding'[18] would ensure that it was this combination of 'extremists' that would strike the deal that would finally bring what, for a time at least, seemed like stable power-sharing government to Northern Ireland.

If Sinn Féin and the DUP were to share power with one another that would require a resolution of the 'decommissioning' issue that had bedevilled previous Stormont administrations. On 28 July 2005, the Provisional IRA announced that it had disbanded and destroyed its weaponry.[19] While the structures of the paramilitary organisation would remain in place and elements of its armoury would surface from time to time, a semblance of decommissioning was sufficient to remove the most fundamental obstacle in the path of Sinn Féin and the DUP reaching an accommodation. In October 2006, the British and Irish governments convened talks in the Scottish town of St Andrews, aimed at the restoration of devolved government in the six counties. During the negotiations, Sinn Féin made a commitment to support the recently (re)formed Police Service of Northern Ireland (PSNI), while the DUP agreed that it was willing to share power with republicans. The St Andrews Agreement that emerged out of the talks paved the way for the Northern Ireland Assembly to begin operating again after a hiatus of five years. A fresh round of elections confirmed that Sinn Féin and the DUP would dominate the incoming executive, and on 8 May 2007 the new coalition partners were unveiled before an audience of the global media. The presence of an unusually large contingent of international journalists in the Great Hall at Stormont was guaranteed by the prospect of witnessing the two principal positions in the restored Northern Ireland Executive being filled by a pair of notoriously bitter erstwhile rivals. The spectacle of the Revd Ian Paisley and Martin McGuinness trading jokes and evidently enjoying one another's company simply beggared belief for anyone who remembered a mutual rancour stretching back over several decades.[20] Indeed, only a year earlier the ageing evangelical firebrand had stated publicly that no one worthy of the name 'unionist' would ever enter government with Sinn Féin.[21] A characteristic facility for historical amnesia would, however, allow the Democratic Unionist leader to strike a deal with Martin McGuinness to restore the Stormont institutions. And so, in the early summer of 2007, this unlikely pairing of the most irascible voice of fundamentalist unionism and the former chief of staff of the Provisional IRA would join forces to begin the most stable period of devolved government that Northern Ireland had enjoyed in half a century.

Those remarkable scenes signalling the return of devolved power to Stormont created an afterglow that perhaps overstated the degree of political progress achieved in Northern Ireland. In the minds of people living elsewhere in particular, the sight of Paisley and McGuinness evidently at ease with one another created an impression of stable government that would long outlast the relatively brief stretch of time that the pair actually spent in office together. The 'honeymoon period'[22] enjoyed by the strange bedfellows heading the new coalition would, in fact, last barely a year. The jocular nature of his relationship with the former chief of staff of the Provisional IRA inevitably offended many of Ian Paisley's core supporters, and in short order he would be deposed from his leadership roles in both the church and the party he had founded.[23] In June 2008, the veteran evangelical preacher stepped aside as leader of the DUP to be replaced by his long-standing political apprentice Peter Robinson. The promotion of this rather more taciturn figure would bring a distinctly cooler tone to relations between the parties of government at Stormont. And over time the various often emotive issues that still inflame Northern Irish political life would test that already fragile relationship to the limit.

Neoliberal consensus and culture clashes

While the new coalition partners would, as we shall see, often find themselves divided over matters of culture and identity, they would swiftly find common cause when it came to issues of social and economic policy. In the period between 2002 and 2007, when the Stormont institutions were suspended, the New Labour government sought to extend the remit of the Private Finance Initiative in Northern Ireland.[24] This led to the creation in 2003 of the Strategic Investment Board, with the brief of securing private capital in the funding and execution of public infrastructural projects such as building schools and hospitals. When the new coalition partners took office, they did so, therefore, in a context where the Blair administration had placed social and economic policy in a distinctly neoliberal frame. As a party from the right of the political spectrum, the DUP was always likely to embrace this turn towards the marketisation of public goods. Rather more surprising was that an ostensibly 'socialist' party like Sinn Féin would prove just as convinced as their unionist counterparts by the dogma that allowing private capital to take the lead in relation to certain critical forms of public provision would result in greater efficiency and prosperity. This 'unusual unanimity'[25] was keenly expressed in the unflagging support of both coalition partners for the Private Finance Initiative. By 2017, the year when Sinn Féin and the DUP parted company acrimoniously, there were no fewer than 31 Public Private Partnerships (PPPs) in Northern Ireland, with a total value of some £1.73 billion.[26]

The commitment of both unionists and republicans in government to neoliberal strategies was also revealed in what often appeared to be the *one big idea* shared by the coalition partners. Over the course of a decade in power, Sinn Féin and the DUP consistently took the line that if corporation tax were to be reduced to 12.5 per cent, in line with the Irish Republic, Northern Ireland would be able to replicate the success of its neighbour in attracting multinational investment. Many economic experts counselled otherwise. The financial consultants PricewaterhouseCoopers, for instance, argued that the proposed cuts in corporation tax were unlikely to induce much greater levels of foreign direct investment in Northern Ireland, counsel that was echoed in the findings of the Stormont assembly's own research team.[27] The parties in government were, however, content to ignore advice that was widely available in house and out, electing instead to cling to the comforting fiction that the 'magic bullet'[28] of yet more tax breaks for multinational capital would pave the way to economic recovery.

While the coalition partners would often find common cause on matters of social and economic policy, they were of course altogether less likely to see eye to eye on those issues that are the more traditional fare of Northern Irish political life. On 3 December 2012, Belfast City Council discussed a Sinn Féin motion stipulating that the Union flag would no longer be flown constantly over City Hall and would instead appear only on eighteen designated days, bringing it into line with public buildings elsewhere in the UK. The decision of the centre-ground Alliance Party to support the proposal tipped the balance in its favour, allowing it to pass by a margin of 29 votes to 21. As the council reached its controversial decision, there were violent scenes outside City Hall as a large gathering of unionist protesters, drawn in part by 40,000 leaflets distributed beforehand by both the DUP and the UUP,[29] vented their anger and clashed with riot police. This would prove to be the first of many heated demonstrations against the new flag protocol. Over the next four months, there were almost 3,000 separate incidents in which mainly youngsters from working-class unionist communities took to the streets to air their grievances. It was apparent from the outset that the flag protests had tapped into a deeper well of anger within those loyalist neighbourhoods that had never enjoyed the 'peace dividend' of economic prosperity promised when the GFA was signed.[30] By the time the disturbances ran out of steam in the spring of 2013, 411 people had been processed by the courts for alleged criminal offences and 160 officers had been injured in a policing operation costing £22 million.[31]

The febrile mood within sections of the unionist community manifested in the flag protests would become evident again a few months later when the Orange marching season reached its annual climax. In previous years, a bitter and seemingly intractable dispute had developed in north Belfast over a parade from Ligoniel Orange Lodge passing the edge of the republican Ardoyne district on its way to and from the Twelfth of July celebrations. In the summer of 2012, a ruling by the Parades Commission that the Orange Order be allowed to follow this contested route provoked widespread anger among republicans. As the loyalist bandsmen returned past Ardoyne, there were sustained scenes of violence as the police came under attack from often very young males who seemed, in part at least, to be under the influence of local dissident republican figures. The rioting that scarred the summer of 2012 would lead the Parades Commission to reach a compromise ruling the following year. While the Ligoniel Orange Lodge would be allowed to pass the shops that fringe Ardoyne early on the morning of the Twelfth of July, they would not be granted permission to return via the same route. The decision was greeted with indignation by the Orange Order and, coming quick on the heels of the decision to restrict the flying of the Union flag over Belfast City Hall, fed into a growing sense among many working-class unionists that they were the casualties of an escalating 'culture war'.[32] On the evening of 12 July 2013, when members of the Ligoniel Orange Lodge sought to return along their 'traditional' route, they were stopped by a heavily fortified police line on Twaddell Avenue, on one side of the roundabout that informally marks the sectarian interface with Ardoyne on the other. What followed, inevitably, was a prolonged and at times frenzied assault on the PSNI that continued long into the night. Amid dramatic scenes, one indelible image of a young loyalist brandishing an Ulster flag being propelled by water cannon from the bonnet of a police Land Rover would become a favourite of news agencies around the world.[33]

The flags dispute and the ongoing controversy over Orange parades in north Belfast would place even greater pressure on the already strained relations between the coalition partners at Stormont. Throughout the course of 2013, Sinn Féin and the DUP found themselves increasingly at loggerheads, and it seemed for a time that there was a danger that the government might fall. In an effort to avoid that eventuality, in the autumn the Obama administration sent Dr Richard Haass and Professor Meghan O'Sullivan to Belfast to initiate talks among the five main local parties. The pair would spend more than three months overseeing intense negotiations designed to break the impasse on issues concerning flags, parades and how to deal with Northern Ireland's troubled past. As with many before them, the efforts of

Haass and O'Sullivan to broker a deal between the local parties would come to nothing. On New Year's Eve 2013, it was announced that no agreement had been reached on the outstanding issues and the two US diplomatic figures who had chaired the discussions prepared for their flights home.[34]

Welfare 'reform' and the Stormont House Agreement

The tensions festering within the Stormont Executive over matters such as flags and parades would in time be compounded by an issue rather less familiar to Northern Irish political life. The story of how welfare 'reform' came to Northern Ireland is recounted in some detail in Chapter 7, and hence we will limit ourselves here to a brief sketch. When the Conservatives returned to power in 2010 in a marriage of convenience with the Liberal Democrats they did so against the backdrop of the worst global recession in eighty years. The majority Conservative administration chose, predictably, to rehearse the almost hegemonic idea that the 'credit crunch' was the result not of unregulated financial speculation but rather of supposedly excessive levels of state expenditure.[35] This diagnosis cleared the ground for the introduction of the 2012 Welfare Reform Act. Billed as an attempt both to simplify the social security system and to 'make work pay', critics have suggested that the new regime is in fact more complicated than its predecessor and acts to deprive some of most vulnerable within British society of essential financial support.[36] As the most radical assault on the welfare state since its creation has taken hold, versions of poverty have surfaced that had not been seen for several generations. Perhaps the most sobering statistic capturing the impact of austerity in the UK is that 1.9 million food parcels are now distributed each year in what remains one of the wealthiest societies on the face of the planet.[37]

The advent of the Welfare Reform Act would shed light once more on the ideological fissures among the principal parties of government in Northern Ireland. While the DUP readily endorsed the new regime, their coalition partners expressed their total opposition to measures that were likely both to impact most gravely on the republican heartlands and to tarnish their credentials as an anti-austerity party that had been nurtured so assiduously south of the border. As a result, when proposals to introduce the Welfare Reform Act came before the Stormont Executive, the Sinn Féin ministers around the table dismissed them out of hand. Given that social security measures are among those devolved to the Northern Ireland Assembly, there was at least the prospect that the UK region with the highest dependency on state benefits[38] might be spared the draconian new regime.[39] The British government would make it clear, however, that welfare 'reform' was to operate throughout every region of the UK and that it was prepared to use financial sanctions to ensure that outcome. As central government began to act on those threats – in the 2014–15 fiscal year alone, some £87 million was withheld from the block grant to Northern Ireland[40] – republicans sharing power in Stormont would be compelled to rethink their previously implacable opposition to the new order of welfare 'reform'.

When the Stormont assembly resumed after the 2014 summer recess, it was apparent that the Northern Ireland executive now faced a sequence of challenges that threatened its very future. Not only were Sinn Féin and the DUP required to deal with the controversies over flags and parades that are the traditional staples of local politics, they were now confronted with the rather less familiar class issues arising out of Westminster's insistence on welfare 'reform'. As the threat grew of government grinding to a halt in Northern Ireland, the British Secretary of State Theresa Villiers and Irish Foreign Secretary Charlie Flanagan convened another round of talks in the grounds of the Stormont estate in September 2014. Eleven weeks of negotiation would on this occasion prove sufficient for the local parties to strike a deal. Finalised in November 2014 and published the following month, the Stormont House Agreement would address some of those ethno-national disputes that were threatening the political stability of Northern Ireland. The text of the deal allowed for the creation of a Commission on Flags, Identity, Culture and Tradition and raised the prospect of powers for regulating parades being devolved to the Stormont Assembly. In addition, the agreement marked some progress in the critical and often neglected area of dealing with Northern Ireland's violent past. The terms of the deal allowed for the creation of a Historical Investigations Unit to examine unsolved deaths from the Troubles and the establishment of an oral history archive giving members of the public the opportunity to record their experiences of the conflict.

While the Stormont House Agreement dealt with those ethno-national preoccupations with which Northern Ireland has become synonymous, it also addressed certain 'bread and butter' issues that are less frequently the substance of political life in the region. Indeed, what was perhaps most significant about the document was that for the first time ever a political deal had been brokered in the six counties that placed class issues up front and centre, albeit in the most reactionary manner. The first section of the Stormont House Agreement was, significantly, one addressing issues of 'finance and welfare'. In signing the deal, the local parties committed themselves to cutting both social security ('welfare changes') and jobs in the state sector ('public sector reform and restructuring'). While the text of the agreement required the Westminster government to provide an additional £2 billion in funding for Northern Ireland, that sum would in all likelihood have been quickly overtaken by the reductions in public spending envisaged elsewhere in the document.

The advent of the Stormont House Agreement meant then that both of the principal parties were now committed – the DUP in principle, Sinn Féin in practice – to the introduction of social security cuts that would have a devastating impact on the poorest sections of one of the UK's poorest regions. This common purpose would become apparent at a meeting of the Stormont executive in January 2015 when the coalition partners joined forces to vote through a budget allowing for welfare 'reform'.[41] The 'neo-liberal turn'[42] on the part of the Sinn Féin leadership would lead both to internal dissent and to stinging criticism from their main electoral rivals, the SDLP, who had adopted a more radical and consistent position on changes to the social security system. These pressures would ensure that by the time the Welfare Reform Act came before the Assembly on 9 March 2015, republicans had experienced another change of heart. When it came time to vote on the proposed legislation, the Sinn Féin MLAs in the chamber astonished their coalition partners by opposing the bill before them.[43] Amid a welter of mutual recrimination, the fault-lines within the Northern Ireland executive became even more apparent than before.

The already fractious relationship between Sinn Féin and the DUP would soon become more perilous still when the return of political violence to the streets of Northern Ireland begged fundamental questions of the nature and the status of the peace process. On 12 August 2015, Kevin McGuigan was shot dead outside his home in the nationalist Short Strand district of east Belfast, apparently in retaliation for the murder of the senior republican figure Gerard 'Jock' Davison three months earlier. According to the authorities, McGuigan's killers were almost certainly members of the Provisional IRA.[44] The very real possibility that republicans were responsible for the murder represented perhaps the greatest challenge that the Northern Irish Executive had faced to date. When the DUP had agreed to enter government with Sinn Féin it had done so on the assumption that the Provisional IRA had disbanded and decommissioned its weapons. Events in the summer of 2015 would, however, confirm the widespread suspicion that the structures of the paramilitary organization were still intact and that it retained the capacity for occasional acts of violence. It was simply untenable that the DUP would continue in power with Sinn Féin if it were established that the latter's armed wing remained in existence. Once the authorities attributed the death of Kevin McGuigan to the Provisional IRA, therefore, it seemed there was little prospect that the coalition partners could remain in office together. As the Stormont executive teetered on the brink of collapse once more, the British Secretary of State Theresa Villiers convened yet another round of talks between the local parties.

A fresh start?

The urgency of the situation in which party negotiators found themselves this time around would appear to have concentrated minds to good effect. The new round of discussions that began in September 2015 would reach what seemed to be a successful conclusion two months later. In view of events the previous summer, it was inevitable that the agreed text that emerged from the negotiations would focus largely on dealing with the activities of paramilitary organisations. The signatories of A Fresh Start reaffirmed their commitment to the Mitchell Principles on the pursuit of political goals through purely non-violent means.[45] For its part, the British government signaled greater seriousness of purpose in dealing with the remnants of organised violence in Northern Ireland. Westminster pledged to spend some £160 million over the next five years to improve security in general and £25 million to combat paramilitary groupings in particular. The text of A Fresh Start also provided for the implementation of several commitments made in the Stormont House Agreement signed only a year before. In particular, the new deal committed all of the parties once more to the implementation of the Welfare Reform Act, with £585million of existing funds at the disposal of the Stormont executive being made available to 'mitigate' its initial impact. Mindful of the previous failure of the Stormont assembly to implement 'welfare reform', those who framed A Fresh Start were unwilling to leave matters to chance on this occasion. The new deal required that the implementation of the Welfare Reform Act the Stormont institutions would in this instance cede their legislative powers to Westminster. On 18 November 2015, the Northern Ireland Assembly duly voted by a margin of 70 to 22 to allow this to happen. Five days later, the British parliament passed the relevant legislation signaling that the new order of welfare 'reform' already endured for several years in other UK regions would now be extended, albeit in mitigated form, to the six counties as well.

While the agreement that emerged from Northern Ireland's latest political crisis would promise 'a fresh start', the rather more likely prospect would be more of the same. With welfare 'reform' in place and a public pledge to the use of purely peaceful political means reaffirmed, Sinn Féin and the DUP were now in a position to resume their duopoly of power in the six counties. The assembly elections held in May 2016 confirmed once more the political dominance of the coalition partners. In the last election before the number of members returned to the assembly fell from 108 to 90, the DUP secured 38 seats and Sinn Féin 28. While the headline figures in the 2016 assembly election evidently augured well for the two parties, there were, however, certain underlying trends that might have given them pause for thought. One was the continuation of a long-running pattern of falling voter turnout. In 2016, a mere 55 per cent of those entitled to vote actually did so, a full fifteen per cent lower than in the first Assembly election eighteen years earlier.[46] A second was the possible kindling of political alternatives to the competing ethno-national agendas that have traditionally dominated Northern Irish political life. Most significantly, the 2016 elections saw emergence of the People Before Profit Alliance as a small but credible electoral force providing a radical critique of the austerity measures about to be administered by Sinn Féin in particular under the guise of welfare 'reform'. The left-wing grouping emerged with two seats, even managing to top the poll in the republican citadel of west Belfast. While voter apathy and the challenge of a nascent Left opposition may have given some concern to the mainstream parties, and to republican strategists in particular, the outcome of the 2016 assembly elections would nonetheless be one that overwhelmingly confirmed the political status quo in Northern Ireland. When Sinn Féin and the DUP renewed their vows as coalition partners, the likelihood was that they would put their recent troubles behind them and spend the next five years colluding once more in the 'sectarian carve up'[47] that has routinely passed for governance during the peace process. As it turned out, the new Stormont Executive would in fact last a mere matter of months. While the latest collapse of the devolved institutions would be widely attributed to a local political scandal, its origins might more accurately be traced to questionable political developments elsewhere in the UK.

'Cash for ash' and the Brexit conjuncture

On 9 January 2017, deputy First Minister Martin McGuinness cut a frail figure as he informed journalists gathered at Stormont that he was resigning from the post. The ostensible cause of this latest crisis in Northern Ireland's power-sharing experiment was what had originally seemed a fairly innocuous project to encourage the use of more environmentally friendly energy sources. Under the terms of the Renewable Heating Incentive (RHI) scheme, homeowners and businesses that moved away from burning fossil fuels were, quite remarkably, given £1.57 for every £1 spent on alternatives, with those using wood chip receiving more than £2 for every £1 invested.[48] In effect, therefore, some people in Northern Ireland were actually being paid to (over)heat their homes and premises, hence the phrase 'cash for ash'. The politician who had introduced the RHI scheme was Arlene Foster during her stint in the Department of Enterprise, Trade, and Investment. In December 2015, Foster had taken over as leader of the DUP and the following month assumed the position of First Minister, replacing Peter Robinson who had moved aside after a sequence of scandals in his personal and business affairs. Her promotion ensured that when the RHI controversy broke in earnest it would reach the very highest levels of government in Northern Ireland. In the closing weeks of 2016, stories began to surface of canny farmers heating empty barns[49] in order to avail of 'cash for ash' and estimates suggested that the total cost of the scheme might eventually amount to as much as £490 million.[50] Initially, the 'instinctive reaction' of Sinn Féin appeared to be to 'keep Stormont together'[51] and the party seemed reluctant to capitalise on the increasingly precarious position of First Minister Arlene Foster. As the scandal continued to gather momentum, however, republicans began to demand that the DUP leader step aside to allow a public inquiry into the RHI scheme. While her predecessor Peter Robinson had agreed to such a move in 2010 when alleged financial improprieties associated with his wife threatened his credibility as First Minister, Foster refused to countenance stepping down, claiming it was not for republicans to dictate who headed her party.[52] On 19 December 2016, the DUP leader survived a vote of no confidence in the Assembly and when Stormont broke for Christmas the future of the power-sharing executive once more seemed in considerable doubt. The dramatic announcement that Martin McGuinness would make early in the new year would of course bring a certain clarity to proceedings.

The dominant narrative surrounding the most recent collapse of power sharing in Northern Ireland tends to lay the blame squarely at the feet of an RHI scheme that over time created insurmountable divisions between the two main parties of government at Stormont. This version of events certainly contains an element of truth, but it fails to tell the whole story. While republicans managed to pin almost all the blame for the 'cash for ash' scandal on their partners in government, they too played an important supporting role in the evolution of the controversial green energy scheme. The period that Michelle O'Neill served as Minister for Agriculture would, for instance, see her department organise no fewer than 58 separate meetings promoting the opportunities of the RHI scheme to an evidently receptive farming community.[53] In addition, the public inquiry into the controversial green energy project chaired by Sir Patrick Coghlin unearthed correspondence indicating that the then south Belfast MLA Máirtín Ó Muilleoir lobbied successfully for the scheme to be prolonged, an extension that alone cost £92 million.[54] The track record of certain key figures in Sinn Féin – and not least that of the future leader of the party in the Stormont assembly – indicates then that republicans were not in fact opposed to the 'cash for ash' initiative for much of its period in existence and suggests that their subsequent vehement objections to the project owed rather less to political principle than to political opportunism. In order to understand the dramatic, and largely forgotten, change of heart that overtook republicans in relation to the RHI scheme we need to leave behind all those lurid tales of boilers running all night in empty barns in rural Northern Ireland and turn our attention instead towards rather more seismic developments elsewhere in the UK.

On 23 June 2016, a slim majority of UK voters took the historic decision to leave the European Union. Although the discussions that preceded the Brexit referendum rarely even mentioned Northern Ireland and most people (56 per cent) living there actually voted to remain part of the EU,[55] it would soon become apparent that the six counties would be the region most gravely affected by this dramatic political development. The subsequent, often fraught, negotiations between the UK government and the EU authorities raised at times the very real prospect of the return of a physical frontier on the island of Ireland. One potential outcome of the talks was that a border that had long since become invisible because of the peace process might once more be marked by customs posts and fortifications reminiscent of the dark days of the Troubles. The prospect of a 'hard Brexit' inevitably served to radicalise opinion across the breadth of nationalist Ireland. A border that barely registered in mainstream political debate previously has once more become a 'live issue',[56] and support for a united Ireland that only recently appeared at an 'all time low'[57] seems to be have gained ground.[58] While republicans played little role in the debates that preceded the referendum on EU membership – indeed, Sinn Féin did not even register with the Electoral Commissioner to campaign on the matter[59] – they would be among the principal beneficiaries of its outcome. In the climate of ever more favourable ideological flux that followed the Brexit vote, Sinn Féin clearly decided to pursue a more radical political strategy that manifested itself not least in the adoption of a more abrasive tone when dealing with their erstwhile partners in government at Stormont.

One of the more remarkable features of the decade in which Sinn Féin shared power with the DUP was that it often appeared to be the former that was a great deal more committed to making the relationship work. A republican movement that had for a quarter-century engaged in 'armed struggle' in order the destroy the institutions of government in Northern Ireland now seemed to be willing to go to great lengths to ensure their continuation. This commitment to the peace process was embodied most obviously in the most senior republican figure serving in the Stormont executive. It often appeared that deputy First Minister Martin McGuinness was on a personal mission to reach out to the unionist community. The most resonant of the many gestures of reconciliation that the Derry republican would make came in June 2012 when he greeted Queen Elizabeth II in public for the first time in the Lyric Theatre in Belfast. Few images summed up more vividly the progress that Northern Ireland appeared to have made during the peace process than that of the former Chief of Staff of the Provisional IRA sharing pleasantries with the head of the House of Windsor.[60] These remarkable gestures towards healing the wounds of the past, however, would not always be reciprocated fully. In particular, the refusal of First Minister Arlene Foster to attend the keynote commemoration in Dublin marking the centenary of the 1916 Rising was viewed dimly within republican circles.[61] This seeming asymmetry ensured that there was a growing feeling among elements within Sinn Féin that the party had become too accommodating in its dealings with an often abrasive DUP, a conciliatory disposition that came to be dismissed in some quarters as 'project Martin'. In the changed ideological circumstances signalled by the Brexit referendum, the republican leadership would apparently come to decide that the climate was right to adopt a rather more aggressive political strategy.[62] This shift in tone was evident at a meeting in the Felons' Club in west Belfast on 7 January 2017 addressed by then Sinn Féin leader Gerry Adams, where there was rapturous applause when the call came to 'bring the [Stormont] institutions down now'.[63] The first public intimation of the new republican strategy would come just two days later. In announcing his resignation as deputy First Minister, an ailing Martin McGuinness was also signalling the end of the particular project of reconciliation he had sustained over the previous decade. While the republican movement had in effect sidelined one of its most revered contemporary figures, the advent of this palace coup was concealed by the Derry veteran's deteriorating health which required him to withdraw from front line politics and which would lead to his death a mere two months later.

The more belligerent republican strategy unveiled in the Felons' Club would become further apparent in the run up to the 2 March 2017 assembly elections necessitated by the recent collapse of the Stormont executive. On this occasion, Sinn Féin secured 60,000 additional votes and came within 1,300 of becoming the largest party in Northern Ireland. In terms of seats gained, the existing gap of ten between the former coalition partners had been whittled down to just one and for the first time ever a Stormont assembly had been returned without a unionist majority.[64] The sectarian logic of Northern Irish political life would inevitably mean that the electoral success of Sinn Féin would invite a response from the other ethno-national bloc. Consequently, the Westminster elections held in June 2017 had the feeling of a proxy border poll in the context of Northern Ireland. While Sinn Féin would gain 15,000 more votes than last time out, that creditable performance was eclipsed by the more substantial advances made by their main political rivals. The DUP would receive almost 70,000 additional votes and secure ten Westminster seats, allowing the party to enter a controversial 'confidence and supply' arrangement that would see the Conservatives remain in power in return for the promise of £1.5 billion in new funding for Northern Ireland.[65]

The outcome of the pair of elections held three months apart in 2017 did not seem to augur well for the prospect of political progress in Northern Ireland. Both of the main political parties had been amply rewarded by the electorate for their belligerent disposition towards one another and that tone would carry over into subsequent negotiations between them. In the period after the 2017 Westminster election, the British and Irish governments would initiate yet more rounds of talks between Sinn Féin and the DUP. What emerged as the largest bone of contention in these discussions was the repeated call of republicans for the introduction of an Irish language act. This demand represents in part a matter of principle. While Irish is the first language of only one in every four hundred people in Northern Ireland,[66] it has nonetheless a genuinely widespread symbolic significance throughout the nationalist community. The call for an Irish language act should also be seen, however, as an astute strategic calculation on the part of republican negotiators. According to Dr Richard Haass, when he convened talks in Northern Ireland in the closing months of 2013, linguistic issues ranked as only a 'tertiary' concern for the Sinn Féin negotiation team.[67] The recent promotion of the Irish language to the top of the republican agenda represents in part an acknowledgement that demands for its introduction play well with a nationalist audience not least because they constantly bring out the worst in the unionists sitting across the table. One of the moments that accelerated the collapse of the last power-sharing government was when DUP Minister for Communities Paul Givan decided to withdraw £50,000 in funding from Líofa, an organisation that brings children from poor neighbourhoods to the Gaeltacht to learn Irish.[68] The apparent spitefulness of this act evidently touched a nerve within a nationalist community whose mood was hardly improved when First Minister Arlene Foster commented subsequently that to give further grants to Irish language groups was to 'feed the crocodile'.[69] Ever since that gaffe, the issue of Irish has assumed an even more heightened figurative power for nationalists, symbolising as it does the cultural pride even of those who do not speak the language and summoning as it does the worst cultural prejudices of political unionism. A party as astute as Sinn Féin was unlikely to fail to spot the suddenly even greater political capital flowing from agitation for an Irish language act and it came as little surprise then that the call for its introduction would emerge as the principal 'red line' issue for republicans during the negotiations convened after the collapse of the Stormont executive.

In the opening weeks of 2018, it appeared once again that Sinn Féin and the DUP might finally be on the verge of resolving their political differences and striking a deal that would allow the restoration of the devolved institutions. Media speculation reached fever pitch on Monday 12 February when the British Prime Minister and the Irish Taoiseach arrived in Belfast in what appeared to be a presage of imminent political progress. Both Theresa May and Leo Varadkar would, however, leave Stormont empty-handed. Two days later, the DUP leader Arlene Foster announced that the finalised political deal that journalists believed to exist had only ever been a draft document and that this had now been rejected by her party. In a series of increasingly heated exchanges, Sinn Féin countered that the text under discussion was in fact a final agreement and that their prospective partners in government had now reneged upon it. All of the detail that would emerge subsequently appeared to bear out the republican version of events.[70] This latest setback in the Northern Irish peace process apparently owed its origins to shifts in the balance of power within the principal party of unionism that occurred after the Westminster elections the year before. The DUP team at Stormont seemed willing to sign off on a political agreement that would see the creation of language acts for both Irish and Ulster Scots, a symmetry that was designed to conceal the fact that Arlene Foster was now effectively going back on her previous insistence that there would be no 'stand-alone' legislation for the Irish language. This deal was vetoed, however, by the party's ten MPs at Westminster, a grouping whose power had grown substantially since the 'confidence and supply' arrangement made with the Conservatives the previous summer.[71] With a seemingly feasible agreement now dead in the water and relations between the two main parties once more in a state of disrepair, Northern Ireland returned again to its accustomed condition of political stalemate.

'The first signs of a diversification'?

In August 2018, Northern Ireland attained the unenviable status of being the democratic polity that has gone the longest period in peace time without a serving government. Although the intransigence of Sinn Féin and the DUP brought electoral rewards in the short term, it was always likely to invite certain dangers as time moved on. As what appeared initially to be a temporary malfunction in the power-sharing experiment settled into a seemingly intractable political stalemate, public disaffection inevitably gathered ground. In particular, there was a widespread sense of grievance that politicians elected to an assembly that was no longer sitting were entitled to draw most of their generous salaries and expenses. This growing mood of alienation would sharpen palpably on 18 April 2019 when Lyra McKee was shot dead by dissident republicans aiming at police officers raiding homes in Derry's Creggan district in advance of a controversial Easter commemoration. In the aftermath of the murder, a succession of public figures claimed that the tragedy was the result of the political vacuum that had been allowed to develop in Northern Ireland. This critique found its most arch and public expression at the ecumenical funeral of the journalist and author held a week after her death in Belfast's St Anne's Cathedral. Marking the bleak irony that the politicians of various hues seated before him had not met in talks for quite some time, Fr Martin Magill drew a standing ovation when he issued the following stinging rebuke: "Why in God's name does it take the death of a 29-year-old woman with her whole life in front of her to get us to this point?"[72]

The mood of public disillusionment so starkly evident in the days after the death of Lyra McKee would become even more manifest during the three elections held in the eight months that followed the tragedy. The local government elections on 2 May 2019 took place in an 'antagonistic, divisive atmosphere'[73] which facilitated Sinn Féin and the DUP in retaining their position as the two principal forces in Northern Irish political life. While the Democratic Unionists saw their share of the vote grow one per cent, they lost eight of the 130 seats secured last time around. Ironically, although Sinn Féin actually saw their vote share drop by almost one per cent, they managed to hold on to all of the 105 seats won previously in Northern Ireland's eleven council chambers. The local government elections held in the early summer of 2019 appeared then to have confirmed the political status quo in Northern Ireland. If we look more closely at the composition of council chambers in the region, however, it seems that we might just be witnessing 'the first signs of a diversification'[74] in the political culture of the six counties. This nascent change owes its origins largely to certain critical changes that have overtaken Northern Irish society since the end of the Troubles. These are explored in considerable detail later in the book – see Chapter 5 – and hence are only examined briefly here for the purposes of illustration.

The era of the peace process has witnessed important shifts in the identities and issues that animate the residents of Northern Ireland. Over time, there has been evidence that many people in the region have begun to question and even discard the twin ethno-national affiliations that traditionally have dominated cultural life in the six counties. The Northern Ireland Life and Times Survey, for instance, has mapped a steady decline in the number electing to call themselves 'unionist' or 'nationalist'.[75] Indeed, in the 2018 edition of the opinion poll, the proportion of people who eschew these traditional cultural identities reached fifty per cent for the first time.[76] The period since the end of the Troubles has also seen the rapid secularisation of a society that within living memory recorded the highest levels of church attendance in the Western world.[77] This trend is especially apparent among those fortunate enough to remember little or nothing about the conflict. While some young people in the region remain preoccupied by traditional ethno-national issues such as flags and parades, many of their peers would prefer to devote their energies to rather more universal issues such as climate change, gay, transsexual and reproductive rights, university fees, precarious employment and the housing crisis. These liberal, secular concerns have rarely been reflected in the priorities of the dominant parties in Northern Ireland and on those occasions when they have actually featured in Stormont debates the contributions from the floor have often illuminated the innate conservatism of local political life. Take, for instance, the issues of gay marriage and a woman's right to choose. The fundamentalist Protestant roots of the DUP ensure that there are many in the party who share the conviction of former Westminster MP Iris Robinson that homosexuality is an 'abomination'.[78] This prejudice would lead the Democratic Unionists to use the supposedly exceptional mechanism of the 'petition of concern' on no fewer than five occasions in the Stormont Assembly to prevent the introduction of legislation allowing people of the same sex to marry in Northern Ireland.[79] While their principal partners in government have often expressed their support for 'gay marriage', this political commitment has at times proved entirely dispensable. In the ill-starred negotiations that concluded in February 2018, for example, it became evident that Sinn Féin were willing to sign off on a deal that made no mention of the rights of sexual minorities which they had previously claimed to cherish as a matter of principle.[80]

The issue of women's reproductive rights, inevitably, casts the two principal parties of government in no less reactionary a light. The evangelical religious convictions of many in the DUP ensure that the party has remained unequivocally opposed to the abortion rights that women in Great Britain have enjoyed for the last half-century being extended to Northern Ireland. What is perhaps less widely acknowledged is that their coalition partners have, until quite recently at least, also assumed an essentially conservative position on matters of reproductive rights. It was only when it became clear that the campaign in the Irish Republic to amend the Constitution to allow for legal terminations had become unstoppable, for instance, that Sinn Féin came to adopt a more explicit and consistent stance in support of a woman's right to choose.[81] The position adopted by the two main parties in Northern Ireland on the issues of gay marriage and abortion rights – opposition by the DUP on grounds of religious principle, equivocation by Sinn Féin on grounds of political pragmatism – has inevitably served to frustrate the introduction of these essential hallmarks of any modern, secular society. It was entirely predictable then that the granting of these civil rights would only occur once the Stormont assembly had been suspended. In the summer of 2019, the Labour MPs Stella Creasy and Conor McGinn introduced bills allowing for same-sex unions and abortion in Northern Ireland that passed comfortably through the House of Commons, much to the fury of the Democratic Unionists present.[82] On 11 February 2020, Robyn Peoples and Sharni Edwards became the first same-sex couple to wed in Northern Ireland, providing a ready metaphor for the remarkable social transformation that has occurred in the region since the end of the conflict.[83] Then, on the final day of March 2020, legislation came into effect allowing for the first legal terminations ever to take place in the six counties.

While the relevant legislation may well have caught up finally with the realities of the modern, secular society that has begun to flourish in Northern Ireland, the same cannot perhaps be said of many of the region's elected representatives. The possibility that the mainstream political parties are no longer able to accommodate the identities and issues that animate many Northern Irish people would begin to become apparent in the May 2019 local government elections. The polls would show small but potentially significant gains for the Greens and People Before Profit, who now comprise a sizeable progressive bloc in Belfast city council. Both parties have sought to advance agendas that looked well beyond the conventional 'narrow ground' of Northern Irish politics, articulating support for civil liberties such as gay marriage and a woman's right to choose, as well as a concern about the perils of climate change and the neoliberal assault on the welfare state, respectively.[84] The most eye-catching performance during the local and European elections was, however, that of the Alliance Party. The centrist political philosophy of Alliance emphasises a shared identity transcending the traditional binaries of 'unionism' and 'nationalism', and advocates relatively liberal positions on matters of gender and reproductive rights. This ideological profile allowed the party perhaps to tap into that growing constituency of people in Northern Ireland, and the young especially, who apparently wish to cast off the traditional tags of 'unionist' and 'nationalist' and to explore the more fluid identities and greater personal freedoms that have come with living in an ever more secular society. The burgeoning appeal of Alliance would be confirmed in the local government elections when the party secured twelve per cent of the vote, winning 53 seats including two in the previously unchartered territory of Derry and Strabane District Council.[85] Even greater success was to come three weeks later in the final election to the European parliament to include candidates from the UK. While the poll held on 23 May 2019 would once again see Sinn Féin and the DUP placed first and second on first preferences, both parties experienced a drop in their vote relative to the previous EU election. This decline was especially dramatic in the case of Martina Anderson, with the republican candidate losing more than 30,000 votes compared to her last outing. The main talking point of the European election was, however, the unprecedented performance of the Alliance candidate. Naomi Long secured a seat with almost nineteen per cent of first preferences, and in the process recorded the best ever performance in the history of her party.[86]

The conditions that allowed the electoral hegemony of Sinn Féin and the DUP to be challenged in the local and European elections had, if anything, become even more favourable by the time of the snap Westminster poll held six months later. In the months that led up to the general election, the mood of public disaffection at the seemingly endless stalemate among the local parties turned darker still. Among the catalysts for this growing popular disillusionment was the sequence of revelations emerging in relation to the scandal that had, ostensibly, brought down the Stormont executive. While the public inquiry into the RHI scheme had produced a steady drip of information concerning the 'cash for ash' controversy, this would become a flood with the publication in October 2019 of a surprise best seller recounting in painstaking detail the entire sorry tale. In his book *Burned*, Sam McBride provides a damning account of how business had been done between the partners in the previous power-sharing government. Over the course of almost 400 pages, the journalist reveals that the mode of governance operating at Stormont had entailed widespread incompetence, endemic bullying and occasional corruption. Among the many peculiar practices that McBride documents are that expensive commissioned reports recommending that the RHI scheme be abandoned were simply ignored, ministerial meetings went, as a matter of course, unrecorded, ministers proposed legislation to Stormont they had not even read, and special advisers were effectively the power behind the thrones of those the public might have naively thought to be running the country.[87] Many of the malpractices identified in *Burned* would be confirmed subsequently in the findings of the public inquiry chaired by Sir Patrick Coghlin. Widely anticipated for many months, the Coghlin report had the misfortune to be released on 13 March 2020 – the day when a very public row broke out between Executive members over whether to follow the Dublin government's closure of schools as the coronavirus crisis gathered speed – and hence made almost no political impact whatsoever.[88]

The revelations concerning the RHI scandal continued to mount at a time when the impact of the political logjam on the social fabric of Northern Ireland was becoming ever more painfully apparent. In the period after the collapse of the Stormont executive, civil servants took over the everyday running of the region but lacked the executive authority to make critical policy decisions. The inevitable outcome was that over time there were funding shortfalls leading to a sharp deterioration in crucial public services. As the waiting lists for hospital appointments grew ever longer, nurses began industrial action aimed at restoring pay parity with their counterparts in other UK regions.[89] In the popular imagination, the nurses' strike became an instant metaphor capturing the chaos and injustice of this rather precarious moment in recent Northern Irish history. Members of the public approached in the street by journalists and asked for an opinion on the current state of affairs would routinely express their anger that health workers were not being paid enough for doing their jobs at a time when politicians were being paid rather greater sums for *not* doing theirs.

In this climate of growing popular dissatisfaction, it was always likely that the two former parties of government in Northern Ireland would experience electoral reprisals when the polls opened on 12 December 2019 and so it was to prove. The principal casualty of this darkening of the public mood would prove to be the Democratic Unionists. The party would see its vote drop almost 50,000 compared to its previous Westminster triumph, and lose two seats, in North and South Belfast. More importantly, the return of new Conservative leader Boris Johnson with a majority of 80 seats meant that the power the DUP had previously been able to exercise over the British government had now evaporated. The era of 'confidence and supply' had effectively granted the party a veto on those aspects of any prospective Brexit deal deemed injurious to the unionist cause. If the Democratic Unionists had been unnerved by the prospect of a 'backstop' while Theresa May was in office, they were downright appalled by the agreement that her successor chose to broker with Brussels. The Ireland and Northern Ireland Protocol that was so critical to the Withdrawal Agreement that Boris Johnson negotiated in October 2019 would see the six counties remain a de facto part of the EU's single market and customs union, creating the prospect of what would in effect be a trade border running through the Irish Sea.[90] That the Conservative Prime Minister would choose to sunder the Union in this manner was held to be all the more treacherous because he had quite explicitly courted favour with the DUP, even giving a barnstorming speech to a receptive audience at their party conference a year earlier. With Boris Johnson seemingly ensconced firmly in power for the foreseeable future, the painful realisation began to dawn among Democratic Unionists that they had been hoodwinked into backing a political project they now saw to pose an imminent and perhaps even existential threat to the UK. Not for the first time, a group of unionist politicians had learned the hard way that those who exercise power at Westminster are only too prepared to treat Northern Ireland as 'a place apart' when the moment becomes opportune.[91]

While the 2019 general election was catastrophic for the DUP, it was, at first glance at least, rather kinder on their former partners in government. Sinn Féin had, after all, managed to emerge from the election with the same number of seats, seven, that it held beforehand, and the historic capture of North Belfast by John Finucane, son of murdered solicitor Pat, put a distinctly positive gloss on proceedings. A closer examination of the republican performance would, however, suggest some grounds for concern. The overall number of votes won by Sinn Féin was very sharply down, almost 60,000, compared to the last Westminster election. It is worth bearing in mind as well that two of the party's existing seats, Fermanagh and South Tyrone and South Down, are marginal, while it is unlikely that the circumstances that saw the SDLP step aside in favour of a fellow 'Remain' candidate in North Belfast will exist again, making that seat potentially vulnerable next time around also. A relatively small shift in the electoral wind could be sufficient to reduce their current total of seven seats to four, a prospect suggesting that Sinn Féin might well have been in rather poorer shape than their net loss of zero in the 2019 general election would indicate. What should really have given the party pause for thought though was the collapse of its support in the Foyle constituency, an outcome already foreshadowed in the local government elections. While Sinn Féin candidate Elisha McCallion had taken the seat under controversial circumstances[92] in 2017, this time around her vote was halved to just under 10,000, barely a third of the figure polled by the victorious candidate, SDLP leader Colum Eastwood.

As sections of the electorate registered their disquiet at the intransigence of the two principal parties of government in Northern Ireland, the scene was set for Alliance to build on the advances made in the twin elections held six months earlier. The cross-community party would more than double its support compared to the previous general election in 2017, receiving some seventeen per cent of the ballots cast. In East Belfast, party leader Naomi Long would run the sitting DUP MP Gavin Robinson close, and in North Down the Alliance candidate Stephen Farry took most commentators by surprise when he claimed the seat recently vacated by the Independent Unionist Lady Sylvia Hermon.[93] This notable success in Northern Ireland's most affluent constituency sheds some light on an especially crucial source of the growing support enjoyed by Alliance in recent elections. While the unionist community is often depicted as overwhelmingly behind the move to take the UK out of the EU, the reality is rather more nuanced. In the Brexit referendum, a sizeable minority of unionist voters, around two in five, voted in fact to 'remain'.[94] This substantial swathe of the unionist population – often presumed to be liberal in terms of cultural disposition and broadly prosperous in terms of class profile – has, however, been poorly represented within mainstream politics. Those unionists who voted to 'remain' are often alienated, at times acutely embarrassed, by members of the DUP who routinely give voice to the crudest forms of cultural prejudice in their response to issues of personal and sexual freedoms and the crassest modes of British nationalism in their support for the Brexit project. Given that the Ulster Unionists had taken a position of opposition to the UK rescinding its membership of the EU, that party might well have offered a voice to the more liberal strands within unionist opinion. In the aftermath of the Brexit result, however, the UUP had moved towards a pragmatic acceptance of the referendum outcome, a strategically disastrous decision that would render it more or less indistinguishable from its larger competitor in the eyes of the unionist electorate.

This specific confluence of circumstances would prove ideally suited to Alliance making substantial electoral gains once more. The success of the centre-ground party in the 2019 Westminster election hinged largely on its ability to tap into that section of the unionist community who increasingly feel that their views are not expressed by the traditional voices of political unionism.[95] With a progamme that emphasised personal freedoms, expressed the wish to remain within the EU, and posed no challenge to the constitutional status quo, Alliance were well placed to capture votes among liberal, middle class unionists who have at least some sense of themselves as Europeans. The context in which this aspect of the centre ground party's appeal would become evinced most starkly was, predictably, North Down. Among the many things that make Northern Ireland's 'gold coast' unusual is that it was the only predominantly unionist constituency to both vote 'remain' in the 2016 referendum and return a politician to Westminster in the 2017 general election, Sylvia Hermon, who was opposed to the Brexit project. An area that is clearly home to many unionist voters disaffected with the direction of the mainstream pro-Union parties was always likely to provide fertile ground for a resurgent Alliance Party and so it was to prove. The result in North Down should perhaps then be regarded less as a political upset, as many commentators suggested at the time, than as another important reminder that there exist within the unionist community profound and long-standing differences of opinion that the Brexit referendum has merely served to sharpen and illuminate.

'New Decade, New Approach?'

The outcome of the December 2019 general election clearly signalled a strong desire within the general public for an end to a political stalemate that had seen the Stormont assembly suspended for close to three years. Chastened by a sharp decline in their electoral support, both Sinn Féin and the DUP were forced to return to the negotiating table in a rather weaker position than before. The balance of power in the new talks process that began in the days immediately after the general election was tilted further away from the former parties of government at Stormont by the calibre of the figures representing the British and Irish governments. Westminster appointee Julian Smith provided the citizens and politicians of Northern Ireland with the 'unfamiliar spectacle of a deft and engaged Secretary of State'[96] who forged a formidable partnership with his Dublin counterpart, Tánaiste Simon Coveney. In the weeks either side of Christmas 2019, the pair would exploit the weakened hand of Northern Ireland's two largest political parties with no little skill. During the talks, both Sinn Féin and the DUP were reminded that in the absence of a new political deal there would have to be Assembly elections that would almost certainly see the parties suffer yet further losses. Smith and Coveney further sought to concentrate the minds of Northern Ireland's notoriously intransigent politicians when they took the bold step of making public the terms of a potential new agreement and demanding that the parties sign up to them. In a memorably adroit move, the Tánaiste and Secretary of State hosted a press conference to reiterate this demand just before 10pm on Thursday 9 January 2020 with a suitably vacant Stormont parliament buildings as a backdrop. Mindful of the darkening public mood caused by the ongoing political stalemate, all of the major local parties would declare their support for Northern Ireland's latest political deal within the next twenty-four hours. Their swift compliance ensured that on Saturday 11 January 2020 the first full meeting of the Northern Ireland Assembly in more than three years took place in an atmosphere so apparently harmonious that the casual onlooker might reasonably have wondered how its record breaking suspension had occurred in the first place.

The political settlement that allowed the Stormont institutions to resume working would, not for the first time, promise a *fresh start* in Northern Irish political life. In the course of its sixty-two pages, the document with the optimistic title *New Decade, New Approach* covers an almost bewildering diversity of topics. The prospective programme for government, for instance, identifies targets as many and varied as 'removing paramilitarism, ending sectarianism, transforming health and social care, reforming education, ensuring households have access to good quality, affordable and sustainable homes, addressing climate change, creating good jobs and protecting workers' rights'. While the new political deal touches on a great diversity of topics, there are really two principal issues that form its core. First, the text of *New Decade, New Approach* sets out to address the deeply dysfunctional mode of conduct associated with the previous coalition government that came to light during investigations into the RHI scandal. With a view to 'rebuilding the trust of citizens' there will be a new way of doing things marked by 'greater transparency and improved governance'. In more specific terms, there will be proper record-keeping, details of ministers' meetings will be published, and measures to prevent bullying and protect whistle-blowers will be introduced. Acknowledging the abuses of power that characterised the previous incarnation of the Stormont parliament, the new agreement pledges to install a code of conduct for special advisers and to ensure that the controversial 'petition of concern' will in future be used 'only in the most **exceptional circumstances and as a last resort**' (bold in original).

Second, the text of *New Decade, New Approach* seeks to acknowledge and advance the diversity of cultural identity and expression that exists in Northern Ireland. Using vocabulary reminiscent of the GFA, the document underlines '**parity of esteem, mutual respect, understanding and cooperation**' (bold in original) as core values that should shape the future of the region. This commitment to a pluralist society finds various expressions but is most crucially apparent in those measures aimed at resolving the dispute over the status of the Irish language that had constantly bedevilled attempts to restore the institutions of government in Northern Ireland. Although the terms of the agreement provide for an 'Office of Identity and Cultural Expression' that will host Commissioners for both the Irish and Ulster Scots languages, it is immediately apparent in the text that it is only the former that will have any real significance. The principal role of the Commissioner for Irish will be to 'protect and enhance' its use by public authorities. A 'translation hub' will be created to assist official agencies, and the repeal of the Administration of Justice (Language) Act (Ireland) dating from 1737 will allow Irish to be used in the Stormont Assembly and to register births, deaths, marriages and wills.

The provisions contained in *New Decade, New Approach* certainly appear a reasonable attempt to resolve those political differences and failures of governance that have derailed the Northern Irish peace process over recent years. Although the advent of this most recent political agreement has been broadly welcomed, anyone reading its terms might have been tempted to speculate why it took so very long for such a deal to be struck. After all, when Sinn Féin brought down the power-sharing executive, they did so on the grounds that Arlene Foster was refusing to stand aside while a public inquiry was conducted into the RHI scandal. And during the multiple rounds of talks that followed the collapse of the institutions, republicans insisted that there could be no return to government in the absence of an Irish language act. The terms of *New Decade, New Approach* meet neither of those demands that Sinn Féin for so long insisted were 'red lines'. The party has returned to share power even though the DUP leader never stood aside while the RHI inquiry fulfilled its remit and in spite of the fact that the new political deal, for all the advances towards cultural parity that it promises, contains no Irish language act *per se*. All of those who were adversely affected by the suspension of Stormont – the nurses striking for pay parity, the patients enduring record delays for operations, the unemployed and disabled facing the 'cliff edge'[97] of the end of social welfare mitigation – might be forgiven then for wondering what precisely those more than one thousand days of political stalemate were all about.

Whither Northern Ireland?

In the first flush of their new romance, the five parties at the helm of government in Northern Ireland were keen to establish that things are being done rather differently than before. At the outset, at least, the tone between members of the Executive was very deliberately respectful, and the ministers recently installed at Stormont were at pains to establish that they were working hard to undo some of the damage that had accumulated over the three years the institutions remained in suspended animation. While the new multi-party power-sharing government has remained keen to give the impression of running a tight and steady ship, there are of course several forces with the potential to blow it off course. Some of these threats to the new-found political stability of Northern Ireland assume the guise of contingencies that are hard to predict in advance. One critical case in point was the outcome of the general election in the Irish Republic that took place not even a month after the restoration of the Stormont assembly. After a disastrous sequence of elections in 2019, Sinn Féin enjoyed a late surge that saw them attract more first preferences than any other political party.[98] The electoral high water mark of the modern republican movement south of the border has the potential to have major repercussions in Northern Ireland as well. Buoyed by their record performance in the elections to the thirty-third Dáil, Sinn Féin immediately stepped up their calls for a border poll, a demand whose likely reiteration will almost certainly place regular strain on the party's relations with their unionist partners in government. Furthermore, the outcome of the Irish general election meant that there was now the very real prospect that republicans would at some point in the near future realise their long-standing strategic goal of holding office in both Dublin and Belfast. While the resistance of Fine Gael and Fianna Fáil to allowing republicans into government will mean that Sinn Féin will remain on the opposition benches throughout the current Dáil term, it is widely assumed that the party will exercise power in Leinster House sooner rather than later. That eventuality would mean that in any political negotiations between the two governments and the Northern Irish parties that might lie ahead, Sinn Féin would be represented on both sides of the table. While unionists were quite content to enter a talks process where they had a 'confidence and supply' arrangement with one of the national governments supposedly acting as honest brokers, they are likely to call foul when required to begin any future negotiations in which Sinn Féin would have an even closer relationship with the other state actor claiming to be a dispassionate arbiter. The seismic recent political developments south of the border would seem, then, to have heightened even further Northern Ireland's already substantial potential for political paralysis in the future.

A second challenge to the stability of the new power-sharing government that falls into the category of the contingent hails from rather further afield. As we finish this book in late September 2020, the COVID-19 pandemic sweeping the world has already claimed many more lives in Northern Ireland than even the dread year of 1972 when the Troubles reached their peak. The arrival of a virus that we are told repeatedly has no respect for the boundaries or sensitivities associated with ethno-national affiliation offered the coalition partners at Stormont a potentially historic opportunity to establish their willingness and ability to work together in the face of a common enemy. In practice, however, the COVID-19 crisis has merely laid bare the divisions and mistrust that exist among the political forces that exercise power in Northern Ireland. As we illustrate in greater detail in Chapter 8, the response of the local political parties to the pandemic has at times appeared to be guided rather less by the universal principles of scientific knowledge than by the altogether more parochial imperatives of ethno-national feeling. While unionists on the Executive have insisted that any public health strategy must mimic that of the other UK regions, nationalists have countered that it would be wiser to follow the lead of the Dublin government. This fundamental difference of opinion has given rise to a whole sequence of running battles on issues such as the closure of schools and businesses, the deployment of British troops to construct field hospitals, the balance between public health and economic recovery, the opening of cemeteries to allow the recently bereaved to mourn their loved ones, and on and on.

The tensions festering within the Stormont Executive would be exacerbated further by the events that followed the death of veteran republican Bobby Storey in late June 2020. When the funeral cortège of the senior IRA figure processed through west Belfast, a huge crowd gathered to pay their respects. This quite explicit breach of public health protocols was made even more problematic by the presence of deputy First Minister Michelle O'Neill, who had spent the previous three months giving daily press conferences expressly forbidding large public gatherings.[99] A further layer of controversy would soon be added to proceedings when it emerged that Storey's remains had been taken to Roselawn Cemetery in predominantly unionist east Belfast, and that several other grieving families had been denied access while the republican veteran was cremated. In the days that followed the funeral, the Sinn Féin leader in the Assembly resisted repeated calls to apologise for her conduct, prompting First Minister Arlene Foster to suggest that she should consider her position and to refuse to appear with her in public. Thus began a political stand-off that would last until the autumn and would end, predictably, with a little 'constructive ambiguity'. In mid-September 2020, Michelle O'Neill issued an apology of sorts, expressing her 'regret' at the controversy that followed the Storey funeral.[100] This equivocation would prove sufficient to allow Arlene Foster to save face, and after a gap of ten weeks the First and deputy First Ministers resumed their daily media briefings addressing, primarily, the ongoing coronavirus crisis. Although the Stormont Executive has now returned, for the time being at least, to some version of equilibrium, the controversy over the passing of Bobby Storey illustrates especially starkly that even in the face of the most serious public health crisis in living memory, local politicians seem unable to break with type. Indeed, it often seems as though the coming of the pandemic has merely given Northern Ireland's parties yet more proxies through which to act out their long-standing differences on a range of other matters. While the scale of the crisis is likely to ensure that the coalition partners will refuse to keep calm but carry on regardless, it remains hard to see how this particular model of government can survive the return to whatever will pass for 'normal' once the plague recedes.

Although some of the forces that threaten the stability of the latest Northern Irish political settlement are hard to predict, there are a couple of crucial ones that are hiding in plain sight. The first is the very definite prospect that the census of population to be conducted in 2021 will reveal that there are more people who might be designated 'Catholic' in the six counties than people who might be called 'Protestant'. The ramifications of such a demographic shift are not of course easy to foretell. As we will illustrate at various stages in the book, there is no straightforward association between ethno-religious affiliation and constitutional aspiration in Northern Ireland. The complexities of that relationship will be jettisoned, inevitably, by those with an interest in doing so, and in the ever more heated atmosphere that will accompany the increasingly insistent calls for a border poll, a whole range of political possibilities may begin to take form. Not all of these will necessarily be malevolent, it should be said, but there will be some that will threaten to take Northern Ireland back to a dark passage in its recent history to which no one should ever wish to return.[101]

The second self-evident potential threat to the political stability of Northern Ireland is those forces of constitutional chaos that have been summoned by the historic decision of the UK to leave the EU. In the initial negotiations that followed the Brexit referendum, the prospect of a 'hard border' evidently inflamed nationalist opinion, rekindling an interest in the unification of Ireland that would previously have been inconceivable. However, during the subsequent talks that produced (what was presumed to be) the definitive Withdrawal Agreement – and the crucial Protocol on Ireland and Northern Ireland therein – it was agreed that the customs frontier that would come into existence would run not along the Irish border but rather down the Irish sea. The deal that was struck between London and Brussels, therefore, promises to consign Northern Ireland once more to its traditional status as mere antechamber of the Union, operating economic regulations that are closer to the state to the south to which it does not belong than to those of the state to the east to which, in principle at least, it does. While most unionists may well have voted in favour of leaving the EU, many have now come to the bitter realisation that Brexit has the potential to threaten the current boundaries, and perhaps even the very existence, of the UK.

Although the deal struck between the EU and UK negotiators in October 2019 was widely cast as marking the final resolution of the various disputes that have punctuated the Brexit saga, we should perhaps have anticipated that there would be at least one further twist in this most circuitous of plots. In September 2020, as we were putting the finishing touches to this book, the British government announced the introduction of an Internal Market Bill that would potentially give Westminster the power to override the Ireland and Northern Ireland Protocol that had, finally, allowed the Withdrawal Agreement to be signed. According to seasoned Brexit observer Chris Grey,[102] were the proposal to become law it would mean that 'the UK government could unilaterally change or do away with customs formalities on goods travelling from Northern Ireland to Great Britain, and unilaterally remove the role of EU law and regulation in state aid policy in Northern Ireland'. That the introduction of the Internal Market Bill represented a deliberate attempt to breach international law was acknowledged quite explicitly in Secretary of State Brandon Lewis' quixotic statement to the House of Commons that the prospective legislation would infringe the Withdrawal Agreement but only 'in a very specific and limited way'.[103] The most common reading of this dramatic turn of events depicts the apparent volte-face of the Johnson administration as simply a calculated gamble to strengthen London's hand in the negotiations with Brussels that began in early September 2020 that mark the end of the post-Brexit 'transitional period'. Another school of thought suggests that the appearance of the Internal Market Bill signals the moment when British Prime Minister Boris Johnson has acceded finally to those ideological zealots within and without his party who wish the UK to leave the EU without an agreement on future trading relations. The advent of a 'no-deal' Brexit would, of course, raise the prospect once again of a 'hard border' that has the potential to place even greater pressure on Northern Ireland's already troubled peace settlement.

When recommending the Internal Market Bill to the House of Commons, Boris Johnson insisted that the prospective legislation 'should be welcomed by everyone who cares about the sovereignty and integrity of our United Kingdom'.[104] Not for the first time, the British premier disclosed a remarkable, and indeed unwitting, facility for irony. While it remains to be seen how the seismic recent events at Westminster will play out, it seems reasonable to assume that the course on which the current Conservative administration has embarked will only exacerbate the already fractious relations between the constituent elements of the UK. The period of acute political flux that began with the Brexit referendum and shows no sign of abating will, inevitably, have an especially dramatic impact on that region which has often seemed to exist merely as the 'secret garden' of the British state. As preparations are made to mark its centenary, the constitutional status and political fortunes of Northern Ireland appear even more precarious perhaps than at any other stage since its foundation.

Notes

1 Northern Ireland Statistics and Research Agency, *Northern Ireland Annual Tourism Statistics 2018* (Belfast: NISRA, 2019). Available at: www.nisra.gov.uk/news/northern-ireland-annual-tourism-statistics-2018. Accessed 7 September 2020.
2 Phil Ramsey, Stephen Baker and Robert Porter, 'Screen production on the "biggest set in the world": Northern Ireland Screen and the case of *Game of Thrones*', *Media, Culture & Society*, 41(6), (2019), 845–62.
3 The entire session is recorded for posterity at www.youtube.com/watch?v=ERnJOEZW7nc. Accessed 12 January 2020.
4 Eamonn O'Kane, 'The Perpetual Peace Process? Examining Northern Ireland's Never-ending, but Fundamentally Altering Peace Process', *Irish Political Studies*, 28(4) (2013), 515–35, p. 531.
5 Glenn Patterson, *Backstop Land* (London: Head of Zeus, 2019), p. 64.
6 Peter Shirlow and Colin Coulter, 'Enduring problems: the Belfast Agreement and a disagreed Belfast', in Marianne Elliott (ed.), *The Long Road to Peace in Northern Ireland: Peace Lectures from the Institute of Irish Studies at Liverpool University* (Liverpool: Liverpool University Press, 2007), pp. 207–23.
7 Susan McKay, *Bear in Mind These Dead* (London: Faber & Faber, 2008), p. 164.

8 O'Kane, 'Perpetual Peace Process?', p. 516.
9 John Nagle, 'Between Conflict and Peace: An Analysis of the Complex Consequences of the Good Friday Agreement', *Parliamentary Affairs*, 71(2) (2018), 395–416, p. 399.
10 Arthur Aughey, *The Politics of Northern Ireland: Beyond the Belfast Agreement* (London: Routledge, 2006), pp. 129–30.
11 Peter Shirlow and Brendan Murtagh, *Belfast: Segregation, Violence and the City* (London: Pluto Press, 2006), p. 43.
12 Jon Tonge, *Northern Ireland* (Cambridge: Polity Press, 2006), p. 200.
13 Henry McDonald, 'How IRA spy scandal spelt the collapse of Stormont', *Guardian*, 6 October 2020. Available at: www.theguardian.com/uk/2002/oct/06/northernireland.ireland1. Accessed 15 August 2020.
14 Arthur Aughey, *The Politics of Northern Ireland: Beyond the Belfast Agreement* (London: Routledge, 2005), p. 179.
15 Nagle, 'Between Conflict and Peace', p. 401.
16 Jocelyn Evans and Jon Tonge, 'Social class and party choice in Northern Ireland's ethnic blocs', *West European Politics*, 32(5) (2009), 1012–30, pp. 1016–17.
17 O'Kane, 'Perpetual Peace Process?', p. 527.
18 Ibid., p. 526.
19 Nagle, 'Between Conflict and Peace', p. 401.
20 Siobhán Fenton, *The Good Friday Agreement* (London: Biteback Publishing, 2018), p. 278.
21 McKay, *Bear in Mind These Dead*, p. 372.
22 Nagle, 'Between Conflict and Peace', p. 405.
23 Patterson, *Backstop Land*, p. 46.
24 Mark Hellowell, David Price and Allyson Pollock, *The Use of Private Finance Initiative (PFI) Public Private Partnerships (PPPs) in Northern Ireland* (Belfast: Northern Ireland Public Service Alliance, 2008), p. 9.
25 Goretti Horgan and Ann Marie Gray, 'Devolution in Northern Ireland: A lost opportunity?', *Critical Social Policy*, 32(3) (2012), 467–78, p. 475.
26 Her Majesty's Treasury, *Private Finance Initiative and Private Finance 2 projects: 2017 summary data* (London: Her Majesty's Treasury, 2017).
27 Horgan and Gray, 'Devolution in Northern Ireland', p. 475.
28 Denis O'Hearn, 'How has Peace Changed the Northern Irish Political Economy?', *Ethnopolitics*, 7(1) (2008), 101–18, p. 112.
29 Paul Nolan, Dominic Bryan, Clare Dwyer, Katy Hayward, Katy Radford and Peter Shirlow, *The Flag Dispute: Anatomy of a Protest* (Belfast: Queen's University, 2014), p. 9.
30 Kevin Hearty, 'The Great Awakening? The Belfast Flag Protests and Protestant/Unionist/Loyalist Counter-memory in Northern Ireland', *Irish Political Studies*, 30(2) (2015), 157–77.
31 Ibid., p. 10.
32 Donna Halliday and Neil Ferguson, 'When Peace is Not Enough: The Flag Protests, the Politics of Identity & Belonging in East Belfast', *Irish Political Studies*, 31(4) (2016), 525–40, p. 527.

33 Gerry Moriarty, 'Orange Order again banned from Ardoyne march', *Irish Times*, 18 July 2013. Available at: www.irishtimes.com/news/politics/orange-order-again-banned-from-ardoyne-march-1.1467540. Accessed 17 September 2020. Subsequent protracted negotiations between the Orange Order and the Crumlin Ardoyne Residents' Association would ensure that the bandsmen would complete the return leg of their journey in the early morning of 1 October 2016, more than three years after it began.
34 BBC News, Northern Ireland: Richard Haass talks end without deal', 31 December 2013. Available at: www.bbc.com/news/uk-northern-ireland-25556714. Accessed 17 September 2020.
35 Mark Blyth, *Austerity: The History of a Dangerous Idea* (Oxford: Oxford University Press, 2013).
36 Philip Alston, 'Statement on Visit to the United Kingdom, United Nations Special Rapporteur on extreme poverty and human rights', London, 16 November 2018. Available at: www.ohchr.org/en/NewsEvents/Pages/DisplayNews.aspx?NewsID=23881. Accessed 15 September 2020.
37 These figures were provided by the charitable organisation The Trussell Trust. Available at: www.trusselltrust.org/news-and-blog/latest-stats/end-year-stats/. Accessed 15 September 2020.
38 Christina Beatty and Steve Fothergill, *The Impact of Welfare Reform on Northern Ireland* (Belfast: Northern Ireland Council for Voluntary Action, 2013).
39 Mike Tomlinson, 'Risking peace in the "war against the poor"? Social exclusion and the legacies of the Northern Ireland conflict', *Critical Social Policy*, 36(1) (2016), 104–23, p. 105.
40 Ibid., p. 107.
41 Chris Gilligan, 'Austerity and consociational government in Northern Ireland', *Irish Studies Review*, 24(1) (2016), 35–48, p. 42.
42 Nagle, 'Between Conflict and Peace', p. 404.
43 Gilligan, 'Austerity and consociational government', p. 42.
44 Fenton, *The Good Friday Agreement*, p. 92.
45 In January 1996, Senator George Mitchell set out six principles of non-violence that were to guide the subsequent peace talks that he chaired. Acceptance of these principles on the part of Sinn Féin, coupled with the restoration of the Provisional IRA ceasefire, was a prerequisite for the admission of republicans into the negotiations process.
46 Brendan O'Leary, 'The Twilight of the United Kingdom & Tiocfaidh ár lá: Twenty Years after the Good Friday Agreement', *Ethnopolitics*, 17(3) (2018), 223–42, p. 227.
47 Nagle, 'Between Conflict and Peace', p. 403.
48 Sam McBride, *Burned: The Inside Story of the 'Cash-for-Ash' Scandal and Northern Ireland's Secretive New Elite* (Newbridge: Merrion Press, 2019), pp. 66–7.
49 While some individuals certainly turned a tidy profit from the RHI scheme, its principal beneficiary was, predictably, a major multinational enterprise. It

has been estimated that 'about half' of the boilers installed under the 'cash for ash' project were owned by farmers raising poultry for Moy Park, Northern Ireland's largest private-sector employer, which has retained its local name but is in fact owned by the Brazilian agribusiness JBS. Ibid., p. 294.
50 Nagle, 'Between Conflict and Peace', p. 408.
51 McBride, *Burned*, p. 252.
52 O'Leary, 'Twilight of the United Kingdom', p. 230.
53 McBride, *Burned*, pp. 70–1; BBC News, 'RHI scandal: Michelle O'Neill defends her role promoting scheme', 30 January 2017. Available at: www.bbc.com/news/uk-northern-ireland-38794777. Accessed 18 September 2020.
54 McBride, *Burned*, pp. 208–9.
55 Fenton, *Good Friday Agreement*, pp. 226, 259–65.
56 Ibid., p. 247.
57 John Nagle, 'The Repositioning of Irish Nationalism in Northern Ireland: An Examination of Consociationalism and Devolution in Identity Change', *Ethnopolitics Papers*, 21 (2012), p. 23.
58 O'Leary, 'The Twilight of the United Kingdom', pp. 233–9.
59 Sean Haughey and James Pow, 'Remain reaffirmed: the 2019 European election in Northern Ireland', *Irish Political Studies*, 35(1) (2020), 29–45, p. 6.
60 Nagle, 'Between Conflict and Peace', p. 405.
61 Gerry Moriarty, 'Arlene Foster accused of 'narrowness' over 1916 events', *Belfast Telegraph*, 11 January 2016. Available at: www.irishtimes.com/news/ireland/irish-news/arlene-foster-accused-of-narrowness-over-1916-events-1.2491674. Accessed 15 September 2020.
62 Fenton, *Good Friday Agreement*, p. 290.
63 Brian Rowan, 'Sinn Féin meeting that brought political crisis to a head', *Irish Times*, 23 January 2017. Available at: www.irishtimes.com/news/politics/sinn-fpercentC3percentA9in-meeting-that-brought-political-crisis-to-a-head-1.2947919. Accessed 18 September 2020.
64 Patterson, *Backstop Land*, p. 74.
65 Fenton, *Good Friday Agreement*, p. 307.
66 Northern Ireland Statistics and Research Agency, *Census 2011: Key Statistics for Northern Ireland* (Belfast: NISRA, 2012), p. 17.
67 John Manley, 'Irish language act was only "tertiary" element in Haass talks', *Irish News*, 28 September 2017. Available at: www.irishnews.com/news/politicalnews/2017/09/28/news/irish-language-act-was-only-tertiary-element-in-haass-talks-1147657/. Accessed 18 September 2020.
68 O'Leary, 'Twilight of the United Kingdom', p. 230.
69 Patterson, *Backstop Land*, p. 73.
70 Gerry Moriarty and Pat Leahy, 'Leaked papers show draft agreement between DUP and SF', *Irish Times*, 20 February 2018. Online at: www.irishtimes.com/news/ireland/irish-news/leaked-papers-show-draft-agreement-between-dup-and-sf-1.3399566. Accessed 17 September 2020.
71 Fenton, *Good Friday Agreement*, p. 321.
72 Patterson, *Backstop Land*, p. 124.

73 Lisa Claire Whitten, '#LE19 – a turning of the tide? Report of local elections in Northern Ireland, 2019', *Irish Political Studies*, 35(1) (2020), 61–79, p. 66.
74 Ibid., p. 71.
75 Ibid., pp. 73–6.
76 Northern Life and Times Survey, 2018 edition. Available at: www.ark.ac.uk/nilt/2018/Political_Attitudes/UNINATID.html. Accessed 17 September 2020.
77 Claire Mitchell, 'Religious change and persistence', in Colin Coulter and Michael Murray (eds), *Northern Ireland after the Troubles: A Society in Transition* (Manchester: Manchester University Press, 2008), pp. 135–55.
78 Patterson, *Backstop Land*, p. 56.
79 Ibid., pp. 66–7.
80 News Letter, 'Sinn Fein criticised by LGBT group over same-sex marriage plans', *News Letter*, 23 February 2018. Available at: www.newsletter.co.uk/news/sinn-fein-criticised-lgbt-group-over-same-sex-marriage-plans-345516. Accessed 20 September 2020.
81 Daniel Finn, *One Man's Terrorist: A Political History of the IRA* (London: Verso, 2019), p. 223.
82 Peter Walker and Rory Carroll, 'MPs vote to extend abortion and same-sex marriage rights to Northern Ireland', *Guardian*, 9 July 2019. Available at: www.theguardian.com/uk-news/2019/jul/09/mps-vote-to-extend-same-sex-marriage-to-northern-ireland. Accessed 13 September 2020.
83 Gerry Moriarty, 'First same-sex marriage takes place in Northern Ireland', *Irish Times*, 11 February 2020. Available at: www.irishtimes.com/news/social-affairs/first-same-sex-marriage-takes-place-in-northern-ireland-1.4170502. Accessed 15 September 2020.
84 Whitten, '#LE19 – a turning of the tide?', pp. 70–1.
85 Ibid., p. 71.
86 Haughey and Pow, 'Remain reaffirmed'.
87 McBride, *Burned*, pp. 21, 25–6, 60, 331, 327.
88 The full text of the RHI Inquiry is available here: www.rhiinquiry.org/report-independent-public-inquiry-non-domestic-renewable-heat-incentive-rhi-scheme. Accessed 25 September 2020.
89 Rory Carroll, 'Northern Ireland nurses strike over pay and patient safety', *Guardian*, 18 December 2019. Available at: www.theguardian.com/society/2019/dec/18/northern-ireland-nurses-strike-over-pay-and-patient-safety. Accessed 12 September 2020.
90 Katy Hayward, 'The Revised Protocol on Ireland/Northern Ireland', 19 November 2019 (Belfast Queen's University). Available at: http://qpol.qub.ac.uk/the-revised-protocol-on-ireland-northern-ireland/. Accessed 14 September 2020.
91 Colin Coulter, 'The culture of contentment: the political beliefs and practice of the unionist middle classes', in Peter Shirlow and Mark McGovern (eds), *Who Are 'the People'? Unionism, Protestanism and Loyalism in Northern Ireland* (London: Pluto Press, 1997).
92 There were allegations from both the SDLP and the People Before Profit Alliance

that Sinn Féin's 2017 victory in Foyle came on the back of widespread electoral fraud. While various members of the public claimed their votes had been stolen, no prosecutions have resulted. Leona O'Neill, 'Claims of Foyle vote theft mount – SDLP to meet with Electoral Office', *Belfast Telegraph*, 13 June 2017. Available at: www.belfasttelegraph.co.uk/news/northern-ireland/claims-of-foyle-vote-theft-mount-sdlp-to-meet-with-electoral-office-35819530.html. Accessed 25 September 2020.

93 Belfast Telegraph, 'North Down: Alliance "elated" with Stephen Farry's shock victory', *Belfast Telegraph*, 13 December 2019. Available at: www.belfasttelegraph.co.uk/news/politics/general-election-2019/north-down-alliance-elated-with-stephen-farrys-shock-victory-38781817.html. Accessed 15 September 2020.

94 Haughey and Pow, 'Remain reaffirmed', p. 39.

95 Ibid., p. 42.

96 Rory Carroll, 'From bitter stalemate to smiles at Stormont: how the deal was done', *Guardian*, 13 January 2020. Available at: www.theguardian.com/politics/2020/jan/13/from-bitter-stalemate-to-smiles-at-stormont-how-the-deal-was-done. Accessed 15 September 2020. In spite of his role in brokering a return to devolved government, Julian Smith would be ousted as Northern Ireland Secretary in the cabinet reshuffle in February 2020. Journalists have speculated that Smith's removal from the Northern Ireland Office was due, variously, to the inclusion in the *New Decade, New Approach* agreement of a commitment to introduce within 100 days legislation to address 'legacy' issues, a move that raises the prospect of further British soldiers standing trial, as well as to his opposition to the UK leaving the EU.

97 Cliff Edge Coalition NI, *Submission to the Joint Inquiry into Welfare policy in Northern Ireland* (2019). Available at: www.nicva.org/article/cliff-edge-ni-coalition-submission-to-the-joint-inquiry-into-welfare-policy-what-are-the. Accessed 15 September 2020.

98 Rory Carroll, 'Sinn Féin declares victory in Irish general election', *Guardian*, 11 February 2020. Available at: www.theguardian.com/world/2020/feb/10/sinn-fein-declares-victory-irish-general-election. Accessed 12 September 2020.

99 Gerry Moriarty, 'Storey funeral fallout: Executive safe for now but things could turn toxic', *Irish Times*, 2 July 2020. Available at: www.irishtimes.com/news/politics/storey-funeral-fallout-executive-safe-for-now-but-things-could-turn-toxic-1.4294772. Accessed 18 September 2020.

100 Niall Deeney, 'Bobby Storey funeral: Michelle O'Neill's comments "far from the apology" demanded by Arlene Foster', *News Letter*, 10 September 2020. Available at: www.newsletter.co.uk/news/politics/bobby-storey-funeral-michelle-oneills-comments-far-apology-demanded-arlene-foster-2967120. Accessed 19 September 2020.

101 Patterson, *Backstop Land*, p. 98.

102 Chris Grey, 'The descent into political insanity', Brexit blog, 11 September 2020. Available at: https://chrisgreybrexitblog.blogspot.com/. Accessed 19 September 2020.

103 Denis Staunton, 'Westminster sketch: Commons bewildered as Brandon Lewis drops bombshell', *Irish Times*, 8 September 2020. Available at: www.irishtimes.com/news/world/uk/westminster-sketch-commons-bewildered-as-brandon-lewis-drops-bombshell-1.4350081. Accessed 18 September 2020.

104 BBC News, 'Brexit: Boris Johnson says powers will ensure UK cannot be "broken up"', 14 September 2020. Available at: www.bbc.com/news/uk-politics-54153302. Accessed 18 September 2020.

2

Fragmented, staggered and inept: addressing the legacy of the Troubles

Introduction

The demand for truth and justice by victims and survivors is an integral part of any post-conflict transitional process that seeks to meaningfully address *and* deal with conflict-related trauma and hurt. While the 1998 Belfast or Good Friday Agreement (hereafter GFA) had up until recent times drawn plaudits home and abroad as a prudent model of conflict resolution, the fact remains that unlike many other regions emerging from the aftermath of protracted armed conflict, Northern Ireland has proven to be something of an exception with regard to the legacy of the past. The unprecedented political reconciliation between unionism and nationalism at an institutional level – particularly in the period of relatively stable devolved government between 2007 and 2016 – deflected attention from the reality that approaches to legacy and reconciliation have been at best fragmented, staggered and inept, leaving thousands of citizens without truth, acknowledgement and accountability.[1] Despite the cursory commitments to addressing the issue of victims in the 1998 peace accord, no state-led, formal structure or process was stipulated or established. If anything, in the intervening years the state has been zealous in removing itself from direct involvement in devising comprehensive approaches to legacy. Matters are further complicated given that the objectives of Northern Ireland's endeavours to deal with the past remain ambiguous and disputed. Do they seek accountability; truth recovery; social reconciliation; retribution and prosecution; provide lessons for future generations; supports and services for victims?[2] While some suggest drawing a line under the past once and for all, the notion that vast swathes of Northern Irish society will embrace and engage in a collective amnesia is simply unthinkable and unworkable. Moreover, the reality is that 'truth' recovery is taking place via a plethora of unofficial and official means.[3] Given the powerful and ubiquitous shadow cast by the legacy over the present, many contend that Northern Ireland has no choice but to accept that the past must be dealt with.[4] Like so many other aspects of Northern Ireland's post-Troubles endeavours, expectations among its citizens regarding legacy were elevated by political rhetoric and numerous negotiated agreements that have hitherto failed to fulfil their obligations and commitments. In contrast to the inertia and often outright unwillingness of political elites to address comprehensively the legacy of past violence, community-led initiatives are prolific and often highly effective, particularly those using the law to pressurise the state into holding inquiries, largely into cases where state involvement is alleged.

Although there exists a lack of consensus on a concise starting point for the peace process, we are more than 25 years on from the first paramilitary ceasefires of 1994. It is self-evident that the evolving peace process has proved as durable as the 30 years of violence that preceded it. It is also a process replete with complexities, controversies and many significant milestones. Therefore, given the scale and breadth of the peace process and its constituent parts, this chapter is not intended to be an exhaustive overview of the innumerable efforts at dealing with legacy, nor is it a chronological detailing of the numerous twists and turns that occurred throughout the peace process.[5] Such a task is beyond the scope of a single chapter. What it does seek to do is to tease out the complexities surrounding the issue of legacy in Northern Ireland. In doing so, the chapter argues that Northern Ireland requires a holistic approach whereby state and non-state endeavours work to mutually cooperate and reinforce each other in ways that support practices of social reconciliation and peace-building. It first outlines a transitional justice approach located in a framework of societal reconciliation. It then goes onto critically appraise some of the various initiatives deployed in dealing with the legacy of the past. The chapter then examines the prospect of a formalised, overarching truth commission as a possible way of addressing legacy in a comprehensive way, before finally examining the legacy proposals outlined in 2014 Stormont House Agreement (hereafter SHA) and the recent *New Decade, New Approach* document. While the discussion that follows details a wide range of legacy initiatives, the common thread running throughout is that many of Northern Ireland's endeavours to address the past, though by no means all, are embedded in processes of assigning culpability and blame, rather than reconciliation and transformation. Thus, although reconciliation is of course contested, the chapter contends that until legacy is reframed as a process that is transformative, conciliatory and mutually beneficial, it will largely remain a communicative platform for expressions of recrimination, mistrust and oppositionality. While the prospect of dealing with the past and even the establishment of a truth recovery process presents significant challenges, the prospect of a present (and a future) that is continually vexed with regular, fragmented disclosures about the past is equally daunting[6].

Transitional justice and reconciliation

The predominance of liberal approaches to conflict resolution means that invariably the principal concerns of those charged with devising a new 'post-conflict' landscape are issues such as state security, sovereignty, law and order, democratic governance and functioning capitalist economies. The establishment and delivery of such approaches requires a political, cultural and discursive framework which legitimises this 'negative peace', that being the absence of military violence, and recasts it as universally beneficial for all. The power of those who propagate the ending of armed actions as signifying a 'post-conflict' context resides in their capacity to package functioning forms of democratic governance, free-market capitalist economies, and the establishment of law, order and retributive justice for past atrocities and abuses as signifying a successful post-conflict transition. In contrast, 'peace-building' processes tend to concentrate less on 'political reconciliation' and more on repairing broken relationships, emphasising the build-up of trust between former adversaries and centring their focus on social reconciliation. Transitional justice plays an important part in this process, with an emphasis on ensuring accountability, truth-telling and justice as part of a long-term path to reconciliation. While often associated with conventional formats of retribution and apportioning blame and punishment, transitional justice as a field, however, has broadened significantly in recent decades, encompassing both judicial and non-judicial modalities, and remains overwhelmingly concerned with addressing the needs and interests of victims and survivors and with repairing and transforming social relations in the aftermath of war. Of importance to transitional justice scholars is the work of Johan Galtung[7] and John-Paul Lederach,[8] which distinguished between a 'negative' and a 'positive' peace. While the former adheres strictly to conventional ideas around ending armed conflict, or more specifically the 'absence' of armed violence, the latter speaks to the 'presence' of social justice, therefore expanding our understanding of harms, and the importance of addressing such harms as a central feature of reconciliation.

Justice in the Kantian liberal tradition finds expression through liberal democratic structures, human rights, and of course the rule of law, invariably dispensed using some type of retributive punishment. Conversely, a conflict transformation approach centres on harms, relationships, healing, dialogue, rehabilitation and community participation. Lederach[9] contends that reconciliation first needs relationships; people need to find the opportunity and space to express to and with one another the trauma of loss and their grief at that loss, and the anger that accompanies the pain and the memory of injustices experienced. Therefore, acknowledgement is decisive in the reconciliation dynamic. Acknowledgement through hearing one another's stories validates experiences and feelings and represents the first step towards restoration of the person and the relationship. The issue with reconciliation in Northern Ireland is that it has become something of a 'buzz-word'; its ubiquity and omnipresence matched only by its lack of clarity and precision by those who deploy it. All too often reconciliation is ill defined and conceived of in many ways; some see it as a policy, some as simply rhetoric, others as a practice or a process, consequently with little attention as to how reconciliation can be practically achieved and/or measured. For Lederach, reconciliation is not a process or a policy, but a social space where encounters between former enemies can engage in issues of truth, justice, mercy and peace. For reconciliation to be effective, the humanity of the 'other' group must be recognised; a new moral order needs to be created that reflects cooperation between two competing groups; stereotypes and generalisations need to be adjusted; communicative purposes that build trust and facilitate mutually beneficial cooperation are required.[10] For example, Luc Huyse argues that there are three stages towards reconciliation: replacing fear by non-violent coexistence, building confidence and trust, and moving towards empathy. For him, empathy also does not imply forgiveness or absolute harmony, and does not exclude feelings of anger. To achieve these objectives, Huyse argues that a variety of mechanisms are required, including truth-telling, reparations, restorative justice and processes to promote healing.[11] Similarly, after their comprehensive review of the literature, Brandon Hamber and Gráinne Kelly[12] conclude that reconciliation should best be viewed as a voluntary process which involves addressing conflictual and fractured relations through a number of practical interwoven strands. Transformation is premised on the assumption that the conflict relationships can shift from mutually destructive, unstable and harmful expressions towards a mutually beneficial and cooperative basis. Given that social conflict occurs within the boundaries of structures and systems, it also assumes the transformation of system and structure by building on the energy and impact of conflict itself.[13] These include developing a shared vision of an interdependent and fair society; acknowledging and dealing with the past; building positive relationships; significant cultural and attitudinal change; and substantial social, economic and political change. In sum, the current field of transitional justice has expanded significantly beyond conventional processes of attaining truth and justice, with a distinct focus on restorative practices centred on dialogue and transforming social relations. In the context of deeply divided societies such as Northern Ireland, reconciliation requires a type of 'social learning' among former antagonists, namely a transformation of the entrenched system of antagonistic identifications, hostile relationships and divisive belief systems underpinning intergroup violence.[14] Despite a broad consensus that Northern Ireland has not adequately dealt with the legacy of its conflict, its peace process is replete with a vast range of initiatives, both state and non-state, and judicial and non-judicial. Exploring some of these enables a better understanding of workable practices that are restorative and transformative of social relations in the specific context of Northern Ireland.

Dealing with the past?

The GFA and its 2006 follow-up, the St Andrews Agreement, are still widely lauded as both pragmatic and largely successful forms of post-conflict settlements. It would be churlish and disingenuous to dismiss the painstaking work and progress achieved since 1998. Their relative success (certainly up to the most recent crisis and suspension of power-sharing governance in January 2017), however, should not and does not preclude critical interrogations of its flaws and limitations. While political stability at an institutional level bedded down from 2007 onwards, the priority afforded to 'political reconciliation' was never replicated with regard to societal reconciliation, furnishing a post-agreement landscape bereft of any overarching mechanism to address the legacy of the past. In the chasm created by the dearth of a comprehensive approach to legacy, there emerged in its place a piecemeal approach by state and non-state actors, including public legal inquiries (the Bloody Sunday Inquiry, the Cory Collusion Inquiries, the Independent Commission of Inquiry into the Dublin and Monaghan Bombings), the Historical Enquiries Team (HET), the establishment of a police ombudsman, community and grassroots initiatives (the Ardoyne Commemoration Project (ACP), the EPIC Report, the Eolas Report, the Time for Truth Campaign), legal challenges (private prosecutions, civil actions, right-to-life cases under the European Convention on Human Rights), policing initiatives (for example the Patten Report, the Stalker/Sampson Inquiry, the Stevens Inquiry) and victim-centred initiatives (the Bloomfield Report, the Report of the Consultative Group on the Past), among others. Given that many persons affected by conflict-related trauma in Northern Ireland were exposed to numerous traumatic events,[15] it is unlikely, therefore, that a single, one-size-fits-all mechanism such as a truth recovery commission will fully uncover 'truth', let alone address trauma and hurt. The needs and interests of victims are plural and diverse: some wish to pursue protagonists through the criminal justice system; others wish to have their hurt and experiences publicly acknowledged; others seek to uncover the full circumstances in which they were injured or how their loved ones died; some wish for public apologies, or other acts of public remembrance.

If we accept the differing, and often competing, experiences, needs, perspectives and interests of those who have experienced violent conflict, then multiple ways of dealing with the past will be necessary.[16] This section critically examines a range of important initiatives in Northern Ireland, though by no means all.

Legal mechanisms and criminal prosecutions

In Northern Ireland, many victims and their families require accountability and justice, seeking prosecutions for those involved in the killing or harming of loved ones. The establishment of the HET in 2005 as a specialist police unit to re-examine upwards of 2,000 killings during the Troubles represented a significant initiative to address those demands. As part of a recurring pattern throughout the peace process, its formation was a government reaction to the prolific actions of civil society groups demanding fresh investigations into unsolved killings. From its very inception however, the HET stated that prosecution was likely in only a small number of cases. While we of course fully respect the rights of victims and their families to pursue judicial and legal processes in their quest for justice and accountability, the likelihood of securing prosecutions (of either state and non-state actors) is significantly reduced due to a number of factors, including the workload of legacy cases for the police service; the time that has lapsed; the reality that some of those involved have since died; and the destruction of most paramilitary arms, thus depriving vital forensic evidence.[17] Additionally, while a paper trail exists for state actions (although often concealed from the public through national security protocols or in other instances, deliberately destroyed), there is no equivalent information held by paramilitary groups or legal authority to demand such information is provided.[18] The issue of prosecutions is further compounded by the reluctance and refusal of all actors to the conflict to disclose the full truth of their roles and deeds. Moreover, while certain facts and aspects will undoubtedly emerge in the legal realm, criminal prosecution processes are incapable of meeting other important needs of victims and survivors. For instance, a criminal trial will not examine the justifications or reasons offered by perpetrators. A healing-centred 'dialogue' between victims and persons involved in inflicting harm is also ruled out in judicial processes. Criminal prosecution trials focus solely on individuals, and so questions about organisational culpability, as well as wider structural or other contextual factors, are also left unchallenged and unexplored. Furthermore, under the terms of the GFA, even in those cases where convictions are secured, those jailed will spend a maximum of two years in prison. In the case of Northern Ireland, the semantics of criminal prosecution appear anchored in symbolic forms of retribution rather than the dispensation of justice.

An obvious impediment to the progress of the HET is the fact that the voluminous workload of unresolved Troubles killings falls on the shoulders of the already overstretched Police Service of Northern Ireland (PSNI). Former PSNI Chief Constable George Hamilton has consistently stated that the issue of dealing with the past should not be a police matter, adding that it is 'impossible to investigate the past and police the present'. The doleful statistics from the HET's work certainly attest to the ineffectiveness of police investigations into legacy. After the first 1,850 case reviews by the HET there were 11 prosecutions and 2 convictions. At the time of its dissolution in 2014, the HET had examined 2,422 cases, of which 1,706 were completed, 658 left open (and of which 290 were in assessment), 70 in allocation and 298 in review.[19] Moreover, the HET was of course not without its controversies. Opponents of PSNI historical inquiries centred on suspicions of bias in cases where killings had been at the hands of state forces. The presence of former Royal Ulster Constabulary (RUC) officers within the teams of investigating officers led to accusations of the 'police investigating themselves'. Recent revelations in 2019 regarding PSNI failure to disclose full information and documents related to a series of loyalist killings to the Police Ombudsman[20] have once again positioned policing as a political issue, calling into question its capacity to investigate legacy in an independent and impartial way. Added to this are unionist fears of a 'legacy imbalance', with a widespread perception regarding a disproportionate investigative focus on killings by state forces. The proposed replacement for the HET, the Historical Investigations Unit, so far has not defined how it will deal with such a low conviction rate. According to Patricia Lundy,[21] while the HET was a bold and innovative move in policing terms, it did not have the capacity to deal comprehensively with a macro-approach to legacy cases.

Truth recovery and accountability: community-led initiatives

Despite the rather bleak appraisals of state-led approaches such as the HET, justice and accountability, however, can be understood in ways beyond the narrow confines of criminal prosecutions or institutional truth-seeking processes such as truth commissions. According to transitional justice principles, alternative forms of justice that meet the needs of victims include truth recovery processes, oral testimonies, official acknowledgement, and the establishment of an authoritative record of past violence.[22] Given this, many victims and others traumatised by the conflict have turned to grassroots endeavours, with the help of community-based groups, in establishing facts regarding the circumstances of past killings. Research from other post-conflict regions indicate that community-based initiatives, or 'bottom-up' approaches to truth recovery, are prolific and effective, the Gacaca process in Rwanda being a pertinent and widely cited example. The Recovery of Historical Memory Project or 'Proyecto de Recuperación de la Memoria Histórica' (REMHI) in Guatemala, which operated between 1995 and 1998, collected more than 5,000 testimonies and documented over 55,000 human rights violations. Using qualitative interviews, their research sought not only 'facts' but also the experience, trauma and impact of war crimes and other human rights violations. Perhaps most significant is that the REMHI conducted its research alongside the UN-led Commission for Historical Clarification (CEH), and is widely accredited with acting as a salient counter to some of the many blind spots and limitations in the more formalised CEH process.[23] This model of truth recovery obviously overlaps considerably with a formal truth-commission approach, but there are, however, some important distinctions. Historical clarification commissions are concerned with historical processes rather than legal ones and tend to have fewer legal powers of compulsion. Ultimately their aim is to generate a relatively definitive and agreed historical narrative rather than to apportion blame to individuals.

Therefore, it is important to establish a link between oral testimonies and some sort of established account to bring social and political 'weight' to recorded acts of storytelling. Healing Through Remembering (HTR) and WAVE Trauma have, quite rightly, earned much cross-community respect and credibility for their work with victims and survivors. The former, created in 2001, works with a range of actors and organisations to deal with the legacy of the conflict. While HTR has five specific themes for dealing with legacy, including a network of commemoration, a day of reflection, storytelling, truth recovery and a living memorial museum, their emphasis is on acknowledgement and 'storytelling'. It is no coincidence that the last major government-led initiative for dealing with the past, the Independent Consultative Group for Dealing with the Past (CPNI), also known as Eames–Bradley, intimated the use of the HTR strategies as viable and credible modes of truth recovery.[24] As proposed by HTR and advanced also within the SHA, the creation of a Commission of Historical Clarification could examine the causes, context and consequences of conflict, but with less emphasis on either victims or those who had been involved in past acts of violence. The Commission's primary objective would be on devising an independent and authoritative historical narrative about what occurred during the conflict and why, in order to encourage a broader sense of collective (rather than individual) responsibility for what happened. Developed by an independent body over a defined period of time, it would produce a definitive narrative that would limit misperceptions and disagreements about what actually happened. As a major stumbling block in Northern Ireland, a definitive account of the conflict is warranted. Without doubt such an endeavour would be less sensitive politically, be less expensive, and could be the start of a broader public debate on what happened.

In addition, there is an abundance of grassroots initiatives that seek to engage in truth seeking, some of which are cross-community. Civil society has led the way, engaging in a plethora of 'bottom-up' truth-recovery approaches which have been used as an effective tool to apply pressure on the state to address certain past instances or to campaign for a future public inquiry.[25] As recommended by the 1998 Bloomfield Report,[26] the Northern Ireland Office established the Victims Liaison Unit, which channelled central state funds into local areas and community groups to meet a range of physical, psychological and cultural needs, identified by victims of violence and their advocates as necessary to their well-being.[27] As was the case in other regions enveloped in armed conflict, many grassroots and community groups in Northern Ireland emerged and proliferated because of a mistrust of the state and/or the historical links to discrimination and deprivation at the hands of the state.[28] In the aftermath of political violence, community-based initiatives regarding truth recovery are also motivated by a belief that the state lacks the willingness, capacity and independence to engage in meaningful truth recovery processes. Moreover, such grassroots initiatives provide the space for engagement between conflict protagonists and victims, whereby dialogue and relationships can be meaningfully built, which have potentially cathartic outcomes for both parties. Notwithstanding, such approaches are often localised and therefore lack the wider public acknowledgement component associated with centralised truth recovery processes.

Despite this, localised forms of truth recovery do play an important role in transforming societies emerging from conflict, and Northern Ireland has widely used storytelling, oral recordings and archives, as well as witness programmes, as important means in the quest for public acknowledgement. Despite the obvious polarised positions on addressing legacy in Northern Ireland, the Disabled Police Officers' Association, the Pat Finucane Centre, the ACP, HTR, the One Small Step Campaign, Sinn Féin and the Falls Community Council – all of whom represent a range of disparate, perhaps even contradictory political interests – were united to the extent of seeing the value of storytelling for individual and societal healing.[29] The advantages of storytelling by victims are demonstrated by the rehumanisation of people humiliated by violence or the establishment of a culture of respect for human rights throughout society. Many victims have regarded the telling of such stories as essential, either in terms of their recovery and healing or in terms of bearing witness to atrocity so that future atrocities can be avoided, and so storytelling offers effective and practical ways of dealing with the horrors of the past.[30] Processes of oral testimonies via storytelling have gained in popularity and are an effective vehicle in the pursuit of acknowledgement. The opportunity and ability to narrate one's own story, as a means to secure recognition, has become associated with a transition from the condition of being a (passive) victim into that of an (active) survivor.[31]

According to Claire Hackett and Bill Rolston, unofficial storytelling mechanisms have numerous strengths: victims get to tell their story in its own right, in a sympathetic atmosphere, where they can gain confidence and receive acknowledgement and validation. In these settings, also, their story can be very powerfully and fully communicated and can collectively articulate the need for a societal response, while also producing complex and multi-layered accounts. Moreover, such mechanisms can facilitate a real sense of empowerment for the individual storyteller, most notably when the story is an expression of agency not just of the individual but also of the collective seeking justice. Arguing for a Habermasian form of communicative dialogue, Kirk Simpson contends that public storytelling can allow for victims to 'take back' their self-pride and their self-worth, and assume their place as an intrinsic part of the conflict transformation.[32] They are processes that are, of course, not without their limitations and difficulties. Cillian McGrattan situates the recent rush towards 'storytelling' as a deliberate political act to displace highly contentious legacy issues away from the formal political arena into the more amicable community setting of oral testimony. While acknowledging the important role of testimony, the emphasis on 'grassroots truths' may work to hamper the stated policy goals of transparency, proportionality and accountability in this area of dealing with the past. In other words, the traditional law-and-order apparatus of due process and forensic evidence will be substituted with an approach to justice based on relative and subjective forms of 'truth', that intuitively feel to be (in)correct, regardless of facts and evidence.[33]

In the absence of an overarching state-led mechanism to deal with the facts and evidence, however, many of those individuals and communities affected by Troubles-related violence devised their own structures and processes. The initial paramilitary ceasefires in 1994 paved the way for much communal reflection and acts of remembrance. Launched in that same year, *An Crann*/The Tree collected thousands of personal testimonies with the objective of telling and hearing complex and often contradictory accounts of the Troubles, in order to stimulate dialogue towards healing and reconciliation. Cross-community organisations such as WAVE Trauma and HTR advocate for and extensively use oral storytelling as a key component in their approaches to trauma and loss. WAVE Trauma's 'Witness Programme' allows space for the public (students, journalists, researchers and academics) to hear first-hand stories from victims and survivors in an unstructured format. Established in 1999 to document the first-hand experiences of the conflict, the Falls Community Council's oral history archive *Dúchas* illustrates the transformative potential of bottom-up storytelling to include various stories not only between divided communities, but also differences from within the community, which often reveal disparities and conflictual accounts within single communities. The interviews are collated in an on-site digital archive that contains both the voice recordings and the interview transcripts, thus representing an invaluable public resource. For Hackett and Rolston, one of the key achievements of the *Dúchas* archive is that the storytellers are not reduced to their experience of loss and trauma but are the subjects of their own story. The agency and cathartic outcomes of articulating conflict-related harms are of course tempered by the reality that such endeavours have the potential to exacerbate or reignite feelings of pain, loss and hurt, as well as the obvious danger of exacerbating already polarised conflict narratives. While any personal recounting of conflict-related harms is imbued with potential risks, evidence suggests that public acknowledgement of the individuality of the dead and the particular circumstances of their deaths also augments the emotional work of healing and mourning, mobilised by a desire to keep alive the name and value of the deceased.[34] Published in 1999, the 1,600-page tome *Lost Lives* detailed the names, biography and circumstances of all those killed in the Troubles and became a popular, if unlikely, bestseller. Out of print for over a decade, remarkably, copies of the book are sold online for anywhere between £500 to £1,000, much to the abhorrence of its authors.[35] The book's success, nevertheless, is testament of the societal need and desire for public acknowledgement of those killed in the Troubles.

The Ardoyne Commemoration Project (ACP) is a striking case in point and was established in 1998 as a reaction to the perceived lack of attention to victims of state violence in the Bloomfield Report. The project identified all the members of the Ardoyne community killed as a direct result of political violence between 1969 and 1998 (99 in all)[36] and gathered testimonies from the closest next-of-kin of each victim, culminating in a 543-page book (Ardoyne Commemoration Project 2002). The project was particularly mindful of the importance of local and grassroots ownership and involvement.[37] A fundamental feature of the project was that for many research participants, this was the first time they had publicly spoken about their loss. In addition, the ACP recovered new details and circumstances regarding the death of loved ones. While deemed a successful community-based initiative, many participants conceived the ACP as a precursor for a more comprehensive, formal truth recovery process. Though such endeavours have their limitations, they nonetheless propose a model of significant potential to others, which constitutes an important intervention by those seeking public acknowledgement that provides an important public platform and forms the basis for the building of trusting relationships.[38]

Alongside the voluminous truth recovery and commemorative groups and organisations, victims groups also proliferated during the post-ceasefire years, primarily as a direct response to the increasing needs of victims. Before 1997, the British state had virtually no policies at all with regard to victims of the Troubles.[39] The aims of most victims groups are to represent the victims of violence, to provide mechanisms and capacities to tell their stories, and to promote their interests by lobbying for funding, and other kinds of support.[40] While there are many cross-community victims groups, perhaps WAVE Trauma and HTR the most distinguished, it is unsurprising that many victims groups tend to align themselves broadly along ethno-national fissures, thus serving the particular needs of either Catholics and nationalists on one hand, or Protestant and unionists on the other. The desire to promote what are believed to be 'forgotten' or 'silenced' victims of the conflict, however, invokes a series of competing and often polarised perspectives on the conflict from various victims' groups and organisations. Disputed experiences and perspectives of previous harms invariably produce relationships of antagonism, not reconciliation. Nationalist victims' groups pre-date 1997 and proliferated in the aftermath of the 1998 agreement. The notion of victimhood appeared more apposite for nationalists as they were the minority group in the state with widespread acceptance that they suffered various forms of discrimination.[41] Unlike unionism, nationalist victims' groups had a clear point of focus, that being the role of the state in direct killings and indirectly through collusion with loyalists. The largest nationalist victims' group, Relatives For Justice, was established in 1991 by relatives of those who lost loved ones at the hands of state forces and loyalist paramilitaries, and the organisation offers a range of supports and services to all the injured and bereaved. It is primarily concerned with issues of transitional justice and truth recovery. While the Pat Finucane Centre acts on behalf of all families and is keen to emphasise that its remit is not restricted to any one community, much of its work has been in the assistance of those whose loved ones were killed by state forces directly or through collusion with loyalist paramilitaries. The Bloody Sunday Justice Campaign pre-dated the 1994 ceasefires and 1998 agreement. The decision in January 1998 by then Prime Minister Tony Blair to hold a second inquiry into the events of January 1972 was widely interpreted as a confidence-building measure for the nationalist community, as well as the mounting 'new evidence' which completely discredited the original Widgery Inquiry published in April 1972. Cases involving allegations of state killing or state collusion dominated much of the nationalist victims agenda, with similar demands for fresh, independent inquiries into issues such as the Force Research Unit, the activities of Ulster Defence Association (UDA) state agent Brian Nelson, the 1988 killing of lawyer Pat Finucane, among others. In response to and under the weight of mounting evidence, in 2003 the British government appointed retired Canadian judge Peter Cory to examine evidence relating to the cases of Pat Finucane, Robert Hamill, Rosemary Nelson and Billy Wright, all suspected levels of state collusion.

While unionist victims groups were initially slow to emerge, again the post-1998 period witnessed a plethora of new associations which sought to demonstrate that the 'real victims' were those Protestants killed by republican paramilitaries. Unionists' endeavours seeking truth and accountability have historically been hampered by the fact that they are seeking some form of redress from non-state, illegal paramilitaries. Unlike republicans and nationalists, who have directed their energies and activism regarding legacy towards the British state and state forces, unionists and unionist narratives regarding legacy have been deprived of a centralised, official body on which to pursue and advance their needs and interests. In reaction to the perceived imbalance in dealing with legacy cases, unionist victims groups such as Families Acting for Innocent Relatives (FAIR) and Families Against Intimidation and Terror (FAIT) emerged from the mid-1990s onwards, focusing their energies on the victims of republican violence. Other 'localised' groups, such as West Tyrone Voice and FEAR Fermanagh, specifically centred their energies and support on those Protestants displaced and forced to abandon their homes because of IRA violence and/or intimidation. Given the fact that much of the British government's actions on dealing with the past are in reaction to nationalist demands and campaigns, many unionist political parties and civil society groups are vociferously opposed to any type of truth commission, dismissing it as a mechanism to further the republican agenda of 're-engineering the narrative' of the past. The demands of unionist victims' groups have tended to centre on criminal prosecutions for paramilitary offences and the provision of services to meet the practical and everyday needs of victims and survivors.

Acknowledgement and public apologies

In light of the grassroots work of victims, survivors and victims' groups, acknowledgement by state and non-state actors for past abuses and hurt is a central component in addressing some of the pain, loss and trauma. While accountability via a judicial court case can in some instances mitigate feelings of anger and animosity regarding past injustices,[42] public acknowledgement can be effective in repairing many broken relationships in Northern Ireland by conferring public recognition of pain, trauma and loss. Such public expressions can be apologies, museums and monuments, among other things. Given the centrality of acknowledgement for their ability to restore dignity and assist in the healing process,[43] public apologies have been cited as bringing benefit to victims by restoring dignity, repairing hurt and conferring acknowledgement. It is, however, largely superficial unless accompanied by a wider suite of measures including policy changes, legal changes and guarantees of accountability.[44] Denial is inherent to the practice of violence – denial of others' suffering creates the framework for legitimising violence against the other. True reconciliation is the ability to acknowledge the suffering of others, to demonstrate empathy and compassion without recourse to denial or explanatory forms of apology. Though forgiveness is a highly personal and of course difficult issue, nonetheless Northern Ireland has witnessed a small number of instances of forgiveness and apology, one of the most notable being that of Gordon Wilson, whose daughter Marie was killed in the 1987 IRA Enniskillen bombing which killed eleven Protestants at a Remembrance Sunday service. In the immediate days after the killing, Wilson stated his forgiveness for those who killed his daughter. The emergence of Sinn Féin as a political force in the 1980s meant that the republican movement now had a 'public face' to justify and condone IRA killings. While Sinn Féin members consistently defended IRA actions by attributing blame to 'British Occupation' or 'colonialism', the 1987 IRA bombing of Enniskillen and the magnitude and humility of Gordon Wilson's forgiveness signified one of the first public utterances of 'regret' from republicans. In the aftermath of the bombing, Gerry Adams warned the IRA that it had to be 'careful, and careful again' with regard to how it pursued its campaign in the future. By 1993, Gerry Adams was more critical, describing the IRA Shankill bombing on 23 October 1993 as 'wrong' and a 'tragedy'. In 2002, on the thirtieth anniversary of the Bloody Friday bombings in Belfast, the IRA issued a statement apologising for the killing of what it termed 'non-combatants' in that atrocity. Apologies and utterances of regret such as these are met with a variety of responses, ranging from scepticism to outright contempt. However, Tom Donnelly, whose sister was killed on Bloody Friday, said he was overwhelmed by IRA's 2002 statement, which he said gave him hope for the future, while others dismissed it as 'half-hearted'.[45] As part of their ceasefire declaration on 13 October 1994, the Combined Loyalist Military Command stated that 'in all sincerity we offer the loved ones of all innocent victims ... abject and true remorse'. The significance of the message was perhaps only eclipsed by the messenger. It was delivered by former Ulster Volunteer Force (UVF) leader Gusty Spence, previously jailed for his part in the 1966 murder of Peter Ward, a Catholic barman who went with some friends to the Malvern Arms off the Shankill Road. Many consider the killing of Peter Ward to be the first fatality of the Troubles. At the release of the report of the Saville Tribunal into British army killings on Bloody Sunday in Derry in 1972, the then British Prime Minister David Cameron's unequivocal apology went a long way towards meeting broad nationalist demands for truth and justice associated with the atrocity.[46]

Statements such as these are often mired in ambiguity; all actors to the conflict – republican, loyalist and state forces – are careful with the language deployed in public utterances of regret and apology, many of which are often replete with contingencies and discursive constructions of contextual and causal explanations. Any critical appraisals of organisational statements of apology are incomplete without an understanding that the legitimacy surrounding overall actions during the Troubles must be safeguarded at all costs.[47] For instance, all IRA apologies speak of regret for the killing of 'non-combatants', a strategy which permits enough enabling space to still legitimise their overall campaign. The attitudes and approaches to the past by the British state are also carefully regulated to protect a narrative depicting their role in the conflict as neutral arbitrator caught between the two squabbling sectarian tribes. Notwithstanding the fulsome and unambiguous 2010 apology by the then British Prime Minister, David Cameron, for British army actions on Bloody Sunday, the British government has consistently placed obstacles in the way of full, independent, public inquiries into cases involving serious and compelling evidence of state collusion between members of the British security forces and loyalist paramilitaries.[48]

For many families and survivors, forgiveness can seem a step too far, even an act of betrayal. Undoubtedly, the issue is further complicated by the fact that no party to the conflict in Northern Ireland has sought forgiveness. Many utterances of apology or regret, by republicans, loyalists or the state, are embedded in an overarching narrative which seeks to justify the violence undertaken. Public statements of regret by all actors to the conflict have largely fallen short of what could be interpreted as genuine remorse, not least in avoiding the specific use of the word 'sorry'. While the instances of public apology are a welcome development, they raise questions as to what extent an apology needs to be linked to discernible and meaningful acts of reparation and justice.[49] A genuine apology must include acceptance of responsibility, accountability, sincerity and regret for the acknowledged wrongdoing, as well as the stated intention to avoid repetition of the offence.[50] What occurs in Northern Ireland, however, are instances of 'explanatory apologies' – these being apologies which also seek to defend previous actions or behaviours.[51] Though civil society has taken the lead through an impressive range of processes and mechanisms which address many post-conflict societal needs, the issue here is that they are fragmented and often localised forms of 'truth-telling'. The commonality across many of these eclectic endeavours nevertheless is, broadly speaking, an aspiration for public acknowledgement of hurt and the opportunity for 'storytelling'. On that premise, some have suggested that the most obvious mechanism to overcome the piecemeal nature of legacy in Northern Ireland is the establishment of a centralised, formal truth commission.

A truth commission for Northern Ireland?

Given the parallels drawn between Northern Ireland's peace process and those elsewhere in the world, the idea of a formal truth commission for the region has been persistently debated since the signing of the 1998 peace accord. While there exists a wide variety of ways in which to examine and deal with the legacy of armed actions, truth commissions have garnered much attention for their ability to deal with the legacy of conflicts. Between 1974 and 1999, some forty truth commissions were undertaken, t of which were created in the last decade of that period.[52] Advocates of a formalised truth commission for Northern Ireland have looked at post-conflict societies elsewhere, most notably Chile and South Africa, emphasising the capacity of truth commissions to confer acknowledgement, reveal facts about past violence, engender accountability and provide a platform for storytelling, and its potential for reparations and reconciliation.[53] In particular, the South African Truth and Reconciliation Forum in the 1990s remains widely lauded, despite the many critiques and flaws identified since. In addition, several reasons specific to Northern Ireland have been put forward in favour of a truth commission: the continuing revelations about the past which are hindering confidence in reform and preventing politics and society from building a stable future; concerns raised regarding the suitability of the existing approaches to dealing with the past, not least concerning their financial cost; and the burden placed on the PSNI, coupled with issues regarding its impartiality and independence.[54] Regardless of the compelling reasons offered in favour of a truth commission, extensive research among citizens and political elites in Northern Ireland reveal pervasive ambiguity and a general wariness that a vigorous examination of the past has the potential to reinforce antagonisms and divisions.[55]

Truth commissions are official bodies established to explore and shed light on past violence, human rights abuses and violations, and have come to be regarded as a vital part of the process of conflict transition. As officially promoted truth recovery mechanisms, they can open up sanctioned spaces for building complex, multi-dimensional perceptions of the 'other' by improving access to the others' perspectives and experiences.[56] Without a formal vehicle, the divergent and conflicting accounts will disseminate in chaotic and piecemeal ways, thus absorbing political energy and goodwill, and effectively continuing the 'war by other means'.[57] The notion that 'revealing is healing' within official truth recovery processes is anchored in the belief that private grief and trauma has a public value. As argued so efficaciously by Marie Breen-Smyth, it is more accurate to describe truth recovery processes as a service that victims (and perpetrators) perform for society, rather than a service provided for their benefit. Unquestionably, truth commissions can and do play an important (and potentially cathartic) role in providing a recognised space for public acknowledgement and empathy for conflict-related trauma. According to John Brewer, truth commissions focus on the past, provide a comprehensive account of past abuses, exist for a limited time only, possess varying authority to access the truth, and finally, they typically conclude with a final, 'authoritative' account of the past. Such processes, however, are far from unproblematic and often enmeshed in a range of complex problems, including: the independence of the process; the role of the state; terms of reference for the inquiry; the witnesses and actors called to testify; amnesties for perpetrators; the societal impact of the process; forms of retribution and/or reparations; and the obvious potential for re-traumatising victims and survivors. The danger with a state-led monopoly on dealing with the past is the value and faith placed in what are effectively one-size-fits-all prescriptions that neglect the heterogenous nature of those persons collectivised under the term 'victims'. The idea of 'dealing with past' within a formal process problematically assumes that endeavours to address trauma and hurt through truth recovery can be neatly book-ended with a predetermined start and endpoints, and perhaps most importantly, will produce a finished, authoritative outcome. While governments and international interventions seek a relatively expedient approach, reconciliation and the reparation of damaged relations require long-term processes and commitments.

Notwithstanding these complexities, undoubtedly, the overarching problem with truth commissions resides in the positivist epistemological belief that value-free, empirical facts exist and can be collated to reach a final, objective 'truth'. For instance, in the case of the South African Truth and Reconciliation Commission, it received over 20,000 statements but could not definitively prove most things unless the perpetrator claimed responsibility – as most, inevitably, did not.[58] Guatemala's experience of the Recovery of Historical Memory occurred against a backdrop of undisclosed files. The terms of reference and boundaries of inquiry profoundly shape the process and outcomes of truth commissions. The Chilean Commission focused on disappearances but not human rights abuses, and so delivered a partial truth regarding the conflict there.[59] There is of course a precedent for independent, outside control, the most famous example being the El Salvadorian case which proceeded under the auspices of the UN. Truth commissions typically hear a selection of victims; a 'sample' that can claim to be representative of the major different groups of victims. In major conflicts such as those in South Africa or Argentina, there were considerable practical problems in recording and hearing the story of every victim.

The key problematic assumption, therefore, is that a single or absolute truth exists out there, waiting to be recovered. There are of course many competing experiences and narratives on the past, generating a plurality of truths. While inter-communal differences are unsurprising, even within relatively homogenous communities and movements, there exists a myriad of contrasting perspectives on the same events, thus problematising the positivist idea of an existing, absolute truth. While there are empirical facts about the conflict, nonetheless memories, perspectives and meanings attached to those events are malleable and profoundly shaped by social interactions in the present. Take, for example, the events of Bloody Sunday in Derry on 30 January 1972. Broadly, the Saville Report released in June 2010 uncovered what are generally accepted facts about the events of the day and, most importantly, affirmed the innocence of the victims and wounded. However, within the hundreds of testimonies across an eclectic range of witnesses emerged both complimentary and contrasting memories, some nuanced, others vast. Across the inquiry, there were, therefore, undeniable facts that were backed by rigorous evidence, but there also existed a wide range of experiences, perspectives and memories of that day. What is perhaps most important about the Saville Inquiry is that for the families it was never about recovering the truth. As they saw it, they and the wider community in Derry already knew 'the truth'. What they wanted, as with most victims in truth recovery processes, was an official acknowledgement of that truth.

Furthermore, admissions of responsibility and culpability that emerge through formal truth recovery processes are tempered by pre-agreed amnesties or the inadmissibility of testimonies in any future criminal prosecutions. The likelihood of perpetrators 'owning up' to previous deeds is of course shaped by many contextual factors: where risks of prosecution exist, chances of perpetrators taking responsibility remains low, but in circumstances of a restorative process, with an emphasis on forgiveness and repairing broken relationships,[60] the prospects of disclosure by former combatants is much higher.[61] The 'price' for disclosure is of course amnesty.

The unfortunate reality of armed conflict is that victims are often faced with a stark choice, between more information or 'truth' on the one hand and justice on the other.[62] Again, the case of Bloody Sunday illustrates the complexities and frustrations experienced by families of victims through a formal truth recovery inquiry. Despite securing a plethora of compelling new evidence and the exoneration of their loved ones through the Saville Inquiry, prosecution services decided in March 2019 to prosecute just one soldier, Solder F, much to the dismay and disappointment of the victims' families, their supporters and wider nationalist and republican victims groups. While expressing messages of solidarity with the families, the distinct muteness from Sinn Féin on the prosecution of Soldier F perhaps divulges their real preference for some formulation of an amnesty for all 'actors to the conflict'.

The Eames–Bradley Report of the Consultative Group on the Past did recommend the establishment of a 'Legacy Commission' as a truth recovery model for Northern Ireland, but the thrust of the report's argument was lost in the political quagmire over its recommendation of a £12,000 payment to all victims of the conflict, including non-state combatants. While the idea of a truth commission was again mooted in the Haass–Sullivan talks in 2013, there are some who suggest that the gulf of trust between all parties to the conflict – loyalist, republican, British state – is indicative of an overall lack of confidence in political structures and processes to deliver an investigation into the past.[63] Broadly, both main nationalist parties, Sinn Féin and the Social Democratic Labour Party (SDLP) have historically advocated some type of a formal truth commission. Sinn Féin published a series of policy documents articulating their desire for a centralised truth commission and so republicans were more likely than any other party to back the idea that the primary aim of any truth commission should be 'to get the story straight about what happened during the conflict'.[64] Given their long-standing links with the African National Congress (ANC) and the anti-apartheid struggle, republicans were keen to push for a South African-style truth commission. In contrast, the foundation of unionist opposition resides in their belief that any truth commission is ultimately a fundamental component of the republican agenda to 'rewrite' the narrative of the conflict to legitimise their violence, and in doing so, seeks a political and moral equivalence between non-state perpetrators and innocent victims. The political parallels constructed by republicans between the apartheid regime in South Africa and unionist rule in Northern Ireland only serve to reinforce unionist fears that they will be cast in the 'Afrikaner' role in any truth commission, thus scapegoated as the oppressors and instigators of the violence. Moreover, senior loyalists have openly criticised historical inquiries and any form of truth commissions as potentially destabilising for the peace process and wider loyalist support for it.⁶⁵ Unionist fears regarding a truth commission are also shaped by international examples where truth commissions have overwhelmingly focused on the actions and abuses perpetrated by the state. The vociferous demands from nationalist and republicans regarding truth about state violence have engendered a widespread unionist perception that the demand for a truth commission is a 'nationalist issue' and the outworkings of any such commission will ultimately be a vilification and witch-hunt of state security personnel.⁶⁶ The significant divergence in attitudes between unionism and nationalism towards any possible truth commission does little to engender the enabling conditions in which a formalised truth commission is likely to emerge.

Additionally, the post-conflict situation that pertains to Northern Ireland is markedly different from that which existed in El Salvador or South Africa, where truth commissions were devised and deployed. Northern Ireland's conflict did not end with a clear-cut victor; its 1998 peace accord largely ended armed actions and to a large degree settled the constitutional question via the consent principle and cross-community power-sharing. However, competing narratives regarding the legacy of political violence and issues related to parades, flags and emblems are testament to the fact that the conflict continues through other means. Opposition to a truth recovery process also reflects concerns about the issue of criminal justice proceedings. As with other regions emerging from armed conflict, the price of a truth commission in Northern Ireland will undoubtedly be an amnesty of some sort. For many victims, such a move is too high a price for relinquishing the pursuit of retributive justice. From the perspective of protagonists, the idea of being held publicly accountable for past deeds is also not an enticing prospect, with some fearing reprisals, stigmatisation and other repercussions. While the use of truth commissions has increased exponentially in recent decades, with more than twenty established since 1973, the issue in Northern Ireland, as in most regions emerging from the aftermath of armed conflict, is that the demands for truth and accountability far outweigh the willingness of those with the relevant information to disclose it.⁶⁷ For those advancing the proposition of a formalised truth commission for Northern Ireland, the demands for the 'truth' are primarily driven by a desire to obtain selective 'facts' to legitimise a carefully constructed narrative regarding their role and actions during the Troubles. All actors in the conflict – republicans, loyalists and the British state – have invested too much political and moral capital in promoting their particular versions of the 'truth' to risk negotiating the rigours of a centralised truth commission. Furthermore, there is ample evidence that many citizens lack confidence in the ability of political institutions and society in general to withstand an investigation into the past, perhaps indicating a latent concern that the 'conflict is not over'. In other words, the risks posed by a comprehensive exposure of truth and acknowledgement are too great.[68]

Despite this, the latest data sets from the University of Liverpool NI General Election Survey (2019) indicate that since 2017 there has been a significant shift in favour of a truth and reconciliation commission among the public. In 2017, 31.5 per cent agreed or strongly agreed with the creation of such a body. This has now risen to 45.7 per cent. When removing those who did not express an opinion, the proportion who wish for a truth and reconciliation commission rises to a formidable 73.6 per cent. Among supporters of the two main political parties, Sinn Féin's share of voters who support a truth and reconciliation commission has risen from 33.4 per cent to 58.1 per cent. When removing those who did not express an opinion, the share who wish for a truth and reconciliation commission rises to 90.4 per cent. The proportion of Democratic Unionist Party (DUP) voters who support a truth and reconciliation commission has risen from 34.3 per cent to 49.1 per cent. When removing those who did not express an opinion, the share who wish for a truth and reconciliation commission rises to 73.4 per cent.

According to Smyth, while there is little systematic evidence of the benefits and outputs of truth commissions, undoubtedly, they can and do serve some useful purposes, including assisting with rewriting the history of the past and the acknowledgement of victims' suffering. Invariably, however, truth is always traded for justice, with amnesties used to incentivise the participation of protagonists. There are of course many other alternatives to truth commissions. Other processes, such as implementing security-sector reform, transforming police and military institutions, addressing the issue of ex-combatants, memorialisation, opening archives, building museums, rewriting official histories, offering apologies and building the interrelationship between transitional justice and development, are all now considered part of the wider field of transitional justice.[69] While many believe that Northern Ireland may not withstand a centralised, overarching truth recovery commission, others have pointed to the successes and future opportunities in localised forms of truth recovery as a distinct method to navigate the divisive terrain of the past in ways that do not reproduce divisions.[70] This chapter contends that while a centralised, formal truth commission could play an important role as part of a holistic package of measures, it is self-evident that, unlike other post-conflict regions, a truth commission would be severely limited by Northern Ireland's zero-sum endeavours with legacy. Given the conflicting (and often irreconcilable) viewpoints and antagonisms that permeate approaches to the past, the outcomes of any formalised truth commission process would likely exacerbate contestation rather than promoting dialogue, engagement and social reconciliation.

Agreements, fresh starts and new approaches

In comparison to the ineffectual and disparate nature of Northern Ireland's legacy endeavours, the 2014 Stormont House Agreement represented the most promising and comprehensive approach to date. Although initially scuppered by Sinn Féin on issues related to welfare reform,[71] the SHA proposals on legacy were effectively front and centre once again with the 2015 Fresh Start Agreement (FSA). The SHA sets out three strategies and related frameworks that include the Independent Commission on Information Retrieval (ICIR), the Historical Investigations Unit (HIU) and the Implementation and Reconciliation Group (IRG). The ICIR is designed as an independent body to collect evidence on deaths where people can 'privately learn' how their loved ones were killed. Information and evidence collected will not be disclosed to law-enforcement or intelligence agencies and will be inadmissible in civil and criminal proceedings. Evidence and members will be given immunities and privileges under international law and will be exempt from freedom of information requests, data protection and related legislation. Though the ICIR holds much potential, Sinn Féin and the SDLP have expressed major reservations about the withholding of information by the British state on its role in the conflict on the grounds of 'national security', particularly in relation to collusion with loyalist paramilitaries. Moreover, it is acknowledged that the ICIR will not have the same investigatory powers as the HIU or the capacity to ascertain the authenticity of the information provided.[72]

The HIU effectively takes over from the now defunct HET (and the Police Ombudsman), and will effectively be the primary mechanism for investigating past killings in Northern Ireland only with a view to seeking possible future prosecutions. It has been designed to have clear disclosure powers and the capacity to compel state agencies to deliver relevant papers and evidence to assist its various investigations. The HIU, however, will ultimately face the same myriad of obstacles that plagued the HET, as outlined earlier in this chapter. More ominously, while the UK government pledged that it would make full disclosure to the HIU, it also added that 'no individuals are put at risk, and that the government's duty to keep people safe and secure is upheld', once again raising nationalist and republican suspicions regarding full disclosure.[73] The IRG, whose membership will comprise academics, will oversee themes, archives and information recovery in order to produce a report or timeline regarding conflict-related violence. It is assumed that it will operate without political interference, although the bulk of nominees will be nominated by political parties. According to the SHA, the chair shall be a person of independent and international standing and will be nominated by the First Minister and deputy First Minister. The other appointments will be nominated as follows: DUP – 3 nominees, Sinn Féin – 2 nominees, SDLP – 1 nominee, UUP – 1 nominee, and Alliance Party – 1 nominee and one nominee each from the UK and Irish governments. Perhaps most significant is its commitment to support wider reconciliation efforts, by recognising a plurality of conflict-related narratives. A fourth and final key institution of the SHA that is often overlooked is the proposal for an Oral History Archive (OHA), which could provide an important platform for personal storytelling and public acknowledgement. While broadly welcome, providing an oral history platform for personal testimonies without rigorous historical evidence or context leaves the door ajar for a rewriting of the conflict narrative, particularly by former paramilitaries seeking to justify their use of violence. Despite the relative potential within the SHA and FSA, Shirlow contends that

> there is no sense that its [SHA] outplaying will mend the social fabric of a divided society. The structures of it are for the location of truth (which is disputed) without any notion of how, beyond victims' needs (which are disputed), what information disclosure will mean in terms of societal recovery.[74]

In other words, there is little discernible connection between the proposed SHA mechanisms and the transformation of social relationships.

Despite the initial broad welcome given to the SHA legacy proposals by most parties and the two governments, attempts at implementation floundered amid concerns regarding (non)-disclosures from the British state, coupled with the deteriorating relationship between the DUP and Sinn Féin, and a widespread unionist perception regarding an 'imbalance' in legacy investigations, believing a disproportionate focus on state killings. The SHA and FSA legacy proposals were of course shelved in the wake of the collapse of the power-sharing institutions in January 2017. Nevertheless, there have been successful attempts to bypass the political paralysis through pursuit of promised funding for dealing with a backlog of legacy inquests, some dating as far back as 1971. Despite the collapse of power-sharing in 2017, Northern Ireland's interminable undertakings with the past continued in its typical disparate and idiosyncratic way with new and ongoing developments, including: the Ballymurphy Massacre Inquest; the decision in March 2019 to prosecute a former British soldier, Soldier F, with murder for some of those killed on Bloody Sunday; and the decision to extradite John Downey, who previously received one of the controversial 'On The Run' letters to IRA suspects, issued by the British government under Tony Blair.[75] In July 2019 the Lord Chief Justice, Sir Declan Morgan, ruled that the PSNI had not honoured the 'legitimate expectation' of victims' families when the force pledged to conduct a rigorous investigation into allegations of police collusion with the notorious UVF Glenanne unit, which operated in mid-Ulster in the mid-1970s.

Significantly, in February 2019 the permanent secretary of the justice department, Peter May, announced that a Legacy Inquest Unit would be set up within the coroner's service to process legacy inquests. In 2016, the Northern Ireland Chief Justice, Sir Declan Morgan, requested £50 million from the power-sharing Executive to address the backlog, but the funding was blocked by the then DUP First Minister Arlene Foster. Throughout 2018 and 2019, with the prospect of prosecution of former British soldiers looming, the Ministry of Defence, members of the Conservative Party, media outlets and veterans' groups, among others, have actively lobbied for a 'statute of limitations' for soldiers who served in Iraq, Afghanistan and, of course, Northern Ireland. The central demand here is an amnesty. Such a proposition, according to many legal scholars, would have long since been established but for the fact that an amnesty for state forces will also extend to republican and loyalist paramilitaries, something many people in Northern Ireland will simply not countenance.

In July 2019, the Northern Ireland Office concluded an assessment of more than 17,000 responses across Northern Irish society as part of its Legacy Consultation initiative. The overarching finding from its consultation is that a clear majority are not in favour of any statute of limitation or amnesty for Troubles-related killings. While the consultation represents the first major public input into legacy by those affected by the trauma of conflict, the publication of the report was not matched by any discernible mechanisms or policy recommendations. The report received a largely subdued response, with many commentators dismissing it as both lacklustre and a political exercise in optics to fill the current political vacuum. In January 2020, the *New Decade, New Approach* initiative by the British and Irish government set about the rebuilding of Northern Ireland's power-sharing structures. While the document covers an array of issues, it is remarkable that the issue of legacy receives a pithy few sentences on page 48 of a 62-page document. In it, the British government will, 'within 100 days, publish and introduce legislation in the UK parliament to implement the Stormont House Agreement, to address Northern Ireland legacy issues'. The government will now start an intensive process with the Northern Irish parties, and the Irish government as appropriate, to maintain a broad-based consensus on these issues, recognising that any such UK parliament legislation should have the consent of the Northern Ireland Assembly.[76] On page 62, the Irish government reaffirms its financial commitment to reconciliation work, particularly in marginalised, border communities. It also states its 'commitment to working with the UK government to support the establishment of the Stormont House Agreement legacy institutions as a matter of urgency, including by introducing necessary implementing legislation in the Oireachtas, to deal with the legacy of the Troubles and support reconciliation, meeting the legitimate needs and expectations of victims and survivors'.[77] Unquestionably, legacy and the past were very much a subordinate issue in the deal to restore the Stormont institutions. In a document primarily concerned with structures of governance and identities and cultures, the cursory instances of attention amounted to little more than reaffirmations of previous positions. In sum, the *New Decade, New Approach* committed to legislating for the SHA within 100 days.

The feasibility of such a commitment is circumvented by Boris Johnson's manifesto promise to end 'vexatious' prosecutions of former servicemen. In April 2020, Secretary of State for Northern Ireland Brandon Lewis proposed the establishment of a new single body to primarily focus on information recovery and reconciliation rather than investigating Troubles-related killings. Widely interpreted as a departure from the SHA, some have objected to what they see as a mechanism to shield members and former members of the British army. In contrast to the HIU envisaged under the SHA, Lewis' proposal seeks to place greater emphasis on gathering information for families, retrieving knowledge before it is lost as opposed to seeking prosecutions. While not totally ruling out investigating into killings, Lewis is largely echoing much of the rhetoric from Boris Johnson and others in the Conservative Party who wish to see an end to what they term 'vexatious claims that undermine our armed forces', and more worryingly, is widely interpreted as preparing the ground for some sort of blanket amnesty for state forces. The incongruity of delivering on SHA mechanisms on the one hand while also pursuing what is effectively a form of amnesty for state personnel on the other, hardly bodes well for a genuine, holistic breakthrough on legacy any time in the near future.

Conclusion

It is over twenty-five years since the pivotal paramilitary ceasefires, and despite the advent of the Bloomfield report, Eames–Bradley and the SHA/FSA proposals, the issue of legacy and addressing the hurt and trauma of victims and survivors is consistently contingent on political stability and other interests, as opposed to constituting a moral and political imperative. Not only have Northern Ireland's efforts at legacy largely failed to deliver discernible improvements for many individuals, families and communities, but they have also exacerbated post-Troubles relationships, where according to the Police Ombudsman Dr Michael Maguire, 'competing narratives of the past in Northern Ireland are more polarised now than ever before'.[78] The post-ceasefire period gave way to a new landscape enmeshed with competing and deeply held perspectives on the thirty years or more of political violence. In such circumstances, memories of war became weapons in a war over memory.[79] Calls for a general amnesia or 'drawing a line under the past' is not an option, as legacy will likely remain embedded in the cultural and political framework, thus creating an inherent volatility which at best will lead to instability, mistrust and poor inter-communal relations, and at worst leaves intact a reservoir for potential future violence.[80] The staggered and piecemeal approach to dealing with and addressing the legacy of political violence, as documented in this chapter, raises questions for those who propagate a beguiling but oversimplistic reading of the GFA as a 'work of genius'. The reality, however, is that not only did the peace deal not put in place any mechanisms for dealing with victims, but it also failed to define the term 'victim'. The consequences of this omission (deliberate or not) has reverberated over the last 20 years with real-world impacts for those who continue to live with the harms of the Troubles.

At the time of writing – late September 2020 – the scheme to administer the 'Troubles Pension'[81] remains stymied by controversy and contestation regarding eligibility for the scheme, thus delaying the commencement of payment and compounding the suffering of those affected by the conflict. The scheme was due to open for applications on 29 May 2020, but was initially delayed by a dispute over who will fund it, with estimated costs of at least £100 million in the first three years.[82] Beyond the funding dispute, Sinn Féin initially declined to nominate a Stormont department to run the scheme because of concerns over the fact that those with convictions of more than two and a half years will be excluded from applying, thus precluding many republicans and loyalists. Moreover, the party also claimed the scheme would significantly benefit British army veterans. While it is envisaged that a judge-led board will decide who qualifies for the scheme, the British government insists it would only apply to people who were injured 'through no fault of their own' and insists that government can directly intervene if it disagrees with any decision by the board. In August 2020, the High Court in Belfast ruled that the Northern Ireland Executive Office was acting unlawfully in delaying the introduction of a compensation scheme. Despite the ruling, it is unlikely that any payment will proceed until early 2021 at the earliest. The former Victims Commissioner Judith Thompson – who was neither reappointed nor replaced when her term concluded in August 2020 – has contended that the issue at stake is beyond the monetary payment; the pension is fundamentally concerned with acknowledgement, respect and value. The victims' pension issue is of course embedded in a wider, adversarial framework regarding the contestation of defining victims and thus assigning 'innocence' and 'culpability'. The failure to agree what victimhood means is undeniably a product of a peace accord that deliberately eschewed the issue, thus bequeathing a vacuum which enabled antagonistic and competing narrative formations that ultimately compound the issue of legacy and deflect energy and focus from devising genuinely transformative measures capable of redressing harm.

The absence of a formal state-led approach to legacy and insufficient levels of social reconciliation, coupled with a lack of victims' supports and services, ensures that for many victims the 'post-conflict' landscape represents a continuum of violence, hurt and trauma, despite prevailing declarations regarding 'peace and prosperity'. According to Lederach,[83] the idea of reconciliation suggests meaningful engagement and discernible changes in previously adversarial relationships. Reconciliation, therefore, requires an acknowledgement of trauma, in all its manifestations, and genuine endeavour to seek truth recovery in ways that build towards healing that trauma. Commissioning a formal and centralised truth recovery process alone to meet the requirements of liberal peace models or in furthering a particular political agenda is facile and unproductive. For Shirlow,

> the intention of such structures and approaches is that they will be a panacea to victims' needs when the correct institutional fix and structures of governance are delivered. Such thinking downplays that such fixes are not identified by political actors as being sites of trauma recovery or conflict transformation but as structures within which to apportion blames and re-enact the conflict and its polarity.[84]

Moreover, this chapter echoes the 2002 report by HTR, which stated that there is 'no single treatment for the healing process', but rather that a multiplicity of actions and approaches are required. Approaches to legacy in Northern Ireland require holistic and interrelated mechanisms. The 'tools of truth recovery' must be eclectic, mutually supportive and 'healing-centred', and meet the needs and interests of victims.

It was not the purpose of this chapter (even if there had been enough space) to come to a definitive answer to the complex challenge of Northern Ireland's issue of legacy. Rather, the primary objective was to critically evaluate some of the past initiatives, while also appraising some of those proposed for future endeavours. There are some who perhaps understandably wish to 'draw a line underneath the past', insisting that the barriers to dealing with legacy are too complex, too sensitive, and are ultimately insurmountable. Notwithstanding the degrees of validity in such claims, it is judicious to bear in mind that we were also told in the 1970s and 1980s that the conflict itself was too complex and, ultimately, intractable. Conflict-related hurt and trauma will continue in Northern Ireland, and in many instances will increase with the new reality of intergenerational trauma. Unlike Northern Ireland's power-sharing institutions, the trauma, loss and pain daily endured by victims cannot be 'suspended' or 'pulled down'. The human cost of this failure is immeasurable, and the passage of over 20 years since the 1998 accord is a damning indictment of a peace agreement that deliberately eschewed the painful and difficult issues of legacy. The idea of confronting a violent past and the uncovering of difficult and often harrowing suffering were deemed too high a risk for the nascent and precarious peace. Perhaps the greatest single shortcoming in the last 25 years of the peace process was to place the arduous task of dealing with legacy in the hands of local parties, where any endeavours with the past would be framed by the contested politics of victimhood and culpability. As potently illustrated by the case of Northern Ireland, the growing body of literature on transitional justice contends that, first, there is no 'right moment' to face the horrors of past violence, and, second, there is no one-size-fits-all approach which will meet the diverse needs and interests of victims and those traumatised by the conflict, which include a considerable range of emotional, health and psychological support services. While there are understandable and often vast differences regarding victimhood, or legacy mechanisms and initiatives in Northern Ireland, there are, however, other grounds for optimism. For instance, there is a broad consensus that Northern Ireland contains many traumatised citizens, families and communities. Much of the research conducted over the last 20 years also indicates that those caught up in the conflict wish to know more about the context and circumstances of the violence that has affected them and their loved ones. Furthermore, there is undoubtedly a broad agreement among the population that the provision of essential emotional, physical and psychological supports and services should be adequately funded, staffed and accessible by all those traumatised by the 30 years of violence.

The issue of dealing with the past, however, should not be monopolised by the political process or be wholly contingent upon it. Any critical appraisal of legacy processes must be based on a broader understanding of truth recovery and transformation. The issue of dealing with the past in harm-centred and transformative ways is a fraught balancing act. The eclectic initiatives through which victims and survivors articulate their memories, needs and perspectives are anchored in practices and processes that are often confrontational, selective, and serve to reinforce the antagonisms central to the conflict. Despite this, confronting the past, with all its pain and complexity, also holds the potential to create new forms of dialogue and understanding that can lead to re-evaluations and new comprehensions that are truth-seeking in genuinely non-adversarial ways. Seeking truth and confronting the legacy of violence, whether through centralised formal commissions, bottom-up approaches or a combination of both, must be viewed not as a single panacea to legacy but as part of a broad suite of measures which include a discernible link with social reconciliation.

Notes

1 Though much of the violence that characterised the 'Troubles' occurred in the six counties of Northern Ireland, it is important to acknowledge that there were many significant acts of violence in Great Britain, the Republic of Ireland and in some instances, mainland Europe throughout the conflict. Indeed, the worst day of the conflict in terms of death toll entailed events that took place south of the Irish border. On 17 May 1974, bombs planted by loyalists in Monaghan and Dublin claimed the lives of thirty-three civilians. Therefore, while much attention is understandably concentrated on victims in Northern Ireland, it is also important to bear in mind victims in the Irish Republic, Great Britain and further afield.
2 A central feature of the problem in dealing with legacy in Northern Ireland concerns victims and victimhood. The visceral debates and exchanges regarding what constitute 'real victims' remain proxies for the construction and maintenance of competing narratives which essentially are concerned with assigning culpability for the violence of the Troubles. Unfortunately, a discussion of this important issue was beyond the scope of this chapter. For a critical overview of victims and victimhood see Erika Bouris, *Complex Political Victims* (Bloomfield, CT: Kumarian Press, 2007). For texts directly dealing with victimhood in Northern Ireland see Sarah E. Jankowitz, *The Order of Victimhood: Violence, Hierarchy, and Building Peace in Northern Ireland* (London: Palgrave Macmillan, 2018) and Graham Dawson, *Making Peace with the Past? Memory, Trauma and the Irish Troubles* (Manchester: Manchester University Press, 2007).
3 Patricia Lundy, 'Paradoxes and Challenges of Transitional Justice at the "Local" Level: Historical Enquiries in Northern Ireland', *Contemporary Social Science*, 6(1) (2011), 89–106.
4 John D. Brewer, *Peace Processes: A Sociological Approach* (Cambridge: Polity Press, 2010); Dawson, *Making Peace with the Past?*; Brandon Hamber, 'Dealing with painful memories and violent pasts: towards a framework for contextual understanding', in Beatrix Austin and Martina Fischer (eds), *Transforming War-Related Identities* (Berghof Handbook Dialogue Series, 2015); Patricia Lundy and Bill Rolston, 'Redress for Past Harms? Official Apologies in Northern Ireland', *International Journal of Human Rights*, 20(1) (2016), 104–22; Marie Smyth, *Truth Recovery and Justice after Conflict: Managing Violent Pasts* (London: Routledge, 2007).
5 For a thorough and insightful account of the peace process, see Fergal Cochrane, *Northern Ireland: The Reluctant Peace* (New Haven, CT: Yale University Press, 2013).
6 Smyth, *Truth Recovery and Justice after Conflict*.
7 Johan Galtung, 'Violence, Peace and Peace Research', *Journal of Peace Research*, 6 (1969) 167–91.

8 John Paul Lederach, *Building Peace: Sustainable Reconciliation in Divided Societies* (Washington, DC: United States Institute of Peace Press, 1997).
9 Ibid.
10 Donald G. Ellis, *Transforming Conflict: Communication and Ethnopolitical Conflict* (Oxford: Rowman & Littlefield, 2006).
11 Cited in Brandon Hamber and Gráinne Kelly, 'A Place for Reconciliation? Conflict and Locality in Northern Ireland', *Democratic Dialogue* (Belfast, 2005).
12 Ibid., p. 21.
13 John Paul Lederach, *Preparing for Peace: Conflict Transformation Across Cultures* (New York: Syracuse University Press, 1995), p. 18.
14 Nevin T. Aiken, 'The Bloody Sunday Inquiry: Transitional Justice and Postconflict Reconciliation in Northern Ireland', *Journal of Human Rights*, 14(1) (2015), 101–23.
15 Finola Ferry, Edel Ennis, Brendan Bunting, Samuel Murphy, David Bolton and Siobhan O'Neill, 'Troubled Consequences: A Report on the Mental Health Impact of the Civil Conflict in Northern Ireland' (Belfast: Commission for Victims and Survivors, 2011).
16 Hamber, 'Dealing with painful memories and violent pasts'.
17 Patricia Lundy, 'Paradoxes and Challenges of Transitional Justice at the "Local" Level: Historical Enquiries in Northern Ireland', *Contemporary Social Science*, 6(1) (2011), 89–105.
18 Peter Shirlow, 'Truth Friction in Northern Ireland: Caught between Apologia and Humiliation', *Parliamentary Affairs*, 71 (2018), 417–37.
19 Ibid.
20 Gerry Moriarty, 'PSNI fails to disclose information about killings by loyalists', *Irish Times*, 14 February 2019. Available at www.irishtimes.com/news/crime-and-law/psni-fails-to-disclose-information-about-killings-by-loyalists-1.3792857. Accessed 4 April 202. In February 2019, Northern Ireland's Police Ombudsman Michael Maguire called for an independent review to be carried out after 'significant, sensitive information' about Troubles killings that he had requested was not supplied to him by the PSNI. The discovery was made during the Ombudsman's investigation into the Ulster Defence Association (UDA) attack on Sean Graham's bookmakers on the Ormeau Road in Belfast in 1992, in which five people were killed. While PSNI Deputy Chief Constable Stephen Martin 'deeply and sincerely' apologised and said the non-disclosure was not deliberate, victims' families and organisations such as Relatives For Justice said it undermines their confidence in the PSNI to fully cooperate with legacy investigations.
21 Lundy, 'Paradoxes and Challenges'.
22 Ibid.
23 Priscilla B. Hayner, *Unspeakable Truths: Facing the Challenge of Truth Commissions* (London: Routledge, 2001).
24 CPNI, 'Report of the Consultative Group on the Past/Robin Eames & Denis Bradley, Co-Chairs of the Consultative Group on the Past' (Belfast, 2009).

25 Lundy, 'Paradoxes and Challenges'.
26 The Bloomfield Report *We Will Remember them* was the culmination of a commission established by the British government in November 1997 to 'to look at possible ways to recognise the pain and suffering felt by victims of violence arising from the troubles of the last 30 years, including those who have died or been injured in the service of the community'. It was headed by former Stormont civil servant Sir Kenneth Bloomfield and delivered its report in 1998. The report made a series of recommendations, including greater compensation for victims of violence and their support groups, an official victims ombudsman, the creation of physical memorial such as a garden or park, the future establishment of a Truth and Reconciliation Commission and a Memorial Day for victims, and improved employment opportunities for victims. While the report was welcomed by most political parties, it was criticised by Sinn Féin and the wider nationalist community for its failure to address the concerns of relatives of people killed by the security forces.
27 Dawson, *Making Peace with the Past?*
28 Kevin Cassidy, 'Organic Intellectuals and the Committed Community: Irish Republicanism and Sinn Féin in the North', *Irish Political Studies*, 20(3) (2005), 341–56.
29 Claire Hackett and Bill Rolston, 'The Burden of Memory: Victims, Storytelling and Resistance in Northern Ireland', *Memory Studies*, 2(3) (2009), 355–76.
30 Ibid.
31 Dawson, *Making Peace with the Past?*
32 Kirk Simpson, *Truth Recovery in Northern Ireland: Critically Interpreting the Past* (Manchester: Manchester University Press, 2009), p. 67.
33 Cillian McGrattan, 'The Stormont House Agreement and the New Politics of Storytelling in Northern Ireland', *Parliamentary Affairs*, 69 (2016), 928–46.
34 Dawson, *Making Peace with the Past?*
35 *Belfast Telegraph*, 'Lost Lives co-author disgusted by "obscene" resale price of book', 11 October 2019. Available at: www.belfasttelegraph.co.uk/news/northern-ireland/lost-lives-co-author-disgusted-by-obscene-resale-price-of-book-38585237.html. Accessed 12 March 2020.
36 The project was criticised by some for excluding members of the RUC, British army and other state forces who were killed in Ardoyne over the course of the conflict.
37 Patricia Lundy and Mark McGovern, 'Community, "Truth-Telling" and Conflict Resolution: A Critical Evaluation of the Role of Community-Based "Truth-Telling" Processes for Post-Conflict Transition. A Case Study of the Ardoyne Commemoration Project' (Belfast: Northern Ireland Community Relations Council, 2005).
38 Lederach, *Building Peace*.
39 John Nagle and Mary-Alice C. Clancy, *Shared Society or Benign Apartheid? Understanding Peace-Building in Divided Societies* (Basingstoke: Palgrave Macmillan, 2010).
40 Dawson, *Making Peace with the Past?*

41 Nagle and Clancy, *Shared Society or Benign Apartheid?*
42 Nigel Biggar, *Burying the Past: Making Peace and Doing Justice after Civil Conflict* (Washington, DC: Georgetown University Press, 2001).
43 Lundy, 'Paradoxes and Challenges'.
44 Patricia Lundy and Bill Rolston, 'Redress for Past Harms? Official Apologies in Northern Ireland', *International Journal of Human Rights*, 20(1) (2016), 104–22.
45 Rosie Cowan and Nicholas Watt, 'IRA Says Sorry for 30 Years of "Civilian" Deaths', *Guardian*, 17 July 2002. Available at: www.theguardian.com/uk/2002/jul/17/northernireland.northernireland2. Accessed 26 February 2020.
46 Nevin T. Aiken, 'The Bloody Sunday Inquiry: Transitional Justice and Postconflict Reconciliation in Northern Ireland', *Journal of Human Rights*, 14(1) (2015), 101–23.
47 Stephen Hopkins, 'Sinn Féin, the Past and Political Strategy: The Provisional Irish Republican Movement and the Politics of "Reconciliation"', *Irish Political Studies*, 30(1) (2015), 79–97.
48 Dawson, *Making Peace with the Past?*
49 Lundy and Rolston, 'Redress for Past Harms?'
50 Ibid.
51 Shirlow, 'Truth Friction in Northern Ireland'.
52 These figures are provided by Brandon Hamber, cited in Bernadette C. Hayes and Ian McAllister, *Conflict to Peace: Politics and Society in Northern Ireland over Half a Century* (Manchester: Manchester University Press, 2013).
53 Brewer, *Peace Processes*; Dawson, *Making Peace with the Past?*; Hamber, 'Dealing with Painful Memories and Violent Pasts'; Smyth, *Truth Recovery and Justice after Conflict*.
54 Cheryl Lawther, 'Unionism, Truth Recovery and the Fearful Past', *Irish Political Studies*, 26(3) (2011), 361–82.
55 Brewer, *Peace Processes*; Jankowitz, *Order of Victimhood*; Lawther, 'Unionism, Truth Recovery and the Fearful Past'; Simpson, *Truth Recovery in Northern Ireland*; Smyth, 'Truth, Partial Truth and Irreconcilable Truths: Reflections on the Prospects of Truth Recovery in Northern Ireland', *Smith College Studies in Social Work*, 73 (2003), 205–20; Smyth, *Truth Recovery and Justice after Conflict*.
56 Smyth, *Truth Recovery and Justice after Conflict*.
57 Ibid.
58 Brewer, *Peace Processes*.
59 Ibid.
60 Dawson, *Making Peace with the Past?*
61 Smyth, *Truth Recovery and Justice after Conflict*.
62 Ibid.
63 Lawther, 'Unionism, Truth Recovery and the Fearful Past'.
64 Lundy and McGovern, 'Community, "Truth-Telling" and Conflict Resolution'.
65 Lawther, 'Unionism, Truth Recovery and the Fearful Past'; Lundy, 'Paradoxes and Challenges'.

66 Ryan Gawn, 'Truth Cohabitation: A Truth Commission for Northern Ireland?', *Irish Political Studies*, 22(3) (2007), 339–61.
67 Shirlow, 'Truth Friction in Northern Ireland'; Smyth, *Truth Recovery and Justice after Conflict*.
68 Lawther, 'Unionism, Truth Recovery and the Fearful Past'.
69 Hamber, 'Dealing with painful memories and violent pasts'.
70 Lundy, 'Paradoxes and Challenges'.
71 One of the most remarkable aspects of the SHA is that while it did indeed outline mechanisms for dealing with legacy, much of the text of the agreement centred on 'bread and butter' issues, primarily what was termed 'welfare reform' as part of the British government's austerity cuts. While initially supporting the SHA, Sinn Féin subsequently blocked the passage of the Welfare Reform Bill (a fundamental component of the SHA) at Stormont in March 2015. Though Sinn Féin stated that its actions were motivated by a desire 'to protect the vulnerable and safeguard current and future welfare claimants under the control of the executive', it would be reasonable to concur that the difficult and contradictory balancing act of opposing cuts in the Republic of Ireland as a party of opposition, while at the same time implementing them as a party of government in Northern Ireland, offers a more plausible explanation.
72 Shirlow, 'Truth Friction in Northern Ireland'.
73 Ibid.
74 Ibid., p. 420.
75 In 2014 the prosecution of John Downey, who was charged with carrying out the 1982 IRA Hyde Park bombing that killed four soldiers, collapsed when it was discovered that he had been sent a letter of reassurance by the British government that he would not be prosecuted. Beginning in 1999, what became known as the 'On the Run' scheme involved the British government sending letters to more than 200 republican paramilitary suspects, stating a lack of evidence to form a prosecution, and informing them that they were no longer wanted by the police for alleged offences during the Troubles. It was effectively a secret, side-deal between the then prime minister and Sinn Féin, something Tony Blair later defended as lawful and essential to keep the peace process on track. The revelations in 2014 were greeted with outrage and disbelief by many families of IRA victims in Britain and Northern Ireland.
76 The *New Decade, New Approach* Deal, January 2020. Available at: www.dfa.ie/media/dfa/newsmedia/pressrelease/New-Decade-New-Approach.pdf Accessed 12 March 2020.
77 Ibid.
78 *Irish News*, 'Police Ombudsman calls for proper debate on legacy of the Troubles', 7 August 2018. Available at: www.irishnews.com/news/northernirelandnews/2018/08/07/news/police-ombudsman-calls-for-proper-debate-on-legacy-of-the-troubles-1401926. Accessed 21 September 2020.
79 Dawson, *Making Peace with the Past?*
80 Smyth, 'Truth Recovery and Justice after Conflict'.

81 The 'Troubles Pension', devised in 2014 and signed into law by the UK government in January 2020, seeks to provide pension-like payments to victims of the Troubles who were physically or psychologically injured. The 'pension' will be paid every year for the rest of their lives, with payments ranging from £2,000 to £10,000 (depending on the 'degree of disablement'). The scheme does not use the 2006 Victims and Survivors Order definition, which identified a victim or survivor as someone who has been 'physically or psychologically injured as a result of or in consequence of a conflict-related incident', as it made no reference regarding an individual's culpability, therefore potentially leaving the door ajar for former actors to the conflict.
82 *Irish Times*, 'End "shameful stand-off" over pension for Troubles' victims, Johnson told', 3 June 2020. Available at: www.irishtimes.com/news/ireland/irish-news/end-shameful-stand-off-over-pension-for-troubles-victims-johnson-told-1.4269647. Accessed 21 September 2020.
83 Lederach, *Building Peace*.
84 Shirlow, 'Truth Friction in Northern Ireland', p. 420.

3

Conflict-related prisoners: the perpetual trap of criminalisation

In the previous chapter, we discussed the fate of victims of violence, and now we turn to those imprisoned during the conflict. Conflict-related prisoners are, for some, the embodiment of violence, and hold overall responsibility for the Troubles. So strong is this interpretation that those incarcerated during the conflict remain disbarred through legal mechanisms of control, censure and exclusion. There has been obvious leadership from within the ex-prisoner community, but also high levels of exclusion, illness and difficulties coping with intrusive memories and other traumas. Whether they are contributing to peacemaking or highly isolated and cut adrift, there is insufficient knowledge regarding their position, outcome or place within society.

Prisoner release was probably on a par with policing reform as one of the most contentious issues that arose from the Good Friday Agreement (hereafter GFA). The political representatives of conflict-related prisoners such as Sinn Féin, the Ulster Democratic Party (UDP) and the Progressive Unionist Party (PUP) had sufficient influence to argue convincingly that the release of prisoners would advance the delivery of demobilisation and disarmament. While sitting at the heart of wider Disarmament, Demobilisation and Reintegration (DDR)[1] strategies at that time, the onset of decommissioning and disarmament has led to a decline in the status and influence that the prisoner community had in relation to the two governments. Holding weaponry or using violence, such as in the Canary Wharf bombing, was a reminder of such influence.[2] After the ceasefires, prisoners' representatives were fêted during visits to Downing Street and Leinster House, as they were consulted at nearly every turn and tweak of the then emerging peace process.

After decommissioning, that access was diminished without the achievement of reintegration. Paramilitary groups experienced the slow burner of decline in influence over government policy, which meant that the ending of criminalisation linked to the convictions that they held was not achieved. This was a form of conflict transition in which participants responded to peace-building demands and the wider clamour for violence to end without achieving one of their fundamental aims of having their role in the conflict considered as legitimate rather than as a form of terrorism. Despite the outcry over prisoner releases and the sense that they were part of a reward culture for 'good behaviour' on the part of people well capable of acting otherwise, or the tail wagging the dog, few have considered that those holding conflict-related convictions remain in the same place today in legal terms as they were when the conflict came to an end.

Conviction in the courts was a societal cutting-off point, and marked the maintenance of the wider authority of both the Irish and British states to define paramilitary groups as criminal. In terms of a point of demarcation, those who were sentenced under conflict-related provisions remain categorised as 'terrorists' and have not been provided with the same rights, entitlements and equality provisions as other citizens. There has been no erasure of the consequences of holding a criminal conviction and no rights given to the former prisoner community. Conflict-related prisoners are disbarred from normal fair-employment provisions, travel, insurance, charity roles and, at times, company directorships. This is the same as it was in 1998. The structures of criminalisation have, as we show below, endured with life-affecting consequences.

In simple terms, once the weapons were handed in the process of reintegration was stifled. There were vague nods in the direction of assistance to enter work and, indeed, funding for former prisoner groups, but at no time have the legally defined forms of exclusion that undermine full citizenship been altered. As often noted by former prisoners, 'at one time they (the governments) would have sent a limousine to pick us up for talks. Now they wouldn't even pay a bus ticket!'[3]

The early release of conflict-related prisoners after the GFA was unpopular. The Northern Ireland Life and Times Survey in 2000 examined support for early prisoner releases and showed that a mere 12 per cent were supportive, with higher, but minority, support among Catholics (31 per cent) compared to Protestants (4 per cent). It may be that the early release provisions were in societal terms the only 'price' that was going to be paid. That toxic relationship between conflict-related prisoners and the peace process is generally embedded in the view that they bear primary responsibility for the suffering, harm and violence of the Troubles period. Although there are communities and groups who do not share that analysis, there is no doubt that conflict-related prisoners are excluded from full citizenship and that they endure stigma and legal consequences linked to their 'criminal' status.[4] There has been no formal reintegration of prisoners, as convictions are neither spent or, unlike other post-conflict societies, quashed via transitional justice processes. In Northern Ireland, former conflict-related prisoners remain in a purgatorial state of conditional citizenship that has prevailed throughout and beyond the conflict.

In some senses, those with conflict-related backgrounds have undertaken very supportive roles in the peace process. The Ulster Defence Association (UDA) in Lisburn, who rebranded as Resurgam, have established one of the largest social economy hubs in Northern Ireland. They operate a range of social housing and economy schemes and support over 120 jobs. In addition, they are involved in anti-sectarian work and have done much to challenge racism and prejudice. Tar Isteach, a republican group in north Belfast, supports over 800 families per year who have complex social, economic and health needs, and have challenged prejudice and promoted inter-community partnership. Both loyalists and republicans have done much to quell riots and challenge the youth aggression that often leads to violent sectarian confrontation. Without doubt, such work has defined and led peace initiatives and sustained the decline in sectarian antipathy and violence. Former loyalist prisoners remove flags from outside Catholic churches, have developed music-based programming with immigrants, and have undermined those committed to a return to violence. Republicans, via their networks, have used their experience of violence and imprisonment to dilute the allure of masculinised identities within hard-to-reach and at-risk youth communities. Such tangible and accountable contributions to society are barely known beyond each community's respective fold. Media and sections of academia remain fixated with the violence of the past or the nefarious activities of drug dealers and others who remain involved in criminal acts. Little space has been offered up to those who operate to secure and reproduce peace and social justice. Furthermore, the result of such work has not been paralleled by proper reintegration mechanisms.

Conflict-related prisoners are an increasingly tricky proposition for Sinn Féin. They have been vital to that party's transition in terms of supporting the peace process, canvassing and endorsing the transition to social democracy. They have undermined slippage to dissident groups and, despite their failure to gain reintegration, have remained generally loyal to their movement. However, republican ex-prisoners have started to call upon Sinn Féin to end its demand for prosecutions for all involved in the conflict. Many now view the prosecution of security force members as simply a reproduction of the state's aim to present the conflict as criminal. This is not merely an attempt to protect themselves from possible prosecution. Former IRA prisoners, as well as their loyalist counterparts, contend that prosecutions of state-force members, an aspiration of Sinn Féin, means that the status of criminality and the reasoning that those who used violence broke the law maintains the conflict as merely transgressive acts. Further prosecutions simply mean that the conflict remains understood as non-political. This critical difference of opinion probably explains why fewer conflict-related prisoners now canvass for Sinn Féin during elections. This is a real and evident division that speaks to the wider sense among former prisoners of being slowly abandoned, an emotional response probably not that dissimilar to that held by former soldiers and police officers.

In the discussion that follows, we examine the ongoing nature and impact of criminalisation and evidence that legacy issues are not merely those of truth-seeking but also those that stretch into the present. That stretch is so great that more than twenty years after the GFA not only are those with convictions undermined by their criminal status, but so too are their children, and even their grandchildren. What we are evidencing is a process that highlights the failure of Northern Ireland to not only cope with a destabilising past but to also resist the redefinition of the boundaries of that conflict.

After the Good Friday Agreement

There is no sense of a wider societal desire for an amnesty on terrorism-related offences much beyond the ex-prisoner community. Even Sinn Féin, the political centre of the republican movement, signed up to the conditions set out in the GFA that conflict-related violence between 1973 and 1998 would, on prosecution, lead to a sentence of up to two years, and that the criminalisation of conflict-related offences would remain. They, like other political parties and many victims' groups, have maintained the proxy war of allegation and counter-allegation in which their former comrades and others face investigation and possible prosecution decades after the conflict ended. Beyond early release, the GFA promised:

> The Governments continue to recognise the importance of measures to facilitate the reintegration of prisoners into the community by providing support both prior to and after release, including assistance directed towards availing of employment opportunities, re-training and/or reskilling, and further education.

Such financial support did materialise, as did substantial EU funding, but more than two decades after the GFA, conflict-related prisoners remain over three times more likely than the rest of the working-age population to be in the receipt of at least one benefit, and over two-thirds are in receipt of sickness/incapacity or unemployment benefit, or their equivalents, under the new order of 'welfare reform'. It is evident that trauma, alcoholism and drug dependency form part of the problem in terms of integration or full citizenship, but it must also be considered that former conflict-related prisoners face many social barriers due to ongoing criminalisation and vetting.[5]

However, the 'assistance' mentioned in the GFA was neither a responsibility nor a prerogative, and it remained paralleled by the maintenance of limitations on conflict-related prisoners regarding legal entitlements. The agreement's clauses linked to principles of mutual respect, equality, social inclusion and parity of esteem did not, and never were intended to, stretch to the former prisoner community. The early release of prisoners (around 2 per cent of those who hold conflict-related convictions), the funding of conflict-related prisoner groups and even provisions such as the Guidance Principles (GPs)[6] did not change the fact that convictions remained criminal.[7] This lack of legal change is mirrored in wider processes of peace-building that have not led to truth recovery, amnesty, reparations and, ultimately, an agreed approach to reconciliation. As Ní Aoláin reminds us, Northern Ireland is not some model of peacemaking allied to 'extraordinary *jus post bellum* law' as it remains fixed within the laws set during the conflict.[8]

The consequences of conflict-related convictions are extensive, with over a dozen legally defined vetting restrictions on employment that have also had intergenerational impacts upon the children and grandchildren of those formerly imprisoned. Adoption, insurance, working for charities and holding certain posts are each vetted. In short, for former prisoners the conflict is not over, and residual criminalisation that entrenches and perpetuates social and economic marginalisation remains. Since the GFA, conflict-related convictions have become associated with an institutional 'closing off' of the opportunity, and indeed the right, to become full citizens. The placing and reproduction of a significant section of the ex-prisoner community into social exclusion is centred upon a peace process that has not delivered meaningful reintegration.[9]

Normally, in societies emerging from conflict, the aim is to deliver social justice and thereby undermine the causes of conflict through removing any differentiation between combatants and civilians. In Northern Ireland, however, no such process has emerged. Therefore, the resources required both financially and legally have not been developed in order to progress a set of practices that aid the transitional flow from criminalisation to restored rights. At the beginning of the conflict, Northern Irish society was based upon social and civic membership divided between those who held full citizenship, such as the right to vote, and those who did not. At the end of a conflict that was instigated by the denial of citizenship rights, there remains, ironically, a clear distinction between those who are full and secondary citizens, respectively. Again, terms such as 'parity of esteem' and 'mutual respect' ring hollow in this context.

It is, therefore, a fiction to consider that conflict-related prisoners have been reintegrated. However, sectional readings and antipathy towards ex-prisoners generates the myth that somehow conflict-related prisoners have more human rights or are protected more from the GFA than victims.[10] This enabling fiction has no basis and former prisoners have received no rights or entitlements since the agreement was signed. Any claims such as these are emblematic of the power and intrinsic persuasiveness of an impression of fact and a desire to make unconfirmed statements that shape conflict-centred division.[11]

As noted, the criminalisation of ex-prisoners sits within the enduring narratives that they have sole responsibility for the conflict. However, those imprisoned generally maintain a form of non-admission of guilt. For them, the legitimacy of their acts was conditioned by state abuse, discrimination and sectarian governance. Those who oppose such a position claim that non-state actors can only be offered full citizenship through acts of repentance, regret and a rejection of the legitimacy of their acts. Neither form of legitimacy-claiming has led to concession nor renegotiation of the laws of criminalisation, as there is assumed to be no equivalence between these morally defined ideologies. Each not only upholds its own narrative but also aims to stigmatically shame those who disagree. This is a common feature of the perpetuation of conflict through symbolically violent means. The maintenance of criminalisation has shifted from a security/moral concern to a purely moral call for shaming, the rejection of the value of ex-prisoners' reintegration and, in some instances, a refutation of their peacemaking efforts.

It is evident that the debate on conflict-related prisoner reintegration is no longer centred upon security concerns, but is instead outplayed within either a rejection or a reproduction of a stigmatised status. The fixedness of that debate is rooted within the arguments and conditions of victimhood, the demand for penitence or its rebuttal. Evidently, for many conflict-related prisoners, demands for remorse are unjustified, as they delegitimise agency from its original context. This is not to deny regret and harm-causing, but to apologise, for some, would be an acceptance of ideological folly. Stigmatic shaming and rejections of non-state violence comprehend that violence as merely violating, transgressive and abusive. As Shirlow explains:

> Despite evident differences between those who uphold stigmatic shaming and apologia there are strategic similarities between them. Both operate a catalogue of approaches including denial, blame shifting, accusation, evasion of responsibility and provocation. Blame casting through stigmatic shaming and apologia is conditional for several reasons. Both perform public address, allegation and counter-allegation, forms of self-defence, posturing, symbolic violence, bolstering of constituency value, sentimentality and being above doubt. The difference lying in the selection of evidence advanced to either promote stigmatic shaming or its rejection.[12]

The inability of either to attain authority over the 'other' means that the rhetoric of derision, disparagement and criticism remains. The duality of ideological standpoints is tied to legacy and remains associated with a desire to only offer a pathway that is based upon unyielding to what are considered unpalatable legitimacies. As neither can offer acceptance of the demands of the 'other', the upkeep of vetting laws signposts how the new political elite remains fixated upon prosecutions and punishment, even when some of their supporters remain locked in the criminalisation and vetting nexus.

When examining the legal conditions that disbar ex-prisoners from full citizenship rights, we locate an inconsistency between wider processes that have attained equality and power-sharing between antagonistic groups and the enduring forces and structures of extensive ex-prisoner vetting. The contradiction of a peace process that has brought power sharing and an expansion of equality legislation and policing reform, while maintaining previous legal impediments that undermine the societal inclusion of conflict-related prisoners, suggests the existence of a proxy war in which the past continues to be replayed. The legacy of the conflict plays such a major role in the politics of Northern Ireland that it becomes nearly impossible to speak of that society as being post-conflict. Reintegration is not only contested but generally remains undelivered.

It is estimated that at least 25,000 people hold conflict-related convictions, and when added to related fines and parole this equates to somewhere between 13.5 per cent and 30.7 per cent of males aged 55 to 64 years and 5.4 per cent and 12.2 per cent of males aged 65-plus.[13] Further evidence that the commitment to reintegration has been largely ineffective is provided in two long-term surveys.[14] Between 2005 and 2015, there was no progress in terms of the percentage of conflict-related prisoners in paid employment. In fact, the share of conflict-related prisoners who were in receipt of employment benefits had grown from 57 per cent to 71 per cent over that period. Moreover, the proportion of those who had failed to gain a post because of their conviction rose from 53 per cent to 74 per cent. A mere one in five who had declared a conviction had found work. Conflict-related prisoners are now more than three times more likely to be in receipt of working-age benefits and are three and half times more likely to be unemployed compared to the average for the electoral ward in which they live. Within the same surveys, the strongest correlation with ill health, both physical and mental, was not the length of imprisonment but the duration of unemployment. Symptoms of trauma and the use of anti-depressants were nearly twice as high among unemployed conflict-related prisoners compared with those who were in work. A significant body of evidence shows that the barring of conflict-related prisoners from work destabilises their health and produces a financial burden upon the state. Many conflict-related prisoners continue in a state of welfare dependency and legal entrapment.

Maintaining shaming and criminalisation

The issue concerning ex-prisoner rights is linked to the binary between inclusive modes that argue for a transitional process that restores full citizenship, and the counter-argument that the removal of criminalisation is amnesty-like and an implicit recognition of the legitimacy of non-state violence. Rights which are at the level of the individual are imagined in Northern Ireland as group rights. Victims, prisoners and others may be groups, but the law concerning them does not endorse group rights but instead upholds or denies the rights of individuals. There are no victim group rights. Victims and survivors have a right to demand that the state investigate crimes and to be informed of those investigations, as is the case with any citizen. Regarding prisoners, there are no group rights. The early release of prisoners was on licence, and some were not released. The sense that there are group rights is only to be expected in a society so heavily affected by civil strife and political violence.[15] Criminalisation has not been removed and, therefore, reproduces modes of exclusion that were designed in the 1970s regarding employment and other vetting legislation. Conflict-related prisoners are rooted in their classification as criminal, and live within what hard-edged laws are maintained by a highly emotive legacy of past violence. Although arguing over whether former conflict-related prisoners should have conventional rights and privileges is considered normal political behaviour in Northern Ireland, it does stretch into the realms of the bizarre when those arguments concern claims that ex-prisoners hold rights that they actually do not have. However, we should not make light of the point that such erroneous claims are simply the act of misunderstanding the law. Instead, they are purposeful and, as with the victims debate, formed by an intention to distort fact. The reason for that is to maintain Northern Ireland in a fractured and proxy war moment.[16]

Therefore, conflict-related prisoners remain under exclusionary codes and laws of vetting that maintain an impediment to opportunities and engagement as competent members of society. The establishment of vetting laws was partly related to removing access to work from those holding convictions so as to reduce the capability of access to security sites or information useful to targeting individuals such as employment records. That was generally linked to cases where paramilitaries had gained employment in organisations such as banks, or human resource positions through which they could secure employee and customer information such as addresses, especially regarding those in the security forces and the prison service. Such information was also collected to map the layout of security and other sensitive sites. It was also part of the overall fabric of criminalising conflict-related offenders and reducing the previous, although ad hoc, categorisation of them as holding a prisoner-of-war status.

Such vetting laws first arose in 1976 and remain within the Fair Employment and Treatment (Northern Ireland) Order (FETO, 1998), namely, Section 2 (4), which states that

> In this Order any reference to a person's political opinion does not include an opinion which consists of or includes approval or acceptance of the use of violence for political ends connected with the affairs of Northern Ireland, including the use of violence for the purpose of putting the public or any section of the public in fear.

The wording of the last phrase is a direct link to the definition of 'terrorism' contained in a series of enactments relating to emergency provisions in Northern Ireland. The effect of that article is that no person holding a conflict-related conviction enjoys fair employment and equality of rights in relation to job applications and employment. This has been proven, post-GFA, in the courts, most notably in the judgement McConkey and another *v.* The Simon Community (Northern Ireland) (2009) UKHL 24 and the court's decision that Article 2(4) of FETO (1998) specifically limits the protection against discrimination in employment that the order seeks to prevent. As that case illustrated, holding a conflict-related conviction is still construed as a political opinion supportive of violence, even though the judges stated that they did not believe the appellants still held such opinions. Therefore, even a renunciation of violence does not preclude an employer's right to reject conflict-related prisoners as both applicants and employees.

Ultimately, employers can vet applicants and use discretionary application to those with a conflict-related conviction. Similar provisions, although they are not required, given the blanket coverage of FETO, are made under amendments to the Transport Act Northern Ireland (Transport Act NI) 1967, the Rehabilitation of Offenders Order (Northern Ireland) 1979 and its amendments, and the Safeguarding and Vulnerable Groups (NI) Order 2007. There are also other vetting checks that can disbar those with conflict-related convictions. These include the Counter Terrorist Check (CTC), which is mandatory for any person employed in posts involving proximity to public figures, access to any information or material that would be sought by proscribed groups, or unaccompanied access to any sites such as military bases, police stations or other places such as civil, industrial or commercial premises that would be viewed as being at particular risk from infiltration or attack.

A Security Check (SC) is the most used process through which to gain security clearance. It relates to those who will have access either as a direct employee, or as an employee of a contractor, who would have access to information classified as a state secret on a regular or occasional basis, working in a security site while unsupervised. An SC includes information regarding personal files, staff reports, sick-leave returns and security records, the checking of spent and unspent convictions and a security service (MI5) records evaluation.[17] Developed Vetting (DV) is the most inclusive security clearance. It is required for 'long-term, frequent and uncontrolled access to top secret information or assets ... or in order to satisfy requirements for access to material originating from other countries and international organisations'. As with each of these security clearance checks, information will be required for natural parents, adoptive parents, foster parents, stepparents, legal guardians, siblings, grandparents and a partner's father and mother. This has led to cases of intergenerational vetting where individuals who do not have convictions have been disbarred from employment, especially in the police and army, due to a relative's conflict-related conviction, even if that person such as nephew, niece or grandchild has no social interaction, or even knowledge, of the individual in question.

The impact of this exemption of conflict-related prisoners from normal equality provision via vetting laws is unquantified, and there is no official mechanism to provide any evidence regarding the impact of the GFA's commitment to reintegration. Thus, there is no information on the position of conflict-related convictions by any government department or agency that maps the impact of the promises made in the agreement – another example of hollow commitments.

The omitted 'R' within 'DDR'

DDR generally speaks to post-conflict maintenance and peacemaking. It aims to remove violence, improve the security situation and promote a process through which combatants are given other means of economic and social inclusion. Those processes can also provide space for much-needed dialogue and reconciliatory efforts that support interdependence and relational change between previously adversarial groups. A key feature of DDR mechanisms is that reconciliation and transition should be time-bound and should lead to all preceding disciplinary and security structures being removed in order to move into a post-conflict situation. In Northern Ireland, such structures remain in existence.

A significant body of work points to how enduring criminalisation has undermined the commitments outlined in the GFA.[18] That research has also shown that qualifying paramilitary prisoners who were members of organisations on ceasefire remain central to readings of legacy and the reproduction of conflict. Those who wish to maintain criminalisation or who objected to early prisoner releases have tended to overlook that less than 10 per cent of those convicted between 1968 and 1997 have returned to prison. This compares to a general recidivism rate nationally of around 60 per cent. Moreover, few have taken the time to examine the conflict transformation and other work in which former conflict-related prisoners engage. As Peter Shirlow and Kieran McEvoy have noted:

> The range of work in which politically motivated former prisoners are or have been involved includes: direct service such as counselling and training for ex-prisoners and their families; capacity building in local communities; ex-prisoner self-help initiatives including conflict related tourist programmes delivered by former combatants; community based anti-poverty and anti-racist work; resolving disputes at interface areas and concerning contested marches; community based restorative justice as alternatives to punishment violence; youth diversionary work; initiatives on dealing with the past including truth recovery, developing relations with former enemies and victims of violence and devising forms of memorialisation and commemoration; equality and human rights campaigning, and a host of other related activities.[19]

A UDA-aligned ex-prisoner group (Lisburn Partnership Strategy) has evolved into a community and social capacity-building organisation that now employs over one hundred people.[20] The body works with republican communities and has a track record of engaging with migrants from Eastern Europe and elsewhere. The group has achieved much in terms of social housing delivery and steering young people away from sectarianism. Despite this and other accomplishments, the former conflict-related prisoner communities remain structurally and legally excluded, based upon their convictions as being criminals. Ultimately, the peace process has failed to deliver the R of DDR, despite processes that brought an end to violence through a series of stages that aim for transition into peaceful and democratic means. Conflict-related prisoner groups have used the resources at their disposal to build a commitment to peace and the transformation out of conflict. Building trust, as they do, between communities that have been in conflict has been vital to the sustainability of the peace agreement. These groups have actualised the pledge of purely peaceful political action enshrined in Section 4 of the GFA Declaration of Support:

> We reaffirm our total and absolute commitment to exclusively democratic and peaceful means of resolving differences on political issues, and our opposition to any use or threat of force by others for any political purpose, whether in regard to this agreement or otherwise.

They have, further, advanced the cause of demilitarisation at the heart of the peace deal:

> All participants accordingly reaffirm their commitment to the total disarmament of all paramilitary organisations. They also confirm their intention to continue to work constructively and in good faith with the Independent Commission, and to use any influence they may have, to achieve the decommissioning of all paramilitary arms within two years following endorsement in referendums North and South of the agreement and in the context of the implementation of the overall settlement.

In terms of the overall structure of DDR, two strands have been achieved. First, the Independent International Commission on Decommissioning (IICD) was established to oversee the disposal of paramilitary weapons in Northern Ireland, as part of the peace process. The Commission was composed of General (Ret.) John de Chastelain, Chairman, from Canada, Brigadier Tauno Nieminen from Finland and Ambassadors Donald C. Johnson and Andrew D. Sens from the United States. Its objective, which was achieved, was to facilitate the decommissioning of firearms, ammunition and explosives, by consulting with the two governments, the participants in the ongoing negotiations in Northern Ireland, and paramilitary and other relevant groups. It devised and presented to the governments a set of proposals on how to achieve decommissioning, facilitating the process by observing, monitoring and verifying decommissioning, receiving and auditing arms, and reporting periodically on progress.

In terms of demobilisation, the Independent Monitoring Commission (IMC), established in 2003 and led by Lord Alderdice, was also founded by agreement between the British and Irish governments. The IMC concluded its operations on 31 March 2011 when it had achieved the remit of monitoring any continuing activity by paramilitary groups, as well as the commitment by the British government to a package of security normalisation measures. It also handled claims by political parties in the Northern Ireland Assembly concerning any Minister, or another party in the Northern Ireland Assembly, that was not committed to non-violence and exclusively peaceful and democratic means, or issues raised concerning any Minister, or party, who failed to observe any other terms of the pledge of office.

However, the issue of reintegration had no such structure until 2010. This led to the formation of the Review Panel: Employers' Guidance on Recruiting People with Conflict-Related Convictions,[21] which operates via a tripartite structure comprising an independent chair and representatives from the Confederation of British Industry (Northern Ireland), the Irish Congress of Trade Unions and the Executive Office. In its terms of reference, the Review Panel is tasked with considering individual cases, building up evidence regarding the acceptance and adoption of the Guidance Principles, and producing progress reports on the impact of that guidance. Since its first report, the Review Panel has continued to promote the employers' guidance and meets regularly to discuss and examine the barriers to employment due to applicant vetting. Those principles aim to assist employers follow best practice in recruiting people with conflict-related convictions and to relate those principles to those holding convictions/offences listed in the relevant schedules to the various Emergency Provisions (Northern Ireland) Acts pre-April 1998. The Review Panel recognises that the transposition of the Guidance Principles will be for employing organisations and their human resource professionals, and that they operate and promote the basic code that any conviction for a conflict-related offence that pre-dates the GFA (April 1998) should not be taken into account unless it is materially relevant to the employment being sought.

The Review Panel also promotes an understanding of the systemic, structural and attitudinal barriers that affect those with conflict-related convictions as they relate to employment and access to goods, facilities and services, and in so doing advances the concept that the onus on demonstrating incompatibility would rest with whoever was alleging it and the seriousness of the offence would not, per se, constitute adequate grounds for disbarring someone. It also encourages an employer when they have ruled out a conflict-related prisoner at any stage of their job application/employment or service provision that he/she should be given the opportunity to outline his/her perspective before a final decision is taken. These principles recognise that the guidance needs to be understood in conjunction with existing legislative obligations and employment-related criminal record checks, and do not ask employers or service providers to give preferential treatment to ex-prisoners with conflict-related convictions, as that would run counter to fair employment and equality legislation. Rather, the guidance aims to ensure that a conviction is not taken into account unless it is materially relevant to the post or service in question and that only after interview, when the successful candidate for employment has been chosen, should the issue of a conviction be considered. This is set within three possible scenarios. First, if the candidate does not possess a conviction, the appointment is made. Secondly, if the candidate has declared a conviction, but the employer considers that it is not materially relevant to the post, the appointment is made. Finally, if the candidate has declared a conviction and the employer considers that it is, or could be, materially relevant, and is manifestly incompatible with the post, then the appointment is not immediately offered. Moreover, the Review Panel encourages employers to contact candidates who are not appointed/dismissed to explain the decision taken, and to permit an unselected candidate the opportunity to speak to them about the decision made and, at that time, provide supporting evidence in regard to his/her case and how they believe it is not materially relevant. In essence, the Review Panel exists to ensure that deselected candidates and those barred/vetted have an opportunity to represent their complaints and concerns. A problem identified when the Guidance Principles were conceived was the increasing use of online application processes. Whether using online recruitment or more traditional recruitment processes, it is important that these procedures are applied consistently.

Overall, the Guidance Principles urge that whichever format of recruitment is used, the fact that an applicant has a conflict-related record should not play a part in any decision-making regarding their application until the individual has successfully gone through a selection process. In accordance with best practice, application forms should normally not require a criminal record declaration except where the job is covered by rehabilitation of offenders legislation. However, security checks are sometimes used by employers for posts not considered under the law as requiring such vetting. Many application forms request information on criminal prosecutions which can lead to applicants not passing the first stage of the application process when they disclose a conviction. Therefore, those with conflict-related convictions fall foul of an electronic system which has no capacity to consider material relevance, good character or the candidate's ability. Given the indiscretion of vetting and barring mechanisms, it is important to note that those who have adopted the Guidance Principles have found the approach helpful. It is also an approach that helps both design and aid reintegration and the recognition of the pursuit of a post-conflict society. It is based upon the following central principle of the Review Panel:

> that conflict-related convictions of 'politically motivated' ex-prisoners, or their membership of any organisation, should not generally be taken into account [in accessing employment, facilities, goods or services] provided that the act to which the conviction relates, or the membership, predates the GFA. Only if the conviction, or membership, is materially relevant to the employment, facility, goods or service applied for, should this general rule not apply.[22]

However, if the Guidance Principles and related advice are to be effective, they must be placed in the context of various processes that define conflict transformation. That has included processes of DDR which aim to remove the tensions and capacity for future conflict, senses of alienation that drive conflict and the sharing of approaches to achieve broader forms of reconciliation. Therefore, reintegrating conflict-related prisoners into the labour market is a key factor in reducing exclusion from routine and normal activities within the life cycle. It is also key to reducing the financial and related problems associated with providing unemployment and related benefits.

However, the Review Panel was never accorded the same legal and scrutiny capacity as the IMC and IICD. Although the Panel eventually gained agreement from the Northern Ireland Assembly to advance the decriminalisation of fair employment law, this is now not to happen, if at all, before 2022. The capacity of the other bodies was notable. In 2004, the IMC recommended that funding should be withdrawn from Sinn Féin due to IRA activity. That proposal was applied by the Secretary of State for Northern Ireland and signposted how an oversight body could achieve legally enforceable penalties. Without doubt, the disarmament and demobilisation bodies created a seismic shift in the security situation. However, despite some ability to affect change, the Review Panel was not presented with the same premeditated and enforceable authority. This unevenness in approach is symptomatic of a broad swathe of opinion that was supportive of ending conflict and achieving security, but less enamoured by the desire to remove legal barriers to conflict-related prisoner reintegration.

In its two reports, the Panel provided evidence that existing legislation and broader approaches do not support reintegration as outlined in the GFA. They are of the opinion that an opportunity exists to support reintegration through legislative change. Such a step will help to reduce a significant burden on welfare and other benefit systems and will increase the opportunity to raise taxpaying and other contributions. If people with conflict-related convictions are unable to secure posts for which they are qualified, this removes the capacity to aid post-conflict economic growth and to transfer ex-prisoners out of unemployment/underemployment and into work. For argument's sake, if 10,000 people with conflict-related convictions or their relatives are dependent upon the welfare system due to vetting and disbarring and the total cost of delivering/receiving income-related benefits was, conservatively, set at £5,500 per head, then the total bill would be some £55 million per annum, or over half a billion pounds per decade. As the Review Panel has noted:

> Significant public funds were spent upon education and labour market training during imprisonment. It is therefore problematic that the principle of such expenditure which was to aid re-entry into the labour market is undermined by FETO and other vetting practices. It is highly problematic that government has never, to our knowledge, evaluated the cost upon the exchequer of the impact of vetting and disbarring legislation upon public resources and in not doing so they are not taking rehabilitation seriously. To understand the cost upon the exchequer of the impact of vetting and disbarring legislation upon public resources the Government should undertake a full review of the costs of FETO and vetting upon welfare and other related expenditure.[23]

The Review Panel is tasked with overseeing the GPs and monitoring the soft-law provisions of the GFA and St Andrews Agreement and their effect in upholding and delivering conflict-related prisoner reintegration. If there was no positive impact of these arrangements, then the Panel was obliged to explain why and offer alternative measures. In their two reports, the Panel highlighted the failure of these arrangements to work and posited the need for more effective arrangements. The second report of the Panel led to two relatively significant changes prompted by the FSA. The first, in 2017, was acceptance of the GPs by the Northern Ireland Civil Service and agreement by the Executive Office to amend Section 2 (4) of FETO. Amendments to FETO will still not remove the capacity to vet ex-prisoners to excepted posts under rehabilitation and offenders' legislation, but its reform is important, as the Order is the only purposeful conflict-related form of vetting legislation.

The Review Panel has called for vetting to be better understood as having foreseeable effects, and that if these laws undermine reintegration, then, as is the case in transitional practice, adequate proposals must be considered that such laws must determine their necessity, in this case regarding the security situation, over time. The Panel has questioned, through detailed analysis and case-study presentation, the authorities' failure to create the means to measure the impact of vetting laws and the commitment to do so. Where the Panel posits an evaluation of the necessity of vetting law in a changing environment of demobilisation and disarmament, the proponents of vetting have relabelled necessity away from the security framework to one in which necessity is morally dependent and can only be removed when conflict-related offenders admit guilt. The agency of stigmatic shaming is for the maintenance of a criminal status to prevent equal status under discrimination law.

One of the fundamental issues regarding the question of DDR as raised by the Review Panel is that the government at no point has measured the impact upon those with conflict-related convictions when accessing/not accessing employment. It holds no data on the number of persons with conflict-related convictions who are disbarred from employment irrespective of their suitability for that employment. Moreover, the government set no benchmark through which to measure the number of persons with conflict-related prisoners who are removed from employment, even when they have disclosed their conviction(s) and have failed to test the impact of FETO upon family life in terms of poverty, social marginalisation, social fatalism, stigma and exclusion. Ultimately, they have not even measured how the impact of failing to gain work or remain in work due to legislation places a financial burden upon the welfare and other benefits system.

The reality of vetting

We look here at a series of case studies in which vetting has operated. In each case, employers have used the law to either bar or remove individuals from posts. There are in each case few examples of due process or any right of appeal. The first case concerns a male in his late fifties who worked continuously for around twenty years for an environmental group in west Belfast. He was imprisoned from 1975 to 1987 and had been convicted when aged 19. This individual has incurred no convictions or been investigated for any offences since he left prison. His employer noted that the standard of his work was exemplary, especially given his leadership role in managing other employees and volunteers. His work generally involved litter management and environmental upgrading within a socially deprived community. The employee had, for that employer, declared his conviction when appointed and had been vetted by AccessNI security checks.[24] He had made full disclosure to his employer who, via their own risk assessment, considered him suitable for employment and working with young people, volunteers and other employees. His work for several years had been funded by a grant from the Department of Social Development (DSD). In 2013, the grant ended and his employer successfully tendered to continue the same work for the DSD. The extended project was accompanied by subcontract arrangements which meant that all employees fell under the terms and conditions of Northern Ireland Civil Service (NICS) employment. This meant an additional AccessNI check had to be completed and forwarded to the Department of Finance and Personnel (DFP). The DFP advised his employers that he was unsuitable to continue in his employment due to his conviction. The Review Panel contacted AccessNI about this case, who advised that the post fell under the conditions of an enhanced disclosure that relates to working with those in care homes, domiciliary care, childminding and access to vulnerable children.

A conviction should not automatically preclude an individual from employment and there need to be arrangements that would consider the material relevance of the conviction to any post. It was confirmed that the individual had submitted two AccessNI checks (one for his original post with his employer and a second one when the contract changed to the DFP) and that the funders could have requested an enhanced disclosure on the grounds that he was working unsupervised and was supervising others within a regulated activity. The Review Panel sought to determine with the DFP how the decision had been taken and on what basis the individual posed a risk to vulnerable people. The DFP reiterated that the law offered insignificant transparency over decisions, especially concerning how the material relevance of the conviction was determined. His employers clearly stated that they did not concur with the DFP's decision, and argued that they did not agree with the interpretation that his convictions were materially relevant given his good character, work ethic and experience. They contacted the DFP, who advised that they could not discuss the case because of data protection and said that there was no right of appeal. The employer drafted a letter to the DFP supporting their employee, and the DFP, who were also contacted by the Review Panel, stated that the individual would be provided with an opportunity to submit a 'statement of disclosure'. The DFP considered this an opportunity to provide additional information to allow their panel (comprising three civil servants) to make an informed and materially relevant decision. Following the submission of a statement of disclosure for the case to be reviewed, the DFP panel upheld their original decision that the employee was unsuitable for employment on the project. The following was received by the Review Panel from the DFP:

> A basic security clearance was a condition of the DSD contract. Because DFP have found him unsuitable for the DSD contract this does not stop him being employed elsewhere by his employer. Although, it was clear that his employment is for the same role he worked under during the contractor's previous grant funding. It was a decision of the designated department to carry out checks. A DFP panel met to discuss the security clearance issue and in light of this asked him to complete a statement of disclosure. The individual concerned had originally failed to submit a statement of disclosure as he was unaware of what its nature and meaning was. Therefore, his case was judged on the information available and refused employment. The additional and permitted disclosure did not change the decision and DFP have stated that there are no grounds of appeal.[25]

The individual was dismissed and the DFP declined a request to meet the Review Panel. The Panel publicly stated their concern that this meeting did not take place and is not aware why the decision to disbar was taken, given material evidence regarding the employee's work record and other information regarding good character.

In September 2014, prior to this case, the Review Panel met with the DFP Corporate Human Resources (HR) regarding the Employers' Guidance. At this meeting, the members of the Panel were reminded of the view and the decision taken by the then Minister of Finance and Personnel that NICS vetting arrangements relating to recruitment were appropriate and adequate. They were further advised that this remained the position. Since then, the legislation has extended the vetting arrangements for civil servants to include Ministers' Special Advisers.[26] The DFP advised that during the application process for NICS recruitment careful consideration is given to convictions and spent convictions but that the approach does not differentiate between conflict-related and non-conflict-related convictions. They further advised that no one is ruled out simply based on a conviction, as all convictions are judged in line with criteria and a risk matrix, and each case is judged on its own merits. In cases where a potential employee has passed the selection process on the basis of the merit principle and a conviction is identified as part of the AccessNI check, the individual is invited by Corporate HR to provide a statement of disclosure which gives them the opportunity to put their convictions into context and to provide testimonials. They advised that at that time they were unaware of any cases where a decision has been taken not to employ an individual in the NICS because of a conviction. They reiterated that Corporate HR are only involved in the vetting process if there is a referral, in which case they would apply the risk matrix.

In respect of applying the risk matrix, it was stated that several factors are taken into consideration, such as the seriousness of the offence, whether there had been any repeat offences, and how long ago the offence had taken place. The DFP were asked if they held figures on the number of individuals who had been refused employment because of a conflict-related conviction and the Review Panel was advised that this information was not captured or held across the twelve departments. The Panel stated that they would consider that capturing such information would be a recommendation in their second report and that said information should be held and traceable under freedom of information legislation. Its members were also concerned that it was stated that the process was considering factors regarding character but that no evidence, even regarding how many disclosures there had been, was held or available. The DFP advised that the NICS policy was compliant with the Rehabilitation of Offenders legislation. In addition, they indicated that the NICS always, despite having no evidence on how many persons with conflict-related convictions passed through the application system successfully, attempts to be fair and reasonable in accommodating individuals. It was also stated that in some cases, if a materially relevant conviction arose among existing employees, that they would consider redeployment rather than dismissal, depending on the circumstances of the case. Additionally, it was posited that the NICS needs to ensure that those it employs are entirely suitable for public service, and this often requires careful consideration and judgement. In 2018, after significant pressure from the Review Panel, the NICS adopted the Guidance Principles and have begun a policy of encouraging applications from conflict-related prisoners.

In the second case, a woman in her mid-fifties who received a conflict-related conviction in respect of a firearms offence in 1982 when she was 22 years old had successfully secured employment, in 2014, through a parenting programme operated by a major children's charity in conjunction with a university located in Great Britain. Her employment with the charity was to facilitate trainers to support a parenting programme and her employer in Northern Ireland was fully aware of her conviction and did not feel, given her experience and excellent track record, that there was any material relevance in her conviction regarding undertaking this new position. Her past employment had been related to issues of anxiety and stress management and she was well placed to undertake any tasks that involved working with children or vulnerable persons. Despite her having declared her conviction to her employer, the new post required that an AccessNI Basic Check be completed. On completion, she was informed by the charity's head office (in Great Britain) that she could not proceed with her employment as the check had flagged up her conviction. Two staff from headquarters came to Northern Ireland to interview her and discuss her conviction, and how she came to be working on the programme. After an eight-week period she was informed that her offer of employment would be withdrawn as she would be working with children. As noted previously, a Basic Check is not suitable for such regulated activity assessment. During her interview, she clearly stated that she had several years' experience of delivering massage and stress management techniques in both primary and secondary schools and had also worked in catering in a local school. Her experience of working with children and vulnerable persons was not deemed relevant to the post from which she was dismissed. It also did not seem to matter that she had undertaken previous work for the employer to whom she had disclosed her convictions. The Review Panel contacted the employer regarding the Guidance Principles. They asserted that they did not have a blanket ban on those with conflict-related convictions and it was confirmed that the charity's review team undertook what they proposed was an extensive review and risk assessment which confirmed their right to decline the services of those with criminal records. This, they claimed, was due to the employee's role not serving 'the best the interests of the charity or its beneficiaries'. The Panel sought clarification regarding what these interests were, but received no reply.

The bizarre nature of vetting is exemplified in the case of these two individuals who, post-conviction, had become social economy and community leaders. Each had been employed in the community sector for over fifteen years and had worked as Operations Managers and then Managing Directors of community resource centres. Their posts involved working with various disadvantaged groups in economically deprived areas. The resource centres they led were tasked under Neighbourhood Renewal to tackle problems such as educational underachievement, physical and economic regeneration and employment issues. In December 2013, their organisations submitted bids for social economy training projects. Both were named in respective applications to receive capital funds from the Social Investment Fund to purchase buildings in which each social economy project would operate. They received significant capital funding to rehabilitate vacant buildings.

In subsequent tenders to Invest NI and the DSD, both organisations received funding for posts to deliver the social economy hubs that they had established. Each was named as the new social economy hub/enterprise Operations Manager, with four additional staff to work on each project. The contract for these posts was awarded on the condition of an AccessNI check being undertaken. The four staff passed these checks, but the two conflict-related prisoners were referred to the DFP for review. Both were advised that they could not work on the project as a result of their AccessNI check, and both organisations had to arrange for others to deputise during review of their initial rejection as post-holders. The Review Panel met Invest NI, who advised that they have no issues with ex-prisoner organisations and had engaged with the groups in the past through other of their training projects. In fact, Invest NI sat on the board for the social enterprise hub, along with representatives from the DSD and the Department of Enterprise Trade and Investment. The Review Panel was also informed that Invest NI were asked to take the lead on the procurement/regulation of the hub regarding the location and capability of the individuals to be employed and the organisation leading the project. Invest NI confirmed to the Panel that the decision to list generic baseline clearance as a requirement in the tender for employment was based on two considerations: the nature of the service to be delivered to a potentially wide range of groups – mother and toddler groups and youth groups, including children and vulnerable adults – and the range of delivery agents and their professional ability. Invest NI confirmed that, based on these two considerations, baseline clearance was considered an appropriate requirement and that any offences issued on an AccessNI check would be taken into consideration. Baseline clearance, which showed unspent convictions, ruled them both out based on the Protection of Children and Vulnerable Adults (POCVA). These two individuals had organised significant capital investment, run youth groups and homework clubs in a voluntary capacity and chaired the boards on the social economy hub on which the organisation sat and which subsequently barred them from the project that both had co-designed.

One further case involves a young woman who had undertaken training and assessment to join a police constabulary in England. Her uncle had been a life-sentence prisoner from a loyalist background. When he had been arrested her father had taken the family to England as he did not want to be associated with his brother's activities. She had never met her uncle and knew little about him. When her uncle died her father did not attend his funeral. There had been no contact with her uncle since he had been arrested. In her police training she had achieved top grades within her cohort. She claims that in the final week of her training two senior officers took her out of class and presented a file containing information on her uncle. She made it clear she knew nothing about him or his convictions and that she had never spoken to, never mind met, her uncle. She was told to collect her belongings, that her training was over and that she would not be graduating. This individual had no right of appeal and is one of several who have been barred from joining the police or army due to a conflict-related conviction held by a parent, uncle/aunt or grandparent. In this case, the question of due process, the right to challenge and the implication that she was not a person of trust is emblematic of how the past stretches long into the present and, potentially, the future.

Each of these case studies highlights the inconsistency of approach taken by the authorities which produces many peculiar situations, and not least those where two individuals could have responsibility for significant capital grant funding but could not work in the facility for which capital funding was awarded. Each example shows a critical disjuncture from wider efforts to facilitate people with conflict-related convictions, even regarding participation in community development and peacemaking activities. Such evidence sends out a negative message to communities that individuals who have been involved in long-term and dedicated community work, or who are working with vulnerable persons, are now precluded from such undertakings.

Conclusion

The GFA's commitment to prisoners presented a quasi-commitment to reintegration despite the public outrage that early release, under licence, caused. The commitments therein provided for some flexibility in enactment and assisted the response to a complex situation. Such accommodation was not based upon removing the structures of criminalisation. The two sovereign governments did enough to carry loyalists and republicans over the line, and once their respective organisations had disarmed and demobilised they no longer had the authority to shape the political process without returning to armed conflict. Even Sinn Féin has not called for amnesty provisions or the removal of criminalisation, but instead has focused on a vague call for a truth commission.

The failure or, more significantly, refusal to remove vetting laws means that contestations over a ruptured and disruptive past remain. There is no agreed societal or statutory response to the past and how to solve the variant interpretations of it. The landscape of assistance to conflict-related prisoners is ruptured, at times ad hoc, and funding is coming to an end. A salutary lesson in which those who engaged in the conflict have generally ended up mired in trauma, dependency or a sense of being used and forgotten. As Northern Ireland moves on, conflict-related prisoners remain in the same category of denied citizenship that began on the first day they went to prison. This is emblematic of the failure to heal the past by moving beyond punitiveness. For a conflict to end, its structures and exclusions have to be timebound.

Notes

1 See United Nations Disarmament, Demobilization and Reintegration Resource Centre. Available at: http://unddr.org/iddrs.aspx. Accessed 1 February 2020.
2 The IRA's bombing of Canary Wharf in 1996 targeted London's financial district. Two years after the same organisation's ceasefire, its capacity to cause over £100 million of damage, kill two people and injure forty more was indicative of its power to force the pace of negotiations between the IRA and the British government.
3 This phrase, and variations on it, were used by paramilitaries from various groupings in conversation with one of the authors.
4 Barry Vaughan, 'Punishment and Conditional Citizenship', *Punishment & Society*, 2(1) (2000), 23–39; Louise Mallinder, *Amnesty, Human Rights and Political Transitions, Bridging the Peace and Justice Divide* (Oxford: Hart, 2008); Jos Berghman, 'The Resurgence of Poverty and the Struggle against Exclusion: A New Challenge for Social Security?', *International Social Security Review*, 50 (1997), 3–23.
5 For surveys on conflict-related prisoners see *Tar Isteach: A Survey of Conflict-Related Prisoner's Needs*. Available at: www.researchgate.net/publication/270794317_Tar_Isteach_A_Survey_of_Conflict-Related_Prisoner's_Needs. Accessed 2 February 2020; Alan Bruce, Tommy McKearney and Oliver Corr, Innovative Intercultural Learning in Post-War Environments: Conflict Transformation Education in Northern Ireland (Monaghan: EXPAC, 2009); Community Foundation for Northern Ireland, 'Taking "Calculated" Risks for Peace II' (Belfast: CFNI, 2003); Jim Crothers, 'EPIC Research Document 2: Reintegration – the Problems and the Issues' (Belfast: EPIC, 1998); Clare Dwyer, 'Risk, Politics and the "Scientification" of Political Judgement: Prisoner Release and Conflict Transformation in Northern Ireland', *British Journal of Criminology*, 47(5) (2007), 779–97.
6 See www.gov.uk/government/uploads/system/uploads/attachment_data/file/136651/st_andrews_agreement-2.pdf, www.executiveoffice-ni.gov.uk/publications/employers-guidance-recruiting-people-conflict-related-convictions. Accessed 2 February 2020.

7 For more details, see www.reviewpanel.org/what-is-ddr/laws-of-vetting-accessni/. Accessed 2 February 2020.
8 Fionnuala Ní Aoláin, 'Remarks by Fionnuala Ní Aoláin', *Proceedings of the Annual Meeting (American Society of International Law)*, 106 (Confronting Complexity) (2012), p. 341.
9 McConkey and another *v.* The Simon Community (Northern Ireland) [2009] UKHL 24 Available at: www.publications.parliament.uk/pa/ld200809/ldjudgmt/jd090520/conkey-2.htm. Accessed 6 January 2021.
10 Ibid.
11 Peter Shirlow, 'Mythic rights and conflict-related prisoner "re-integration"', *Capital & Class*, 43(1) (2019), 40.
12 Ibid., p. 42.
13 Ruth Jamieson, Peter Shirlow and Adrian Grounds, *Ageing and social exclusion among former politically motivated prisoners in Northern Ireland – Report for the Changing Ageing Partnership* (CAP, 2010). Available at: www.researchgate.net/profile/Peter_Shirlow/publication/265108320_Ageing_and_social_exclusion_among_former_politically_motivated_prisoners_in_Northern_Ireland/links/545b8e3b0cf249070a7a73fd.pdf. Accessed 2 February 2020.
14 Peter Shirlow, Brian Graham, Kieran McEvoy, Féilim Ó hAdhmaill and Dawn Purvis, *Politically Motivated Former Prisoner Groups: Community Activism and Conflict Transformation* (Belfast: Northern Ireland Community Relations Council, 2005). Available at: http://epic.org.uk/images/custom/uploads/129/files/PMEPP-Final%20-Version.pdf, accessed 14 January 2021; Peter Shirlow and Ciaran Hughes, *Tar Isteach: A Survey of Conflict-Related Prisoner's Needs* (Belfast: Tar Isteach, 2015).
15 Peter Shirlow, 'Truth friction in Northern Ireland: Caught between apologia and humiliation', *Parliamentary Affairs*, 71(2) (2018), 417–37.
16 Shirlow, 'Mythic rights and conflict-related prisoner "re-integration"', 44.
17 See https://webarchive.nationalarchives.gov.uk/tna/+/http://www.mod.uk/DefenceInternet/AboutDefence/WhatWeDo/SecurityandIntelligence/DVA/DefenceVettingAgencyFrequentlyAskedQuestionsTheVettingProcess.htm. Accessed 16 December 2020.
18 Clare Dwyer, 'Dealing with the Leftovers: Post-Conflict Imprisonment in Northern Ireland', *Prison Service Journal*, 175 (2008), 3–12; Brian Gormally and Kieran McEvoy, *Release and Reintegration of Politically Motivated Prisoners in Northern Ireland: A Comparative Study of South Africa, Israel/Palestine, Italy, Spain, the Republic of Ireland and Northern Ireland* (Belfast: NIACRO, 1995); Adrian Grounds and Ruth Jamieson, 'No Sense of an Ending: Researching the Experience of Imprisonment and Release upon Republican Ex-Prisoners', *Theoretical Criminology*, 7(3) (2003), 347–62; Ruth Jamieson and Adrian Grounds, *Facing the Future: Ageing and Politically Motivated Former Prisoners in Northern Ireland and the Border Region* (Monaghan: EXPAC, 2008); NIVT, *A Level Playing Field: The Final Evaluation Report of the Work of Politically-motivated Ex-prisoner Self-help Projects Funded by the Peace Programme* (Belfast: NIVT, 2001); Peter Shirlow, *The State they are Still In. Republican*

    Ex-Prisoners and their Families: An Independent Evaluation (Coleraine: University of Ulster, Social Exclusion Research Unit (2001); Peter Shirlow, *Politically Motivated Former Prisoners: Evaluation of the Core Funding Project 2006–2008* (Belfast: Community Foundation for Northern Ireland, 2008); Peter Shirlow and Kieran McEvoy, *Beyond the Wire: Former Prisoners and Conflict Transformation in Northern Ireland* (London: Pluto Press, 2008).
19 Shirlow and McEvoy, *Beyond the Wire*, p. 86.
20 The ideas of transition and conflict transformation among paramilitary and former prisoner groups are not broadly known within public or policy discourse. Examples include: '"Taking Responsibility": Conflict Transformation and the Loyalist Paramilitaries of Northern Ireland', available at www.scribd.com/doc/27603/Progressive-Unionist-Party-Principles-of-Loyalism-Document, accessed 17 December 2020; Shirlow et al., *Politically Motivated Former Prisoner Groups*; Coiste na nIarchimí, *Submission to the Panel of Parties of the NI Executive, also known as 'The Haass Talks', on Dealing with the Past*, on behalf of the Executive Committee and members of Coiste na nIarchimí, available at: http://news.bbc.co.uk/nol/shared/bsp/hi/pdfs/17_12_13_coiste_haass.pdf; Bill Rolston, *Review of Literature on Republican and Loyalist Ex-Prisoners* (Belfast: University of Ulster Transitional Justice Institute, 2011), available at: www.executiveoffice-ni.gov.uk/sites/default/files/publications/ofmdfm_dev/Review-of-Literature-on-Republican-and-Loyalist-Ex-Prisoners.pdf, accessed 1 February 2020.
21 Available at: www.reviewpanel.org/. Accessed 1 February 2020.
22 Ibid.
23 Ibid.
24 See www.nidirect.gov.uk/information-and-services/accessni-criminal-record-checks/apply-accessni-check; www.nidirect.gov.uk/index/information-and-services/crime-justice-and-the-law/accessni-criminal-recordchecks/accessni-applications.htm). Accessed 1 February 2020.
25 See www.reviewpanel.org/. Accessed 1 February 2020.
26 The Civil Service (Special Advisers) Act (Northern Ireland) (2013) (SPAD Act), as passed in the Northern Ireland Assembly, ensures that any person with a serious criminal conviction of five years or more may be legally excluded as a special adviser.

4

Ghosts of our lives: spectres of the past in recent Northern Irish cinema and television

Introduction

In the era of the peace process, a great many glossy promotional films have appeared that are aimed at potential tourists, both at home and abroad, and seek to depict Northern Ireland as a place that has moved on from its violent past. Belfast, in particular, is cast as a multicultural, perpetual-motion city, driven by ceaseless consumption and populated, it often appears, solely by the young and the beautiful.[1] Shorn of its former associations, the Northern Irish capital takes its place as merely another destination for yet another weekend break in what could be more or less any metropolis in the Western world.[2] While these slick advertisements have continued to multiply, over time they have been required to compete with other moving images providing a rather more critical reading of how far, and in which direction, Northern Ireland has travelled since the end of the Troubles. As we saw in Chapter 2, Northern Irish politicians have largely been unwilling or unable to deal with the 'legacy issues' that stem from almost three decades of conflict. In contrast, scriptwriters for both the big and the small screen have become ever more prepared to summon the 'ghosts' that continue to haunt a region with a notoriously violent recent history. Around the tenth anniversary of the Good Friday Agreement (hereafter GFA), there began to emerge a series of dramas for cinema and television that focused ever more explicitly upon those – and perhaps *that* – lost during the conflict and the transition to peace. In calling our attention to the spectres that attend the feast of the region's new political dispensation, these productions issue a timely reminder that for all the progress that has undoubtedly been made, Northern Ireland remains, in John Hewitt's indelible phrase, a 'ghost-haunted land'.[3]

'A delightful setting for romantic comedy'

The conflict in Northern Ireland would inevitably prove fertile ground for scriptwriters based in Hollywood and beyond. Over the course of the Troubles, the region would be depicted on the silver screen in a constant, glaringly disproportionate stream of films typically operating within the constraints of the thriller genre and invariably fixated on the activities of the Provisional IRA. In these productions, the violence happening in Northern Ireland was often depicted as atavistic rather than political, with republicans represented as animated rather less by the ideologies of Irish unification than the pathologies of the 'dark Celtic soul'.[4] As the conflict came to an end, however, these increasingly hackneyed thrillers began to go out of fashion and were replaced by a series of rather gentler, more optimistic films. A region that had in the recent past been portrayed as a place of senseless tribal violence would in short order become a 'delightful setting for romantic comedy'. In the late 1990s, as the peace process appeared finally to bear fruit in the guise of the GFA, a whole stream of films in this genre began to appear, among them *With or Without You* (Michael Winterbottom, 1999), *The Most Fertile Man in Ireland* (Dudi Appleton, 1999), *An Everlasting Piece* (Barry Levinson, 2000) and *Wild About Harry* (Declan Lowney, 2000).

The focus of these films released as the century turned no longer falls on the 'men of violence' but rather on what Greg McLaughlin and Stephen Baker term the 'ordinary people' of Northern Ireland.[5] Those who remain engaged in paramilitary activity are cast not as objects of fear but rather as figures of fun. The republican who appears at the door of a neighbour who is one of the toupée makers in *An Everlasting Piece*, for instance, seems to believe that his balaclava will conceal his identity, even though his voice is instantly recognisable to people who have known him all his life.[6] And in the distinctly flaccid comedy *The Most Fertile Man in Ireland*, the pair of paramilitaries from across the communal divide competing for the services of the title character to enhance their community's chances of victory in the region's demographic dogfight are both exposed in the end as suitably impotent.[7] Those men of calibre who were once in the ranks of the paramilitaries are shown to have now chosen a different course. The figure of 'O' who appears in the charming coming-of-age drama *The Mighty Celt* (2004) might be seen as paradigmatic here. Having spent more than a decade 'on the run' after a gunfight with British soldiers in which he was injured and his best friend killed, O returns to a west Belfast enjoying the relative normality of the peace process. Shrugging off the goading of dissident republicans with quiet exasperation, the lapsed republican opts not to return to the 'armed struggle' but rather to build a new life with his former romantic interest and her son, of whom he comes to learn he is, almost inevitably, the father.

In opting for a life of domesticity, O joins the ranks of the 'ordinary people' who are the heroes and heroines of the steady slew of films that appeared in the years immediately following the GFA.[8] The characters who appear in these features are preoccupied by distinctly quotidian matters and seem indifferent, at times hostile, to the incendiary political issues that had hitherto dominated films devoted to Northern Ireland. These plain folk are animated not by the 'constitutional question' but rather by the desire to make a living, start a family, or repair a marriage damaged by serial infidelity. The backdrop against which these everyday dramas are played out is one far removed from that which dominated the films of the Troubles era. The films that emerged during the early years of the peace process depict a 'new Northern Ireland'[9] that is prosperous and progressive. Once portrayed as a 'pariah city'[10] on screen, Belfast is transformed in the films that mark the turn of the century into an affluent 'commerce-driven city of glass'.[11] This optimism about the present leads almost inexorably towards a certain disposition towards the past. A sensibility common to the films under consideration here is the belief that Northern Ireland is 'moving on' and needs to draw a line under its recent troubled history. This conviction is articulated most explicitly perhaps in the film *Wild About Harry* in which the title character, once a political radical, has settled into a comfortable career as a local celebrity television chef whose many infidelities have led his wife to initiate divorce proceedings. After an unprovoked beating at a late-night petrol station, Harry blacks out and wakes up in hospital to find that he has lost his memory. He cannot recall anything after the age of 18 and has, in effect, returned to the person he was before the Northern Irish conflict began.[12] With all memory of troubles both personal and collective now 'magically excised',[13] Harry has the opportunity of a fresh start, rebuilding his relationship with his wife and children and reclaiming a certain verve for life jaded by all those years of bad living. While this attempt at a new life is not without its pitfalls – his wife proceeds with the divorce when he appears to relapse into former questionable habits – the film ends on a defiantly positive note, with the prospect of a reconciliation between the former partners clearly on the cards.

The amnesia that conveniently allows Harry to erase his past and move on with his life offers an instantly legible prescription for how Northern Ireland should proceed at a critical early stage of the peace process.[14] The contention that we need to draw a line under the past is one that has always enjoyed some currency in the region and indeed was expressed, albeit *sotto voce*, in the text of the GFA itself. In the opening lines of the text, the signatories agree that they should 'never forget' those who were killed or injured in the conflict or their families, but that the best way to honour the dead is through a 'fresh start' or 'new beginning'.[15] The loading of the Agreement towards the future rather than the past has arguably found expression in public policy over the course of the two decades since the accord was struck. As we explored at length in Chapter 2, the new political dispensation in Northern Ireland has never managed to find a way to come to terms with the region's recent violent history. There have of course been critical moments when the British state has facilitated public scrutiny into civilian deaths at the hands of its military personnel. Most crucially, the public inquest into Bloody Sunday, established in the same year as the GFA was signed, reported some twelve years later that those killed in Derry that day in January 1972 were entirely innocent, prompting then Prime Minister David Cameron to make the historically unprecedented concession that the conduct of the Parachute Regiment had been 'unjustified and unjustifiable'.[16] For all the undoubted significance of the 'political exorcism'[17] that was the Saville Inquiry, such occasional public tribunals cannot of course compensate for the lack of a more comprehensive truth and reconciliation process. In the absence of such a mechanism, there remain tens of thousands of people in Northern Ireland who continue to be traumatised because they do not know what happened to their deceased friends and relatives and/or who bears responsibility for their deaths.

The failure of the Northern Irish political class to deal adequately with what have come to be known euphemistically as 'legacy issues' has drawn criticism from various quarters. The argument that a peaceful political future requires that we face the traumas of our violent political past has been made insistently by a network of grassroots organisations of 'exceptional longevity and passion' often demanding justice for relatives and neighbours killed in the conflict.[18] Another place where what Graham Dawson terms 'the ghosts of history' are recalled is in the dramas scripted for cinema and television in recent years.[19] This critical turn in the visual representation of Northern Ireland appears to date from the release in 2008 of the film *Hunger*, and has subsequently found expression in a series of productions for the big and small screen that stretches right up to the present day. It began, in other words, within a year of that seemingly historic moment when Ian Paisley and Martin McGuinness stunned audiences at home and abroad by agreeing to share power with one another. At first glance, the timing of this palpable shift in how Northern Ireland is depicted in cinema and on television might appear a little ironic. It was, after all, just at that moment when the region seemed, finally, to be facing a future of stable consocational government that film-makers began to summon repeatedly the spectres of its violent past. In hindsight, however, the rather mournful tone of many of the films that appeared in the period after Sinn

Féin and the Democratic Unionist Party (DUP) agreed to share power appears distinctly prescient. One of the principal issues that would plague the partners in government would be how to deal with the past. Although the parties would seek to resolve their differences in the 2014 Stormont House Agreement as well as the Fresh Start deal struck the following year – overlooking, of course, that the haste for *a fresh start* might well have been the source of many of their problems in the first place – the matter of 'legacy issues' would never be resolved adequately and would add its weight to the cluster of difficulties that would eventually bring down the power-sharing Executive. When the devolved institutions were restored finally, in January 2020, these issues would once more become a bone of contention, with the introduction of a pension for victims of the conflict delayed yet further due, in part, to the dispute between unionist and republican politicians over who would be eligible for the scheme. Looking back across the years since Sinn Féin and the DUP first consented to enter office together, it often appears that the dramas of the period on the big and small screen represent a premonition of the troubles that would flow from the failure to deal with the spectres of the past. These diverse but often mournful films and television programmes, in other words, issue a warning to politicians, and others, not to forget the ghosts that are all about us, an injunction to acknowledge before it is too late that Northern Ireland exists in a perennially perilous state that might be deemed 'hauntological'.

Learning to live with ghosts

The concept of 'hauntology', in its recent incarnation, derives from Jacques Derrida's examination of the cultural world in the immediate aftermath of the end of the Cold War. The demise of the Communist project, Derrida suggests, has created a sense of loss reflected in a widespread mood of mournfulness. The spectres that remain from the dream of a genuinely egalitarian future are unlikely to disappear any time soon. Living at the 'end of history', Derrida observes, requires us to 'learn to live with ghosts'.[20] One of the most engaging attempts to explore the 'hauntology' that defines the modern world appears in the writings of the late cultural theorist Mark Fisher.[21] In a collection of essays entitled *Ghosts of My Life*, Fisher observes that the triumph of the neoliberal project signalled the demise of other, more progressive visions of the future. This closing down of ideological space – what Franco Berardi terms 'the slow cancellation of the future' – has ensured that beneath the glossy surfaces of late capitalism there is a pervasive mood of 'melancholia'.[22] The term is employed here in a manner akin to Sigmund Freud, denoting a mode of grieving in which the bereaved refuses to relinquish the lost love object, a refusal that gives rise to certain pathologies. One of these disorders, Fisher suggests, expresses itself in the pervasive and debilitating nostalgia of the contemporary culture industries in general, and popular music in particular. While the calling card of pop was once its facility for 'future shock', it now seems haunted by its own past, constantly retreading and reissuing the songs and styles of a previous golden age. The 'anachronism and inertia'[23] of contemporary popular music proves emblematic of an ever more ubiquitous nostalgia that increasingly deprives time of all meaning. In an age where the hits of yesteryear are seamlessly interchangeable with those of today, it often feels that is no genuinely *contemporary* popular music, that there is no 'now'.[24]

Fisher is suitably withering in his depiction of the 'extraordinary accommodation towards the past'[25] that defines mainstream popular culture in the early twenty-first century. He does, however, discern the existence of certain modes of contemporary pop music that, while formally nostalgic, are politically progressive nonetheless. Fisher is especially fervent in his praise of certain figures producing experimental electronica, and in particular those associated with the Ghost Box record label. The hallmark of these artists is an 'overwhelming melancholy' that stems from their preoccupation with how analogue technologies 'materialised memory', especially in the 'crackle' of the stylus on vinyl. That Fisher regards the 'hauntology' of these forms of electronica to be progressive hinges on a very specific understanding of what is meant by the term 'spectre'. As Derrida notes,[26] the most famous appearance of the noun comes in the opening line of the *Communist Manifesto*: 'A spectre is haunting Europe – the spectre of Communism.' The use of the term here reminds us that the spectral is not merely retrospective, but prospective as well. The figure of the spectre is a disembodied manifestation of that which has passed but also that which has still to come to pass. In the words of Martin Hägglund, it is at one and the same time both the 'no longer' and the 'not yet'.[27]

It is, in part, the multi-temporal nature of the spectral that informs Fisher's celebration of the 'hauntology' of certain versions of contemporary electronica. In their use of analogue technologies from a bygone age, these artists are seeking, Fisher insists,[28] to summon not merely the spectres of the past but also those of the future. Their intention, in other words, is not to return to some previous sepia-toned era but rather to reclaim and reanimate the political dreams of 'popular modernism' that germinated in those years before the neoliberal revolution. The melancholia that informs the artists that orbit around the Ghost Box label articulates, then, not an unwillingness to relinquish the past but rather a refusal to abandon the 'lost futures' that once dwelled there. The 'hauntology' of these cultural forms may well represent a form of nostalgia but it is, in the words of the late Pete Shelley, a 'nostalgia for an age yet to come'.[29]

The ideas that Mark Fisher developed in his writings on 'hauntology' provide a valuable – if, perhaps, at first glance unlikely – conceptual framework in which to examine recent dramas for the big and small screen dealing with Northern Ireland. The films and television series that have appeared over the last decade or so, as we shall see, often depict the region as haunted by the spectres of a conflict that has never quite been put to rest. These moving images, moreover, often reveal a certain sense of nostalgia, not only for the past but also for the future, or at least for a future that once seemed possible but was lost somewhere along the way. In the analysis that follows, we will set out to illustrate how these themes have played out both in the cinema and on television. We begin our discussion with what is perhaps the most celebrated, and indeed controversial, film concerned with Northern Ireland to have appeared since the end of the Troubles.

'But I knew I did the right thing by that wee foal'

The directorial debut of British visual artist Steve McQueen, *Hunger* brought a radical arthouse sensibility to one of the most controversial passages of the Northern Ireland conflict. A film in three discrete parts, the opening sequence offers the viewer a 'visceral'[30] reminder of the squalor and violence that accompanied the campaign for recognition as political prisoners initiated by republican inmates in 1976. The film opens with some sparse text providing a little context for the prisons dispute, accompanied by the sound of Catholic women rattling bin lids on the street outside their homes, by that stage a traditional means of protest and a warning to republican volunteers of the presence of British military personnel. This cacophony of sound will prove to be an aberration in a film largely characterised by prolonged periods of silence.[31] The opening passage sees the arrival of a young republican Davey Gillen in Her Majesty's Prison Maze/Long Kesh.[32] Having declared he is a political prisoner and will refuse to wear an inmate's uniform, Gillen is issued with a blanket and assigned a cellmate who is participating in the long-running 'dirty protest'. As the new arrival struggles to adjust to the gloom, his revulsion at the sight of excrement smeared on the walls mirrors that of the audience. For all its privation, this space will soon prove to be one of comparative refuge. When prisoners are removed so that their cells can be power-cleaned by men in 'prophylactic suits',[33] the warders seize the opportunity to brutalise and humiliate those ostensibly in their care. The first time we encounter the central figure of Bobby Sands, he is being dragged into the corridor where he is repeatedly beaten before having his hair roughly shorn and his body scrubbed clean with a yard brush. When the prisoner is eventually dumped head first back in his cell, he turns to look at the camera, his arms extended and his face freshly bruised. This will prove to be the first of many occasions when 'the resemblance to Christ is obvious'.[34]

The end of the opening passage of *Hunger* is signalled by the murder of a prison officer who is visiting his elderly mother in a care home. Suffering from dementia, the woman does not flinch even when spattered with the blood of her own son, who comes to rest in her lap, in an image that calls to mind the *pietà*.[35] We are then returned to the prison to eavesdrop on a conversation between Bobby Sands and a parish priest from west Belfast to whom he refers only as 'Dom'. In this 'daringly extended'[36] scene of almost 24 minutes scripted by playwright Enda Walsh,[37] we watch from the sidelines as Sands discloses that the decision has been made to escalate the prison protest by calling a hunger strike. The two men argue back and forth about the morality and utility of this course of action. The priest goads Sands that he is motivated by a vainglorious desire for martyrdom, but the republican counters that the hunger strike is motivated by the desire to create a 'new generation' willing to join the 'armed struggle'. As the argument reaches a stalemate, the camera moves to focus solely on Sands, who begins to recount an incident he claims to have happened when he was a 12-year-old boy. In Donegal for a cross-country race, he was part of a group of boys from Belfast and Cork who stumbled across an injured foal in a stream. While the others postured about how best to put the animal out of its misery, the young Sands chose to act, holding its head under the water until it drowned. His actions led to a beating from a Christian Brother, but this was deemed a small price both for securing the respect of his peers and for acting in the interests of the stricken animal: 'But I knew I did the right thing by that wee foal.' In this monologue, the communal enterprise that was the hunger strike becomes a solo mission, and the motivation for embarking on this course of action becomes one straight from a familiar Hollywood playbook. Bobby Sands ceases to belong to a group of political prisoners and is cast instead in the role of the maverick who 'rides alone'[38] so beloved of screenwriters down the generations.[39]

After the 'avalanche of dialogue'[40] that defines the middle passage of *Hunger*, the film proceeds in almost total silence. This final segment documents the last days of Bobby Sands in the hospital wing in 'excruciating detail'.[41] As the hunger strike proceeds, Sands' body begins to consume itself. His eyesight fails, his back is covered in suppurating wounds, he discharges clotted blood into the pristine white toilet bowl. As Sands moves in and out of consciousness, an apparition appears at the foot of his bed in the guise of his 12-year-old self. The boy stares unblinking at the camera, in a gesture to the closing scene of François Truffaut's celebrated *400 Blows*,[42] a film already referenced the previous year in the final frames of Shane Meadows' *This is England*. In these agonising closing scenes, Sands undergoes a predictable transformation that had already been signalled earlier in the film. The prolonged suffering of the republican prisoner clearly echoes the Christian fable of *The Passion*, and the presence of his mother watching over him from his bedside merely heightens those connotations. In a hospital room illuminated by sharp, clear light, Sands makes the 'Christ-like transcendence to pure image'.[43] As he finally approaches death, the figure of his younger self makes another appearance. We see the 12-year-old Sands running alone along a path beside a river. He stops to catch his breath and looks quizzically behind him, possibly wondering where the other harriers are, before deciding to run on alone.

On its initial release, *Hunger* enjoyed 'enormous critical success',[44] with director Steve McQueen winning the 2008 *Caméra d'Or* at Cannes for best debut feature. The 'formally experimental'[45] nature of the film stood in stark contrast to most previous films devoted to Northern Ireland, which rarely strayed from the stylistic clichés of the thriller or the romantic comedy. Its many admirers often point towards the film's bold use of sound and silence,[46] as well as its willingness to dwell for 'almost unbearable'[47] stretches of time on seemingly innocuous details: a prisoner toying with a fly, snowflakes melting on the grazed knuckles of a prison officer, a warder casually brushing streaks of urine seeping from under cell doors.[48] While *Hunger* drew many critical accolades, it also attracted no little political controversy. This was entirely to be expected, of course. In its choice of subject matter, the film had, after all, elected to summon perhaps the most prominent of the many spectres associated with the Northern Irish conflict. When interviewed, director Steve McQueen sought to resist any claims that the film was 'political', countering that it was simply concerned with 'human' issues of identity and forbearance, universal themes that ensured the film had a relevance for other, more contemporary sites of political incarceration a long way from Northern Ireland, most notably Abu Ghraib and Guantánamo Bay.[49]

These assurances of the essentially apolitical nature of *Hunger* would inevitably fail to convince many of its critics. Writing in the *Daily Mail*, Chris Tookey[50] argued that the film was 'pro-terrorist propaganda', adding a predictably puerile flourish in the claim that the feature amounted to nothing less than a 'love letter' to Bobby Sands. A rather more considered version of this argument would come from Fintan O'Toole of the *Irish Times*. O'Toole[51] argued that the central flaw of the film lies in its collusion in the representation of the hunger strike as an event that was aesthetic rather than political. In framing the event in this way, the film obscures crucial elements of the wider context in which it occurred, with the journalist and cultural critic alleging (wrongly in the latter instance, at least) that the script fails to acknowledge that the prisoners had often been convicted of violent crimes and that the prison protests saw the deaths of more warders than inmates. With these pivotal details neatly removed from view, O'Toole insists, the film becomes focused on the aesthetics of human commitment and endurance. In doing so, the film simply cannot avoid repeating a narrative scripted for it in advance by the hunger strikers themselves. This reading finds its academic equivalent in the work of Cillian McGrattan. In removing the 1981 hunger strikes from their appropriate context, McGrattan asserts,[52] Steve McQueen transforms 'the historical record into a morality tale' and in the process produces 'a re-politicising, propagandistic exercise in myth-making'.[53]

This accusation that *Hunger* represents a politically partisan work has been countered by several writers. The case for the defence here typically entails a simple reiteration of many of the claims that its director has made for the film. *Hunger* is held to be a film that is only coincidentally 'about' Northern Ireland, with the sparseness of the historical context provided in the opening and closing credits offered as evidence of the drama's distance from the particularity of the place in which it is set. Rather than being concerned simply with the Troubles, the film is depicted as dealing with rather weightier and more universal concerns that transcend the narrow confines of the six counties. This attempt to disconnect *Hunger* from the specificities of its chosen locale and subject matter reaches particularly absurd heights when John Lynch[54] claims that director Steve McQueen 'has not made a film about Bobby Sands at all'. A rather more plausible version of this argument comes in a thoughtful article by Rebecca Graff-McRae. In her essay, she ponders why it is that the republican movement has been rather more ambivalent towards a critically revered film like *Hunger* than a more artistically limited work dealing with the same subject matter such as *H3* (Les Blair, 2001). The answer, Graff-McRae suggests, is that the former offers a 'universalistic perspective' that ends up 'erasing the political context of the strikes'. The outcome of this erasure is that *Hunger* 'ruptures Sinn Féin's exclusive claim to ownership of the event and its political legacy', and consequently the film does not feature prominently on what she terms the republican movement's 'official commemorative playlist'.[55]

While the competing readings of *Hunger* outlined above certainly enjoy widespread currency, neither of them offers a satisfactory account of the film's politics. Although an assertion made with some regularity, the insistence of Graff-McRae and others that the film's 'universalist perspective' erases the specific context of the Northern Irish hunger strike simply fails to square with the facts of the matter. This is, after all, not a film about someone who bears a passing resemblance to Bobby Sands who finds himself in gruelling circumstances similar to those of Bobby Sands. This is, rather, a film that is very specifically, and indeed entirely explicitly, *about Bobby Sands*. Those who claim that *Hunger* is not really concerned with Northern Ireland but rather with more universal issues of human rights and fortitude tend to point to a paucity of historical detail provided to viewers of the film. In reality, however, the explanatory text that bookends the film is comparable to that provided in most dramas 'based on real events' and is certainly sufficient for a reasonably engaged viewer to follow closely what is happening on screen. Furthermore, there are several key moments in the drama that operate effectively as exposition scenes to orientate the viewer not already familiar with all the relevant historical detail, not least the 24-minute central passage in which the arguments for and against the hunger strike are explored at quite extraordinary length. In short, it makes no sense at all to suggest that *Hunger* is a film that is only tangentially or coincidentally connected to Northern Ireland. This is a film about very specific people in very specific circumstances in a very specific time and place. Admittedly, the impressionistic style[56] of the film can suggest otherwise at times, but the fact remains that this is a drama that locates itself in a very particular historical context and that gives its viewers sufficient information to orientate themselves accordingly.

It is perhaps the quite explicit specificity of *Hunger* – rather than the allusive 'universalism' identified by the likes of Graff-McRae – that explains why the film might well pose difficulties for at least some within the republican movement. Over recent decades, the leadership of Sinn Féin has sought to fold the hunger strike into the subsequent trajectory of republican political strategy. The deaths of ten young working-class men in the summer of 1981 are portrayed as the catalyst that allowed republicans to secure the electoral gains that would, in time, nurture a mass political movement with the confidence and stamina to enter into devolved government in Belfast, a move depicted invariably as a mere staging post on the road to a united Ireland.[57] Gerry Adams has often been at pains to underline that the dead hunger strikers would have fully approved of the republican peace strategy. Addressing a twenty-fifth anniversary rally, for instance, the then Sinn Féin President commented that in negotiations with the British government he often felt his side of the table to be 'rather crowded' with figures from the pantheon of the republican dead: 'There's Bobby, and Francis Hughes, there's Mairead, and Maire Drumm.'[58] These quite explicit attempts to integrate the hunger strikers, among others, into the narrative of the peace process, however, have never quite managed to be entirely persuasive. The 'renewing death ritual'[59] initiated by Bobby Sands and his fellow inmates is frequently cast as a critical but entirely consistent juncture in the evolution of a political strategy given retrospective coherence in the relentless revisionism of the republican leadership. In reality, however, the hunger strike represented a singular moment of 'profound rupture'[60] in the 'long war' that was the Northern Irish conflict. The very explicit purpose of the prisoners was, after all, not to create the conditions of a prospective peace – as the republican leadership would now have us believe – but rather to spark an 'apocalyptic'[61] escalation in an actually existing war. And for a time it appeared that the republican inmates' ambitions might well be realised. The hunger strikes would, after all, spark rioting in working-class Catholic neighbourhoods on a scale not seen since the start of the Troubles, and in the three months that followed the death of Bobby Sands alone some 31,000 plastic bullets were fired by members of the security forces.[62]

George Legg[63] has suggested that *Hunger* captures something of the genuinely transgressive character of the hunger strike only to squander this insight in the final third of the film, when the prisons dispute comes to be framed in the 'exhausted imagery of myth and martyrology'. While there is certainly more than a grain of truth in this criticism, the film does still offer the viewer an indelible sense of what it is that makes Bobby Sands, in a certain sense at least, such a disruptive character in current republican narratives on recent Northern Irish history. It is this quality that ensures that while the hunger striker represents its principal modern icon, he also remains a deeply troubling figure for many at the helm of contemporary republicanism. Bobby Sands is at one and the same time the (dis)embodiment of all of the ideals that republicans claim to hold dear and an omnipresent, nagging reminder of how far they have fallen from those cherished, foundational ideals. He is, in other words, the spectre at the feast of a republican movement long since professionalised and co-opted into the 'hollow, depleted, and apathetic'[64] politics of the 'new Northern Ireland'. And the film that summons that spectral presence with greatest verve and imagination is, without question, *Hunger*.

In our earlier discussion, it was suggested that the spectre exists not only as the 'no longer' but the 'not yet'. The power of *Hunger* derives in large measure from its facility to summon the troubling figure of Bobby Sands in both of these tenses simultaneously. In his prison writings, Sands revealed an eschatological impulse, a conviction, that is, that the catastrophes of the present are a prerequisite of the triumphs of the future. This particular sensibility was reflected in his famous dictum *tiocfaidh ár lá* ('our day will come') and in his insistence that 'our revenge will be the laughter of our children'.[65] In the agonising final segment of *Hunger*, we watch Sands waste away until on the sixty-sixth day without food he passes on, with his mother at his bedside. In that fateful moment when he breathes his last, the image that flits across his imagination is that of his 12-year-old self.

While this might appear to be a figure from the past, it might be seen more accurately perhaps as one from the future. The boy running along the river path, after all, pauses at the precise moment that Sands expires but continues to run on even after he has passed away. In metaphorical terms, the figure of his juvenile self might be read, then, as suggesting that Sands – or, more precisely perhaps, the political ideals he is often held to embody – will experience some version of an afterlife. The dead hunger striker represents not merely the actuality of a political revolution in the past that failed, but also the possibility of a political revolution in the future that might have a different fate. He exists, then, as a spectre that gives form not only to the 'no longer' but also the 'not yet'.

It is in part this Janus-faced figurative power that enables Sands to remain such a profoundly unsettling figure for so many, and not least perhaps for those now at the helm of the republican movement. The spectre that is summoned in the reels of *Hunger* is one that haunts not only the past but the future as well. The figure of the dead hunger striker, after all, continues to articulate a set of political possibilities far removed from the 'banality'[66] of the peace process to which Sinn Féin has plighted its troth. It is scarcely surprising, then, that the ghost stories that feature in *Hunger* should have proved uncomfortable for some within the republican tradition. When the likes of O'Toole and McGrattan suggest that the film offers a narrative deeply convenient for the republican movement they certainly have a point. The rendition of this crucial passage of the Troubles that appears in *Hunger* obscures, after all, a whole slew of inconvenient truths. It neglects to mention, for instance, that the prisoners depicted so sympathetically on screen were themselves personally involved in often heinous acts of violence conducted in the name of an organisation responsible for more deaths than any other during the Northern Ireland conflict. The film also fails to acknowledge adequately the allegedly Machiavellian role of certain republicans on the outside, most notably Gerry Adams, in prolonging the hunger strikes for electoral gain when a resolution may well have been at hand.[67] It would seem, then, that the cultural critics who contest that *Hunger* makes for comfortable viewing for the republican movement have no shortage of evidence on their side. What these commentators fail to appreciate, however, is that precisely the opposite might well be true at the same time. The figure of Bobby Sands reminds republicans not only of what they believe to be their valiant past but also of what they know now to be their lost future. In re-creating with such vividness the tragic events of the summer of 1981, the makers of *Hunger* conjure up a spectre that continues to haunt many in Northern Ireland, but not least a republican leadership that has long since abandoned the idealism of those who starved themselves to death in pursuit, ostensibly, of a socialist republic in favour of the shabby neoliberal compromises that have been among the more dispiriting hallmarks of Sinn Féin's period in office.[68]

'You are not leaving this country!'

As Martin McLoone[69] has noted, the many cinematic and televisual dramas centred on Northern Ireland that have appeared over recent decades have been marked by the 'relative invisibility' of British military personnel. An important exception to that rule comes in the guise of '71, directed by Yann Demange, which became a box-office success when first released in 2014. Set in the titular year when the nascent 'civil unrest' in the six counties escalated into the 'long war' that would define the Northern Irish Troubles, the film centres on the figure of Gary Hook, a young (presumably) orphaned man from Derbyshire who leaves his younger brother in care to pursue a career in the British army. The new recruits in Hook's platoon are supposed to be shipping out to Germany, but on the eve of departure they are informed that the 'deteriorating security situation' in Belfast means they will be heading there instead. In an attempt to reassure the evidently disgruntled squaddies, the officer making the announcement delivers deadpan the following lines:

> 'I take it you all know where Belfast is? Northern Ireland. United Kingdom. 'Ere. You are not leaving this country!'

On arrival in Belfast, however, it becomes immediately apparent that the fledgling soldiers have in fact done precisely that. Their first full day in the city sees members of the newly arrived platoon lost in west Belfast where they have been assigned to support the RUC in a house search for weapons in a republican neighbourhood. As the police officers proceed to humiliate and brutalise the inhabitants, angry neighbours gather in the street, sparking an inevitable riot. In the chaos, one soldier felled by a flying object has his rifle stolen by a child who scampers off behind the protective cordon of rioters. Hook and another soldier, Thommo, are dispatched to retrieve the weapon, but they are set upon by angry locals, and in the midst of the beating an IRA man emerges from the crowd and shoots the latter squaddie dead. Showered in his friend's blood, Hook takes off through the back streets, pursued by a pair of republicans who turn out, fortuitously, to be rather poor shots. Eventually the soldier takes refuge in an outside toilet where he waits until nightfall before venturing out, camouflaged in a pullover purloined from a convenient washing line, in an attempt to return to barracks. Only in the city barely a day, Hook is completely disorientated, but he happens upon an unlikely guide in the form of a precocious, foul-mouthed young Protestant who offers to bring him to the presumed safety of a pub out of which operates his uncle, a major figure in local loyalist paramilitary circles. When the pair arrive at the bar, they witness something they were not supposed to. In a back room, a member of the Military Reconnaissance Force (MRF) – a covert British intelligence agency skilled in the dark arts of 'counter-insurgency' that operated in Northern Ireland in the early 1970s[70] – based in the same barracks as Hook is priming a bomb for loyalists to plant on licensed premises in a nationalist district of the city. The soldier steps out of the pub in search of a lift back to base and at that moment the explosive device detonates prematurely. In the especially powerful scene that follows, Hook searches through the wreckage for the boy, who has lost both arms and is barely clinging to life, a local woman arranging for him to be ferried to hospital in what seems the vain hope he might survive. Shrouded in ash, his temporary deafness mimicked by the now muffled soundtrack, the soldier stumbles off into the night. Lost once more in a strange and hostile city, Hook does not know which way to turn, until, through the gloom, a diminutive, ghostly apparition beckons him and he follows dutifully. It will not be the last spook that the bedraggled British soldier will encounter on his second night in Belfast.

We next encounter Hook passed out on a street corner, seriously injured from the premature explosion in the loyalist bar. A middle-aged man, Eamon, and his daughter, Brigid, happen upon the unconscious squaddie on their way back to their apartment in the republican Divis Flats complex. Against the pleading of his anxious daughter, Eamon insists on bringing Hook home, and it is only then that the pair realise that they are inadvertently harbouring a British soldier. Realising that their lives are in danger should the fugitive be discovered, they seek to enlist the help of Boyle, an older, relatively moderate figure in the republican movement who we see on various occasions seeking to cool the heels of younger militants itching for battle. It transpires that Boyle is in fact an informant, and he contacts the MRF personnel we have encountered already to come and collect Hook. The younger militants have, however, been tailing the older republican all evening, and having become aware that the missing British soldier is in the vicinity, they eventually capture him and lead him away to what appears to be his certain death. By the time the MRF personnel, supported by several soldiers from Hook's platoon, arrive at the Divis Flats complex, the squaddie is being held in the basement of a abandoned local pub and only remains alive due to the squeamishness of a young republican recruit who cannot bring himself to pull the trigger. When the military intelligence officers storm the bar, it appears that their intention is to save Hook's life, but in reality they are there to ensure they he will never be able to testify as to the provenance of the bomb that devastated the loyalist bar earlier that evening.

The covert operative who delivered and primed the explosive device is the first to arrive in the basement, where he seemingly kills the young republican who could not bring himself to discharge his pistol and then proceeds to strangle the captured soldier. Arriving late on the scene, Hook's platoon leader witnesses what is happening and is about to intervene when two shots ring out. The prostrate young republican who is out of sight has just killed the military intelligence figure, and in the confusion the officer returns fire, killing the fledgling paramilitary instantly.

The closing scenes of '71 feature a summary army tribunal clearly designed to cover up the events that we have just witnessed on screen. The senior officer of the MRF unit provides a menacing presence in these briefings, as the platoon officer is browbeaten into accepting that the facts of what happened in the Divis Flats that night were at variance with what he saw with his own eyes. Still bearing the wounds of his ordeal, Private Hook maintains a stoic silence as his superiors pressure him into endorsing their convenient version of events. This abuse of procedure evidently shatters any remaining faith the soldier has in the army and, like many other protagonists in recent films about Northern Ireland, he makes the decision to leave the world of combat behind and opt instead for a life of domesticity, albeit of a slightly unusual stripe.[71] In the closing frames we see Hook on the boat back to England, tossing his dog tags into the brine. On arrival, he heads straight to retrieve his younger brother from the care home where he left him before departing for Belfast. The film ends with a shot of the siblings seated together on a bus passing through bucolic countryside, on their way to a destination that is unspecified, but which presumably this time really does entail 'not leaving this country'.

As a commercially successful film, '71 reminded a mainstream audience that even a full generation after the end of the conflict, Northern Ireland remains troubled by 'ghosts haunting the spaces of the progressive present'.[72] In most dramas dealing with the region, the British military occupies a marginal position, as though it had been somehow 'above' the armed conflict that raged for a quarter-century. The reality is of course that the British army was a principal player in, and indeed accelerant of, the Northern Irish Troubles. In the course of its longest ever campaign, 'Operation Banner', the British military lost more than 500 soldiers and was responsible for more than 300 fatalities.[73] '71 represents perhaps the most significant recent attempt by film-makers to capture the experience of those predominantly young working-class men who crossed the Irish Sea to serve in the region. In the main, the film provides a distinctly sympathetic portrayal of British soldiers deployed to Northern Ireland. The young squaddies who arrive on the streets of west Belfast are depicted as inexperienced and vulnerable, entirely ill-equipped to police a conflict that they do not understand and which already appears to have spiralled out of control. There are several haunting scenes in '71, but none more so perhaps than when an army patrol returns in the dead of night to recover the body of Thommo, the callow private we saw earlier being shot at close range by a republican gunman while trying to recover a stolen rifle. The body of the young squaddie remains where he fell, his brains scattered across the pavement of a street that is now eerily quiet. The ghosts that haunt '71 are not only those of fallen British soldiers but also those of the almost two thousand civilians[74] who lost their lives in the violence that accelerated in the year that gives the film its title. One of the most shocking scenes is that where the premature detonation of a bomb destroys a pub in a loyalist neighbourhood. For anyone who remembers the events of the Troubles, this moment would instantly call to mind many similar moments of carnage, the attacks on McGurk's Bar or the Bayardo among them.[75] As Private Hook stumbles, shrouded in ash, from the wreckage of the bar, a spectral figure appears through the gloom, the spirit perhaps of the dismembered boy he has just attempted, in vain, to salvage from the ruins of the bombed pub. This fleeting apparition offers a chilling reminder of all the civilians who perished in the bombing campaigns that marked the Troubles, of those who are no longer with us but whose spectral presence remains in the lives of those left behind.

There is at least one further form of ghost that appears in the frames of '71. Among the issues that the film illuminates is the conduct of those military intelligence figures who operated in Northern Ireland during the conflict and indeed beyond, a theme also prominent in other recent feature films such as *Fifty Dead Men Walking* (Kari Skogland, 2008) and *Shadow Dancer* (James Marsh, 2012).[76] These covert operatives, by their very nature, have a certain spectral quality – they are, after all, both there and (officially) not there at the same time – and it is, then, rather appropriate that they are often referred to as 'spooks'.[77] In '71, it often appears that it is these 'spooks' who are the principal figures orchestrating the escalating violence in Northern Ireland. We see, for instance, members of the MRF supplying loyalists with a bomb intended to 'send a message' to republicans that their acts of violence will be met like for like. Later in the film, it transpires that operatives from the group have 'turned' a senior IRA figure and that they are conspiring to have him assassinated and replaced by a newly recruited informant from the younger, more militant ranks of the organisation. While the conspiracy theory that the film seems to provide by way of explanation of the Northern Irish conflict is clearly overstated, it certainly contains a kernel of truth nonetheless. Over time, the scale of covert operations by British military intelligence in Northern Ireland has become ever more chillingly evident. Perhaps the most stunning revelation in this regard came in 2003 when it emerged that the individual who headed the 'nutting squad' responsible for identifying and killing 'touts' within the Provisional IRA, Freddie Scappaticci, was himself a long-standing informant.[78] Those who defend the strategy of running agents within paramilitary organisations insist that the practice has gleaned intelligence that has allowed many lives to be saved. This rationale was projected onto the big screen in 2008 with the release of a film based on the life of Martin McGartland, the title of which makes the claim that his role as an informant within the IRA ensured that there are 'fifty dead men walking'. Those more critical of British military intelligence would counter that their activities in Northern Ireland have cost rather more lives than they have saved. The case against covert operations often points to those moments when the authorities have colluded with loyalist assassins and those when innocent civilians were sacrificed in order to protect agents within paramilitary organisations.[79] A film like '71 offers a genuinely damning indictment of those 'spooks' that operated outside the law and often with seeming impunity throughout the Troubles. In doing so, it provides a critical reminder that there are within Northern Ireland many people who remain deeply haunted by incidents of violence committed by many actors, but not least those who were in the employ, or in the pay, of the British state.

'What is this, the seventies?'

When it first aired on BBC2 in the spring of 2013, *The Fall* was an immediate hit with viewers, drawing the largest audiences that the channel had enjoyed for almost a decade.[80] Set in Belfast, the programme offers a depiction of the urban landscape that, while 'fresh' for the Northern Irish capital, remains, as Charlotte Brunsdon[81] notes, 'generically familiar for the television city: a place where women get murdered'. The series opens as we watch Detective Superintendent Stella Gibson clean her bathroom and remove a cosmetic face-mask before retiring to bed with her laptop to read up on the murder case which, among others, will consume her energies for many months to come. The following morning she is to fly to Belfast to conduct a 28-day review on the investigation into the death of a female architect who happens to be the estranged daughter-in-law of a powerful local unionist politician. While DCI Gibson has no idea yet who is responsible for the murder, the audience has already been introduced to the killer of Alice Monroe. The opening scenes of the series that cast us as voyeurs observing the police officer engaged in mundane domestic chores are intercut with those of the killer, Paul Spector, engaged in his own act of covert surveillance outside the home of his next victim. Like all his previous targets, Sarah Kay is a dark-haired professional woman in her early thirties.[82]

At first glance, the character of Paul Spector appears to be an unlikely serial killer. A seemingly mild-mannered grief counsellor, he is also a married man with two young children and clearly especially besotted with his daughter Olivia. While Spector might not immediately appear to fit the classic profile of a serial killer, an uncharacteristic moment of impetuousness will soon bring him to the attention of the authorities. The next murder that the serial killer has plotted fails to go to plan when the intended victim, Annie Brawley, returns home not alone, as expected, but in the company of her brother. Rather than flee, Spector decides to proceed as planned and in the ensuing struggle stabs the man to death with a pair of decorating shears, later discarded as the killer hastens his escape from the crime scene. An extensive search sees the police retrieve the murder weapon and the forensic evidence reveals the prime suspect to be Paul Spector. Once he is in custody, the true identity of the murderer gradually begins to reveal itself. The harrowing back story that unfolds provides some explanation of the birth of a serial killer, and in the process dredges up some of the traumas that continue to haunt the society that spawned him.

One of the dilemmas facing the makers of *The Fall* was how to deal with the very specific context in which this rather more universal story is set.[83] As Hill has noted, there has been a propensity in contemporary cinema and television dramas set in Belfast to erase the troubled recent past of the city.[84] In these features, the Northern Irish capital is often depicted as a giddy site of conspicuous consumption by a young, cosmopolitan population that could be living in pretty much any Western city in the era of late capitalism.[85] Belfast comes to be marked by a certain 'placelessness' which suggests that it could in fact be 'anywhere but Northern Ireland'.[86] In certain respects, the writers of *The Fall* have followed this recent trend of depicting the city as almost 'placeless, abstract'.[87] Many of the scenes in the series appear to showcase the glossy accelerated consumerism that is the hallmark of the 'new Belfast'.[88] The opening episode, for example, shows the young lawyer Sarah Kay flirting with a male colleague in a chic city-centre bar. Others are set in the various glamorous locations that animate the night-time economy of a Belfast that not so long ago closed down more or less completely in the early evening.[89] We see Spector meet his bogus love interest, the Lolita figure of schoolgirl Katie Benedetto, in an elegant restaurant in the recently minted 'cathedral quarter', while the polyamorous DSI Gibson attempts unsuccessfully to seduce the pathologist Reed Smith in the fashionable surroundings of Bert's Jazz Bar. The programme also showcases the host of new hotels that have sprung up of late in a city that was once famous for the bombing of such enterprises. DSI Gibson has a night of passion with the soon-to-be deceased police officer James Olson on her arrival in the Belfast Hilton, a structure that stands within metres of where the charred remains of the victims of Bloody Friday in July 1972 were shovelled into body bags, and is literally a stone's throw from the once notorious republican district of the Markets. Later, she seems to have relocated to The Merchant – an exclusive hotel fashioned out of a former bank in what was once an almost derelict part of central Belfast – which features in so many promotional videos for the city that its appearance seems almost a legal requirement at this stage.

The three series of *The Fall*, then, feature ample representations of the sites of breathless consumption that define the widely celebrated 'new Belfast'. Indeed, at times the programme comes close to resembling a tourist advertisement, with Stephen Baker noting that, in spite of its 'dark subject matter', official agencies for a time directed potential visitors to the city to the series' website which featured an interactive map of the various locations where filming took place, murder scenes and all.[90] The frequent, seemingly positive representations of contemporary Belfast that appear in *The Fall* sit side by side, however, with others that call to mind the profoundly troubled recent past of the city.[91] On her arrival, DSI Gibson is met by Assistant Chief Constable Jim Burns, a former romantic interest who takes the opportunity to warn her that policing is 'different' in Northern Ireland, more 'political'. Gibson responds with characteristic hauteur, dismissing these claims to the specificity of the region as 'all that my Jesus is better than your Jesus stuff'. The very particular challenges and dangers of policing in Northern Ireland will, however, soon become very apparent. On her way to the police station that will house her investigation, Gibson is chauffeured past many of the landmarks and scars of the Troubles, taken on a journey past the now abandoned courthouse on the Crumlin Road and the principal, imposing peace line in west Belfast, which anyone familiar with the geography of the city would know is neither a logical sequence of travel nor the shortest route to her destination. Arriving eventually at the barracks, she is greeted immediately by a montage of photos of police officers who died in the Troubles, captioned with the phrase 'our murdered colleagues'.[92]

Such moments of political violence have not, however, been consigned entirely to the past. In the second episode of the first season, we see Constable James Olson, fresh from his extramarital tryst with DSI Gibson, return home only to be shot in the street, the killing witnessed by his young son looking on from his bedroom window. The gunmen are suspected to be dissident republicans, associates of two men Olson was in the process of prosecuting for another recent murder. A further threat of violence comes from loyalist paramilitaries still operating two decades after they declared a ceasefire. In a counselling session to ascertain how they are dealing with the loss of their son, Paul Spector asks the former loyalist prisoner Jimmy Tyler and his wife how things are 'in the bedroom'. Once the discussion has concluded, an enraged Tyler pursues Spector into a lift where he informs him that he has done 'bad things', and tells him never to enquire about their sex life again. Suspicious that the grief counsellor may be having an affair with his wife, the evidently *not so former* paramilitary begins a campaign of intimidation that culminates with him shooting Spector, who is in police custody, and guiding officers to the spot in a forest where he has abandoned the abductee Rose Stagg in the boot of a car. At the hospital to which Spector is taken it transpires he is not the only person to arrive with a gunshot wound, leading one of the doctors to make the wryly amusing, but telling, enquiry: 'What is this, the seventies?'

Among the many victims of the 'dark and troubled history'[93] sketched in *The Fall* is, perhaps, the serial killer at the very heart of the drama. As the series unfolds, we discover that Paul Spector is in fact the assumed name of someone who was once Peter Baldwin. His birth certificate reveals Baldwin to have been the result of a romance between a touring British soldier and a local Catholic woman. In nationalist districts, such relationships were anathema, often leading to the women involved being ostracised and publicly humiliated in the guise of 'tarring and feathering'.[94] It was perhaps a blessing in disguise, then, that the relevant squaddie disappeared before his son was born. The place of the soldier was later taken by another man, but he also left while Baldwin was still a young child. On the day of his eighth birthday, Baldwin was informed by his mother that the person he had always thought of as his biological father was not in fact so. Ten days later, he arrived home to find that his mother had hanged herself from the back of her bedroom door. Now effectively an orphan, Baldwin would be shunted between a sequence of care homes on both sides of the Irish border. In one of these, he and the other residents were subjected to repeated sexual abuse at the hands of those responsible for their well-being. Deemed to be 'a very pretty boy' by the paedophile priest in charge of the home, Baldwin would spend an entire year as his primary carnal prey.[95]

The predation to which the child who would become Paul Spector was subjected took place, of course, in the context of the widespread political violence of the Northern Irish conflict, and that association should be acknowledged as rather more than coincidental. Perhaps the most notorious site of sexual abuse of children in care in Northern Ireland was the Kincora Boys' Home in east Belfast. The group of paedophiles who preyed on youngsters living there contained a number of figures from the world of loyalist paramilitarism, some of whom were agents working for British military intelligence. While the abuse happening in Kincora was common knowledge among unionist politicians and covert operatives working for the state, none of those with influence intervened to stop it. Indeed, the latter had a vested interest in the sexual violence continuing, generating as it did the sorts of incriminating evidence that military intelligence agents often consider essential to their trade. There was, therefore, a chain connecting the violence against children taking place behind the closed doors of residential care homes and that happening on the streets outside such institutions. Over time, it would become apparent that the sexual and other violence happening in Kincora was far from an isolated incident.[96] The body set up to examine the abuse to which a large number of Northern Irish children in care had been subjected issued its final report in the summer of 2017, a few months after the Stormont Executive that had created it had ceased to function. The findings of the Historical Institutional Abuse Inquiry make for harrowing reading and map out a network of residential homes across the six counties in which sexual and other forms of violence were rife for much of the previous century.[97]

That the figure of Paul Spector was the product of Northern Ireland's own 'gulag archipelago'[98] provides some clues perhaps as to why he would later become a serial killer. It may well have been the agonies that he experienced as a child that prompted him to visit similar sexual violence on others as an adult. The writers of *The Fall* certainly seem to be interested in this potential explanation at several points in the narrative arc of the programme. On the evening when ACC Burns arrives unannounced and with amorous intent at the hotel door of DCI Gibson, he recounts that he was the officer who arrested the paedophile priest who ran the home in which Spector spent part of his childhood. Seeking to draw a connection between the abuse that Spector experienced and his subsequent career as a serial killer, Burns speculates that 'maybe this murderous fuck is a victim too'.

The speculation that Spector somehow represents an apparition from Northern Ireland's violent past is an interesting notion that the script writers of *The Fall* toy with from time to time but never quite seem able to develop fully. The problematic manner in which this conjecture is handled in the series becomes most starkly apparent in a key scene in the second season where the team of investigating officers are discussing the suspect's birth certificate. When it is revealed that Spector was born on 25 May 1979, ACC Burns reacts as if he has seen a ghost. The perennially harrowed senior policeman appends this disclosure with comments that appear to be couched as explanation: 'The year the Shankill Butchers were sentenced for life imprisonment for 19 murders, the year of Warrenpoint … Bad year.'[99] The inference that these observations invite would seem to be that somehow Spector was preordained to become a monster by the timing of his birth, a 'bad seed' cast to the winds by the violence that drew to a close the most troubled decade in Northern Ireland's most troubled history. The sheer absurdity of the thesis that ACC Burns seems to have just propounded is registered on the face of the unrequited love interest seated across the conference room. Not for the first time in the series, DSI Gibson fixes her superior officer with a look that expresses both contempt and concern that he may well have taken leave of his senses. In hindsight, the scene in which the 'bad year' monologue appears is one of those that alerts us to the decline of a series that had begun with considerable promise. The inability of the writers to decide what to do with the plot line about Spector's background as an abused child proves to be indicative of a wider narrative incoherence, and by the third and final season it becomes ever harder to work out what is actually going on, and why, in the programme. Even an actress as eminently gifted as Gillian Anderson proves unable to salvage the enterprise, and in the final few episodes her character DSI Gibson is reduced to issuing her lines almost under her breath, as if to apologise for a production that has long since lost its way.

For all its ultimate shortcomings, *The Fall* illustrates well the haunted nature of recent representations of Northern Ireland on both the big and small screen. After all, the serial killer at the heart of the drama is – to mark, just once, the excruciating pun of his adopted surname[100] – a spectre from the region's troubled recent history. *The Fall* invites us to remember the suffering of those children scarred by the experience of growing up in residential care in Northern Ireland. It also issues an important reminder that attacks on women – largely overlooked during a conflict that saw so many[101] – remain the single most substantial category of violence in the region.[102] While *The Fall* often sets out to capture the glossy surfaces of the 'new Belfast', there appear at the edge of its frames, then, the ghosts of Northern Ireland's violent past, and, indeed, its violent present.

'Never occurred to me to ask'

The writings of cultural theorist Mark Fisher, as we saw earlier, depict contemporary popular culture as ever more in thrall to the figures and styles of previous eras. This compulsive retrospection has, Fishers insists, engendered a pervasive 'melancholia' that centres on a gnawing 'feeling of belatedness, of living after the gold rush'.[103] In particular, the popular music that has emerged in the twenty-first century has the increasingly haunted air of a cultural form grieving not only for its lost past but also for its 'lost futures'. The pervasive mood of nostalgia identified by Mark Fisher has come to feature in certain of the cinematic and televisual dramas concerned with Northern Ireland that have appeared in the last few years. Released in the spring of 2013, the film *Good Vibrations* sets out to capture a familiar 'utopian moment'[104] amid the seemingly relentless gloom of the Troubles. In the opening narrative, the central figure in the drama, Terri Hooley, recounts the cultural energy and diversity of Belfast before the outbreak of the conflict. In that prelapsarian age, all of the major recording artists of the day came to play in the city, until, that is, 'they stopped coming'. As the 'civil unrest' in the capital escalates, Belfast becomes a 'ghost town' in which all but the most foolhardy abandon the nightlife of the central district for the relative safety of their own ethnically segregated neighbourhoods. The cultural torpor of the city is, however, broken by the arrival of punk rock in the latter half of the 1970s. A flyer posted in his recently opened record store draws Hooley to a gig in the legendary venue The Pound, where his prior scepticism disappears in the face of the politically radical brio of the bands on stage. Intoxicated by the energy in room, as well as several pints of lager, Hooley informs one of the groups, Rudi, that he will release their debut single even though he has no idea how to do so. Reluctant to go back on his word, Hooley hastily invents a label named after his record shop. In the months to come, *Good Vibrations* would release several of the seminal punk singles to emerge from Northern Ireland. The label appears to have struck gold when they put out the classic '45 *Teenage Kicks* by Derry band The Undertones, only for Hooley to sign the band over to the Sire multinational for the price of a second-hand van and an autographed photo of The Shangri-Las that never materialises. This lack of business acumen would in time cost him his home, his marriage and, on more than one occasion, his record store. The film concludes with a concert to raise funds for the ailing Good Vibrations shop. Although the iconic venue of the Ulster Hall is full to the rafters, the event manages to run at a loss because the ever-profligate Hooley has placed so many figures from the local punk scene on the guest list.

The account of the punk era in Northern Ireland that we find in *Good Vibrations* is a hugely positive one that proves entirely familiar. The local punk scene is, not for the first time and, presumably, not for the last, depicted as offering a radical political space that enabled young people in the six counties the opportunity to discard and transcend the stifling ethno-national identities that have traditionally dominated cultural life in the region. This representation is especially explicit in a somewhat ungainly passage in the film, which presumably acts as an exposition scene for viewers unfamiliar with the often vexing particularities of Northern Irish society. At one point, Hooley heads off on the road with a couple of the young bands on his record label for some gigs outside Belfast. On their return journey, the musicians have stopped at the roadside to heed a call of nature when they are confronted by a British army foot patrol. Asked at gunpoint where they come from, the various members of the party call out locations in different parts of the city, signifying that they are drawn from both principal ethno-national traditions. In case this context remains insufficient for an audience from outside the six counties, one of the English squaddies underlines the point by asking Hooley: 'You're telling me some of these fuckers are Protestant and some of them are Catholic?' The harried record store owner offers a suitably ecumenical reply: 'Never occurred to me to ask.'

The glowing representation of the Belfast punk scene as a cultural oasis in the midst of the sectarian warfare of the Northern Irish conflict has been repeated so often that it has long since passed into the realm of mythology.[105] The release of *Good Vibrations* marks the moment where that cherished corpus of legends is trapped in amber and captured for posterity on the big screen. That the folk tales that attend the Northern Irish punk scene are told with such numbing regularity owes a great deal, of course, to the very specific context that nurtured the subculture in the six counties.[106] The flowering of punk, in Belfast in particular, in the latter half of the 1970s represents one of the very few positive passages that can be salvaged from the wreckage of the Troubles. Those who recount time and again all the legendary gigs that took place in the Harp Bar are perhaps yearning for a certain lost moment in time, one very much removed from the high-octane consumerism of the 'new Belfast' symbolised by the Merchant Hotel that stands just around the corner from the repurposed site of the hallowed punk venue. This enduring nostalgia suggests a dark irony that we might wish to reflect upon here. While the Belfast punk scene explicitly set its face against the sectarian enmities that consumed the city at the time, the energy and sense of mission animating the subculture, ironically, presupposed the campaign of political violence against which many of its members railed. This peculiar symbiosis between Belfast punk and the Troubles is dutifully underlined by the writers of *Good Vibrations*. In the closing frames set at the ill-fated fundraiser in the Ulster Hall, Terri Hooley takes to the stage to try to explain the particular force and longevity of punk in the Northern Irish capital, proclaiming: 'New York has the haircuts, London has the trousers, but Belfast has the reason!'

The intimate association between Northern Irish punk and the Troubles reminds us that there is perhaps a certain subliminal darkness in cultural artefacts such as *Good Vibrations* that provide flattering retrospectives on the subculture. In the seemingly endless homages to the Belfast punk scene, there is a palpable yearning for a previous time of energy and authenticity, but that cherished moment is of course inextricably bound up with the political violence happening in the city at the time. What these breathless paeans to the subculture disclose then, perhaps, is a particular longing not just for the heady days of punk but also that frenetic period of conflict that gave the moment such vitality and meaning. Even in the frames of a film as ostensibly genial as *Good Vibrations*, there are occasional glimpses of a certain inchoate longing for Northern Ireland's troubled history. The montage of city-centre explosions that appears at the start of the film, for instance, is intended as a document of the dark days of the 1970s, but those images are curated so lovingly that it feels almost like a family album. Summoning the spectres of the past is always, of course, a perilous business and, as we shall see in due course, the thread of 'Troubles nostalgia' that runs so innocently through *Good Vibrations* finds other, rather more sinister expressions in the 'real world' of contemporary Northern Irish society.

'Don't let the Jaffa bastard hurt me!'

A rather gentler evocation of the dark days of the Troubles comes in the guise of the television series *Derry Girls*. Scripted by local writer Lisa McGee, the show has become an unlikely success with viewers across Britain and Ireland since its first broadcast in early 2018, drawing regular audiences of 2.5 million to make it the most watched programme on Channel Four in recent years.[107] The series follows the adventures of four mid-adolescent Catholic girls from Derry ('or Londonderry, depending on your persuasion'),[108] who are joined by a male relative from across the water ('the wee English fella') who is sent to their single-sex school for his own protection. Set in the mid-1990s, *Derry Girls* marks the key moments in the early stages of the Northern Ireland peace process, the time lovingly curated in period detail and the chart hits of the day. The success of the series has hinged largely on its use of a local sense of humour that is rather lighter than the pitch-black version favoured in Belfast and that calls to mind, a little too deliberately perhaps at times, the whimsical tone of another hit Channel Four comedy, *Father Ted*.

While the tone of the series is in the main light-hearted, it does from time to time have a real satirical edge. One episode pokes fun at the well-intentioned folly of some cross-community schemes, when an attempt to create an ecumenical dialogue between the girls' school and a local Protestant boys' equivalent at an outdoor pursuits centre descends into chaos. Prompted by an 'ice-breaking' exercise to list on a blackboard that which divides and unites them, the pupils gleefully fill the 'differences' column while the 'similarities' one remains glaringly empty. The exercise deteriorates from that point on and ends with the essentially good-natured Clare claiming that the Protestant boy feeding her rope as she abseils is trying to kill her, leading her to yell to her friends gathered below a request that may have required some explanation for viewers outside Northern Ireland: 'Don't let the Jaffa bastard hurt me!'[109] Another episode takes a swipe at the Home Office Order introduced in 1988 which meant that interviews with political figures deemed to be 'terrorists' or their fellow travellers could be broadcast only if their voices were dubbed by actors who often sounded uncannily like them. Watching Gerry Adams being ventriloquised thus on local television, the fantastically self-absorbed Aunt Sarah muses that the authorities will not allow the republican's own voice to be heard because a British audience would simply find it too seductive. The distinctive timbre of the then Sinn Féin President, she insists, makes him sound like a 'west Belfast Bond'. Perhaps the darkest moment of political satire to appear in *Derry Girls* comes in the pilot episode, in which the sweet-natured Clare is observing a 24-hour fast to raise funds to help an Ethiopian child. The rest of the girls seem entirely uninterested in this undertaking, with Erin in particular rather more concerned with persuading someone to accompany her to a gig that evening organised by an older boy on whom she has her eye. Exasperated at the constant pleading, the sharp-tongued Michelle gestures towards the increasingly famished Clare, before suggesting: 'bring Bobby Sands'. It is perhaps a testimony to the good will that the show has generated that this passing, mischievous reference to the dead hunger striker never even seemed likely to become a matter of public controversy.

The armed conflict that provides the backdrop to *Derry Girls* is in the main observed with a certain wry detachment. In the pilot episode of the programme, the extended family of the principal character Erin are gathered around the television on the first morning of the new school year, watching the news about a bomb scare that has led to the closure of one of the bridges across the River Foyle that divides the city in both geographical and sectarian terms. While for many people elsewhere this would be the source of some anxiety, the Quinn family seem to regard it as somewhere between a minor annoyance and an amusing distraction. There is speculation from several quarters that the girls will be unable to arrive on time for school as they will be required to take the 'long way round'. The response of Aunt Sarah is, inevitably, rather more solipsistic. In her trademark deadpan drawl, she expresses some concern that she may not make a midday appointment at a tanning salon on the other side of the river, moving her to issue the classic line: 'Well, I don't know about the rest of ya, but I'm not enjoying this bomb.' Moreover, the various protagonists in the conflict that feature from time to time in *Derry Girls* rarely appear to be especially menacing. In the episode where the girls and their families attempt to leave the city and head for Donegal in a vain attempt to avoid the Orange Order parades, it transpires that an IRA man has stowed himself away in the boot of one of their cars. As the discussion concerning whether they should allow him to remain there while they cross the border takes various twists, the paramilitary Emmett watches on with a bemused equanimity that was scarcely the trademark of republican volunteers while the Troubles raged. Furthermore, while British soldiers are routinely depicted patrolling the walled city of Derry, the girls at the centre of the drama no longer even seem to notice them. On one occasion, the school bus is stopped at a checkpoint and army personnel get on board to conduct a search. To the astonishment of the English character James, the girls barely seem to take any notice of the soldiers until his cousin, the sexually precocious Michelle, notes the transgressive appeal of finding a squaddie attractive and gestures to one of them while asking her friends: 'Do you think if I told him I'd an incendiary device down my knickers, he'd have a look?'

While *Derry Girls* is best known for its gentle, idiosyncratic comedy, at times the series also manages 'great poignancy'.[110] The occasional pathos that features in the programme is best illustrated in the episode that closes the first series. Here we see the adults in the Quinn family gathered once more around the television to hear a local broadcaster announce yet another atrocity. The news that twelve people are dead reduces all of them to stunned silence. The shock is even sufficient to persuade Granda Joe to call a momentary halt to his incessant haranguing of son-in-law Gerry for being from the 'Free State'. As the closing credits are about to roll, the patriarch approaches the southern Irish man and gently places a hand on his shoulder as they watch in mute disbelief. In the penultimate episode of the second series, we once again meet the Quinn adults circling the television, which has on this occasion stopped working. After carrying out a sequence of not terribly technical procedures, Gerry manages finally to coax the screen back into life just as the newscaster is announcing that the IRA have called a ceasefire, beginning at midnight. The news brings the Quinns out onto the street to celebrate the welcome news with their neighbours. Anybody who remembers the period could scarcely fail to be moved by the evocation here of that glorious, sun-blushed day in the late summer of 1994 when it seemed, finally, that the Troubles might just be drawing to a close.

At the heart of *Derry Girls* is a poignant depiction of a specific time and place drawn largely from the autobiographical detail of its writer. The pathos that is such an attribute of the series evokes not merely a particular passage in Northern Ireland's recent history but also the rich possibilities that seemed to exist at that moment. What *Derry Girls* captures well at times is the mood of optimism that was kindled as the peace process gained momentum during the 1990s.[111] That sense of possibility has of course been challenged and largely dissipated during the quarter-century that has elapsed since. In the episodes of *Derry Girls*, our minds are called back to a time when there seemed to be the prospect of a genuinely progressive future for Northern Ireland, one very far removed from the squalid corruption and sectarian squabbling that would come to define the era of restored devolved government in the region. The spectres that the programme conjures up, then, are not only those of a 'lost past' but also those of what often seems to be a 'lost future'.

While the gentle longing for a previous version of Northern Ireland that we find in *Derry Girls* appears entirely innocent, it is worth remembering that it may well be accompanied by an evil twin. As the Belfast novelist Glenn Patterson has noted,[112] there seems to persist in the region a certain 'Troubles nostalgia', even among some people fortunate enough not to remember that baleful period. One of those intent on staging a simulacrum of the Northern Irish conflict may well have been responsible for a tragic event that occurred within sight of the city walls that provides a dramatic backdrop for several scenes in *Derry Girls*. In April 2019, the final episode of the hugely successful second series of the programme aired on Channel Four. Later the same month, the emerging author and journalist Lyra McKee was killed by a stray round discharged as she watched rioting orchestrated by dissident republicans in the Creggan district of the city. McKee had written about the plight of the 'ceasefire babies' who had come of age after the conflict but were yet to reap the benefits of the peace process.[113] It may well have been another member of that same generation who was responsible for her death. While there has yet to be a prosecution arising from the murder, the prime suspect seems to be a male who was only 18 at the time of the incident.[114] The tragic early death of Lyra McKee provides an important reminder that nostalgia can at times assume a poisonous form, that those who are unwilling to 'give up the ghost' of a conflict that should really have been over a long time ago are capable of creating yet more spectres to haunt Northern Ireland.

Conclusion: *Lost Lives*

In their accomplished 2010 survey of the moving images that have sought to capture Northern Ireland during the peace process, McLaughlin and Baker contest that the 'new dispensation' in the region has 'quashed politically engaged film and television drama'.[115] That may well have been true of the often excruciating romantic comedies counselling Northern Irish audiences to leave the past behind that littered the opening decade after the GFA. It is, however, an accusation that could scarcely be levelled at the productions for both the big and small screen that have been released since. In the period since Paisley and McGuinness made the historic decision to share power, there has been a stream of movies and television programmes with a sharp political edge. Writers for both the big and small screen have with some regularity insisted that Northern Ireland remains haunted not only by the regressive past that the GFA was meant to draw to a close but also by the progressive future that the accord was meant to herald but now seems lost. And this 'hauntological' turn in the visual representation of the six counties shows little sign of abating. In October 2019, for instance, film-makers Michael Hewitt and Diarmuid Lavery released *Lost Lives*, a feature that blurs the boundaries between film and documentary and succeeds in the seemingly impossible task of translating into moving images the book of the same name which records all of those who died in the Northern Ireland conflict and stretches to 1,700 pages.[116] The film centres on eighteen of the fatalities in the conflict, with a string of renowned actors reading the relevant entries from the text over images that shift from the carnage of the Troubles to rather oblique images from both rural and urban landscapes. What the suitably elegiac tone of *Lost Lives* signals is the return of that which was only ever barely repressed during the often choreographed optimism that marked the early stages of the Northern Irish peace process. Like so many of the other genuinely haunting, and indeed haunted, features that have appeared since the devolved institutions were restored in 2007, the documentary issues a timely reminder that if the people of Northern Ireland are finally to face a genuinely peaceful political future they must find at last the means through which to acknowledge and exorcise the spectres of their violent recent past.

Notes

1 Here are a pair of advertisements that might be considered representative: one from *Discover Northern Ireland* (www.youtube.com/watch?v=KbctoBGog7I) and the other produced by *Belfast City Council* (www.youtube.com/watch?v=_Kpz6KGF1UE). Accessed 3 September 2020.
2 Stephen Baker, 'Tribeca Belfast and the On-Screen Regeneration of Northern Ireland', *International Journal of Media & Cultural Politics*, 16(1) (2020), 11–26.
3 Quoted in Susan McKay, *Bear in Mind These Dead* (London: Faber & Faber, 2008), p. 11.
4 Debbie Ging, *Men and Masculinities in Irish Cinema* (Basingstoke: Palgrave Macmillan, 2013), p. 132.
5 Greg McLaughlin and Stephen Baker, *The Propaganda of Peace: The Role of Media and Culture in the Northern Ireland Peace Process* (Bristol: Intellect Books, 2010), pp. 72, 83.
6 John Hill, *Cinema and Northern Ireland: Film, Culture and Politics* (London: British Film Institute, 2006), pp. 210, 230.
7 Ibid., p. 223.
8 McLaughlin and Baker, *Propaganda of Peace*, pp. 78–9; Stephen Baker, '"Victory doesn't always look the way other people imagine it": post-conflict

cinema in Northern Ireland', in Yannis Tzioumakis and Claire Molloy (eds), *The Routledge Companion to Cinema and Politics* (Abingdon: Routledge, 2016), pp. 175–85, p. 176.
9 Phil Ramsey, '"A Pleasingly Blank Canvas": Urban Regeneration in Northern Ireland and the Case of Titanic Quarter', *Space and Polity*, 17(2) (2013), 164–79, p. 165.
10 Martin McLoone, *Film, Media and Popular Culture in Ireland: Cityscapes, Landscapes, Soundscapes* (Dublin: Irish Academic Press, 2008), p. 52.
11 Declan Long, *Ghost-Haunted Land: Contemporary Art and Post-Troubles Northern Ireland* (Manchester: Manchester University Press, 2017), p. 31.
12 Ging, *Men and Masculinities in Irish Cinema*, p. 147.
13 McLoone, *Film, Media and Popular Culture in Ireland*, p. 63.
14 Ruth Barton, *Irish Cinema in the Twenty-First Century* (Manchester: Manchester University Press, 2019), pp. 142–3.
15 Colin Graham, '"Every Passer-by a Culprit?" Archive Fever, Photography and the Peace in Belfast', *Third Text*, 19(5) (September 2005), 567–80.
16 Long, *Ghost-Haunted Land*, pp. 20–1.
17 Ibid., p. 36.
18 Graham Dawson, *Making Peace with the Past? Memory, Trauma and the Irish Troubles* (Manchester: Manchester University Press, 2010), p. 14.
19 Ibid., p. 8.
20 Jacques Derrida, *Specters of Marx: The State of the Debt, the Work of Mourning and the New International* (Abingdon: Routledge, 1994), pp. xvii–xviii.
21 Mark Fisher, *Ghosts of My Life: Writings on Depression, Hauntology and Lost Futures* (Alresford: Zero Books, 2014).
22 Ibid., p. 6.
23 Ibid.
24 Ibid., p. 10.
25 Ibid., p. 9.
26 Derrida, *Specters of Marx*, p. 2.
27 Fisher, *Ghosts of My Life*, p. 18.
28 Ibid., pp. 22–5.
29 The lyric appears on the track 'Nostalgia' from the second Buzzcocks album *Love Bites* (United Artists, 1978).
30 John Lynch, '*Hunger*: Passion of the Militant', *Nordic Journal of English Studies*, 13(2) (2014), 184–201, p. 191.
31 Barton, *Irish Cinema in the Twenty-First Century*, p. 152.
32 Like so many things in the region, Northern Ireland's most infamous prison has two names. Originally called Long Kesh when it consisted of a series of Nissan huts dating from its time as a World War II air-force base, the prison was renamed Maze in the mid-1970s to mark its transition to the more regimented place of incarceration in which the hunger strikes would take place. Republicans tend to use the older name in order to resist the erasure of the prison's role in previous infamous moments such as the campaign of internment.

33 Lynch, 'Hunger', p. 194.
34 Alison Garden, 'Proving their "virility"? Steve McQueen's *Hunger* and transgressive masculinity', in Joel Gwynne (ed.), *Transgression in Anglo-American Cinema: Gender, Sex and the Deviant Body* (London: Wallflower Press, 2016), pp. 57–72, p. 59.
35 Ibid., p. 60.
36 George Legg, *Northern Ireland and the Politics of Boredom: Conflict, Capital and Culture* (Manchester: Manchester University Press, 2018), p. 171.
37 Eugene McNamee, 'Eye Witness – Memorialising Humanity in Steve McQueen's *Hunger*', *International Journal of Law in Context*, 5(3) (2009), 281–94, p. 288.
38 Ging, *Men and Masculinities in Irish Cinema*, p. 163.
39 Emilie Pine, 'Body of evidence: performing *Hunger*', in Conn Holohan and Tony Tracy (eds), *Masculinity and Irish Popular Culture: Tiger's Tales* (Basingstoke: Palgrave Macmillan, 2014), pp. 159–70, p. 163.
40 Comment made by the director Steve McQueen in a press release by Maple Pictures, 2008.
41 Adam Melvin, 'Sonic Motifs, Structure and Identity in Steve McQueen's *Hunger*', *Soundtrack*, 4(1) (2011), 23–32, p. 24.
42 Pine, 'Body of evidence', p. 164.
43 Ibid., p. 163.
44 McNamee, 'Eye Witness', p. 281.
45 Lynch, 'Hunger', p. 186.
46 Melvin, 'Sonic Motifs'.
47 Lynch, 'Hunger', p. 194.
48 McNamee, 'Eye Witness', p. 289.
49 Ging, *Men and Masculinities in Irish Cinema*, p. 150.
50 Chris Tookey, 'Hunger: more terrorist propaganda', *Daily Mail*, 30 October 2008. Available at: www.dailymail.co.uk/tvshowbiz/reviews/article-1081911/Hunger-More-pro-terrorist-propaganda.html. Accessed 13 September 2020.
51 Fintan O'Toole, 'Hunger fails to wrest the narrative from the hunger strikers', *Irish Times*, 22 November 2008. Available at: www.irishtimes.com/news/hunger-fails-to-wrest-the-narrative-from-the-hunger-strikers-1.913725. Accessed 10 September 2020.
52 Cillian McGrattan, *Memory, Politics and Identity: Haunted by History* (Basingstoke: Palgrave, 2013), p. 88.
53 Ibid., p. 96.
54 Lynch, 'Hunger', p. 102.
55 Rebecca Graff-McRae, 'Fiction, Encryption, and Contradiction: Remediation and Remembrance of the 1981 Hunger Strikes', *Nordic Irish Studies*, 13(1) (2014), 19–39, p. 26.
56 Gary Crowdus, 'The Human Body as Political Weapon: An Interview with Steve McQueen', *Cineaste* (Spring 2009), 22–5.
57 Daniel Finn, *One Man's Terrorist: A Political History of the IRA* (London: Verso, 2019), p. 207.

58 McKay, *Bear in Mind These Dead*, p. 320. The references here are to the first two men to die in the 1981 hunger strike: Bobby Sands, who, tellingly, requires no surname, and Francis Hughes. The two female republicans mentioned are Mairead Farrell, killed by British undercover soldiers in Gibraltar in 1988 while on active service but unarmed at the time, and Maire Drumm, the former Vice-President of Sinn Féin, who was murdered in her hospital bed by loyalists in 1976.
59 Allen Feldman, *Formations of Violence: The Narrative of the Body and Political Terror in Northern Ireland* (Chicago, MI: University of Chicago Press, 1991), p. 242.
60 Ibid., p. 215.
61 Ibid., p. 254.
62 McKay, *Bear in Mind These Dead*, p. 319.
63 Legg, *Northern Ireland*, p. 176.
64 Ibid., p. 62.
65 McKay, *Bear in Mind These Dead*, p. 319.
66 Legg, *Northern Ireland*, p. 176.
67 Thomas Hennessey, *Hunger Strike: Margaret Thatcher's Battle with the IRA: 1980–1981* (Sallins: Irish Academic Press, 2014), pp. 463–4); Richard O'Rawe, *Blanketmen: An Untold Story of the H-Block Hunger Strike* (Dublin: New Island, 2005).
68 Colin Coulter, 'Northern Ireland's Elusive Peace Dividend: Neoliberalism, Austerity and the Politics of Class', *Capital & Class*, 43(1) (2019), 123–38.
69 McLoone, *Film, Media and Popular Culture in Ireland*, p. 217.
70 Jon Tonge, *Northern Ireland* (Cambridge: Polity Press, 2006), pp. 72–3.
71 Barton, *Irish Cinema in the Twenty-First Century*, p. 157.
72 Long, *Ghost-Haunted Land*, p. 3.
73 Marie-Therese Fay, Mike Morrissey and Marie Smyth, *Northern Ireland's Troubles: The Human Costs* (London: Pluto Press, 1999), p. 169.
74 Ibid., p. 159.
75 The bombing of McGurk's Bar in the republican New Lodge district by loyalist paramilitaries in December 1971 caused the deaths of fifteen civilians, including two children. The bomb attack by republicans on the Bayardo Bar in the loyalist Shankill neighbourhood in August 1975 resulted in the deaths of four civilians and one loyalist paramilitary.
76 Barton, *Irish Cinema in the Twenty-First Century*, p. 157.
77 Thomas Hennessy and Claire Thomas, *Spooks: The Unofficial History of MI5 from Agent Zigzag to the D-Day Deception 1939–45* (Stroud: Amberley Publishing, 2011).
78 Rosie Cowan, 'He did the IRA's dirty work for 25 years – and was paid £80,000 a year by the government', *Guardian*, 12 May 2003. Available at: www.theguardian.com/uk/2003/may/12/northernireland.northernireland1. Accessed 12 September 2020.
79 Anne Cadwallader, *Lethal Allies: British Collusion in Ireland* (Blackrock: Mercier Press, 2013).

80 Caroline Magennis, '"That's not so comfortable for you, is it?": The spectre of misogyny in *The Fall*', in Fionnuala Dillane, Naomi McAreavey and Emilie Pine (eds), *The Body in Pain in Irish Literature and Culture* (London Palgrave Macmillan, 2016), pp. 217–34, p. 217.
81 Ipek A Celik Rappas, 'From *Titanic* to *Game of Thrones*: Promoting Belfast as a Global Media Capital', *Media, Culture & Society*, 41(4) (2019), 539–56, p. 541.
82 Magennis, '"That's not so comfortable for you, is it?"', p. 224.
83 Ibid., pp. 217–18.
84 Hill, *Cinema and Northern Ireland*, p. 191.
85 Matthew Brown, 'Cities under Watch: Urban Northern Ireland in Film', *Éire-Ireland*, 45(1&2) (Earrach/Samhradh/Spring/Summer 2010), 56–88, p. 59.
86 McLoone, *Film, Media and Popular Culture in Ireland*, p. 58.
87 Ibid.; Lindsay Steenberg, '*The Fall* and Television Noir', *Television & New Media*, 18(1) (2017), 58–75, p. 67.
88 Robert Moore, 'Rebranding Belfast: Chromatopes of Post-Conflict', *Signs and Society*, 4(S1) (Supplement 2016), 138–62.
89 Stephen Baker, 'Tribeca Belfast and the On-Screen Regeneration of Northern Ireland', *International Journal of Media & Cultural Politics*, 16(1) (2020), 11–26.
90 Ibid.
91 Steenberg, '*The Fall* and Television Noir', p. 60.
92 Magennis, '"That's not so comfortable for you, is it?"', p. 219.
93 Ibid.
94 Allen Feldman, 'Political Terror and the Technologies of Memory: Excuse, Sacrifice, Commodification, and Actuarial Moralities', *Radical History Review*, 85 (Winter 2003), 58–73, p. 64.
95 Magennis, '"That's not so comfortable for you, is it?"', p. 230.
96 Ibid., p. 229.
97 The full report of the Inquiry is available at: www.hiainquiry.org/historical-institutional-abuse-inquiry-report-chapters. Accessed 7 January 2021.
98 The phrase comes of course from Aleksandr Solzhenitsyn's famous indictment of the constellation of incarceration camps constructed in the Stalin era.
99 The same could also be said of any year in that decade, and, indeed, the one that followed. While 1979 was most certainly a 'bad year' there were in fact six others in the 1970s where the death toll was higher. Fay et al., *Northern Ireland's Troubles*, p. 137.
100 Magennis, '"That's not so comfortable for you, is it?"', p. 220; Steenberg, '*The Fall* and Television Noir', p. 65.
101 Magennis, '"That's not so comfortable for you, is it?"', p. 231.
102 Police Service of Northern Ireland, *Domestic Abuse Incidents and Crimes Recorded by the Police in Northern Ireland: Update to 30 June 2020* (Belfast: PSNI, 2020).
103 Fisher, *Ghosts of My Life*, p. 8.
104 Barton, *Irish Cinema in the Twenty-First Century*, p. 158.

105 Colin Coulter, 'Working for the clampdown: an introduction', in Colin Coulter (ed.), *Working for the Clampdown: The Clash, the Dawn of Neoliberalism and the Political Promise of Punk* (Manchester: Manchester University Press, 2019), pp. 2–3.
106 Martin McLoone, 'Punk Music in Northern Ireland: The Political Power of "What Might Have Been"', *Irish Studies Review*, 12(1) (2004), 29–38; Sean Campbell and Gerry Smyth, 'From shellshock rock to ceasefire sounds: popular music', in Colin Coulter and Michael Murray (eds), *Northern Ireland after the Troubles: A Society in Transition* (Manchester: Manchester University Press, 2008), pp. 232–52.
107 Oonagh Murphy and Laura Aguiar, 'When a 1981 Diary Meets Twitter: Reclaiming a Teenage Girl's Ordinary Experience of the Northern Irish Troubles', *British Journal for Military History*, 5(1) (2019), 49–70, p. 52.
108 Shilpa Ganatra, 'How Derry Girls became an instant sitcom classic', *The Guardian*, 13 February 2018. Available at: www.theguardian.com/tv-and-radio/2018/feb/13/derry-girls-instant-sitcom-classic-schoolgirls-northern-ireland. Accessed 14 September 2020.
109 The 'Jaffa' is a variety of orange, the colour closely associated with the marching traditions of Northern Irish Protestants. The term is hence used as slang to designate someone from the unionist community.
110 Susan McKay, 'The fabulous, feral Derry Girls are the new emblems of Northern Ireland', *The Guardian*, 6 March 2019. Available at: www.theguardian.com/commentisfree/2019/mar/06/derry-girls-tv-northern-ireland-emblems-troubles. Accessed 12 January 2020.
111 Frank Ferguson, 'Home to a Ghost: Ulster-Scots Language and Vernacular in Northern Irish Culture since the Good Friday Agreement', *Przegląd Kulturoznawczy*, 3(37) (2018), 335–47, p. 345.
112 Glenn Patterson, *Backstop Land* (London: Head of Zeus, 2019), pp. 102–4.
113 Murphy and Aguiar, 'When a 1981 Diary Meets Twitter', p. 55; Baker, 'Tribeca Belfast and the On-Screen Regeneration of Northern Ireland'.
114 Ciaran Barnes, 'Lyra McKee murder suspect set to be a dad – teen's baby conceived same week of fatal shooting', *Belfast Telegraph*, 12 August 2019. Available at: www.belfasttelegraph.co.uk/sunday-life/lyra-mckee-murder-suspect-set-to-be-a-dad-teens-baby-conceived-same-week-of-fatal-shooting-38391721.html. Accessed 15 September 2020.
115 McLaughlin and Baker, *Propaganda of Peace*, p. 96.
116 David McKittrick, Seamus Kelters, Brian Feeney, Chris Thornton and David McVea, *Lost Lives: The Stories of the Men, Women and Children Who Died as a Result of the Northern Ireland Troubles* (Edinburgh: Mainstream, 1999).

5

More than two communities: those who are both, neither, other, and next

Different types of differences

Northern Ireland was created in full knowledge of the fact that it would please no one absolutely and displease many people very deeply. Predictably, therefore, Northern Ireland is not a society at ease with itself. The unease that all citizens have in Northern Ireland is primarily centred on its place in the Union of the UK, with some feeling that the Union is too loose and others feeling that it is too close. This means that the grounds on which its democratic system is built are fundamentally unsure. The 1998 Agreement sought to create the basis for peaceful democratic politics by removing the 'existential' things which would have been seen as turning unease into dangerous fear or a sense of being under threat. The principle of majority consent, for example, and the three levels or 'strands' of cooperation in the Good Friday Agreement (hereafter GFA) attempted to create the conditions for fostering essential levels of trust and cooperation between elected representatives.[1] Despite recognising the discomfort of the demos in Northern Ireland, the GFA did not seek to create a new common culture. In a 'normal' democratic society, legitimacy and stability are conferred on a political system by its shared civic culture. The 1998 Agreement approached Northern Ireland as being without such an attribute. Instead, it sought to give parity to different political aspirations and cultural values in Northern Ireland. This is primarily because it holds Northern Ireland to be a society divided by a binary. The GFA does not mention Catholicism or Protestantism, nor does it explicitly reference unionism and nationalism. Instead, it rather coyly refers to 'both communities' or 'two traditions'. This is typically summarised as Protestant/unionist/British and Catholic/nationalist/Irish – as if it is a society split in two, with labels on either side being pretty much interchangeable. In so doing, however, it has allowed us to become neglectful of three things: the differences *within* these blocs, the interconnections *between* them, and the growing proportion of the population who *do not identify* with one or more of the categories they are assumed to fit. A whole generation on from the GFA, it is worth asking whether the future of society in the region will be increasingly experienced and understood in terms of these differences and nonconformities rather than by 'the divide'.

This chapter thus considers the evidence for what Paul Nolan[2] has described as 'the society of minorities'. He argued that there are no overarching majorities, nor indeed stark binaries in Northern Ireland, but instead there are plenty of blurred lines and even common ground. In order to put this to the test, it is worth differentiating between the various categories of identity that are significant here. This can be seen in part through time series data on public attitudes as revealed through the Northern Ireland Life and Times (NILT) Survey conducted by ARK ('Access Research Knowledge' hub, Queen's University Belfast and Ulster University), and also through the Northern Ireland General Election Surveys led by the University of Liverpool since 2010. These data reveal a growing cohort of those who are non-aligned politically, those who are of no religion, those who have dual nationality, and those who were born outside Northern Ireland. They also show a fairly stark generational divide in terms of attitudes and political identities and engagement. In order to assess the significance of these groups who disrupt the 'two communities' thesis, we need to be able to measure identity change in a divided society.

Identities in Northern Ireland

John Coakley provides a helpful typology for assessing attitudinal change which is useful for the purposes of this chapter.[3] He explains that there are three levels in the process of identity formation: the factors which form our background but which we cannot choose as a rule; those which we can choose; and those which are key to the socio-political environment. In the first category comes religious denomination (which in turn is seen to determine which 'community' one is from) and ethnicity.[4] The second is about citizenship and national identity, plus the marker of communal identity which is quite distinct to Northern Ireland, i.e. unionist and nationalist. The third, which is most clearly an 'elective' identity, but which is often treated as indistinct from an 'ascribed' identity, is that relating to an individual's constitutional and political preference, as well as party support. Coakley points out that it is important to make these distinctions between the levels of identity categories because there are fewer people who describe themselves as 'unionist' than those whose preference is for Northern Ireland to remain in the Union.[5] What this chapter explores is not so much the change within these categories but the change between them, i.e. that identity formation in Northern Ireland is more fluid than it has been in the past.

Even with this distinction between the given, the inherited and the chosen aspects of identity, conceptualising identity change is still difficult. Most scholarly literature has focused on classification or categories, not least because in some ways it is easier to analyse the boundaries and lines of distinction than what they separate.[6] In practice, of course, the categories and the meaning they hold are inseparable. This is particularly true in divided societies, or in cases of social conflict. Studies have shown that conflict 'hardens' identity structures because those same structures give people psychological comfort.[7] In situations of peace, even though personal and national identities can remain very much entwined (sometimes necessarily so in the case of consociational models), change in these identities can occur more easily.[8] Jennifer Todd's work has illuminated how the categories of significance in Northern Ireland (e.g. religious community, national identity, constitutional preference) are understood and how they change over time, not least through the ways in which 'individuals transform these composite divisions from within'.[9] As such, one can be Protestant, but what that means in practice can be determined by the individual. Todd's work thus brings agency back into discussions of identity in contemporary Northern Ireland, in particular through what she refers to as 'identity innovation'.[10]

What we can learn from this is that identity change is not something that can be directed from the top down. Categories of identity can continue to be used and applied by the state, but their 'meaning, permeability and salience' can be transformed from the ground up.[11] Furthermore, individuals can together form new spaces in which 'identity innovation' can develop. This will not only happen through greater official recognition of the limitations of the traditional categories but also through more expansive recognition of the emergence of new ones. At the moment, many of these new categories are by default simply 'other' than the long-established ones. Drawing on Coakley's typology, we look now at the data to show trends towards change in and between identity categories in contemporary Northern Ireland. This chapter thus constitutes an overview of identity and attitudinal change in relation to religious, national, ethnic, political and generational categories in post-Agreement Northern Ireland. It concludes by considering the longer-term implications of the consistent patterns in identity formation, as well as the trends of change.

Religious identities: Catholic, Protestant, other and none

Why religious identity is important

Under the first layer of identity formation that Coakley outlined, religious background is a vitally important category in Northern Ireland. There are five broad reasons for this which generally hold true. The first is that people cannot choose which religion they are brought up in – this is something determined by their parents or guardians, and thus seen as being a type of identity that is inherited from generation to generation. Furthermore, religious identity is not merely about a personal faith or even about deeply held values. Religious identification means far more than a demonstration of theological subscription. Religious upbringing also provides a 'world-view', a 'grand narrative' of the world which seeks to explain and guide through the greatest questions of life, including political and social ones. Thirdly, related to this, religion does not simply mark boundaries between communities, but also gives substantive meaning to them by offering a repertoire of common ideas, images and values. Thus, even if they are not observant, individuals' religious beliefs can form a type of cultural memory that can become reconstructed in new social forms.[12] Fourthly, religious upbringing brings a form of socialisation, including directly through institutions (e.g. schools and youth groups as well as churches) that are the most influential on the development of an individual as a social being. And last, but not least, religious background also brings with it a close connection to other people and some of the most marked experiences of 'community'. In sum, religion offers ritual, routine and support networks as well as shared values and practices.

Placing all such influences in the context of Northern Ireland, one can see how important religious background is in identity formation. As well as being soaked through with what Davie referred to as 'vicarious religion' (as in prayers at the start of business in the Northern Ireland Assembly, or the prevalence of clergy delivering the 'thought for the day' on Radio Ulster's flagship morning programme),[13] the close relationship between religion and social structures in Northern Ireland is intrinsically connected to the wider political sphere. Protestantism as an identity (if not an ideology) took on a weighty significance as a result of the state-building practices led by unionists in Northern Ireland in the mid-twentieth century.[14] Boundaries between communities in terms of cultural values, norms and habitus became effectively institutionalised. John Whyte went so far as to claim that religion thus became the basis of separate social structures that keep communities apart in Northern Ireland, citing the example of education as illustrating this.[15] And in a society in which religious observance is still high, religion remains a crucial dimension of identity and community. Churches and associated networks continue to be important in building and sustaining identity and community, in both urban and rural settings. This can be seen in very positive terms, both in terms of social bonding and community cohesion that it offers,[16] and in terms of churches' contribution to wider community and peace-building work.[17] But it has also been viewed in negative terms too. John Fulton, for instance, argued that in some respects the churches 'work together' with the political parties and the two states to keep people divided and thus maintain their power.[18]

For these reasons, there have been strong arguments made to interpret religion as, much more than an 'ethnic marker' or mere label to separate groups, something that is actively used to construct ethnic identity itself. Mitchell described this in terms of the way that 'them' and 'us' distinctions between Catholics and Protestants were brought into explaining personal identities and implicitly justifying political-cultural prejudice.[19] Mitchell's work showing that these views were largely held by those of various ages and of differing degrees of religiosity served to illuminate the claim that 'Catholic' and 'Protestant' is far more than a denominational or ecclesiastical distinction.[20] Added to this, the intergenerational transfer of religious practice in Northern Ireland has no doubt been given a greater significance in light of the history of conflict and segregation. This suggests that the process of secularisation in Northern Ireland is far more complicated than elsewhere. It simply cannot be the case that religion becomes 'epiphenomenal' in this context.[21] Nevertheless, the *social* significance of religious identities can change, and this is in part as a consequence of what these categories are seen to be secondary markers for.

Changing religious identities in Northern Ireland

Northern Ireland remains one of the most religious societies in Western Europe. According to Eurobarometer surveys, while 11 per cent in Britain describe themselves as being highly religious (making it one of the least religious countries in Europe), 24 per cent of adults in Ireland are 'highly religious'.[22] The 2019 NILT Survey shows 25 per cent of respondents indicating that they are highly religiously observant, i.e. they attend a religious service at least once a week. A closer look at these data shows that there are no significant differences between Catholics and Protestants or men and women in this regard, but age is a considerable variable, with only 8 per cent of 18–24-year-olds being highly religious compared to 40 per cent of those over 65.[23] So if the intensity of religious observance is so much weaker among the younger generation, what does this mean for the pertinence of religious identity categories in the future? Fundamentally, the answer rests in the apparent validity of the use of the two community labels, i.e. Catholic and Protestant.

Certainly, there has been a significant change in the relative sizes of these two communities over the course of Northern Ireland's history. By bringing together a diversity of Christian denominations under the heading 'Protestant', we see that, from a 2:1 ratio of Protestant to Catholic when partition took place, the size of the two communities is now about equal.[24] The 2011 census found the population of Northern Ireland to be 40.8 per cent Catholic, 41.6 per cent Protestant, 16.9 per cent none/none stated and 0.8 per cent 'other religion'.[25] What this shows is that around one in five residents in Northern Ireland identify as being *neither* Catholic nor Protestant. To put this in context, the 2011 census for England and Wales had 32.3 per cent and Scotland 43.7 per cent either saying they had 'no religion' or not answering the question (see Figure 5.8).[26]

In Northern Ireland, if any person ticks the 'None' box in response to the question of religious belonging, they have to answer a compulsory question about what religious denomination they were 'brought up in'. Bringing together the data from the two questions, the results in 2011 were that 45.1 per cent were brought up Catholic, 48.4 per cent were brought up Protestant and 0.9 per cent were brought up in an 'other' religion, with only 5.6 per cent being brought up in no religion. From this, we can see that those raised in a Protestant denomination have been more likely than those who grew up Catholic not to continue to identify as religious. Added to the trends of demographic change, the anticipation is that those identifying as Catholic will outnumber those identifying as Protestant by the time of the 2021 census. This is not occurring so much through differential birth rates as higher emigration rates for Protestants;[27] but it is increasingly affected by the growing number of those choosing to disavow any religious identity or affiliation. The NILT surveys have found a steady growth in those identifying as being of 'no religion' over time. This has risen from 9 per cent in 1998, to 13 per cent in 2008, to 20 per cent in 2018. If we look at the age profile of those who describe themselves in this way, the 2019 NILT Survey data indicate that a quarter of those under the age of 24 describe themselves as having no religion, and 37 per cent of those aged 25–34. It is much less common among those over the age of 55.[28] Data from the Labour Force Survey also show that younger people are much more likely to describe themselves as having no religious affiliation (see Figure 5.1).[29]

So, the proportion of the population in Northern Ireland who describe themselves as of no religion is growing; but even more significant in terms of changing significance of religious identity is the fact that, among those who do decide to identify with a religious denomination, there is a growing number who tend not to practise that religion frequently. Indeed, there has

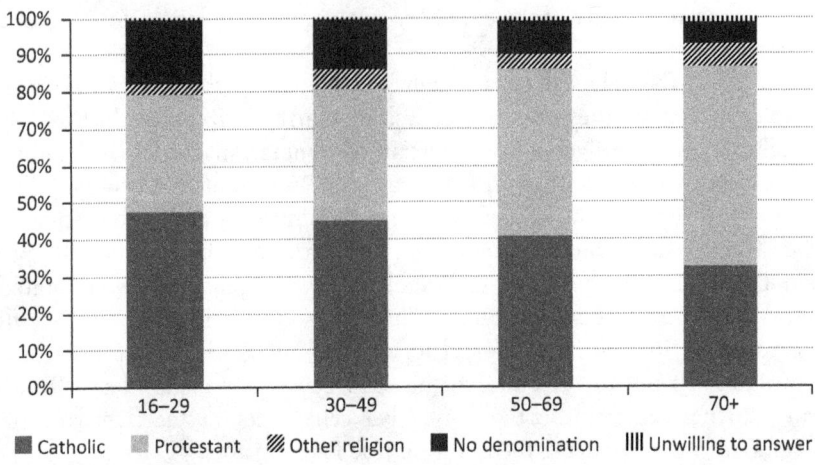

Figure 5.1 Religious identification by age group

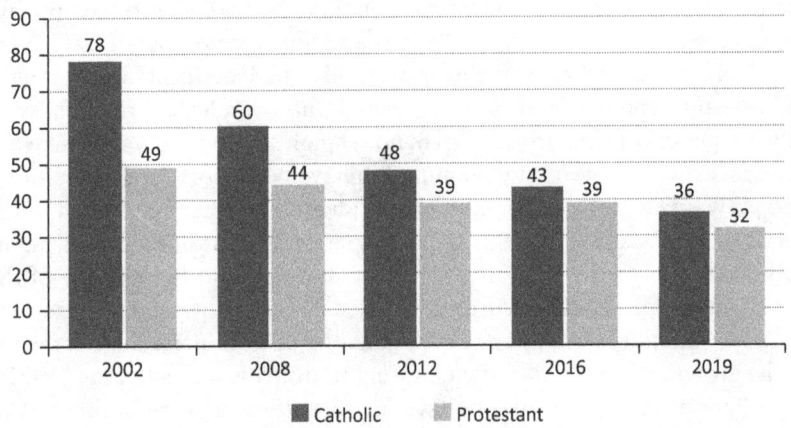

Figure 5.2 Regular church attendance (% attending 2+ times per month)

also been a fairly steady decline in religious observance – and a decline that has happened most sharply among Catholics since the mid-2000s (see Figure 5.2). From 2002 to 2018, the percentage of Catholics who attend mass at least twice a month has halved, whereas the proportion of Protestants who are religiously observant (by these terms) has fallen less sharply, albeit from a lower starting point. What this means is that, while at the turn of the century the Catholic Church could have claimed that 4 out of 5 members of its flock were religiously observant, this is now just 2 out of 5. And, in the same time period, Protestant churches have seen the religiously observant fall from a half to a third of those who claim a Protestant affiliation. As noted above, religious observance is about far more than theological or spiritual matters but also about community bonds, social capital, socialisation and institutional influence. With more people claiming a religious identity than are actively practising it, the social meaning of what it is to be Protestant or Catholic will inevitably evolve.

The generational aspect to the trend of non-observance is significant. According to the 2019 NILT Survey, 12 per cent of those over the age of 65 never go to church and 40 per cent attend at least once per week; in contrast, 22 per cent of adults under the age of 24 never go and only 8 per cent attend at least weekly.[30] The figures of religious observance for young adults in Northern Ireland are still very high, however, when compared to the rest of the UK. This is in part because religious observance, as well as nominal belonging, has historically been higher in Northern Ireland. Looking ahead, however, this would indicate a trend that will have a cumulative effect. Evidence from the British Household Panel Survey and the British Social Attitudes surveys suggests that religious belief does erode at the same rate as religious affiliation and attendance.[31] And this decline is generational. Analysis of the rates at which religion is transmitted from parents to children suggests that absence of religion is almost always passed on, whereas in Britain only about half of parental religiosity is successfully transmitted.[32] If, looking at generational trends, both religious practice and the compulsion towards nominal belonging is diminishing, as it appears to be, what does this mean for Northern Irish society?

Are there common traits and attitudes among those of no religion?

In order to assess the significance of the growing proportion of those who tick the box of 'no religion', it is worth analysing their answers to questions on three other key identifying categories: national identity, constitutional preference and political identity. First, in terms of national identity, we can see that almost equal proportions of Catholics and Protestants say that they hold exclusively Irish and British identities, respectively (Figure 5.3). And there are similar patterns among those who do have religious identities in terms of the mixing of Irish and British identities. However, those who are of no religion are more likely than Catholics or Protestants to describe themselves as having a national identity *other* than British and Irish. Furthermore, they are less likely to hold exclusively British or Irish identities and more likely to have mixed identities, including equally British and Irish identities.

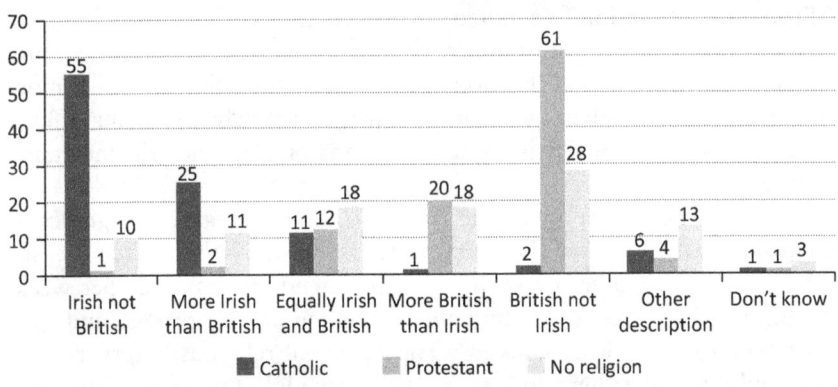

Figure 5.3 National identity and religion (%)

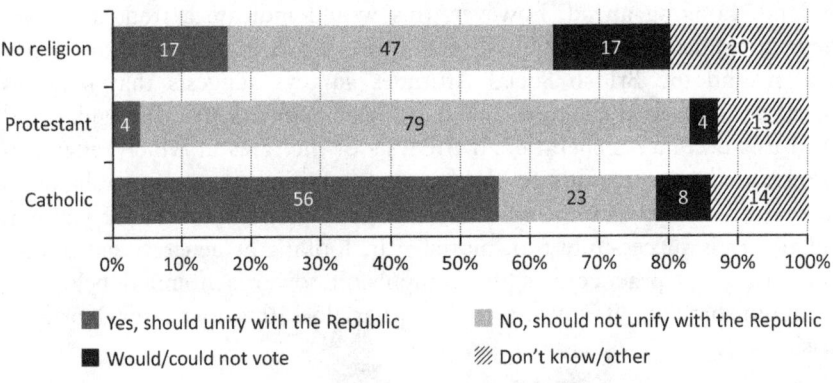

Figure 5.4 Intention to vote in a referendum on Irish unification, by religion

Another category of interest is that of constitutional preference. When it comes to the question of voting in a border poll, we can see that those who are of no religion are halfway between Catholics and Protestants in their favour for remaining in the UK (Figure 5.4). In figures borne out by the 2019 NI General Election Survey, those of no religion are twice as likely to support the Union as to support Irish unification.[33] The most striking finding from this is that 1 in 5 of them say that they would not vote at all. This indicates that those of no religion tend to be in favour of the Union but are also more likely to be keen to actively disassociate themselves from a political question that appears to be divisive. Those of no religion in Northern Ireland, therefore, are not merely indecisive or even reticent (as seen in the fact they are slightly more likely than Catholics to say they don't know how they would vote in a border poll). Indeed, we can assume that some may see the decision not to vote in such a poll as being not an omission but a positive act.

Views on unionism and nationalism by religious identity

Such a position comes in the context of what appears to be steadily growing polarisation among Catholics and Protestants. The NI General Election Surveys indicate that between 2010 and 2019 the share of Protestants who support remaining in the Union grew from 90.3 per cent to 94.5 per cent (notably higher figures than in NILT surveys). In the same period, the share of Catholics who support remaining in the UK declined (from 17.8 per cent to 13.6 per cent – notably lower figures than in NILT surveys).[34] The University of Liverpool NI General Election Survey 2019 found that almost two-thirds of those who do not indicate a preference regarding Northern Ireland's long-term constitutional future are Catholics.[35] This indicates that if there is any shift in their position in either direction, they would have a significant impact upon the results of any future referendum on Irish unification. John Coakley has also noted that 'divided political preferences on the Catholic side contrast with the much more substantial consensus on the Protestant side, stable over time, in favour of the Union'.[36] But he warns against consequently discounting the prospect of a majority for unification. This is because, as he put it, '"soft" Catholic support for the Union, as expressed in recent surveys, might in certain circumstances be converted into "soft" Catholic support for Irish unity'.[37] This, of course, depends on political circumstances. But it also depends on the comfort that people have in certain communal affiliations. And evidence would indicate that it is important to distinguish between these identities and political preferences, as we move on to show now.

While recognising the limitations of quantitative data, as well as the fact they were gathered at a time of political flux across the UK arising from Brexit, NILT Survey findings in 2019 (Figure 5.4) indicate that over half of Catholic respondents would vote for a united Ireland if a border poll were held 'tomorrow' and a nearly a quarter would vote to remain in the UK (i.e. the unionist position). That said, it is quite clear that Catholics are as loath to describe themselves as unionist as Protestants are to self-identify as nationalist, as we can see from Figure 5.5.

As Coakley noted, no community is 'a monolith in its identity patterns and fundamental political priorities, but the Catholic community is more divided in these respects than the Protestant community'. He attributes this to 'the attraction of the existing power structure to sections of an historically subordinate community' being greater than 'the attraction of disrupting the status quo' among the community that has been 'historically dominant'.[38] Coakley further notes that

> At the level of communal affiliation, there is no cross-over between the two sides (virtually no Protestant 'nationalists' or Catholic 'unionists'),

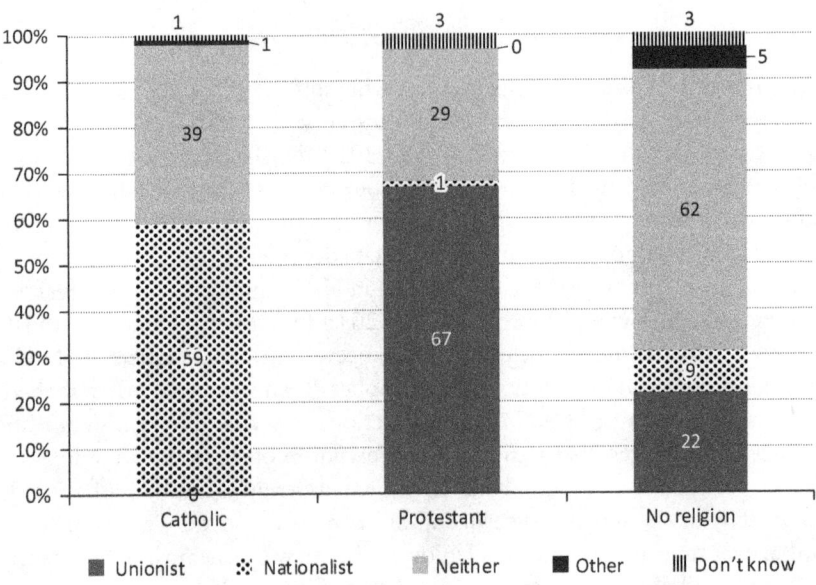

Figure 5.5 Political identity and religious identity

but a significant group within each community refuses to align itself with either label.[39]

To interrogate this a little further, analysis of NILT survey data shows a strong correlation between a clear political ambition for Irish unity and the description of 'nationalist'. Catholics who describe themselves as 'nationalist' tend to subscribe to the tenets of Irish nationalism, i.e. a desire for Irish unity. 'Nationalist' has connotations of in-group identity beyond politics that is important for many Catholics. However, so too does the label of 'unionist'. Thus, although 1 in 4 said they would vote for Northern Ireland to remain in the UK, it is extremely rare for Catholics to feel comfortable describing themselves as 'unionist' (none did so in the 2018 or 2019 NILT surveys, for example).[40] This suggests a toxicity of the label of 'unionist' for Catholics that is a mirror image of the feeling among Protestants for the label of 'nationalist'. But it is worth noting that the label of 'unionist' is also uncomfortable for some Protestants too, including those who hold pro-union preferences. This is despite the fact that there is, overall, more consensus among Protestants about their preferred political outcome, i.e. remaining in the Union, and about their political identity. While 87 per cent of Protestant respondents in the 2019 NILT Survey said that they would like Northern Ireland to remain in the UK, only two-thirds described themselves as unionist.[41] What about those of no religion? Compared against their stated constitutional preferences, we see that both the labels of unionist and nationalist are uncomfortable for many of this cohort. Only half of those of no religion who want to see a united Ireland would describe themselves as 'nationalist', and substantially less than half of those who hold pro-Union views describe themselves as 'unionist'.[42] Those of no religion seem mostly to seek to disavow labels altogether.

To designate as neither unionist nor nationalist is a popular choice among those of no religion, but it is also used by both Catholics and Protestants who don't know how or, indeed, whether they would vote in a border poll. In sum, we see that the label of 'neither' (rather than 'other') is chosen by both Catholics and Protestants and those of no religion who would like to see a continuation of the Union but who reject the identity of 'unionist'. To put it a different way: the label 'unionist' can be uncomfortable for people of all religious identities (including Protestants) who subscribe to the principal tenet of unionism. Secondly, the identity of neither unionist nor nationalist is used by 'undecideds' (Catholic, Protestant and no religion) who do not know how, or even whether, they would vote in a border poll. The data also suggest that there are differences in the way that the terms 'nationalist' and 'unionist' are conceived among Catholics and Protestants, respectively. Together, this would imply that the associations and implications of the terms 'unionist' and 'nationalist' are highly significant beyond the political ideologies and preferences they represent. More broadly, with the steady growth of those saying they are of no religion, particularly among the younger generation, there is a desire to actively disassociate with divisive labels and positions altogether. This brief discussion highlights the problems of assuming the sustained existence of a Protestant/unionist bloc in sharp distinction from a Catholic/nationalist one. Instead, the identities of Protestant and Catholic continue to be important to the majority of individuals but, in reality, they are increasingly difficult to associate with either a clear religious influence/observance or with a strong constitutional preference or political identity. At the same time, there is a growing confidence among the under-45s when it comes to rejecting what are seen as 'divisive' or conflictual identities, including those of religious denomination.

National identities: British, Irish or both?

The birthright to choose

The second level of identity formation that Coakley notes as being of critical importance in Northern Ireland is that of national identity. This has unique significance in Northern Ireland because, as noted above, recognising the equality, legitimacy and validity of both British and Irish identities in Northern Ireland is core to the post-Agreement order. In particular, it formalised the 'birthright of all the people of Northern Ireland to identify themselves and be accepted as Irish or British, or both, as they may so choose'. Indeed, the fact that those born in Northern Ireland can *choose* to be 'British, Irish or both' is fascinating; both British and Irish identity in Northern Ireland are recognised as simultaneously given and elective. In many ways, this is a natural follow-on from the fact that, in Northern Ireland, those traits associated with national identity (language, territory, history, culture) have been so intrinsically shaped by both Britain and Ireland. One of the greatest achievements of the 1998 Agreement was to turn Northern Ireland's existence from being a point at which the identities and histories of Britain and Ireland clash most violently into a society in which these identities can be (at least theoretically) held together as complementary.

In post-Agreement Northern Ireland, in the context of EU membership and the Common Travel Area, the choice to identify as British or Irish or both was primarily one of personal identity and cultural preference. In real terms, there was not a great deal of difference between the two citizenships in Northern Ireland. The choice to be both – in the sense of holding two passports – had not been taken up in great numbers in Northern Ireland in formal terms (standing at less than 2 per cent in the 2011 census). This has changed considerably in the context of Brexit (as is discussed in more detail in the final chapter of this book). For the purposes of this chapter, we want to analyse not so much the citizenship or the rights of those holding British and/or Irish identities but rather what the patterns of this identification are. In particular, we are interested in those who see their Britishness and Irishness as equal and as complementary. Are the British-Irish or Irish-British more likely to come from a particular religious background or to be unionist or nationalist? Digging further into this, we analyse studies of those who self-identify as having a 'Northern Irish' identity to see whether this holds any particular socio-political significance, and whether it can be seen to be a group sharing common characteristics or whether 'Northern Irish' means different things to different people.

A closer look at those who are 'both' British and Irish

We can see from NILT Survey data that a spread and a combination of Irish and British identities is well established in Northern Ireland (see Figure 5.6). More generally, it is more common for people in Northern Ireland to describe themselves in terms of being 'both' British and Irish to varying

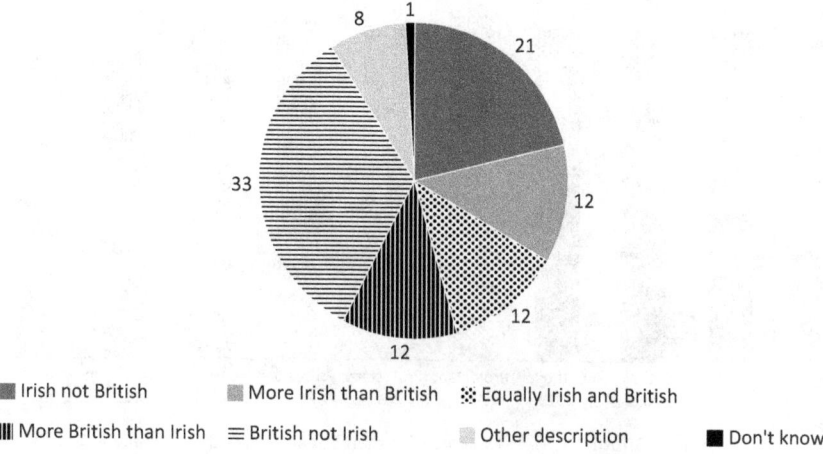

Figure 5.6 Do you see yourself as British or Irish? (%)

degrees (approximately 4 in 10 people) than for them to see themselves as exclusively of one national identity. Looking at this data by age group over the past several years, we see that to be equally British and Irish is not an identity that is very clearly associated with the younger generation. Indeed, those who say they are 'both' British and Irish come from across the generations in almost equal proportions.

One of the reasons behind the 'two communities' thesis is that Catholics are much less likely to say they have a British identity than Protestants, and Protestants are much less likely to say they have an Irish identity than Catholics. It is worth recognising that most of those saying that they are of no religion grew up in a Protestant household; so the fact that they are more likely to have a mainly British rather than mainly Irish identity probably reflects this. Nonetheless, the results belie the idea of a stark binary. According to NILT 2019 survey data, 35 per cent of Protestants claim some Irish identity (down from 51 per cent in 2017) and 39 per cent of Catholics claim some British identity (about the same as in 2017).[43] In both cases, this is predominantly as a 'minor' or 'equal' identity rather than the major identity. The data indicate a trend towards polarisation in more recent years, which we can only speculate is related to the Brexit context. In 2018, 3 per cent of Catholic respondents described themselves as having a predominantly British identity. And it is becoming less likely for Protestants to describe themselves as having any Irish identity. Looking at a decade of results from 2007 to 2019, we can see that there is a growth in the 'other' identity, a growth in the 'Irish only' identity (amongst Catholics) and (since the 2016 referendum) a slight contraction in the proportion of those feeling equally British and Irish (see Figure 5.7).

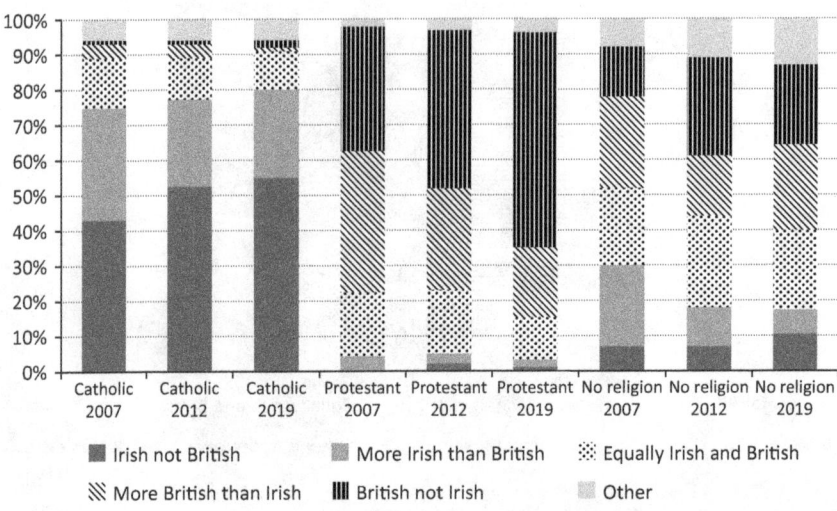

Figure 5.7 National identity by religion (2007, 2012, 2019)

If, instead of religious background, we look at political identities, there are some interesting differences in the patterns of national identities claimed (see Figure 5.8). Unsurprisingly perhaps, we see the sense of exclusive Irish or British identity being very strong (around 70 per cent) for nationalists and unionists, respectively. Those who say that they are 'neither' unionist

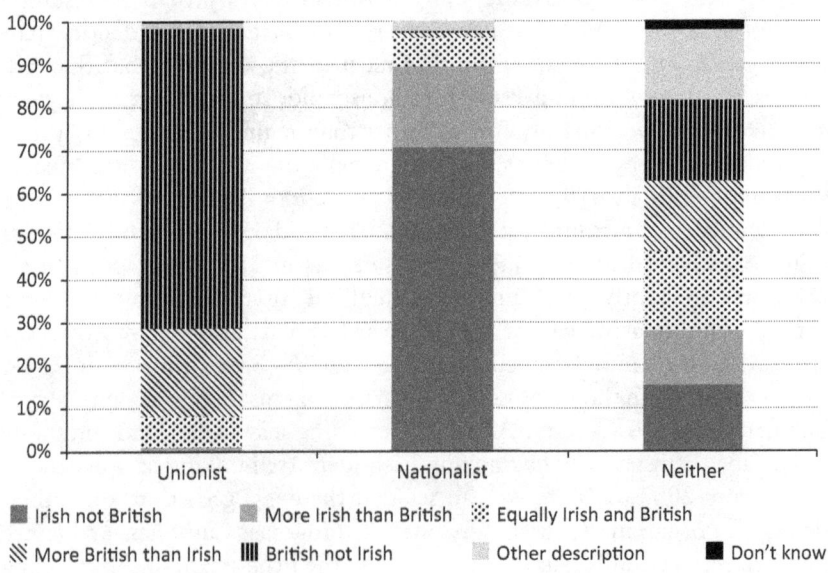

Figure 5.8 National identity and political identity

nor nationalist, thus rejecting the most common but oppositional political identity categories, appear to have a wide spread of national identities, including only British, only Irish and equally both. Indeed, those who describe themselves as 'equally British and Irish' are almost three times as likely to be 'neither' than either unionist or nationalist. This indicates that a statement of being equally British and Irish is most likely to be not completely apolitical but seen as a positive expression of something alternative to the sense of having to be either/or. The fact that some claim British or Irish only identity without the label of political aspiration is interesting and points again to the problem of conflating 'Irish' with 'nationalist' and 'British' with 'unionist'.

The Northern Irish

If those who are 'both' British and Irish do not have a clear political leaning or age or gender or religious profile, maybe there is another category of national identity that is more revealing and significant in contemporary Northern Ireland. Surveys first include 'Northern Irish' as a category in the late 1980s, replacing the earlier category of 'Anglo-Irish' and, later, 'Ulster'.[44] Survey data indicated that around a quarter of the population self-described in these terms in the 1990s, and that this rose in the 2000s to include close to half of young Protestants.[45] In fact, 'Northern Irish' becomes more popular for Protestants after the mid-2000s, while it becomes less so for Catholics.[46] In the 2011 census, the category of 'Northern Irish' was included for the first time, and 1 in 5 people ticked that box. Analysis of the 2011 census data shows that those describing themselves as 'Northern Irish only' are most likely to be Catholic (58 per cent to 36 per cent Protestant). Overall, in 2011, some 31 per cent of Catholics identified themselves as at least in part 'Northern Irish' compared to 27 per cent of Protestants. Survey data would indicate that this pattern would have reversed since, with it being the more popular choice among Protestants. Indeed, Tonge and Gomez claim that events after 2012 (specifically the flags protest)[47] seriously undermined the attractiveness or comfort of a 'Northern Irish' identity for Catholics, suggesting that it is an identity that is more closely affected by socio-political context than other forms of national identity.[48] Another relevant factor is that 'Northern Irish' appears to be most popular among younger Protestants, whereas it is an identity that is chosen by Catholics across the generations.[49] McNicholl and Garry confirm that age is a very clear predictor of Northern Irish identification among Protestants, while for Catholics, 'there appears to be a consistent bell-curve shaped trend with Northern Irishness being preferred by middle aged Catholics compared with both older and younger respondents'.⁵⁰ The younger generation of Catholics tend towards describing themselves as 'Irish'. It seems that we are a long way from 'Northern Irish' being a shared identity for a new generation in Northern Ireland. It would be misleading, therefore, to view this 'Northern Irish' or 'Northern Ireland' identity as one associated with a new, post-Agreement generation.

So, what does it mean to be 'Northern Irish'? In the 2011 census, 21 per cent of people identified as exclusively Northern Irish.⁵¹ The lack of overlap between a Northern Irish identity and a British identity or (even less commonly) an Irish identity indicates that this is not a synthesis of British and Irish national identities but something quite different.⁵² Todd notes that the term 'Northern Irish' is itself 'ambiguous between Irish (Northern variant) and British (from the region of Northern Ireland)' and thus that it holds a certain level of comfort for those of varying political views and backgrounds.⁵³ Putting it another way, Shelley McKeown claims that 'Northern Irish' could mean very different things for Catholics and Protestants, with the former using the term to show their geographical location in the north of Ireland and Protestants using it to give validity of the existence of Northern Ireland itself.⁵⁴ Nevertheless, most academic studies on the Northern Irish identity until the mid-2000s positioned it as a common in-group identity,⁵⁵ emphasising the fact that it can be perceived to be constructively ambiguous, inclusive or, indeed, a 'safe label' when to identify in stronger national identity terms could be seen as problematic.⁵⁶ McNicholl et al. found that the different uses of 'Northern Irish' mean that it can be used for political as well as social ends.⁵⁷ They elaborate:

> the moderate nationalist Social Democratic and Labour Party (SDLP) are more inclined [than Sinn Féin] to discuss ['the Northern Irish'] as a people. That is, 'the Northern Irish' are all of the people in Northern Ireland, regardless of their self-identity. This distinction is also found within unionism. The historically more hard-line Democratic Unionist Party occasionally refer to all people in the region as Northern Irish in an effort to undermine claims of Irishness. The Ulster Unionists are relatively more likely to say it is an identity claim, and so a matter of personal choice. The centrist Alliance party, with its explicitly antisectarian message, use it as part of a moderate political project.⁵⁸

As such, it is slightly problematic to see 'Northern Irish' as counter-culture, a 'new, cross-community identity in a society where nationalisms have a long-running salience and a profound influence on political life'.⁵⁹ Their qualitative research revealed that younger people understand that 'Northern Irish' can be used in political rhetoric just as much as 'Irish' and 'British' can be. But does this mean that 'Northern Irish' is more or less likely to be a category of social or national identity that they are likely to use? To some degree, it depends on other factors.

Closer analysis by Garry and McNicholl shows the political attitudes of the 'Northern Irish' varies according to whether they are Protestant or Catholic. 'Northern Irish Protestants' are not more likely to vote Ulster Unionist Party (UUP) rather than Democratic Unionist Party (DUP), whereas 'Northern Irish Catholics' are significantly less likely to vote for Sinn Féin than those identifying as Irish. However, there are differences between 'British' and 'Northern Irish' Protestants when it comes to constitutional preference. They found that less than a quarter of the latter favour direct rule compared to two-fifths of the former. And differences in constitutional preferences are even more stark among Catholics: support for Irish unity is three times greater among 'Irish' Catholics (59 per cent) than among 'Northern Irish' Catholics (21 per cent). This is borne out when it comes to identification as unionist, nationalist or neither. 'Northern Irish' Protestants are almost equally as likely to be 'neither' or 'unionist', with 'British' Protestants being twice as likely to be the latter. And 'Irish' Catholics are also twice as likely to be nationalist than 'neither' – a pattern directly reversed for those who are 'Northern Irish' Catholics. This indicates that a 'Northern Irish' identity for Catholics is often connected to a political choice or effort to disassociate from a strong nationalist position. In contrast, a 'Northern Irish' Protestant identity is not necessarily an indication of a rejection of, or alternative to, unionism; it is, in no small part, a reflexive response to 'Britishness'. The complexities and ambiguities of a 'British' identity (in England as much as any other part of the UK) perhaps contribute to some Protestants opting for the (at-least-more geographically) straightforward 'Northern Irish'. Garry and McNicholl conclude that, overall, the Northern Irish identity is politically meaningful in the sense that it is related to relatively moderate forms of ethno-nationalism.'[60] They go further and state that 'Northern Irish' people also share some common characteristics: they tend to be more supportive of power-sharing, more supportive of social mixing and more directly experienced in it (with intergroup contact being of significance). Again, this complicates the 'two communities' thesis. We see that 'Northern Irish' is not a catch-all identity but serves a slightly different purpose and has a different meaning for those from different backgrounds. For Catholics of all ages, it may be an effort to be neutral on the constitutional question; for Protestants, particularly of a younger generation, it is a useful alternative to 'British' identity. For neither Catholics nor Protestants does 'Northern Irish' simply mean 'both British and Irish'.

Ethnic differences: minorities and immigrants

An homogenous divided society

One thing that Coakley's typology of the levels of identity formation in Northern Ireland did not fully account for was ethno-racial identity. This is perhaps not surprising given that Northern Irish society has traditionally been so ethnically homogenous. Nonetheless, to understand the role of identity in contemporary Northern Ireland we must account for the fact that people of ethnicities other than 'white' and nationalities other than British or Irish form an integral part of the fabric of Northern Irish society. Unfortunately, the numbers are still too small to be able to gather a representative sample of those who are from 'other' ethnicities and nationalities in public attitudes surveys. This means that what we know about the diversity of Northern Irish society and its socio-political significance rests mainly in the attitudes of the ethnic majority. And that ethnic majority in Northern Ireland is strikingly large. Comparing 2011 census data from Northern Ireland, England/Wales and the Republic of Ireland shows quite how unusual Northern Ireland is, compared to its neighbours, when it comes to ethnic diversity (see Figure 5.9). For a start, the population in Northern Ireland has not grown nearly as quickly nor as significantly as that in the Republic of Ireland. Following on from this, we see that the region has very little ethnic diversity compared to the Republic and to the rest of the UK. The 2011 census of Northern Ireland found it to be 98 per cent white (compared to 99.15 per cent white in 2001), with 89 per cent of the population having been born inside the region and 95 per cent born in the UK or Ireland. In 2018, the Labour Force Survey showed there were an estimated 146,000 non-UK nationals in Northern Ireland, equating to around 7.8 per cent of the population.[61] Although this represents a growth on the figure from the 2011 census of 6.6 per cent from outside the UK, this is still among the lowest share of any UK region, and considerably below the national average (14.3 per cent). The Labour Force Survey statistics from 2018 indicate that non-Irish EU nationals constituted 3.3 per cent of the population and non-EU nationals around 2.7 per cent.[62]

Immigration

The most significant source of immigration to Northern Ireland in the past twenty years has been the European Union. This is partly due to the consequences of the single market, which gives freedom of movement to EU citizens to live, work and study in other EU member-states. But levels of

	Republic of Ireland	Northern Ireland	Scotland	England and Wales
Population	4.58m	1.81m	5.3m	56.1m
Growth since 2001	17%	7%	4.61%	7%
Ethnic minority	15.5%	1.8% (0.8% 2001)	8%	19.5%
Born outside the place of census	12%	11% (9% 2001)	16.7%	13%
English not usual language	11%	3.1%	10%	8%
Average age	36	37	41	39
Age over 65	11.4%	12.8%	16.8%	16.4%
Age under 15	21%	21%	17.3%	17%
Urban population	62%	65%	83%	81.4%
Religion: Christian	87% Christian (84% Catholic; 3% Protestant)	82% Christian (40% Catholic; 42% Protestant)	54% Christian	59% Christian
Religion: None	5.9% (+ 1.6% not stated)	10% (+ 6% not stated)	37% (+ 7% not stated)	25% (+ 7.2% not stated)
Religion: Other	1.9%	0.8%	2.5%	8.4% (4.8% Muslim)

Figure 5.9 Summary of census data (2011) comparison of Northern Ireland, rest of UK and Ireland

immigration have also been clearly affected by the enlargement of the EU in 2004. The holding of a language other than English as a mother tongue is a good indicator of diversity, and here we see that Northern Ireland is 97 per cent English-speaking. It is possible to see the difference made by EU integration by noting that in the 2011 census, of those whose first language is not English, the majority speak EU languages such as Polish (1 per cent of the total population) or Lithuanian (0.4 per cent). Indeed, the enlargement of the EU coincided with the change in the trend of net migration for Northern Ireland, with inflows greater than outflows from 2004 for a period of six years. We can see from Figure 5.10 that the peak of inward migration reached before the economic crash of 2008 has not been matched since, and there is no expectation that it will be matched for the foreseeable future, given the UK's exit from the EU.[63]

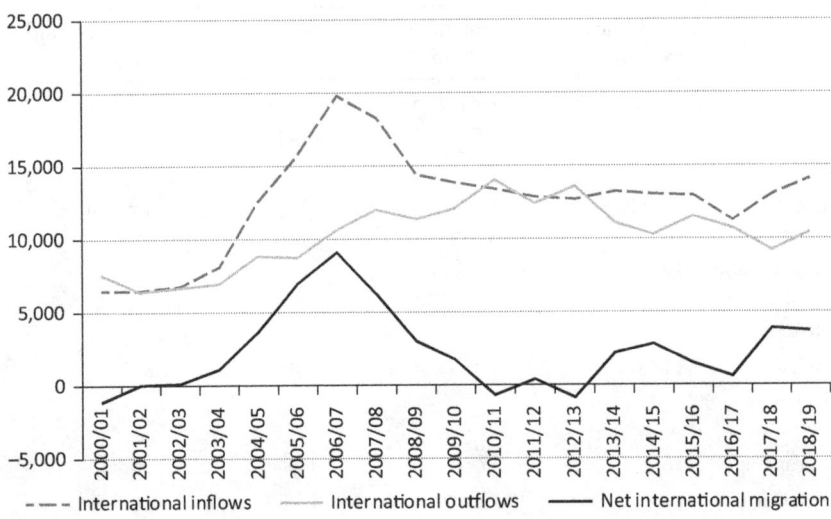

Figure 5.10 Levels of net migration in Northern Ireland, July 2000–June 2001 to July 2018–June 2019

Almost half (45 per cent) of those who migrate to Northern Ireland do so for work. The 131,000 non-UK-born adults in Northern Ireland are more likely to be in employment (66 per cent) and less likely to be economically inactive than the UK-born population.[64] This figure is even greater for EU26 nationals, with 80 per cent in employment, and just 16 per cent economically inactive. Manufacturing is particularly reliant on migrant labour, with over a fifth of the sector's workforce having been born outside the UK. While EU26 migrants are concentrated in manufacturing (many working as plant, process and machine operatives) and hospitality, those from the rest of the world are spread fairly evenly across the spectrum of sectors and employment occupations (including managerial and professional).[65] For such reasons, Northern Ireland's economy is most vulnerable to the negative impact of reduced migration compared to the rest of the UK. In a scenario in which only half the proportion of EU and international workers entered Northern Ireland in the space of two decades than would have been the case if the UK had remained in the EU, the Confederation of British Industry (CBI) calculated that Northern Ireland's GDP would be 9.1 per cent lower than it would otherwise have been.[66] The compounding effect of an ageing population and reduced access to migrant workers will impact some regions more than others, but the overall effect would be negative for Northern Ireland.[67] The vital role played by 'others' in Northern Irish society and economy is not reflected in the attitudes held towards them by the wider population.

Mixed reactions to mixing

The 2019 NI General Election Survey found that half of respondents disagreed with the statement that immigration is 'good for the economy and society'.[68] This is notably different from the findings of the NILT Survey of 2017, which found only around 1 in 10 people disagreeing that migrant workers are good for the economy (see Figure 5.11).[69] Perhaps the difference in the results arises from the difference in the questions posed: perhaps people make a distinction between what is good for the economy and what is good for society.

The attitudes of NILT Survey respondents towards immigrants varies depending on their relationship with them. For example, attitudes to migrant workers remain positive, especially in relation to their contribution to the labour force. Nearly nine out of ten respondents (88 per cent) believe that 'it is good for Northern Ireland that migrant workers come to work as doctors and nurses when there is a shortage of medical staff'. More generally, most respondents say that they would be willing to accept Eastern Europeans, Muslims and Irish Travellers as tourists or local residents. And the overall picture is one of support for refugees, with 62 per cent in 2017 agreeing with the statement: 'I think it is our duty to provide protection to refugees who are escaping persecution in their home country.' Nonetheless, this varies slightly depending on whether those arriving are seen as Muslim or not.[70]

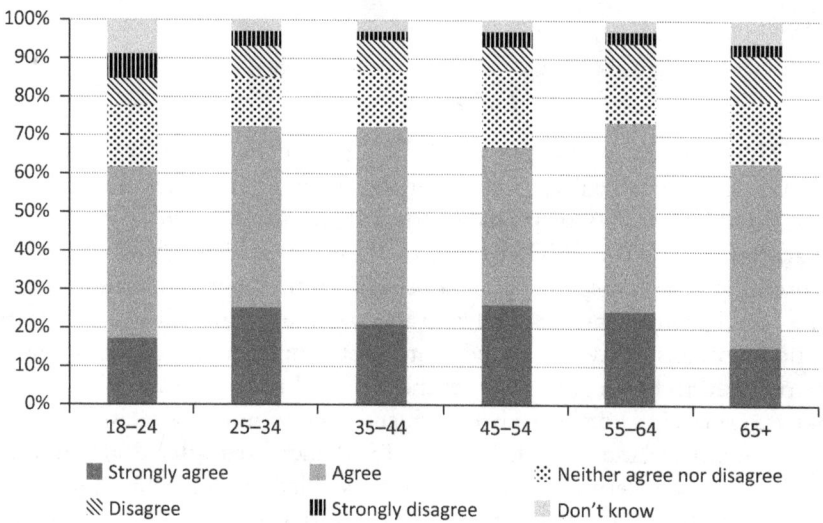

Figure 5.11 'Migrant workers are generally good for Northern Ireland's economy', by age

This perhaps connects to attitudes regarding immigrants as potential family relatives. Interestingly, the 2016 NILT Survey data showed a decline in acceptance of having a member of any minority ethnic group as a relative by marriage compared to attitudes of 2010.[71] Indeed, in the space of six years, acceptance rates for having Eastern Europeans, Irish Travellers and other minority ethnic groups (excluding Muslims) as relatives fell by nearly half. Only 45 per cent of respondents would accept Eastern Europeans as a relative by marriage, while 32 per cent would accept Muslims in that context.[72] The interesting point is that these levels of prejudice, or at least wariness of 'others', are occurring against a background in which there is an increase in the proportion of respondents with friends from ethnic or nationality backgrounds different from their own. However, there is a notable difference in levels of mixing between certain groups, in part a result of the relative size of those groups to begin with. For example, the proportion of respondents having Polish friends more than trebled between 2006 and 2016 from 11 per cent to 37 per cent. On the other hand, in 2016 the majority of respondents reported having rare or no contact with Muslims (75 per cent) or Irish Travellers (79 per cent). Overall, levels of self-reported prejudice against people from minority ethnic communities are low. This contrasts with the fact, however, that at least three-quarters of NILT Survey respondents every year state that they believe there to be racial prejudice in Northern Ireland.[73] Even if they think they are not prejudiced, they believe the dominant impression of Northern Irish society to be one of intolerance. This is borne out by the hard figures for race-hate incidents.

Racism on the rise?

The Police Service of Northern Ireland (PSNI) defines hate crime as 'any criminal offence which is perceived, by the victim or any other person, to be motivated by hostility or prejudice towards someone based on a personal characteristic'.[74] The PSNI defines 'race' or 'racist' hate crimes as being those in which a person is targeted because of their perceived membership of a racial group, which can refer to 'race, colour, nationality or ethnic or national origins'.[75] Even if an incident is not seen to meet the level of severity required to be recorded as a 'crime' it is still recorded (hence the figure of hate crimes is a portion of hate incidents). The number of racist incidents in Northern Ireland recorded by the PSNI increased after 2004, during which time Northern Ireland came to be labelled the 'race hate capital of Europe'.[76] Racist incidents then declined during the period of economic crisis (see Figure 5.12).[77] However, the number almost doubled between 2012 and 2014, peaking at 1,336 incidents in 2013/14. This dramatic rise

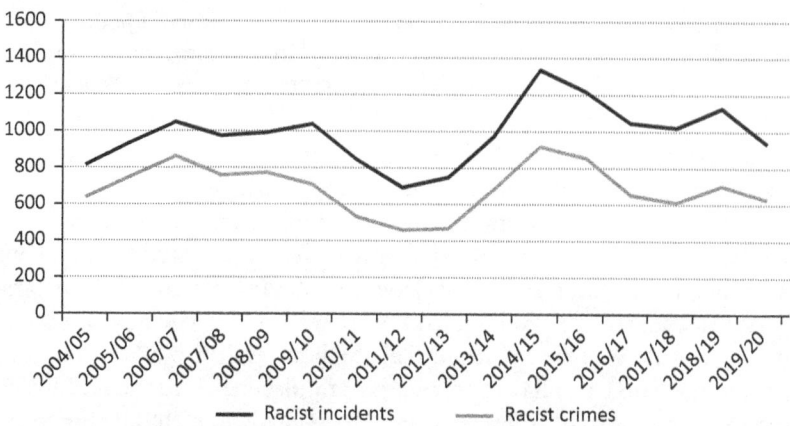

Figure 5.12 Racist incidents and crimes recorded by the PSNI, July 2004–July 2020

occurred during a period in which (as shown in Figure 5.10) there was no significant rise in inward migration, certainly not at the levels experienced from 2004. This would indicate that the levels of inward migration are not in themselves the 'cause' of increased incidents of racist hate crime.

Hate-motivated incidents are not just directed at the new immigrant communities; long-established minority ethnic communities are also victims of prejudice, intimidation and violence. Of the different minority ethnic identities in Northern Ireland, the two main communities are the Jewish community (which originated in the mid-nineteenth century) and the Chinese community (which dates from the 1960s).[78] The Chinese Welfare Association issued a press release in 2004 in response to the rise of hate-crime incidents being recorded by the PSNI: 'we have witnessed the alarming fact that many victims of racial incidents are actually internalizing their experiences and accepting this as a routine part of living as a minority community in Northern Ireland'.[79] This problem has not gone away. Ten years after that statement, Anna Lo, the Chinese-born Member of the Legislative Assembly (MLA) for the Alliance Party, announced she was stepping down from Northern Ireland politics. Ms Lo had come to Northern Ireland in 1974, at the height of the Troubles, and was made an MBE in 1999 for her work with the Chinese immigrant community. For many, she represented the 'new Northern Ireland', but she described her own experiences of blatant and fear-inducing racism as only compounding the sense of a lack of progress in Northern Irish society more broadly:

> I've had enough of the inability of this society and its political leaders to escape from the past. And what's worse is the rising racism in our community.

I have been living here for 40 years and this has forced me out of politics, and made me think about getting out of Northern Ireland altogether. So what must immigrants who have come here only recently think about this place?[80]

Although statistics and studies indicate that anti-immigrant negativity is no more prevalent in Northern Ireland than elsewhere in the UK, Ms Lo's sense of despair and exhaustion at persistent racist intolerance is no doubt exacerbated by the fact that other forms of hate-motivated incidents also remain high in Northern Ireland.[81] Between 2005/06 and 2015/16, sectarian incidents accounted for the largest number recorded under any of the hate motivation strands. These reached their highest level in 2009/10 (at 1,840 sectarian incidents) and have shown a general decline since then. However, the same cannot be said for other types of hate incident, including homophobic incidents. In 2016/17, the number of racist incidents exceeded that of sectarian incidents for the first time. In 2018/19, 1,124 racist hate incidents were recorded, compared to 865 sectarian ones.[82] Regression analyses on NILT Survey data (2005–15) found strong connections between anti-immigrant negativity, sectarianism and perceived neighbourhood segregation. These problems persist in Northern Ireland. Given that higher education, contacts with minority members and (religiously) mixed schooling appear to make people less likely to hold negative views of immigrants, the prospects for significantly countering intolerance from childhood remain low, especially for those from areas of multiple disadvantage. The problem of prejudice in Northern Ireland is not on a downward trajectory.

Political identities: unionist, nationalist and neither

The Good Friday Agreement's binary

Now we turn to the third level of the typology of identity formation, that which is fundamentally elective. Political identity is particularly important in Northern Ireland because, as noted above, it is seen as very closely related to given identities. This is largely because political identity is primarily conceived not in terms of left and right but in terms of constitutional preference, which is, in turn, assumed to grow almost inevitably from an individual's 'given' affiliation. This section of the chapter looks into this in more detail. The political identities upheld in and by the 1998 Agreement are, unsurprisingly, those according to which most political parties in Northern Ireland define themselves, that is, whether they are unionist or nationalist. In simple terms, this is whether they want Northern Ireland to remain in the UK or to become part of a united Ireland. This makes sense for several reasons. First, the GFA was supported and enabled by the two governments of the UK and Ireland, who both have legitimacy as the kin-states for communities in Northern Ireland. Secondly, the agreement both led to and paves the way for constitutional change in Ireland and the UK regarding the status of Northern Ireland. And finally, the GFA was designed through multi-party negotiation. At the time of its signing, the largest two parties were the UUP and the nationalist SDLP. They were joined at the table by eight other parties. Within a few years of the peace deal being signed, the UUP and SDLP had been outstripped by their unionist and nationalist competitors and the smaller parties, with the exception of Alliance, had all experienced serious decline. The GFA strengthened the hand and confidence, then, of unionism and nationalism as the dominant identity markers in Northern Ireland. Indeed, the logic of the 1998 Agreement was to enable a situation in which both nationalists and unionists could feel relatively comfortable. For unionists, this is achieved by the principle of 'majority consent', that is, having Northern Ireland remain in the UK until such a time as the majority of people, as expressed through a referendum, choose for it to become part of a united Ireland. Nationalists were reassured by the fact that the GFA saw the UK government bound to hold such a referendum 'if at any time it appears likely' that a majority of those voting in it 'would express a wish that Northern Ireland should cease to be part of the United Kingdom and form part of a united Ireland'.[83]

The fact that the future of Northern Ireland can, in principle, be determined by the expressed wish of a simple majority in Northern Ireland means that majoritarianism has continued to rationalise a 'two communities' approach to the region. Moreover, it has pushed the main parties in Northern Ireland to treat every election in the region as a proxy border poll, with the matter of whether there are more unionist or nationalist MLAs or MPs, and whether unionism or nationalism 'topped the poll' coming to dominate analysis after every election. The operationalisation of the GFA further legitimates this binary competition in pragmatic terms. The designation of unionist and nationalist MLAs has particular significance in the operation of the agreement. Each member of the Assembly is required to register a 'designation of identity' from the three options of nationalist, unionist *or* 'other'; however, the value of 'other' is somewhat diminished by the fact that most attention is paid to ensuring that the views of those who are nationalist are not vulnerable to being overridden by those who are unionist, and vice versa. This reflects the fact that majoritarianism is not seen to work well in a divided society in which mutual accommodation is required. Strand One of the GFA provides for 'a democratically elected Assembly in Northern Ireland which is inclusive in its membership ... and subject to safeguards to protect the rights and interests of *all* sides of the community'. However, the notion of 'all sides of the community' tends to be reductively viewed in terms of the rights and safeguards of 'both', i.e. those in one of either of the two principal ethno-national blocs. Most decisions of the Assembly are taken by a simple majority vote. However, some 'key decisions' must have cross-community support (although what constitutes a 'key decision' is not defined), which effectively ignores the existence and views of those who are 'other' in the Assembly.[84] As such, some criticise the system for reinforcing divisions rather than diminishing them by placing greater value on unionist and nationalist designations than that of 'other'.[85] A pertinent question is whether the Assembly still resembles the political identities that actually exist in contemporary Northern Ireland.

Unionist/nationalist preference

If we look at NILT Survey data since the 1998 Agreement, we can see that there has been a fairly consistent level of support for Irish unification (nationalism) and for the Union (unionism) since that point (see Figure 5.13). Irish unity has remained fairly consistently the preferred long-term outcome for about 1 in 5 respondents. There are a couple of exceptions to this – in 2001 the figure was 28 per cent and in 2006 some 30 per cent of respondents said that they wished to see Northern Ireland be part of a united Ireland. Those periods were ones of tension and instability in the peace process, with the 2001 survey coming during on-off suspensions of the Assembly and the 2006 survey coming at around the time of the St Andrews Agreement which paved the way to power-sharing government between Sinn Féin and the DUP, confirming the marginalisation of 'moderate' unionism and nationalism in the form of the UUP and SDLP. 2006 was also at the crest of the wave of the economic bubble in the Republic of Ireland, although there is little evidence that this convinced waverers as to the merits of Irish unity. It is notable that support for Irish unity in 2001 appears to come at the cost of preference for the Union, but in 2006 it comes at the cost of preference for 'other' options, such as an independent state. The trend in support for alternatives has considerably declined since 2007, and this is no doubt connected to the fact that the question on preference for the Union was disaggregated from 2007 to allow for answers specifying a preference for direct rule from London or for devolved administration in Belfast. When support for a devolved Northern Ireland within the UK declines, it tends to be accompanied by growing support for direct rule – a striking trend from 2017 onwards when the Assembly was not sitting. These time series data show that support for the Union has remained remarkably steady since the 1998 Agreement, albeit with occasional surprising results. It also shows that big changes in government or the economy in either London or Dublin make little demonstrable impact on people's preferences for Northern Ireland's constitutional status.

The 'neithers'

Since 2006, according to the NILT Survey, the largest portion of people in Northern Ireland identify themselves not as unionist nor nationalist but as 'neither' (see Figure 5.14). This means that the largest proportion of the population do not consider either of the two predominant labels in politics in Northern Ireland to be relevant to them. The trend is one of fairly steady growth of the proportion claiming to be neither unionist nor nationalist, although there has been some fluctuation in this. Before 2018 (where it reached 50 per cent), the peak for 'neither' had been 2012. And the 2019 NI General Election Survey also found the largest share of the electorate to consider themselves as 'neither' unionist nor nationalist.[86] This could be the manifestation of a phenomenon identified by Aphrodite Baka et al., namely that, rather than reflecting pre-existing 'neutrality', the design of the question itself could be producing ambiguity.[87] In some ways, offering an option to be 'neither' unionist nor nationalist is like offering a middle point in a Likert Scale. The decision to pick that middle point could be used to convey a lack of knowledge or a degree of uncertainty. But it could also reflect internal dilemmas on the part of the respondent (for example, the perception of negative associations with the other options), or it could mark a decisive rejection of the assumptions behind the question itself (for instance, that there is a binary divide). What does closer analysis of the data tell us about this group, which is of such significance in terms of it being larger than that of either unionist or nationalist?

By looking in more detail at who is ascribing themselves to this 'neither' category, Katy Hayward and Cathal McManus sought some insights into

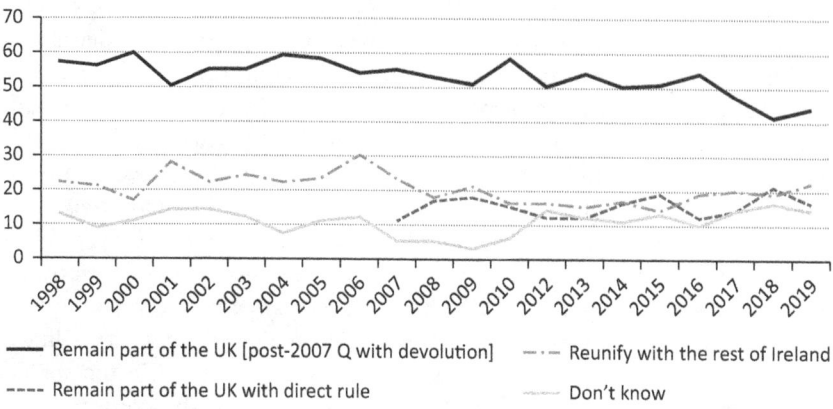

Figure 5.13 What would you prefer Northern Ireland's long-term future to be? (% of total respondents)

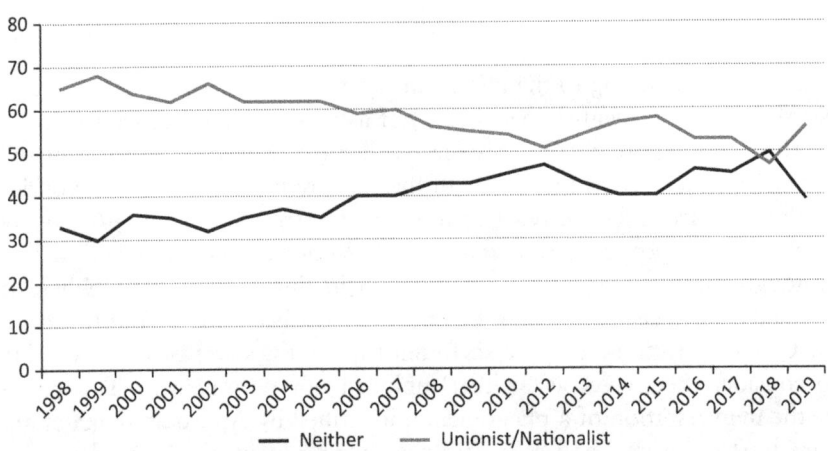

Figure 5.14 Those defining themselves as neither unionist nor nationalist (% of total respondents)

whether those self-reporting as neither can be classified as having some group features or whether it is merely an articulation of dissatisfaction, protest or rejection.[88] They found that the 'typical' person identifying as neither is not only more likely than either unionists or nationalists to be female, but they are also more likely to be younger, of both British and Irish identity (to varying degrees), to have lived outside Northern Ireland, to have some qualification (especially at the highest levels), to have gone to a religiously mixed school, to be in paid employment and to have a relatively high income. By 2018, two-thirds of those with No Religious affiliation were describing themselves as 'neither' in the NILT Survey.[89] This tallies with the findings that those who are 'neither' and those who are of no religion tend to hold more socially liberal views, compared to those identifying with Catholic or Protestant denominations.[90] But do these socially liberal views translate into a form of political activity that could potentially challenge the dominance of the unionist and nationalist parties? In theory, this depends on whether to be 'neither' is an omission, an avoidance or a positive statement of an alternative political identity to the dominant two.

Hayward and McManus conclude that to tick the 'neither' box is primarily 'a rejection of the labels of nationalism and unionism, and of the politics associated with those labels, rather than a clear coherent expression of an alternative way'.[91] This is supported by evidence of their (lack of) political engagement. There has been no dramatic change since 1998 in the spread of support among 'neithers' for the various options on the constitutional question. Devolution within the UK is consistently the favoured outcome, followed by the response of 'Don't Know', which was that of one in four 'neithers' in 2017. That said, part of the issue here is, of course, that the binary union/unity border poll creates no middle ground such as 'neithers' might prefer to see. These findings are confirmed by the 2019 NI General Election Survey, which found that, among those who are neither nationalist nor unionist, the majority stated a preference to stay in the UK. But the overall impression of the 'neithers' is that their political preference is rather less significant than their reluctance to go to the polls at all. Jan Van Deth and Martin Elff argue that an interest in politics, which frames levels of apathy, can be 'the consequence of the apparent saliency of societal and political arrangements'; which implies that if societal and political arrangements do not appear salient to people, then this translates into a lack of interest in politics.[92] The disjuncture between the social and political views held by the neither group and the continued salience of unionism and nationalism in the political system could appear to be translating into a certain level of political disengagement, if not apathy. Only a third of those who are neither unionist or nationalist voted in 2019, according to the University of Liverpool NI General Election Survey. And this is particularly the case among younger people. Around two-thirds of Catholics and Protestants aged 18–44 who do not vote are neither unionist nor nationalist. Indeed, most young people who do not vote are generally from a socially progressive group and do not subscribe to being either unionist or nationalist. What does this mean for the future Northern Ireland, it being in the hands of this younger generation?

Generational differences

New context, new issues

Over a period of ten years, the University of Liverpool NI General Election Surveys have found that major attitudinal divides are not along traditional lines but between younger and older and voters and non-voters – younger people being less likely to vote. Indeed, the majority of those aged 18–29 (52.6 per cent) did not vote in the 2019 UK General Election. Several studies of post-Agreement Northern Ireland have identified increasing differences between political and voting choices across generations. Some have seen this as a consequence of the changing political environment in which different age cohorts have been socialised.[93] Most obviously, younger people are growing up in a society no longer afflicted by the levels and intensity of political violence that their parents experienced. Studies of young people in contemporary Northern Ireland consistently point to the enduring legacy of the conflict. Paul Connolly et al. found that cultural dispositions and prejudice are formed among children from a young age,[94] and Madeleine Leonard has shown that these cultural habits soon translate into the use of sectarian markers – and divergent social worlds – of Catholic and Protestant teenagers.[95] The so-called Agreement Generation (born around or after the time of the 1990s ceasefires) is still affected by this persistent, one might say 'banal' sectarianism,[96] together with the institutionalised segregation of the education system. Differences create wariness and unfamiliarity, particularly so in areas suffering multiple deprivation and still very much affected by the hold of criminality and those who use intimidation to gain community control and compliance.[97] But in a context of peace, that is, without the sense of threat or fear that was no doubt more vivid and widespread in previous generations, community identity is not seen as being something as *politically* relevant to the younger generation as it once was.

Certainly, the 1998 Agreement helped to create an environment in which constitutional political tensions are of less bearing than they were during the conflict, but yet they still constitute the fundamental grounds upon which most political parties campaign and mobilise. This, as noted above, is compounded by the operation of the Assembly itself. The apparent irrelevance of 'the constitutional question' (perhaps up until Brexit, as discussed in the concluding chapter) might help to explain why self-identifying as neither unionist nor nationalist has become increasingly popular among younger adults. This is against a background in which – possibly counter-intuitively – the 'Agreement Generation' were found to be more likely to conflate religion and nationality than the older generation.[98] So younger people do not seem to be 'community-blind', so to speak, but they are less likely to think of religion or nationality as being politically significant. And when it comes to the 'constitutional question', they are not all necessarily uninterested, but they see it as an identity matter rather than an urgent or pressing political concern.[99]

Indeed, away from the typical lines of political identity, we see that there is a growth in liberal attitudes that constitutes 'a profound divide between younger people and their parents and grandparents'.[100] Younger Catholics and Protestants, especially non-voters, generally agree on social and inter-community issues. The most socially liberal group are young Protestant non-voters, followed by their Catholic equivalents. Younger people are significantly more likely to be pro-choice when it comes to abortion (with 52 per cent of 18–25-year-olds saying abortion should be legalised compared to 26 per cent of over 65-year-olds).[101] They are also more likely to be supportive of marriage equality, with younger Protestant non-voters most supportive (73.7 per cent aged under 45), followed by younger Catholic non-voters (62.7 per cent aged under 45), compared to the average of 51.6 per cent.[102] The liberalism of Ireland as well as Britain compared to Northern Ireland is changing the environment for this generation. Similarly, global challenges are also of increasing concern to this age cohort. The vibrancy of the Extinction Rebellion movement in Belfast is also an indication that young people, including schoolchildren, are ready for a different type of politics and political action.

What next with the next generation?

Post-Agreement society in Northern Ireland is, as this chapter has shown, more diverse in terms of communities and identities, and less easy to categorise in binary terms, than it has ever been before. Although growing up in a predominantly white, still religiously conditioned society, the younger generation are more familiar with diversity than their parents or grandparents. It is interesting, then, that NILT Survey data indicate that a greater proportion of 18–24-year-olds than any other age group self-report as being prejudiced against trans people (28 per cent, compared to 15 per cent of 35–44-year-olds).[103] Similarly, 18–24-year-olds are less likely than any other age group to say that they are 'not prejudiced at all' against people from minority ethnic communities (74 per cent compared to 80 per cent of over-65s).[104] However, this is potentially more a reflection of the nature of the question asked. Perhaps younger people are more likely to be honest about their views, or else simply more exposed to the debates about trans identities. When asked questions that uncover opinions about the rights of trans people or the benefits of migration, the results indicate that young people are more liberal and tolerant than the older generations. Opinion surveys among young people in Northern Ireland consistently show that they are generally favourable to enabling greater 'mixing' between communities.[105]

There does appear to be, at least in principle, a willingness among the younger generations – not rare elsewhere but particularly significant in a 'divided society' – to test traditional boundaries. This is because they are increasingly living across those boundaries. Almost a quarter (23 per cent) of 18–25-year olds are living with a partner/married to someone from another or no religion.[106] And, more broadly, the concerns of young people are not only cross-community but transnational. And the challenges that they face are more universal than those of their parents' generation – college fees, the struggle to buy a house, a changed labour market, precarious employment. The 2019 NI Election Survey found that younger people show more confidence when it comes to integration and immigration. And that such views are particularly true of young non-voters. Just 14.8 per cent of Protestant non-voters and 18.6 per cent of Catholic non-voters aged 18–44 agreed that they would prefer to send their children to an own-religion school (compared to the average of 33.4 per cent). Younger Protestant non-voters are particularly relaxed when it comes to the prospect of a close relative marrying someone from a different religion; 83.7 per cent said they would not mind, followed by 69 per cent of Catholic non-voters. We do not have the data to tell us why people choose not to vote – for some this is indifference, for others an aversion to the prevailing political categories and identities. But it is further indication that the party-political system of the GFA does not seem relevant to either the everyday or the existential problems that would look set to be the most pressing policy challenges for the next generation. Morrow's study of a series of these surveys led him to the conclusion that 'this is a generation expectant of change'.[107] The pertinent question is whether they are ready and willing to lead it.

Conclusion

Northern Ireland is a society not just of two communities but of many. What is the long-term significance of this? In sum, we can be sure that those who are of no religion, those who are neither unionist nor nationalist, those are both British and Irish, those who other than white or locally born, and those who are of the next generation will be the ones in whose hands the future of Northern Ireland lies. The overriding impression from analysing the attitudes of, and about, such individuals is that – despite their growing significance – many of them are disengaged from, and disillusioned with, electoral politics in Northern Ireland. But, although the next generation in particular are less likely to vote, less likely to be religiously observant and less likely to oppose mixing and immigration, they are still conditioned by a society in which a binary divide is given predominant significance. They recognise the traditional identities and labels to be important, but important in a negative way, that is, in sustaining division. Indeed, they may be as likely to see Northern Ireland in terms of 'two communities' as previous generations, and simply consider themselves individually at odds with the social norm and unrepresented by its democratic system. Their experience of the 'blurring' or 'irrelevance' of the community divide is assumed to be the exception, and few anticipate unionism and nationalism doing anything other than continuing to exist.

However, in actual fact, the challenge to the 'two communities' model of Northern Ireland is a profound one. Labels of given and of chosen identities will continue to be assigned and assumed. But they cannot remain mere 'labels' for long. The more empty these signifiers become, the less power there is to be found by simply claiming to speak on their behalf. Even if segregated education persists, a growing proportion of Protestants and Catholics who do not practise mean that the churches have less influence – for better or for worse. A growing proportion of those who are committed to the Union but who eschew the label of 'unionist' represents an uphill struggle for unionism to show what it stands for rather than just what it is not. Of course, as Brexit has shown, external factors can quite dramatically disrupt this trend, either to the benefit or the detriment of these political identities. However, in terms of internal legitimacy, unionism and nationalism face a challenge. Growing abstentionism and political disengagement could potentially lead to a serious democratic or constitutional crisis in Northern Ireland in the medium to long term. This would not be of the type that we might traditionally have predicted (and which the 1998 Agreement tried to defuse), but rather of a kind that arises from a growing disjuncture between the democratic institutions and the society they are meant to represent. The challenge for the leaders of unionism and nationalism – both as ideologies and as the communities on which the democratic system is founded – is whether they are able to demonstrate their relevance in a world that is changing under their feet and about their ears.

Notes

1 Institutions and cooperation were formalised in Strand 1 within Northern Ireland, Strand 2 the island of Ireland, Strand 3 between Britain and Ireland.
2 Paul Nolan, *The Northern Ireland Peace Monitoring Report Number Two* (Belfast: Community Relations Council, 2013).
3 John Coakley, 'National Identity in Northern Ireland: Stability or Change?', *Nations and Nationalism*, 13(4) (2007), 573–97.
4 We have slightly adjusted the model used by Coakley in order to accommodate the fact that ethnic identity in contemporary Northern Ireland, including people born here, is a 'given' identity and that it is an important category aside from the typical understanding of 'ethno-national' identity as it is used in this context. For more, see Cillian McGrattan, 'Explaining Northern Ireland? The Limitations of the Ethnic Conflict Model', *National Identities*, 12(2) (2010), 181–97.
5 Coakley, 'National Identity', p. 577.
6 Kanchan Chandra (ed.), *Constructivist Theories of Ethnic Politics* (Oxford: Oxford University Press, 2012).
7 Daniel Bar Tal, *Intractable Conflicts: Socio-Psychological Foundations and Dynamics* (Cambridge: Cambridge University Press, 2013).
8 Daphna Canetti, Julia Elad-Strenger, Iris Lavi, Dana Guy and Daniel Bar-Tal, 'Exposure to Violence, Ethos of Conflict, and Support for Compromise: Surveys in Israel, East Jerusalem, West Bank, and Gaza', *Journal of Conflict Resolution*, 61(1) (2017), 84–113.
9 Jennifer Todd, *Identity Change After Conflict: Ethnicity, Boundaries and Belonging in the Two Irelands* (Basingstoke: Palgrave Macmillan, 2018), p. 28.

10 Ibid., p. 31. See also Joseph Ruane, 'Comparing Protestant-Catholic conflict in France and Ireland: the significance of the ethnic and colonial dimension', in John Wolffe (ed.), *Irish Religious Conflict in Comparative Perspective: Catholics, Protestants and Muslims* (Basingstoke: Palgrave Macmillan, 2014), pp. 146–66.
11 Todd, *Identity Change After Conflict*, p. 232.
12 Danièle Hervieu-Léger, *Religion as a Chain of Memory* (London: Polity Press, 2000).
13 Grace Davie, *Religion in Modern Europe: A Memory Mutates* (Oxford: Oxford University Press, 2000).
14 Steve Bruce, *Paisley: Religion and Politics in Northern Ireland* (Oxford: Oxford University Press, 2007).
15 John Whyte, *Interpreting Northern Ireland* (Oxford: Clarendon Press, 1991).
16 Claire Mitchell, *Religion, Identity and Politics in Northern Ireland* (Abingdon: Ashgate, 2006); Gladys Ganiel, *Evangelicalism and Conflict in Northern Ireland* (Basingstoke: Palgrave Macmillan, 2008).
17 Joseph Liechty and Cecelia Clegg, *Moving Beyond Sectarianism: Religion, Conflict and Reconciliation in Northern Ireland* (Dublin: Columba Press, 2000); Maria Power, *From Ecumenism to Community Relations: Inter-church Relationships in Northern Ireland 1980–1999* (Dublin: Irish Academic Press, 2006).
18 John Fulton, 'Religion and Enmity in Ireland: Institutions and Relational Beliefs', *Social Compass*, 49(2) (2002), 189–202.
19 Mitchell, *Religion, Identity and Politics*.
20 Ibid.
21 Bryan Wilson (ed. Steve Bruce), *Religion in Secular Society: Fifty Years On* (Oxford: Oxford University Press, 2016).
22 Jonathan Evans and Chris Baronavski, 'How do European countries differ in religious commitment?', *FactTank*. Available at: www.pewresearch.org/fact-tank/2018/12/05/how-do-european-countries-differ-in-religious-commitment. Accessed 5 April 2020.
23 *Northern Ireland Life and Times Survey*, 2019. Available at: www.ark.ac.uk/nilt/2019/Background/CHATTND2.html. Accessed 19 September 2020.
24 The 1926 census (none was taken in 1921) shows the Catholic population to be 33.5 per cent of Northern Ireland, with 'other' or 'not stated' constituting 4.3 per cent. Source: *1926 Census of Northern Ireland*, NI Statistics and Research Agency. Available at: www.nisra.gov.uk/sites/nisra.gov.uk/files/publications/1926-census-general-report.pdf. Accessed 17 December 2020.
25 *2011 Census of Northern Ireland*, NI Statistics and Research Agency. Available at: www.nisra.gov.uk/sites/nisra.gov.uk/files/publications/2011-census-results-key-statistics-northern-ireland-report-11-december-2012.pdf. Accessed 5 April 2020.
26 *2011 Census of England and Wales*, Office of National Statistics. Available at: www.ons.gov.uk/peoplepopulationandcommunity/culturalidentity/religion/articles/religioninenglandandwales2011/2012-12-11. Accessed 5 April 2020.

2011 Census of Scotland, Scotland's Census. Available at: www.scotlandscensus.gov.uk/. Accessed 5 April 2020.
27 64 per cent of Protestants and 73 per cent of Catholic school-leavers who go on to university do so in Northern Ireland; the key difference is the proportion who go to Great Britain. Over a third of Protestant school-leavers go to university in Britain, compared to just around a quarter of their Catholic counterparts. *Qualifications and Destinations of Northern Ireland School Leavers 2017/18*, Department of Education NI, Statistical bulletin 4/2019. Available at: www.education-ni.gov.uk/sites/default/files/publications/education/qualifications-and-destinations-of-northern-ireland-school-leavers-20171.._.pdf. Accessed 20 April 2020.
28 *Northern Ireland Life and Times Survey*, 2019.
29 The Labour Force Survey overall estimates the proportion of the population in Northern Ireland as Catholic 42.4 per cent, Protestant 40.7 per cent, those of other religion 4.37 per cent and those claiming no religion 12.6 per cent. *Labour Force Survey 2019*. Available at: www.ons.gov.uk/peoplepopulationandcommunity/culturalidentity/religion/adhocs/11193religiousdenominatio nofresidentsofnorthernireland1995to2019. Accessed 5 April 2020. Notably, a consultation conducted by the NI Statistics and Research Agency (NISRA) in 2019, the Labour Force Survey (LFS) Religion Report, received the highest number of respondents of all the LFS outputs, finding it 'not applicable or not useful'. The Executive Office Religion Report user survey in 2019 asked users about the impact of ceasing to publish the bulletin. As a consequence, it was decided that the LFS Religion Report would not be published in 2020. NISRA (2020). Available at: www.nisra.gov.uk/publications/labour-market-statistics-consultation-2019-0. Accessed 1 October 2020.
30 *Northern Ireland Life and Times Survey*, 2019.
31 David Voas and Alasdair Crockett, 'Religion in Britain: Neither Believing nor Belonging', *Sociology*, 39(1) (2005), 11–28.
32 Ibid.
33 *University of Liverpool NI General Election Survey 2019*. Available at: www.liverpool.ac.uk/media/livacuk/research/heroimages/The-University-of-Liverpool-NI-General-Election-Survey-2019-March-20.pdf. Accessed 5 April 2020.
34 Ibid.
35 Ibid. It should be noted that there is a discrepancy between data collected using face-to-face interviewing as in this survey and those collected via telephone or online methods. The latter types of survey tend to have a significantly higher proportion return of pro-unity views and lower portions of 'don't knows'.
36 John Coakley, 'Public Opinion and the Future of Northern Ireland', *Working papers in conflict transformation and social justice*, CTSJ WP 04–14 (Belfast: Queen's University Belfast, Institute for the Study of Conflict Transformation and Social Justice, 2014), p. 9. Available at: www.qub.ac.uk/Research/GRI/mitchell-institute/FileStore/Filetoupload,450805,en.pdf. Accessed 5 April 2020.
37 Ibid.

38 Coakley, 'National Identity', p. 591.
39 Ibid., p. 591.
40 *Northern Ireland Life and Times Survey*, 2019.
41 Ibid.
42 Ibid.
43 Ibid.
44 Kevin McNicholl, Clifford Stevenson and John Garry, 'How the "Northern Irish" National Identity Is Understood and Used by Young People and Politicians', *Political Psychology*, 40(3) (2019), 487–505.
45 Todd, *Identity Change After Conflict*, p. 56.
46 Jonathan Tonge and Raul Gomez, 'Shared Identity and the End of Conflict? How Far Has a Common Sense of "Northern Irishness" Replaced British or Irish Allegiances since the 1998 Good Friday Agreement?', *Irish Political Studies*, 30(2) (2015), 276–98.
47 Paul Nolan, Dominic Bryan, Clare Dwyer, Katy Hayward, Katy Radford and Peter Shirlow, *The Flag Dispute: Anatomy of a Protest* (Belfast: Queen's University, 2014). Available at: https://pureadmin.qub.ac.uk/ws/files/13748797/The_Flag_Dispute_report_PRINTED.pdf. Accessed 5 April 2020.
48 Tonge and Gomez, 'Shared Identity'.
49 Ibid., p. 286.
50 John Garry and Kevin McNicholl, 'Understanding the "Northern Irish" Identity', Knowledge Exchange Seminar Series 2014–2015 (Belfast: Queen's University Belfast, 2015). Available at: www.niassembly.gov.uk/globalassets/documents/raise/knowledge_exchange/briefing_papers/series4/northern_ireland_identity_garry_mcnicholl_policy_document.pdf. Accessed 5 April 2020.
51 This figure rises to 27 per cent for those saying they are both British and Northern Irish. 2011 Census of Northern Ireland, NI Statistics and Research Agency. Available at: www.ninis2.nisra.gov.uk/public/census2011analysis/nationalidentity/index.aspx. Accessed 5 April 2020.
52 McNicholl et al., 'How the "Northern Irish"'; Karen Trew, 'The Northern Irish identity', in Anne J. Kershen (ed.), *A Question of Identity* (Aldershot: Ashgate, 1998), pp. pp. 60–76.
53 Todd, *Identity Change After Conflict*, p. 56.
54 Shelley McKeown, 'Perceptions of a Superordinate Identity in Northern Ireland', *Peace and Conflict: Journal of Peace Psychology*, 20(4) (2014), 505–15.
55 Bernadette C. Hayes and Ian McAllister, *Conflict to Peace: Politics and Society in Northern Ireland Over Half a Century* (Manchester: Manchester University Press, 2013).
56 Jennifer Todd, Theresa O'Keefe, Nathalie Rougier and Lorenzo Cañás Bottos, 'Fluid or Frozen? Choice and Change in Ethno-National Identification in Contemporary Northern Ireland', *Nationalism and Ethnic Politics*, 12 (3–4) (2006), 323–46.

57 McNicholl et al., 'How the "Northern Irish"'.
58 Ibid.
59 Ibid.
60 Garry and McNicholl, 'Understanding the "Northern Irish"', p. 4.
61 Oxford Economics, 'The Impact of Changes to Migration Policy on the Northern Ireland Economy' (Belfast: Department for the Economy, 2020). Available at: www.economy-ni.gov.uk/sites/default/files/publications/economy/Impact-changes-migration-policy-ni-economy.pdf. Accessed 5 April 2020.
62 Ibid.
63 Source: NI Statistics and Research Agency. Available at: www.nisra.gov.uk/publications/long-term-international-migration-statistics-northern-ireland-2019. Accessed 1 October 2020.
64 Oxford Economics, 'Impact of Changes'.
65 Ibid.
66 CBI Northern Ireland, 'All Together Better: Accessible Labour – a Necessity for Regional Economic Prosperity' (Belfast: Confederation of British Industry, Northern Ireland, 2018). Available at: www.cbi.org.uk/articles/all-together-better/. Accessed 5 April 2020.
67 Ibid.
68 There was no significant difference between Catholic and Protestant respondents, but those of no religion are significantly more likely to agree that immigration is good for society and the economy, i.e. 30 per cent compared to around 25 per cent. *NI General Election Survey 2019*.
69 Source: Northern Ireland Life and Times Survey 2017. Available at: www.ark.ac.uk/nilt/2017/Minority_Ethnic_People/MIGWRK1.html. Accessed 5 April 2020.
70 Lucy Michael and Paula Devine, 'A Welcoming Northern Ireland? Understanding Sentiment towards Asylum Seekers and Refugees', *Research Update 124* (Belfast: ARK, 2018). Available at: www.ark.ac.uk/ARK/sites/default/files/2018-11/update124.pdf. Accessed 5 April 2020.
71 Paula Devine, 'Attitudes to Minority Ethnic Groups in Northern Ireland, 2005–2016', *Research Update 122* (Belfast: ARK, 2017). Available at: www.ark.ac.uk/ARK/sites/default/files/2018-11/update122.pdf. Accessed 5 April 2020.
72 Lucy Michael, 'Racism and Intolerance towards Minority Ethnic Groups in Northern Ireland', *Research Update 112* (Belfast: ARK, 2017). Available at: www.ark.ac.uk/publications/updates/update112.pdf. Accessed 5 April 2020.
73 Paula Devine, 'Attitudes to Minority Ethnic Groups in Northern Ireland, 2005–2016', *Research Update 122* (Belfast: ARK, 2017). Available at: www.ark.ac.uk/ARK/sites/default/files/2018-11/update122.pdf. Accessed 5 April 2020.
74 Police Service of Northern Ireland (PSNI), *Hate Motivation Statistics Definitions and User Guide* (Belfast: PSNI, 2018). Available at: www.psni.police.uk/globalassets/inside-the-psni/our-statistics/hate-motivation-statistics/documents/hate-motivations-definitions.pdf. Accessed 5 April 2020.

75 Ibid. Notably, the PSNI definition of race hate crime includes UK national origins, such as Scottish or English, and the Irish Traveller community, although this is not to be confused with sectarian hate crime, which constitutes a separate category.
76 Colin Knox, 'Tackling Racism in Northern Ireland: "The Race Hate Capital of Europe"', *Journal of Social Policy*, 40(2) (2011), 387–412.
77 PSNI, *Hate Motivation Annual Trends*. Available at: www.psni.police.uk/inside-psni/Statistics/hate-motivation-statistics. Accessed 1 October 2020.
78 Bethany Waterhouse-Bradley, 'Sectarian legacies and the marginalisation of migrants', in Bryan Fanning and Lucy Michael (eds), *Immigrants as Outsiders in the Two Irelands* (Manchester: Manchester University Press, 2019), p. 34.
79 Mary Delargy, 'Language, culture and identity: the Chinese community in Northern Ireland', in Mairead Nic Craith (ed.), *Language, Power and Identity Politics* (London: Palgrave Macmillan, 2007), pp. 123–145.
80 'Only Chinese-born parliamentarian in UK to quit politics over racist abuse', *Guardian*, 29 May 2014. Available at: www.theguardian.com/uk-news/2014/may/29/northern-ireland-chinese-mp-might-leave-province-racist-abuse. Accessed 7 April 2020.
81 Stefanie Doebler, Ruth McAreavey and Sally Shortall (2018), 'Is Racism the New Sectarianism? Negativity towards Immigrants and Ethnic Minorities in Northern Ireland from 2004 to 2015', *Ethnic and Racial Studies*, 41(14) (2018), 2426–44.
82 PSNI, *Hate Motivation Annual Trends 2004/05 to 2018/19* (Belfast: PSNI, 2019). Available at: www.psni.police.uk/globalassets/inside-the-psni/our-statistics/hate-motivation-statistics/2018–19/hate-motivated-incidents-and-crimes-in-northern-ireland-2004–05-to-2018–19.pdf. Accessed 5 April 2020.
83 Northern Ireland Act, 1998 [Schedule 1.2].
84 There are two forms of cross-community support: parallel consent, where more than 50 per cent of MLAs agree to the motion, including more than 50 per cent of each nationalists and unionists; and a weighted majority, requiring the support of 60 per cent of those voting, including 40 per cent of nationalists and 40 per cent unionists.
85 Rupert Taylor, *Consociational Theory: McGarry/O'Leary and the Northern Ireland Conflict* (London: Routledge, 2009).
86 *University of Liverpool NI General Election Survey 2019*.
87 Aphrodite Baka, Lia Figgou and Vasiliki Triga, '"Neither Agree, nor Disagree": A Critical Analysis of the Middle Answer Category in Voting Advice Applications', *International Journal of Electronic Governance*, 5(3–4) (2012), 244–63.
88 Katy Hayward and Cathal McManus, 'Neither/Nor: The Rejection of Unionist and Nationalist Identities in Post-Agreement Northern Ireland', *Capital & Class*, 43(1) (2019), 39–55.
89 Northern Ireland Life and Times Survey 2018.
90 *University of Liverpool NI General Election Survey 2019*.
91 Hayward and McManus, 'Neither/Nor'.

92 Jan W. Van Deth and Martin Elff, 'Politicisation, Economic Development and Political Interest in Europe', *European Journal of Political Research*, 43(3) (2004), 477–508.
93 James Tilley and Geoffrey Evans, 'Political Generations in Northern Ireland', *European Journal of Political Research*, 50(5) (2011), 583–608.
94 Paul Connolly, Berni Kelly and Alan Smith, 'Ethnic Habitus and Young Children: A Case Study of Northern Ireland', *European Early Childhood Education Research Journal*, 17(2) (2009), 217–32.
95 Madeleine Leonard, 'It's Better to Stick to Your Own Kind: Teenagers' Views on Cross-community Marriages in Northern Ireland', *Journal of Ethnic and Migration Studies*, 35(1) (2009), 97–114.
96 Michael Billig, *Banal Nationalism* (London: Sage, 1995).
97 Peter Shirlow and Brendan Murtagh, *Belfast: Segregation, Violence and the City* (London: Pluto Press, 2006).
98 Orla Muldoon, Karen Trew, Jennifer Todd, Nathalie Rougier and Katrina Mclaughlin, 'Religious and National Identity after the Belfast Good Friday Agreement', *Political Psychology*, 28(1) (2007), 89–103.
99 Aobhín de Burca and Katy Hayward, 'The Agreement Generation: Young People's Views on the New Cross-Border Relationship', *Journal of Cross Border Studies in Ireland*, 7 (2012), 23–36.
100 *University of Liverpool NI General Election Survey 2019.*
101 Ibid.
102 Ibid.
103 Gail Neill and Siobhán McAlister, 'The Missing T: Baselining Attitudes Towards Transgender People in Northern Ireland', *Research Update 128* (Belfast: Ark, 2019). Available at: www.ark.ac.uk/ARK/sites/default/files/2019-06/update128.pdf. Accessed 5 April 2020.
104 *Northern Ireland Life and Times Survey 2017.* Available at: www.ark.ac.uk/nilt/2017/Minority_Ethnic_People/UPREJMEG.html. Accessed 5 April 2020.
105 Duncan Morrow, 'Shared or scared? Attitudes to community relations among young people 2003–7', in Dirk Schubotz and Paula Devine (eds), *Young People in Post-Conflict Northern Ireland* (Lyme Regis: Russell House, 2008), pp. 9–20.
106 *University of Liverpool NI General Election Survey 2019.*
107 Morrow, 'Shared or Scared?', p. 16.

6

Rethinking the post-conflict narrative: women and the promise of peace in the 'new' Northern Ireland

Introduction

The Good Friday Agreement (hereafter GFA) marked itself out as significant for its commitment to 'the right of women to full and equal participation in political life'. Moreover, some also lauded the relatively high levels of visibility and participation of women within the wider peace process.[1] Although dominant, state-centric forms of conflict transition claim to be universally beneficial, evidence from the so-called 'post-conflict' period around the world demonstrates a continuity of violence and inequality for women, with many also facing new forms of violent practices. As a society emerging from protracted armed conflict, Northern Ireland is no exception. This chapter explores the position of women in Northern Ireland today, and by doing so seeks to problematise the 'post-conflict' narrative by gendering peace and security. The chapter begins by exploring the field of gender and conflict transition in Northern Ireland. It then moves on to look at women's formal and informal political activism, exploring arguments offered for women's persistent under-representation in formal politics. In advancing a feminist argument that seeks to challenge the gendered nature of peace and security, the chapter then examines the increased levels of gender-based violence that have marked the peace-process era, before finally considering women's security in relation to the struggle for reproductive rights. While these issues are also commonplace in other regions free from the residue of armed conflict and its legacy, 'the combination of challenging patriarchy and the particular impact of living with political violence for such a long time offers a unique voice for feminism in Northern Ireland'.[2]

Given the deeply polarised conditions that define Northern Irish society, women of course do not represent a homogenous bloc, but instead are individuals whose identities, options and experiences are shaped by factors including their age, economic class, race, clan, tribe, caste, ethnicity, religion, sexuality, physical ability, culture, geographic location, state citizenship and national identity, and their positioning in both local and global economic processes. And so we need to be attentive to the differences as well as the similarities among women in the region.[3] This chapter, therefore, does not claim a universal experience for every woman in Northern Ireland. It does, however, cover a multiplicity of issues relevant to many women. Notwithstanding the important fissures of difference between women in the region, unequal power relations between the sexes remain pervasive and largely undisturbed. The diverse issues explored here – from women's political representation to gender-based violence and abortion – are linked and embedded within a structural and cultural gender order which invariably privileges masculinity and male power. Regardless of the rhetoric and widespread sense of optimism in the initial aftermath of the 1998 Agreement, this chapter argues that traditional forms of male power and dominance are a feature of Northern Irish life that remains uninterrupted by the peace process.

Gender and conflict transition

Despite its centrality to the composition and reproduction of ethno-nationalism, gender is rarely viewed as a significant concern within conventional approaches to both war and conflict resolution. Given its assigned subordinate status within nationalism, gender is largely conceptualised as being tangential, not central to conflict. Peace processes, however, are as gendered as wars.[4] A trademark of such processes is that 'women's concerns are still rarely heard, let alone addressed, by policy makers during [formal] peace settlements'.[5] While the ending of armed conflict presents opportunities for men and women, processes of conflict resolution often reiterate gendered stereotypes and inequalities.[6] Gender stereotypes of war and conflict, which typically position women as either 'non-violent' or as simply 'victims', 'undermines their desire to be taken seriously as political players'.[7] Women's apparent propensity for peacefulness, as often expressed in both nationalist discourse and conventional narratives, consistently fails to translate into the hard-political capital required for entry into the 'hard talk' of formal negotiations. For the most part, women's participation in peace processes has been largely restricted to the 'feminised', informal-level, typically cross-community grassroots engagement.[8] While such activism is important and powerful, it nevertheless sits quite comfortably with prevalent stereotypical assumptions of women's innate peacefulness. Gender segregation between formal and informal peace-building augments the prevailing assumption that somehow women, more than men, possess abilities for reaching across the divide in times of conflict, accentuating the myth of women being 'outside' conflict. Furthermore, women's role as peace activists is easily discounted and disregarded as non-political; there is no greater illustration of this dismissal than the fact that despite their seeming innate talent for 'peacemaking', women continue to be universally absent from formal processes of peace negotiations the world over.

During the formative years of the peace process, the broader women's movement was organising around the issue of forthcoming peace negotiations. Members of the Northern Ireland Women's Rights Movement and the Belfast Women's Collective, both of which deliberately eschewed republican or loyalist identities, began agitating on women's right for inclusion in peace negotiations *as* women.[9] Furthermore, women within Northern Ireland's mainstream political parties were also endeavouring to exert some political influence in any future negotiations. Working-class republican women established *Clár na mBan* and began organising to ensure that their voices and demands were not marginalised from the republican agenda in any future peace talks. In particular, their objectives were to push any peace process beyond the traditional confines of simply 'ending armed actions' and to instead pursue an agenda of peace with social justice, particularly focusing on women's role in a post-war society.[10]

The shared frustration among many women in Northern Ireland towards their perpetual exclusion from formal processes found its clearest expression in the establishment of the Northern Ireland Women's Coalition (NIWC). The NIWC formed as a corrective measure to the gender deficit, claiming 'that women could add something to the peace process that men could not'.[11] The coalition energised around notions of female solidarity,[12] urged women to put aside their differing identities in the cause of a unified sisterhood, and focused instead on their shared concerns regarding the absence of women's voices. Due to their avoidance of a position on the 'constitutional question', the NIWC were guided in the belief that the presence of women was in itself enough to bring a different perspective to the debate.[13] From a critical feminist perspective, there is a danger that embracing the 'acceptable' culturally endorsed role of women as peacemakers and bridge-builders risks diluting the overall feminist project. It is a position which 'fails to challenge the very stereotypes of masculinity and femininity which may need to be transformed if conflict is to be managed non-violently'.[14] While women had agitated for women's rights within their own political parties, the formation of the NIWC propelled gender to the forefront of the burgeoning peace process. The uniqueness of an emerging all-female political party within the often inhospitable and inimical field of male-dominated, oppositional nationalist politics caught the media and the public's attention. It is important to recall, however, that their electoral advancement arose primarily by accident rather than design. The 1996 Forum elections included a 'top-up' mechanism in a deliberate attempt to include political parties aligned to loyalist paramilitaries. Based on electoral strength, two seats at the talks table were allocated to the top ten-performing parties. Despite a low but relatively respectful vote for an all-women and brand-new political party, the NIWC's 7,731 votes (1.07 per cent) were enough to secure its two seats at the 1996 multi-party talks.

Testament to their endeavours, the GFA inserted the statutory duty of all public bodies to advance equality in areas such as religion, gender, sexuality and disability. The agreement went beyond political institutional design and sought to address issues of political, civil and citizenship rights. From a gender perspective, the GFA recognises the 'right of women to full and equal participation', as well as the right of all individuals to 'pursue democratically national and political aspirations'. Section 75 of the Northern Ireland Act 1998 imposes a statutory duty on public authorities to promote equality of opportunity between persons who differ in terms of religious belief, political opinion, racial group, age, marital status and sexual orientation, between persons with a disability and without, persons with a dependent and without, and 'between women and men generally'.[15] While the peace process, and specifically the negotiations that led to a political agreement, embodied all the trademark characteristics of an elitist, male-dominated process, the GFA is extolled by some for the ways in which women of various political shades formed strategic alliances to ensure that their voices and interests were represented at the talks.[16] Much has been written on the role the NIWC played in 'representing women' at formal negotiations but equally, thanks to the sustained and imaginative efforts of the women's sector and many other civil-society organisations, the GFA contained significant clauses on the twin rights agenda: equalities and inclusions.[17] It is important also to recognise that others offer a rather less benign account of the GFA negotiations, as nothing more than a classic 'old boys' club' which saw republican and non-republican women alike excluded from them.[18] In particular, the widely celebrated commitment to gender equality remains as it was undoubtedly intended – purely aspirational.

The years following the GFA were characterised by serial suspensions of the Executive in the face of the political standoffs regarding IRA arms decommissioning, as detailed in Chapter 2. Interpretations of the agreement's transformative potential across a myriad of social and political issues were found to be misplaced, as issues such as policing and justice reform, prisoner releases, parades, and conflict legacy issues bequeathed a political realm consumed solely with state-centric concerns. Within this dysfunctional devolution, women were very much the minority players within the Stormont Assembly. Negotiations designed to establish a basis for trust and cooperation culminated with the St Andrews Agreement in

October 2006, paving the way for the restoration of power-sharing in the North. With the NIWC now disbanded in the wake of disappointing election returns, the St Andrews talks were distinctly male-dominated and focused solely on the principles of consociation between what had become the two largest parties, Sinn Féin and the Democratic Unionist Party (DUP). Within this elite-fashioned, male-dominated process, it was not surprising to find that gender equality receded as a political priority.[19] One could argue that gender equality was in fact never deemed a genuine political priority in the first instance, given the lack of political teeth regarding its 'enforcement'. The overall appraisal by many concurs that the political potential within the GFA has failed to translate into discernible gains for women in Northern Irish society.[20] The remainder of this chapter critically examines the position of women and the role of gender in Northern Ireland a generation after the signing of the agreement.

Women's representation in electoral politics

Low levels of female political representation are not unique to Northern Ireland, with a vast body of research revealing male political dominance as a consistent global pattern.[21] The signing and ratification of the GFA in 1998, however, was lauded by many, though by no means all, as a catalyst for a new type of post-Troubles politics in Northern Ireland, with genuine potential for diversity and equality in political life with respect to gender.[22] Though some women have made significant progress in areas of paid employment, public bodies and senior civil service positions, their opportunities for public governance and political representation have stagnated.[23] Despite the commitments enshrined in the 1998 Agreement, Northern Ireland consistently lags behind the UK's other regional assemblies, where devolution in Scotland and Wales has yielded significant dividends for levels of female representation.[24] Historically, Northern Ireland's record on female descriptive representation emerges as distinctively bleak. During the first fifty years of its existence (1921 to 1972), a total of nine women were elected to its devolved parliament, a mere 4 per cent of all elected members during that period. The eruption of armed conflict in 1969 positioned state-centric issues firmly as the primary concerns of Northern Irish political life. The links between militarism and hegemonic masculinity (though women were active protagonists in the conflict also) served to reaffirm the orthodoxy of male political dominance, ensuring that the realm of politics was conceptualised and presented as a thoroughly masculine one. Elections to Westminster lucidly illustrate the predominance of men, with only three female MPs elected in the region prior to the GFA.

In 1998, the prospect of a new chamber comprising 108 Assembly members presented a sizeable and new field of opportunity for women to cultivate political advances. Furthermore, proportional representation (PR) electoral systems have proven to be favourable to increasing levels of female representation.[25] Despite the inimical masculine culture of Northern Irish politics, auspicious omens such as the introduction of a PR electoral system, the presence of the NIWC, and the unambiguous commitment to women's full political participation in the text of the GFA gave grounds that the newly formed political structures were, at the very least, relatively receptive to a new era of female representation. Despite some very recent modest increases, women's formal participation over the course of the last two decades is marked by vast levels of under-representation, where the gendered characteristics of Northern Irish formal politics since 1998 have proven quite resilient to change. Regardless of the spotlight on gender and women's right to political participation during the GFA negotiations, the first 1998 Assembly dolefully indicated 'business as usual', with women comprising 16 per cent of the overall candidates and a paltry 13 per cent of those elected to the new chamber. Due to an increase of female candidates representing Sinn Féin and the Alliance Party (rising by 10 and 11 per cent, respectively), the 2003 Assembly elections produced a modest increase from 14 female Members of the Legislative Assembly (MLAs) in 1998 to 18. Given the rhetorical commitments to women's full and equal political participation, one would expect the sounding of alarm bells within the main political parties in reaction to the dispiriting patterns of women's representation in the new Assembly. The 2003 and 2007 Assembly elections revealed overt stagnation in the political fortunes of women, with just 18 female political representatives elected in both polls. The doleful gender consistencies across several electoral contests are indicative of the low priority afforded by the main political parties to women's equal political representation. Appraisals of Northern Ireland's female representation would be entirely dismal were it not for the modest yet significant upturn in the 2016 Assembly contest. While the number of female MLAs rose to 20 in 2011, a total of 30 female Members were elected to the Assembly in May 2016, representing a 50 per cent increase on 2011. The Assembly elections in March 2017 once again reaffirmed this relatively progressive trend, with women comprising 27 of the now reduced figure of 90 seats, again representing a relatively respectable 30 per cent. The 2016 and 2017 figures stand out as the largest number of female MLAs elected since 1998, but are also important given that they effectively 'stopped the rot' in the dismally low levels of female MLAs up to that point.

Despite their historically low levels of representation in local council elections, success rates for women have gradually increased over time, from 7 per cent in 1977 to 14 per cent in 1997, to 19 per cent in 2001.[26] A gender breakdown of the May 2014 local elections for the 11 new local councils in Northern Ireland indicates a moderate increase of female representation. Of the 906 candidates standing for election, 222 (24.5 per cent) were women; of the 462 elected councillors, 116 were women, representing a relatively impressive 25 per cent, signally a slight increase on the 23 per cent recorded in 2011 for the previous 26 district council system. Of the current 11 local councils in Northern Ireland, 4 had a female mayor/chair and a further 3 had a female deputy mayor/chair elected for the civic year 2015/16, representing 31.8 per cent of posts overall. For 2014/15, under the previous 26 district council system, 26.9 per cent of such posts were held by females. In the 2017 Westminster election, there were 36 female candidates (33 per cent), and a total of 4 female MPs (22.2 per cent) were elected from Northern Ireland. Sinn Féin has 2 female Members, followed by the DUP with 1, and an Independent Member (Sylvia Hermon, North Down). The proportion of female candidates in Northern Ireland for the 2015 Westminster election (24 per cent) increased on the previous election in 2010 (19 per cent). Of the 24 per cent of candidates who were female, the 2015 results, however, saw a downward trend with only 2 elected (11 per cent), compared with 4 elected in 2010 (22 per cent). Despite the decrease in the proportion of female candidates from 33 per cent in the 2017 Westminster election to 27 per cent in 2019, 4 female MPs out of 18 Northern Ireland MPs were elected, representing no change from the 2017 result. Northern Ireland's current standing again remains in stark contrast to the overall UK trend, which saw an increase in female MPs, rising from 23 per cent in 2010 to 29 per cent in 2015. If we take the Westminster election figures in conjunction with the relatively high levels of female representation in the Scottish and Welsh assemblies, it is clear that Northern Ireland remains significantly out of step with its UK counterparts. While Northern Ireland can rightfully boast women as the leaders of three main political parties, the reality is that formal, electoral politics remains thoroughly male-dominated. Despite the optimism engendered by the GFA and its potential for new politics in a 'new Northern Ireland', the unequivocal and persistent trend is a damning indictment of women's low levels of political representation. The matters of causal links and explanatory factors are explored below.

The issues at stake here go beyond the aesthetics of women's presence and visibility. The dearth of critical consideration within political parties towards increasing women's presence and participation, coupled with an inability or unwillingness to implement effective mechanisms to address it, bequeaths a realm of formal politics that lacks a 'critical mass', thus tempering the political effectiveness of those women successfully elected. Though the idea of increasing women's presence and participation is entirely legitimate and laudable, it would however be foolhardy to assume that a quantitative increase in women's formal representation in Northern Ireland automatically equates to an increase in gender equality or feminist-leaning legislation. Additionally, it is important to be mindful of the old adage that 'not all women are feminists, and not all feminists are women'. The idea of a 'critical mass' of female political representatives, however, shifts our analysis from descriptive (numbers of women elected) to substantive (agency; effects of women's presence) forms of representation.

Anne Phillips'[27] theory of 'the politics of presence' suggests that female politicians are best equipped to represent the interests of women, thus highlighting a causal link between descriptive and substantive representation. Although such a contention appears drenched in blind gender essentialism, Phillips' argument is built upon constructed differences between women and men in their everyday lives, such as child-rearing, education and occupation, divisions of paid and unpaid labour, exposure to violence and sexual harassment. The regional assemblies in Wales and Scotland have seen significant progress in increasing women's participation in formal politics, and furthermore, also indicate nascent and discernible improvements from the increase in women's political representation.[28] In the first term of the Welsh National Assembly, Chaney's analysis of the 327 plenary debates found that women parliamentarians had a qualitative impact on the nature of politicking, for approximately half of all debates included discussions related directly to what are broadly considered 'women's issues'. In addition, his research also reveals significant advancement of gender equality and broad feminist issues via their cross-party Equality Committee. Chaney correctly argues for attentiveness to the fissures of difference among women, and in particular, the links between women's presence as elected representatives, their substantive representation and their backgrounds, social class and attitudes, among others. However, women in general are statistically more likely than their male counterparts to use the institutional mechanisms of governance to promote gender equality in policy and law. Increasing women's levels of representation, therefore, goes beyond descriptive representation or visibility; a substantial increase in women as elected representatives has proven to yield significant changes in policy agendas and output.[29] As Ward correctly points out, however, the dominance of the ethno-national cleavages significantly militates against the possibilities of women's 'critical mass', working across opposing party-political lines.[30]

Gender and ethno-nationalist politics: exploring the causes of women's under-representation

Party ideologies

A conventional ideological reading that contrasts progressive nationalism with conservative unionism obscures both the nuanced complexities and overt disparities between the two. Women's rights tend to resonate strongly with the nationalist/republican 'equality' agenda, and moreover, women's eclectic and important roles as combatants and activists within the republican movement ensured that feminism, or perhaps more accurately, republican feminism, was incorporated into their broad ideological canon of Irish nationalism. Although patriarchy and sexism undoubtedly existed within all formations of republicanism, high levels of politicisation and gender consciousness-raising among republican women advanced linkages made between national and gender identities and led to a realisation that they were 'dually oppressed'.[31] Republican women's experiences of sexism and patriarchy during and after the Troubles, however, demonstrate the vexed and often contradictory relationship between republicanism and feminism,[32] and so any generalised claims regarding gender equality and Irish nationalism and republicanism need to be measured and nuanced. Despite the complexities and numerous allegations regarding the cover-up of sexual abuse at the hands of republicans, Sinn Féin is lauded for its exemplary track record in consistently returning the highest percentage of female elected representatives.[33]

While nationalism ensconced gender within the broader nationalist agenda of equality and ending discrimination, feminism was greeted with outright suspicion in many unionist and loyalist circles, where it was deemed a 'dirty word'.[34] The broad church of unionism, including mainstream political parties, moderate unionists, state forces and loyalist paramilitaries, was overwhelmingly concerned with defending and preserving the state (and status quo), therefore limiting the transformative political potential for loyalist and unionist women. In general, loyalist women carried the guns, loyalist men used them,[35] and so women's and men's roles within loyalist organisations mirrored the traditionalist patriarchal social structure.[36] In addition to their conservative outlook, the juxtaposition of republicanism with feminism by some during the 1980s and 1990s ensured that unionism remained at best sceptical of feminism, retaining a strong conservative view on women's roles in society, including party politics.

In contrast to the overtly republican feminist standpoints on a myriad of 'public and private' issues, mainstream unionism has typically offered rather terse and conservative policy positions on women's status. The

DUP position on women has historically highlighted their vulnerability and victim status, and thus generated a party position that women be 'protected' from rape and domestic violence.[37] The party's 2015 Westminster Manifesto and 2016 Assembly Election Manifesto made no specific mention of women or gender equality. While the party typically eschews direct reference to women's political representation, it has nonetheless consistently stated its desire to promote equality for all, including women. Like its DUP counterparts, the Ulster Unionist Party (UUP) is firmly wedded to the merit principle and would oppose any policy of positive discrimination. While the issues of gender and women's political participation have all but disappeared from the recent election manifestos of most mainstream political parties, the Alliance Party has maintained a strong advocacy position right up to the 2016 Assembly manifesto which tackled multiple issues related to gender and women, and made specific mention of establishing 'mentoring schemes to assist women in the public and private sectors, with an aim to increase the number of women in decision-making positions'. The ideological schism between nationalism and unionism therefore orients their respective policies and approaches to women's political participation.

It would be disingenuous and wholly inaccurate, however, to dismiss loyalism and unionism as being entirely inhospitable to progressive feminist politics. Up until the recent election of Arlene Foster as DUP leader, the Progressive Unionist Party (PUP) was one of the few political parties in Northern Ireland to boast a female party leader. Dawn Purvis was elected leader of the small loyalist party in 2007, until her resignation in June 2010.[38] In contrast to mainstream unionist parties, the PUP anchors its ideological outlook in a class-based paradigm, with a central focus on equality and social justice.[39] Moreover, the PUP also marked itself as distinctive by adopting a straightforward pro-choice position on abortion, a seismic and bold move considering both the broadly conservative nature of unionism in Northern Ireland and, of course, the party's unionist/Protestant support base. In addition to the election of Dawn Purvis as PUP leader, Anne Dickson was the leader of the short-lived Unionist Party of Northern Ireland in 1976 until its demise in the early 1980s. Furthermore, Arlene Foster was elected DUP leader and First Minister of Northern Ireland in January 2016. Relatively high levels of women's visibility within unionism and loyalism caution against an over-simplistic dichotomy of nationalism/republicanism as 'good', unionism/loyalism as 'bad'. As will be discussed later in this chapter, surveys consistently indicate high levels of progressive and liberal attitudes among Protestants. While nationalism and unionism display significant points of departure regarding their attitudes to women's roles and status, they nevertheless possess many points of comparison. First, nationalism and unionism remain male-dominated, particularly at a leadership level, where issues such as abortion are considered and delineated through gendered and often socially conservative attitudes. Second, despite a broad suite of available mechanisms available to increase women as candidates and political representatives, not a single political party, unionist or nationalist, has adopted such strategies, opting instead for more incremental, piecemeal changes. Third, both ideologies subsume women's rights and equality within an overarching national movement. In other words, gender equality remains wholly contingent on 'national equality'.

Meritocracy? Candidate selection

The barriers to women's participation in Northern Ireland are attributed to several factors, including the propensity of gender stereotypes, male monopoly of power, gender division of domestic labour and education, training and occupational status, among others.[40] With regard to increasing the selection and recruitment of female candidates, Sinn Féin marks itself out from others through a number of direct strategies. The party reserves 50 per cent of its *Ard Comhairle* (National Executive) seats for women. Furthermore, the party hierarchy has the power to overturn local candidate selections if their overall gender candidacy falls short of its 30 per cent target.[41] The unofficial quota of 30 per cent has a measurable impact, particularly in its Assembly representation, thus positioning the party as one of the most progressive in terms of female representation. As a nationalist party, the Social Democratic and Labour Party (SDLP) is disposed towards a relatively conservative standpoint, adopting a more cautious approach to issues of gender quotas and candidacy. Candidate selection remains embedded in local selection processes, which invariably favour incumbents, typically male MLAs, who also have a strong say in the choice of their running mates.

Despite boasting one of the few political parties in the UK and Ireland with a female party leader, the DUP remains firmly wedded to its formal meritocratic approach, rejecting mechanisms of quotas or positive discrimination. As a result of its endeavours to eschew what it sees as superficial tokenism,[42] the party lags significantly behind in its promotion of female representatives. Up until recent times, the UUP situated the locus of candidate selection power at a local level. In 2007, the party introduced candidate shortlists, constituency primaries and a headquarters-dominated election committee which retained a final decision on candidates.[43] While the shift of selection power from localised associations to the party headquarters is significant, it has yet to make any discernible impact on the dominance of men among its party candidates. The Alliance Party occupies the so-called 'middle ground' in Northern Irish politics, although historically the party was often understood as a 'unionist party' with a small 'u'. The party headquarters takes the lead in candidacy selection and provides an approved list of potential candidates to each constituency organisation, providing the party with a strong female membership among its political representatives. While most parties favour the involvement of headquarters in the selection process, the results have been mixed. This is not, however, to suggest that women are completely absent within unionism. The UUP had its own women's section, and both the UUP and DUP have had female political representatives at Westminster. Notwithstanding, mainstream political parties have demonstrated no initiative or interest in gender equality, and their structural designs do not prioritise the incorporation of gender considerations.[44] This is particularly pertinent when examining the issue of candidate selection processes.

Given the vast discrepancies between men and women in terms of rates of pay, education and the gender division of domestic labour, it is safe to assume that the merit principle, however, is tipped well in favour of male candidates. Given the role of parties as the primary gateway to political representation, the often diverse candidate selection processes remain a significant factor in determining the gender composition of Northern Ireland's public representatives. In particular, reselection of sitting representatives is relatively high in the North, producing a discernible incumbency effect,[45] which typically shifts the balance of favour towards men. Factors such as financial independence and the gender division of domestic labour invariably tip the balance of favour towards men. One of the few effective mechanisms for ensuring an increase in female political representation is the Sex Discrimination (Election Candidates NI) Act 2002, which provides for political parties to positively discriminate in order to increase quantities of female election candidates. Despite the availability of such a provision, not a single political party in Northern Ireland has utilised what is potentially a highly effective mechanism. Unlike ethno-religious equality, however, there is no statutory requirement for parties to promote equality between the sexes, illustrating once again the lack of urgency afforded to gender issues.

Factors beyond the party system

The 'weak supply' of female aspirants to political office is often advanced as a plausible and overarching explanation of the under-representation of women in public life.[46] While it may be tempting to suggest that the dearth of female political representation stems from a lack of interest in formal party politics, research consistently reveals a saturation of female party members at the grassroots level of political parties in the North.[47] For instance, the DUP and UUP boast an impressive record on female party membership, 60 and 50 per cent, respectively.[48] Female presence and participation recede significantly, however, once we begin to move towards the upper echelons of the party machinery. Despite the rhetoric of inclusion and numerous manifesto pledges, there exists a striking gender division of labour within Northern Ireland's main political parties. Empirical research on the day-to-day operations of the region's principal parties largely finds women located in 'behind-the-scenes' work.[49] Research on the republican movement uncovered striking instances of women's 'back-room' work during the GFA negotiations, with men positioned as the primary negotiators. Equally troubling is the emergence of a post-Troubles narrative referring to republican women as the 'backbone of the struggle', much to the chagrin of female republicans.[50] Similar gendered patterns exist within the DUP, with some women just making tea and/or undertaking roles such as treasurer, running constituency offices, canvassing, attending meetings, fundraising and organising events – described internally as the ubiquitous 'backbone roles'.[51] Like the typical patriarchal household, many political parties appear to exhibit a clear gender division of labour, undoubtedly governed by cultural norms and expectations regarding appropriate masculine and feminine roles. Given the high proportion of women within the bottom ranks of the parties, male dominance in the upper echelons is unquestionably facilitated and enabled by women's unpaid, low-status 'domestic' labour within many of Northern Ireland's political parties. While many may occupy such roles out of choice, there is, however, a striking pattern that exhibits the stock-in-trade characteristics of gendered occupational segregation. The concentration of women at the bottom tiers of any political movement undeniably creates, at the very least, a patriarchal culture which only serves to impede women's political progression.

There are also other factors to consider. There are widely held beliefs among the public and political parties of a marked reluctance among women when it comes to being considered for candidacy.[52] There is unquestionably more than a kernel of truth to those convictions, but rather than apportioning 'blame' for the dearth of female representatives or potential candidates, the salient issue is to explore the culture and characteristics of formal politics that repel, or at the very least, dampen women's enthusiasm for state-centric politics. Northern Irish society retains a clear sexual division of labour in the domestic realm, a marked segregation of gender in paid occupational roles, and a prevailing conservative outlook regarding gender roles and sexuality. In this context, it is consistently and almost exclusively women who need to consider the burden of 'work–life balance'. Women's assigned role as primary caregivers, along with a multiplicity of other unpaid domestic tasks, invariably deprives women of the appetite and/or the opportunity to enter formal, paid employment. Moreover, the gender division of domestic labour ensures that men and women do not enter the public realm on an equal footing. Qualitative research among female representatives across all major political parties reveals recurring feelings of guilt among female representatives for 'abandoning' their children, the constraints of a busy public role alongside their unpaid domestic roles, and the unsocial working hours. In addition, there remain other more implicit barriers, including the stigmatisation of those women deemed to have abandoned 'their primary role as mother and caregiver' to pursue a career in the public realm, either as a political representative or in paid employment.

Joanne Nagel's[53] interrogation of nationalism delineates the linkages between ethno-nationalism and normative masculine traits. The institutionalisation of ethno-nationalism within Northern Irish politics, therefore, codifies the arena of formal politics as thoroughly masculine. Enshrining competing ethno-national blocs as the primary political category has thus served to propagate a male monopoly of formal political power while reifying stereotypical masculinity as the 'ideal' form of political engagement. With adversarial masculinity exalted as the primary cultural force, the arena of formal politics in Northern Ireland reinforces masculinity, squeezing out potential spaces for alternative styles and forms of political engagement. The levels of outright sexist abuse and harassment of NIWC Forum and Assembly members is well documented,[54] and is indicative of the hostility meted out to those perceived to have transgressed normative feminine and masculine spheres. The non-position adopted by the NIWC on the constitutional question served to further single the party out as a legitimate target for verbal haranguing, and, often, sexist taunts. In other words, political cleavages other than the dominant ethno-sectarian framework are deemed a threat to the 'stability' of Northern Ireland's adversarial ethno-national blocs. Examining the experiences of NIWC members reveals the narrow and highly gendered ways in which politics is conceptualised by the main players. Those who refuse to conform to either, such as the case of the NIWC, experienced the personal wrath and institutional preclusions which only serve to alienate those who profess an alternative political identity and agenda. Moreover, research on women within the main political parties reveals consistent levels of frustration at the dominance of masculinity, which, they assert, tends to decrease the pace of political progress within the Assembly.[55] Agitating within formal political parties also presents constraints and opportunities. According to Ian O'Flynn,[56] while nationalist and unionist women can and do challenge party policy on gender internally, more often than not this internal struggle is tempered by an overarching allegiance to their ethno-national identity and respective political party.

It is important to state that critical examinations of contemporary formal politics in Northern Ireland uncover little evidence of any formal barriers or explicit gender discrimination.[57] Nonetheless, political institutions – by virtue of their cultures, norms and practices – are not gender-neutral. Formal politics is often viewed by grassroots activists as a system dominated by wealthy, often white, men (and of course sometimes women) vying for power for its own sake and for their own personal gain,[58] and therefore is inimical to the development of feminist politics within the formal sphere. If elite power-sharing enshrines fissures of political difference firmly along ethno-national lines, it follows that adversarial masculinity synonymous with competing ethnic blocs finds a privileged position in the style, substance and culture of Northern Irish politics. Normative masculine behavioural stereotypes are those most cherished in the often belligerent and bruising arena of representative politics. The prevalence of a conservative gender order discursively reinforces the notion that the qualities required and revered within formal politics are quintessentially masculine in character.

Women's civil society and community activism

Given the largely conservative nature of most mainstream political parties in Northern Ireland,[59] women's participation within male-dominated, ethno-national political parties does not necessarily represent the most nascent way of pursuing feminist politics. For many women and for feminists, the formal arena of politics was viewed as another part of the patriarchal order, and one which was so masculine that it was best avoided altogether.[60] Due to the male monopoly and elitist nature of institutional politics in Northern Ireland, women have historically turned to grassroots activism and community politics to exercise some influence over the policies that affect their families, communities and themselves.[61] Globally, many feminists organise either through non-hierarchical autonomous groups and collective actions, or through participation within social movements.[62] Progressive social movements seek to build the collective power of excluded, marginalised or oppressed constituents so that they can access human rights and challenge dominant ideologies and power relations.[63] Formal political parties, imbued with relations of power and hierarchical control, organise for the attainment of state control, and hence, are unlikely sites which will foster a progressive feminist agenda.[64] Despite its valuable supports and services, particularly in some of the most marginalised communities, community activism and civic society organising in Northern Ireland is rarely afforded value or status by the state. In the dichotomy of formal politics and informal activism, power, finance and status firmly reside in the former, with the latter often dismissed as an extension of unpaid domestic labour. In spite of this, examining the informal sphere demonstrates that women in Northern Ireland are not politically apathetic nor merely complacent.

There is a strong history of women organising outside formal political structures in Northern Ireland, providing essential support, training and services in areas of domestic violence, poverty, childcare, education and drug addiction, among many others.[65] Much of the community sector's motivation is the perceived inadequacies of the state; community activism, or what Elizabeth Porter[66] terms the 'situated politics of everyday life', allows women to engage in issues that directly affect them and their communities. With formal politics firmly governed by state-centric and security concerns during the Troubles, it was often community activism and the voluntary sector that filled the void, providing essential supports and services for some of the most marginalised communities. For the most part, this activism was not concerned with aping or paralleling formal structures, but developed as an alternative form of politics, addressing issues that are all too often neglected or excluded by the state. In particular, the sluggish pace of formal politics contrasted sharply with the high velocity of community organising.

Given the highly polarised context in which they developed, it is unsurprising that many of Northern Ireland's women's-sector groups, though by no means all, organised along ethno-religious lines. Nevertheless, feminist and women's cross-community organising is often extolled for demonstrating ways in which women can work across deeply polarised communities, and there were many instances of such throughout the Troubles and beyond. While the theoretical kernel of transversal politics resides with intersectional feminist Nira Yuval-Davis,[67] Northern Ireland has often provided sound empirical evidence of cooperation between women of polarised ethno-national groups.[68] Eilish Rooney,[69] however, takes issue with transversal notions of 'dialogue across difference', arguing that the women depicted, constituted and claimed by the dominant discourse are of course women who appear to be uncomplicated by sectarian or class tensions. Often the women depicted 'fit an ideal picture of one who is not involved in discredited politics; or at least not involved through her agency or consent'.[70] Other scholarly appraisals of transversal politics deem it as an essentialist form of 'lowest common denominator politics',[71] which papers over the conflict experiences of many women in the North and attempts to reduce women's issues solely to those perceived as being universally shared by women.

Regardless, the strong presence of 'transversalism' among some of Northern Ireland's women's groups during the latter years of the Troubles engendered the conditions which resulted in the establishment of the Women's Support Network (WSN) in 1989. According to Gráinne McCoy, the 'opening of a women's centre was viewed by women in many types of campaigns and groups in Northern Ireland as an achievement in its own right and a necessary stage in the process of empowering women'.[72] The WSN today attracts members from several women's centres in Belfast as well other member organisations, including Belfast Women's Training Services and Women's Resource and Development Agency. Also included are members of the public-sector trade unions and another important partner, Women Into Politics. The WSN continues to provide a range of supports and services to community-based women's centres, projects and infrastructure groups and associate members drawn from across the community and voluntary sector who support women, families and communities. In the lead up to the GFA negotiations, the Network and its partners mobilised 400 women's groups across Northern Ireland in a major policy initiative, *Making Women Seen and Heard*. Along with the representatives of people with disabilities, full-time carers, lesbians and gays, people from ethnic minorities, lone parents and other disadvantaged groups, women achieved an explicit commitment in the eventual peace accord to equalities (in the plural), and above all to a right to inclusion and participation in the decision processes of the future Northern Ireland.[73] Moreover, the women's community sector played a vital role in gathering public support for the cross-border referenda on the GFA.

Though informal political activism and formal party politics in Northern Ireland are often depicted as 'two parallel universes',[74] the establishment and relative success of the NIWC provided a vital nexus between women's formal and informal political activism during the years of the peace process. In addition to providing presence and visibility for women during and after the GFA, one of the many vital contributions of the NIWC was the establishment of the Civic Forum, which provided a gateway for community activists and civil-society groups into the Executive. In 2002, however, the Civic Forum ceased to function, following the latest collapse and subsequent suspension of the power-sharing institutions. Much like the rhetoric of equality and the promise of 'new politics', the Civic Forum faded from view as the power play between ethno-national blocs once again eclipsed all other concerns during the suspension years between 2002 and 2007. The dysfunction within institutional politics during this period, marred by distrust over paramilitary weapons, policing and justice, among many other things, sapped the morale of those within the community sector, and reaffirmed their sense of alienation from mainstream, formal politics. Moreover, the diverse spaces and equality agendas created during the GFA were slowly squeezed by the dominance of a state-centric programme for peace and security. The negotiations aimed at restoring stable, power-sharing governance culminated in the St Andrews Agreement in October 2006. With the NIWC now disbanded, the St Andrews talks were distinctly male-dominated and focused solely on the principles of consociation between what had by that stage become the two largest parties, Sinn Féin and the DUP. Within this elite-fashioned, male-dominated process, it was not surprising to find that gender equality receded as a political priority.[75]

Following the demise of the NIWC in 2006, the energy around women's activism once again returned to the civil-society sector, where it remains relatively vibrant and wide-reaching. As the initial tide of optimism regarding women's formal political representation receded, others were identifying new mechanisms for ensuring women's voices are heard. Although the GFA preceded United Nations Security Council Resolution (UNSCR) 1325,[76] the historic development emboldened many women in the community sector, culminating in the establishment of Hanna's House, an all-Ireland feminist network. At a special conference on *Women Delivering Peace & Security* in 2012, members of Hanna's House concluded with the following recommendations:

> women's participation and representation; and gender perspectives on conflict prevention; protection of women and girls; and relief and recovery. In relation to the Good Friday Agreement, participants support the Hanna's House proposal to retrospectively weave UNSCR 1325 into the institutions of the Peace Agreement; to ensure that they set gender targets; and that they have adopted a gender perspective on all of their work.

Funded by Atlantic Philanthropies, Hanna's House was at the forefront of the UNSCR 1325 campaign in Ireland. Despite their many successes, not least their ability in bringing many diverse groups together under a single banner, the reliance on overseas funding also ensured a limited lifespan. Nevertheless, many women's community groups continue to use UNSCR 1325 as a platform in demanding women's right to a voice in any future political and social arrangements. The pressure exerted by Hanna's House and women's civil-society groups on the British and Irish governments yielded significant advancements where both states now have National Action Plans (NAPs) in place for the integration of UNSCR 1325.[77]

Northern Ireland today retains a vibrant and wide-reaching women's community sector. A study commissioned by the Community Foundation in 2001 estimated that there were some 1,071 'traditional' women's organisations active across the North, and 423 'activist' women's groups/centres, with the vast majority of the latter (some 90 per cent) being community-based.[78] The ability of this sector, however, to influence those who wield power in the formal realm remains relatively low, with formal and informal politics still governed by rigid boundaries. Furthermore, the effectiveness of women's community and civil-society activism as a valuable counterbalance to the state is significantly tempered by issues of funding. In exchange for sustained support from the Department of Social Development (DSD), Belfast community centres have to a large extent become service providers. According to Cynthia Cockburn, centre managers must devote a great deal of their time to paperwork if they are to satisfy the authorities and secure resources, and the time and stress involved in this have increased with the downturn in the economy and cuts to public-sector spending. The centres must increasingly compete with each other, and thus cooperation has greatly diminished.[79]

While the women's informal sector continues to work at the coalface of social and economic disadvantage, the prospect of maintaining previously high levels of such community organising is significantly challenged by the dearth of funding available, particularly since the latest collapse in global capitalism. In 2008, the Northern Ireland Women's European Platform (NIWEP) urged the government to develop a specific stream of funding for women's civil-society organisations, particularly in relation to key areas such as training and education. The current agenda of economic austerity, however, is having a negative impact on the government's response to this call, and thus undermines women's community organising. Examinations of women's community activism in recent years have led many to concur that it has become too 'professionalised' and 'NGO-ised', with a distinct loss of the political dynamic present during the 1990s and early 2000s.[80] Understood as a 'generational' shift, contemporary feminist organising in Northern Ireland is increasingly concerned with issues of bodily autonomy and sexuality, rather than with issues of class and material inequalities. Outside the 'official informal sector' women continue to organise as feminists in groups such as Belfast Feminist Network or around single-issue causes in bodies such as Alliance for Choice and Pro Choice NI. This 'post-millennial' feminism, rather than being embedded in working-class struggles in housing estates and workplaces, is a movement mainly of educated women and students, confident in their social networking skills. It has its own priorities – sexuality, reproductive rights, multiculturalism and violence against women – in contrast to the policy-challenging agenda of socialism, inclusion and workers' rights inspired by the former alliance of community centres and trade unions.[81]

Despite the demise of the NIWC in 2006 and the 'NGO-isation' of many, though not all, organisations, the women's community sector has made some inroads in attempting to re-establish a discourse at Stormont around women's policy interests. The NIWEP has established an all-party group at the Assembly on UNSCR 1325 which enjoys the membership of seven different political parties. Unanimously passed in October 2000, UNSCR 1325 reaffirmed 'the important role of women in the prevention and resolution of conflicts and peace-building ... and the need to increase their role in decision-making'. The resolution has been used as a platform by some feminists and women's groups in other regions emerging from armed conflict as a platform and tool for demanding the inclusion of women in all aspects of conflict resolution. Similarly in Northern Ireland, representatives from various political parties are increasingly aware of the need for mechanisms such as UNSCR 1325 and gender quotas that have the potential to deliver greater female involvement in formal politics.[82] While the now defunct Civic Forum offered a platform for grassroots and community input, particularly for women, the failure to resurrect the body alongside the restoration of devolved powers in 2007 is emblematic of the state-centric approach and indifference to alternative modes of political input. The issue of a revived civic panel received a much-needed boost in the recent *New Decade, New Approach* document in January 2020. In the text of the latest deal, the parties commit to putting civic engagement and public consultation at the heart of policy-making. The parties have agreed that the existing Compact Civic Advisory Panel should be reformed to include a renewed membership appointed within six months by way of a Public Appointments process. The parties have also agreed that about one to two issues will be commissioned per year for civic engagement. The Panel will be invited to propose the most appropriate model of engagement for specific issues, including one Citizens' Assembly a year. The issues will be identified by the Executive and, following consideration of the assigned issues, recommendations will be made to the Executive by the Panel. It remains to be seen if the envisaged reformed version of the Civic Advisory Panel can once again provide some meaningful conduit between Northern Ireland's formal and informal political spheres. As EU peace-funding continues to dry up alongside an uncertain post-Brexit landscape, women's community-sector organising in the future will be more dependent on state funding through the Department of Social Protection. Under the Fresh Start Agreement (at A3.9), there is a commitment for the 'development of a programme to increase the participation and influence of women in community development'. As was the case in the 1998 accord, the resounding rhetoric and affirmations in the Fresh Start Agreement are meaningless in the face of the relentless hollowing-out of the women's sector by over ten years of austerity.

Insecurities in 'post-conflict'

Dominant approaches to peace and security typically reflect an androcentric perspective on international relations, and so feminist international relations scholars are centrally concerned with problematising prevailing definitions of security. As women are generally marginal to state-centric power structures, many feminist definitions start with the individual and/or community rather than the nation-state or international political system.[83] The resultant body of scholarly work reconceptualises security as multidimensional and multilevel to include not just military wars but also domestic violence, environmental security, unjust social relations, rape and poverty.[84] Much of traditional, male-dominated security theory assumes that security of the state is a precondition for security of the individual. Many feminists have called for a more 'bottom-up' approach, arguing that gender inequality itself is a direct cause of outbreaks of armed conflict.[85] Without falling into an essentialist cul-de-sac, men and women typically have differing needs, interests and concerns in post-war societies. While the *freedom from* military violence and war is undoubtedly a source of security for women, the *freedom to* access food and shelter, paid employment, education, state services and financial independence, among many other things, is equally important in securing women's post-war lives.[86] In particular, gender-based violence and restrictions on women's reproductive rights remain key sources of women's insecurity in societies emerging from armed conflict.

A vast body of work documenting the many instances of violence against women in the aftermath, and of course during, war challenges the conventional discourse of 'post-conflict' or a 'return to normal'.[87] Given the correlation between decreasing military violence and increasing forms of gender-based violence, 'post-conflict' is exposed as a period of continued violence and insecurity for women, where they remain socially, politically and economically marginalised and exposed to various forms of physical violence.[88] Despite the official rhetoric regarding Northern Ireland's status as the site of a more secure and peaceful dispensation, data collected over the course of the last two decades indicate that violence against women increased exponentially in the immediate aftermath of the paramilitary ceasefires of 1994. The category of 'domestic violence' encompasses a broad range of actions beyond the insidious act of direct, violent assaults and includes emotional, physical, financial, sexual and psychological forms of abuse. The United Nations defines gender-based violence as 'violence that is directed against a woman, because she is a woman, or violence that affects women disproportionately. It includes acts that inflict physical, mental or sexual harm or suffering, threats of such acts, coercion and other deprivations of liberty.' Men are of course also victims and survivors of domestic and sexual abuse, and I do not wish to denigrate or trivialise their narratives and experiences. The statistics, however, reveal an overwhelming gender pattern to domestic violence, both globally and in Northern Ireland: the overwhelming majority of victims are women.

While the GFA is lauded by many for ending decades of 'violence', increased levels of domestic and sexual violence in the aftermath of the 1994 ceasefires and the agreement serve to illustrate the androcentric and state-centric orthodoxies which underpin this partial peace. In Northern Ireland, violence specifically directed against women and girls – rape, trafficking, abuse in the home – appears to be growing rather than diminishing with the 'peace'.[89] The prevailing narrative of a post-war society belies the violent reality of women's daily lives in the region. Statistics from Women's Aid Federation Northern Ireland reveal that 14,714 women and 14,356 young persons and children received refuge between 1999 and 2013. The latest data from Women's Aid for the 2018–19 period indicate that 654 women and 421 children stayed in a refuge; 381 other women were denied access because refuges were full.[90] In the 12 months from 1 July 2018 to 30 June 2019, Police Service of Northern Ireland (PSNI) statistics show there were 31,531 domestic abuse incidents recorded by the police in Northern Ireland, an increase of 912 (3 per cent) on the previous 12 months and one of the highest 12-month periods recorded since the start of the data series in 2004/05.[91] The number of domestic abuse crimes recorded by the police reached 16,575, an increase of 1,496 (9.9 per cent) on the previous 12 months and the highest of any 12-month period recorded since 2004/05. There were 17 domestic abuse incidents and 9 domestic abuse crimes per 1,000 population, the incident rate and crime rate both increasing by one when compared with the previous 12 months. Domestic abuse crimes made up 16 per cent of all police recorded crime, an increase from 15 per cent during the previous 12 months.[92] Overall, in the period between 2004/05 and 2019/20, the annual number of incidents of 'domestic abuse' in Northern Ireland rose from 20,959 to 32,127.[93] By way of comparison, the highest level of assaults with a 'ethno-sectarian' motivation in any given year during that time-frame was 1,840, and by the end of the period the number of such attacks had fallen to 879.[94] Therefore, there are around 37 acts of violence committed by men against women in Northern Ireland today for every one that entails unionists or nationalists assaulting one another. It is clearly evident that the most pressing security threat to women in Northern Ireland since the GFA is not 'terrorism', a hard Brexit, dissident republican or loyalist groups, but rather gender-based violence that in almost 80 per cent of all incidents occurs at the hands of a partner, ex-partner or personal acquaintance. In January 2019, a dissident republican car bomb in Derry made national and international headlines, sparking days and weeks of analysis and discussion regarding this existential security threat. The disparity in attention between certain forms of ethno-sectarian violence and the shocking statistics regarding gender-based violence indicates a gendered hierarchy of violence and harm in Northern Ireland. Threats to women are often depicted as 'stranger danger'; the hyperbole depicting the perils of the public realm (dark alleys, consumption of alcohol in public spaces, and so forth) conceals the 'private hell' that many women endure. In February 2020, the well-known security correspondent for the *Irish News*, Allison Morris, called for stalking legislation to be extended to Northern Ireland after she spoke about the years of harassment she had received from a former partner. The reality is that current or former male partners account for over 80 per cent of domestic abusers in Northern Ireland.

In addition to the insidious effects of domestic violence, various organs of the state are perceived as consistently failing victims and survivors. Research conducted by Women's Aid Northern Ireland and Women's Centres Regional Partnership reveals high levels of reticence in reporting domestic and sexual abuse. Using in-depth interviews and focus groups, victims and survivors recalled their anger and frustration with the criminal justice response, which typically positions domestic violence as a minor crime or misdemeanour, with perpetrators often receiving short or suspended sentences. Others feared that psychological, financial or sexual violence within the 'private sphere' of marriage and intimate relationships would not be taken seriously by state agencies. The trial of four men in March 2018 – in which Irish rugby players Paddy Jackson and Stuart Olding were cleared of raping a 19-year-old woman, and two of their friends, Blane McIlroy and Rory Harrison, were cleared of indecent exposure and perverting the course of justice, respectively – revealed the trauma and burden placed upon complainants of rape and sexual assault. Moreover, the evidence used within the trial – particularly text messages between the defendants – exposed what many believe is a pervasiveness culture of misogyny and sexism. The 2018 trial, however, is not untypical. In 2015, Sir Keir Starmer, former Director of Public Prosecutions in England and Wales, published an independent review which was highly critical of the Public Prosecution Service in Northern Ireland with regard to their handling of allegations of rape and sexual violence by Máiría Cahill and two other victims against former IRA prisoner Martin Morris in west Belfast in the late 1990s. In September 2018, a further independent report by the Police Ombudsman into the same cases found that the victims were 'failed' by a disjointed PSNI investigation and recommended that four officers be disciplined. The traumatic experiences of complainants in both cases have exposed what many believe are structural and cultural flaws within the entire judicial system, and have rightly reignited debate regarding the handling and conduct of rape and sexual abuse allegations in Northern Ireland.

Recommendations from Women's Aid Northern Ireland, legal scholars and Women's Centres Regional Partnership include: the designation of domestic violence as a criminal offence; increased funding for provision of services and supports for victims and survivors; reform of the judicial system to help more women engage positively to take legal recourse and protection; and powers to compel perpetrators to cooperate and take responsibility for their violence. Furthermore, they also highlight the fact that patterns and archetypes of violence can be identified and used to inform women about self-protection and prevention strategies, as well as mainstreaming education about gender relations in order to challenge the prevalent entitlement mindset. Gender-based violence is consistently patterned with discernible causal links and, therefore, cannot be reduced to arbitrary, 'individual' criminal acts. There is a compelling need to anchor all approaches – including support services, legal, academic, judicial and policy – in a framework of equal gender relations.

Societies which normalise, rationalise and institutionalise the subordination of both women and femininity breed a wider culture of power inequalities that threatens the security of many women. Scholarly research on gender and conflict transition has repeatedly uncovered the inextricable links between violent masculinity and the ending of armed actions. In a changing political culture characterised by processes of demilitarisation, the narratives and practices of violent masculinities will reconfigure. Conventional forms of paramilitarism having largely subsided, the energies of violent masculinity found expression in other forms of violence, new and old. While ex-combatants, both male and female, undertook prominent positions in community and grassroots activism, others, however, and men in particular, experienced the cost of war in the form of drug addiction, alcohol abuse, hyper-vigilance and underemployment.[95] Paramilitaries in Northern Ireland remain primary arenas for overt expressions of hegemonic masculinity, shaped by prevailing narratives which conflate the violent protection of defined ethnic groups with normative masculinity. Despite the significant decline of militarism in Northern Ireland, the coalescence of normative masculinity and violence remains a stubborn residue of the Troubles.

The presence of structured gendered inequalities and pervasive gender-based discrimination in a society offers a promising line of inquiry for understanding the causes and utility of widespread gender-based violence.[96] A 2012 UN report found that levels of sexual and gender-based violence are most likely to occur in conditions of women's general subordination, their precarious economic conditions resulting from a lack of security from the state, and the existence and acceptance in culture that women's bodies are objects that belong to men.[97] We are not suggesting that the state is actively complicit in acts of gender-based violence; there are, however, compelling comparative case studies from other regions emerging from armed conflict which demonstrate the linkages between transformations in gender relations at a macro-level and the potential for conflict in intimate partnerships. In her comparison of the peace processes in Northern Ireland and Chiapas, Melanie Hoewer[98] found that while the former prioritised state-centric concerns such as power-sharing government, the latter recognised indigenous women's autonomy, and reversed neoliberal socio-economic processes. In contrast to Northern Ireland, the macro-peace process in Chiapas was informed equally by female and male perspectives, and in doing so created the conditions necessary for challenging community traditions and masculine power, leading to a significant decrease in gender-based violence.

The documented experiences of women's exposure to various forms of violence in the aftermath of armed conflict, in Northern Ireland and globally, undermine the very essence of terms such as 'peace process', 'conflict resolution' or 'post-conflict'. According to John Brewer,[99] terms such as 'post-conflict' are now widely interpreted as being too vague and inadequate, and so he argues for the use of 'post-violence' instead as a descriptor. Given the global pattern of increased post-war gender-based violence, and the inextricable links between conflict resolution and gender power, a question arises: post-violence for whom exactly? The daily reality for many women in Northern Ireland suggests that conventional definitions of violence, peace, conflict and post-conflict are entirely inadequate for the purposes of examining gender relations both during and after armed actions. The vast distance between the prevailing discourse of a peaceful and secure society and the various forms of violence experienced by many women expose both the flaws and the consequences of a peace process that has failed to transform gender relations as an integral part of conflict transition.

Reproductive rights in Northern Ireland

Despite the passage of over twenty years since the GFA, Northern Irish society remains deeply polarised along ethno-religious lines. Perennial division and mistrust between two competing ethno-national blocs remain the overwhelming characteristic of its formal party-political structures. In such circumstances, the issue of abortion provides a truly rare case of cross-community harmony among the assorted political adversaries.[100] While there are of course some differences between their respective policy positions, overall, none of the main political parties advocate for safe, legal and free access to terminations in Northern Ireland. Abortion ostensibly offers a political space where multifarious parties can temporarily park their competing ethno-national identities and, broadly, unite in opposition to women's full reproductive rights. Given the dominance of male-led ethno-nationalism in Northern Irish society, coupled with pervasive forms of religious conservatism, this seemingly unlikely alliance of unionism and nationalism may not be as anomalous as it first appears.

Until very recently, Northern Ireland stood out as one of the few countries in Western Europe where women exercise less control over their reproductive capabilities, including with their fellow citizens in the rest of the UK. In July 2019, Westminster MPs resoundingly voted to extend same-sex marriage and access to abortion to Northern Ireland, to bring the region into line with the rest of the UK, unless the then suspended Executive and Assembly were restored by 21 October 2019, thus decriminalising abortion in Northern Ireland. As of 1 April 2020, abortion services are available in two hospital sites in the region. Until these seismic, recent changes however, access to abortion in Northern Ireland was governed by the Offences Against the Person Act 1861. Section 58 of the Act criminalised any woman who had an abortion, and Section 59 criminalised anyone trying to help a woman to abort. Both actions were punishable by a maximum sentence of penal servitude for life. While the 1967 Abortion Act legalised terminations in certain, limited circumstances in Great Britain, the Act was not extended to Northern Ireland. Consequently, the legislation governing abortion in Northern Ireland resided in laws dating back a century and a half. The only amendment to Northern Ireland's abortion laws occurred as result of the *R. v. Bourne* 1938 case, in which a London surgeon, Alec Bourne, performed an abortion on a 14-year-old girl who was pregnant as the result of rape. The judgement stated that abortion is legally permissible when a doctor is of the opinion that the probable consequences of continuing with the pregnancy will be to make the woman 'a physical or mental wreck'. While the judgement reaffirmed the legal restrictions on women's reproductive rights, it is problematic for several reasons. First, it deprives women of agency and places bodily autonomy in the hands of a medical professional, not women themselves. Second, the stipulated condition 'physical or mental wreck' is ambiguous and open to subjective interpretation, with no clear guidelines. Finally, it speaks volumes as to the status and value of women's 'mothering role' in society. Essentially, it is only in the circumstances in which the 'mother' is pushed to the point where she is physically or mentally incapable of fulfilling her 'true role' that access to abortion is legally permissible. The tragic death of Savita Halappanavar in a Galway hospital in October 2012 illustrates, if further illustration were needed, the perils involved in identifying the point when pregnancy represents a clear threat to the physical and mental well-being of a woman.

In April 2016, Northern Ireland made international headlines, once again, for ignominious reasons. A 21-year-old student was handed a one-year suspended sentence after her flatmates reported the young woman to police for procuring pills on the internet to induce an abortion. In court, her barrister stated that if his client had lived anywhere else in the UK, she would 'not have found herself before the courts'. The court also heard that the young Belfast student tried to travel to England for a termination but could not cover the costs. While Northern Ireland's highly restrictive abortion regime sated those who opposed any changes to it, abortion in Northern Ireland was nevertheless a daily reality. While the 2018 repeal referendum in the Republic of Ireland has amended the constitution,[101] thus allowing for legislation that expands the circumstances for access to abortion, the 'solution' hitherto to abortion in both states has been to export citizens to another jurisdiction. For those who cannot access abortion in Northern Ireland, the only option is to travel abroad, mostly to Britain, incurring costs in the range of £600–£2,000.[102] Such a dispensation invariably discriminates against working-class, immigrant and younger women, due to the costs of travelling abroad.[103] Data published in 2019 by the Department of Health and Social Care (DHSC) showed that 1,053 women from Northern Ireland travelled to Britain in 2018 for a termination, a rise of 192 on the previous year. In a society where women, girls and healthcare workers lived under the threat of criminal prosecution, the reality of abortion in Northern Ireland is also often hidden for fear of stigmatisation, and so the numbers of women travelling outside Northern Ireland may indeed be much greater than the figures suggest.

While Northern Ireland is often (erroneously) characterised as a site of a 'religious war', the coterminous ground between all the main churches is their outright opposition to abortion, typically propagating a misleading narrative that most people oppose abortion. The views of the Protestant churches in Ireland on matters such as divorce, abortion and homosexuality are virtually identical to the Catholic Church, born out of the same social puritanism.[104] Moreover, this religious consensus provides a formidable support base for several powerful 'pro-life', anti-abortion groups – the Society for the Protection of the Unborn Child, Precious Life, LIFE, Christian Action Research and Education Care – that exert considerable influence in the debate. While religious conservatism unquestionably informs the standpoints of some of those opposed to women's reproductive rights, linkages between women's reproductive capacities and the sectarian demographics serve to further embed virulent opposition to abortion on any grounds. While nationalism fabricates a narrative of horizontal comradeship, the gendered constructions of ethno-nationalism position and value women primarily for their symbolic and reproductive roles. The centrality of women as biological reproducers to sustaining ethno-national collectives provides the operative framework for restricting women's access to reproductive healthcare. The dominance of ethno-nationalism and/or religion as primary political identities in Northern Ireland, therefore, ensures that women's health and women's rights remain subordinate to and contingent upon the needs of the ethno-national project. Accessing abortion is, therefore, not only about practical and material rights; symbolically, it subverts the gender fundamentals on which nationalist movements are based. Demanding that women control their own bodies, not the 'nation', strikes a blow at nationalism's ideological bedrock.

This dominance of religious conservatism and polarised ethno-nationalism is of course diffused throughout the formal political system, with all the main political parties vehemently opposed to women's full access to reproductive healthcare. During an Assembly debate on abortion law in June 2000, the proposer of a motion opposing the extension of the 1967 Abortion Act, Jim Wells, implored his fellow MLAs to 'send out this evening a very clear, cross-community message – supported by different parties with different viewpoints – that the people of Northern Ireland totally resist any extension of the 1967 Abortion act to this community'. In May 2008, a letter jointly signed by the leaders of the main churches and the leaders of the four main political parties (the DUP, Sinn Féin, the UUP and the SDLP) was sent to all Westminster MPs asking them not to vote for a proposed amendment that might extend the 1967 Abortion Act to Northern Ireland. The reason offered for such rare instances of consensus among the political parties is a persistent belief that their overall electoral mandate automatically means that they speak for over 90 per cent of the population. The orthodoxy of those who claim that the overwhelming majority of Northern Irish citizens want no change in abortion laws is contradicted regularly by public surveys which consistently reveal a more liberal standpoint on the issue. An Omnibus survey of 1,400 respondents conducted in 2012, for instance, found that 59 per cent believed abortion should be legal in cases of rape or incest. A 2014 survey by Amnesty International which polled 1,013 people found 69 per cent said there should be access to abortion where the pregnancy is the result of rape; 68 per cent said abortion should be available where the pregnancy is the result of incest; and 60 per cent of people thought abortion should be available where the foetus had a fatal abnormality. The latest data sets from the University of Liverpool NI General Election Survey 2019 once again highlight this consistent trend in public attitudes. The survey found that 72.1 per cent supported the right to an abortion under a range of circumstances. Of those who stated a preference, around half supported it 'only when a mother's life was in danger', and around a quarter agreed to 'up to

12 weeks of pregnancy'. Tellingly, non-voters were nearly three times more likely (15.2 per cent) than voters to support abortion up to 28 weeks, and those who did not state a faith were more supportive of abortion at 28 weeks. The survey also showed a generational shift, with those aged 45 or over more supportive if a mother's life was in danger, contrasting with those aged under 45 showing higher levels of support regarding up to 12 to 28 weeks. When asked if the law should allow abortion up to 28 weeks, 15.6 per cent of 18–29-year-olds agreed, compared with just 4.5 per cent of those aged 45–65. While convention typically depicts a socially progressive Sinn Féin and a reactionary and conservative DUP, data sets and surveys reveal similar levels of progressiveness on social and moral issues among Catholics and Protestants, particularly among non-voters. It is of note that there exists a discernible level of detachment between Northern Ireland's elected politicians and its citizens, thus calling into question the monopolisation of these issues by the main political parties. In a polarised society where ethno-national identity assumes primacy, votes cast for parties generally reflect a constitutional/ethnic preference, and so this does not necessarily translate as an automatic endorsement of party positions on issues such as abortion or marriage equality. Considering the consistent patterns within survey data, the claims by some elected representatives of cross-community unity in outright opposition to any change to Northern Ireland's abortion laws seem dubious and disingenuous. The mounting evidence from multiple polls and surveys strongly suggests that the political classes are well out of step with changing public attitudes.

While legislation regulating women's reproductive rights in Northern Ireland was anchored in the Victorian era, the public sentiments of many leading political figures also appear to similarly resonate with another bygone age. The discourse frequently deployed by politicians, church leaders and other commentators consistently denies women their agency, instead depicting them solely as vulnerable victims. All too often, those who oppose changes to abortion access offer their 'sympathy', their 'empathy', their 'concern'. When faced with the harsh realities in which many women in Northern Ireland find themselves, the refrain from political representatives is the need for such cases to be treated with 'sensitivity', 'care' and 'support'. DUP MLA Paul Givan suggested the appropriate approach in all circumstances is to 'protect and provide the best care for mothers': once again women's vulnerability is foregrounded. In his reaction to the 2014 Amnesty International poll, DUP MLA Jim Wells stated that rape is not a valid reason for abortion, insisting that aborting an unborn child was 'punishing' the 'ultimate victim' of the crime. Sinn Féin's position for a number of years has been that it is 'opposed to the attitudes and forces in society, which pressurize women to have abortions, and criminalise those who make this decision'. While republicans tend to position themselves as more liberal on matters of gender and sexuality than their unionist counterparts, their policy position is at best opaque, and again positions women not as agents but as victims of 'attitudes', 'forces' and 'pressures'. Their nationalist cohorts, the SDLP, are supportive of LGBT+ rights but stringently opposed to any changes to the current abortion laws. The UUP, which has in recent years attempted to shift from conservative to liberal positions on such matters, has adopted a 'matter of conscience' stance on issues of marriage equality and abortion. The Alliance Party allows for a free vote for its members on abortion. While there are undeniable differences between Sinn Féin and the DUP on abortion, this, however, should not conceal the overall commonality in both parties' opposition to the strict regulation of abortion in Northern Ireland. The extension of the 1967 Abortion Act to Northern Ireland was one of many key pledges in Tony Blair's New Labour campaign of 1997, although in talks with DUP as potential coalition partners in 2010, Labour also promised not to liberalise abortion. For those who doubt the centrality of gender to the politics of conflict resolution, it is often widely reported that at the time of the St Andrews Agreement in 2007 the British government agreed not to extend the 1967 Abortion Act to Northern Ireland as part of their package to restore power-sharing between unionist and nationalist political parties.[105] Furthermore, there is widespread belief that DUP MPs voted for the Labour government's proposed 42-day terror-suspect detention in exchange for a further affirmation not to extend the 1967 Abortion Act across the Irish Sea. While the British government advocates access to abortion in developing countries, it invariably sees Northern Ireland as something of a special case.

Though the main political parties in Northern Ireland have eschewed confronting the issue of changing Northern Ireland's abortion laws, their reticence has been overridden by decisions taken elsewhere. The 2018 repeal referendum in the Republic of Ireland paved the way for the state to liberalise its restrictive abortion laws, but perhaps equally as important, significantly shaped the debate regarding women's reproductive rights north of the Irish border in several ways. First, the Irish government have already explicitly stated that women in Northern Ireland will have access to any new reproductive healthcare under the provisions of the General Scheme of the Bill to Regulate the Termination of Pregnancy. Second, the huge majority in favour of changing the Republic of Ireland's highly restrictive abortion laws, some 64 per cent, meant that Northern Ireland remained the only region in Western Europe where abortion was illegal, and women were forced to travel. Closer to home, Northern Ireland was, until very recently, distinctly out of step with the citizens in the Republic of Ireland and Great Britain. While Sinn Féin has been unsurprisingly keen to bring Northern Ireland in line with the type of proposed legislation in the Republic of Ireland, declaring that 'the North is next', the DUP were left in a more politically awkward scenario. When it comes to the issue of Brexit, the party is zealous in its belief and demands that there should be no border down the Irish Sea, arguing that there can be no separation between Northern Ireland and Great Britain economically, politically or socially. On the issue of abortion, however, among many other issues, the DUP consistently plays the 'our wee country' card, opposing any change to Northern Ireland's existing laws, and arguing that such matters are 'devolved' issues for local political representatives. Finally, and related to the previous point, the vote for repeal in the Republic of Ireland was demonstrable evidence of a clear gulf between the conservatism of the political classes and the attitudes and opinions of citizens. This is a particularly pressing point for Northern Ireland, where ethno-national allegiances are the dominant indicators of voting patterns and preferences within assembly elections. Rendered a peripheral concern within general elections, it is unsurprising that the issue of women's reproductive rights has never been a 'make-or-break' issue for any government or party during electoral contests. While most major political parties in the Republic deliberately eschewed the issue of abortion or adopted conservative policy positions, the huge vote in favour of repeal is indicative of the need for citizens in Northern Ireland to also have a direct say on this important matter in a way that is separate from the 'everyday' ethno-national issues that tend to dominate elections in the region.

An unforeseen intervention during the latest prolonged suspension of the power-sharing structures, however, overhauled abortion in Northern Ireland and women's access to it. In July 2019, Westminster MPs resoundingly voted to extend same-sex marriage and access to abortion to Northern Ireland, to bring the region into line with the rest of the UK, unless the Executive and Assembly were restored by 21 October 2019. With the Northern Ireland Executive at that time languishing in 'cold storage', seemingly indefinitely, there was little prospect of a return in the foreseeable future. A formal recall of the Assembly by the DUP to block the Westminster legislation was not heeded by Sinn Féin, the SDLP[106] and others, who dismissed it as little more than a futile and ultimately symbolic publicity stunt. On 22 October 2019, abortion in Northern Ireland was decriminalised, meaning that no criminal charges can be brought against those who have an abortion or against healthcare professionals who provide a termination or assist in one. As of 1 April 2020, abortion services are available in two hospital sites in the region. Women's reproductive rights in Northern Ireland have historically been hostage to the overarching primacy of ethno-nationalism. Given that the Assembly is viewed as 'detached' from everyday lives and frequently proven itself as out of step with wider social attitudes, it is perhaps only fitting that abortion rights were secured not in spite of, but because of, its absence.

Those tasked with the transformation of Northern Ireland frequently speak of the need to transform and renegotiate all aspects of society. Women's reproductive rights, however, are actively excluded from that agenda. Women need full access to their reproductive rights if they are to participate as citizens equal to men, and hence Northern Ireland's laws factor heavily in women's unequal status in both symbolic and practical ways.[107] Moreover, not only is women's right to bodily autonomy an issue of human rights, equality and social justice, but also a central component of women's security and well-being.[108] What did Northern Ireland's previously restrictive abortion regime tell us about gender relations? What did it tell us about the status of women in Northern Ireland some twenty years on from the GFA? While women have made impressive gains in paid employment, the real story of gender in Northern Ireland is a perennial patriarchal culture which positions women and feminist politics firmly on the periphery of its peace and security agenda. Restrictive regulation of abortion in Northern Ireland was historically a form of social control and a form of gender control.

Conclusion

While comparative scholars continue to debate the idea of a 'Northern Ireland model' fit for export, incorporating a critical gender analysis lays bare the androcentric and state-centric tendencies among those who propagate the notion that the current dispensation signifies a 'society at peace'. Gender provides politicians, academics, practitioners and stakeholders with a more holistic vision of what violence and peace looks like, and those who refuse to acknowledge the importance of gender will continue to yield a partial and limited vision of conflict transition. The political flux generated by constitutional uncertainty during the GFA negotiations was a unique opportunity for the insertion of women's rights and formal representation in the new post-agreement Northern Ireland. Despite the robust and unambiguous commitments in the text of the GFA, the primary architects of the peace process situated gender and women's issues as peripheral to the main priorities of guns and government. The complete absence of gender and women's rights from the subsequent St Andrews (2006) and Hillsborough (2010) talks is emblematic of the indifference towards gender equality. Although Northern Ireland can rightfully boast women as the leaders of three main political parties, the realm of formal electoral politics, however, remains what is has always been: a 'cold house' for women in Northern Ireland.[109] Given the protracted nature of intra-state conflicts, peace processes seldom deliver in rapid time periods. The passage of over twenty years since the peace deal was struck is more than ample time in which women's political participation in Northern Ireland should have yielded significant growth. While the recent Assembly elections of 2016 and 2017 recorded some much-needed increases in representation, nevertheless they remain modest and well off the pace of the UK's other regional assemblies.

While gender equality was left in the hands of male-led political parties and their idiosyncratic procedures, equality between nationalist and unionist was endowed with the full might of institutional power. Weighted voting, petitions of concern and other vetoes, and 50:50 recruitment for the new police service, among other things, demonstrate that while parties baulked at such equality measures for women, they were zealous and prolific champions of such methods when it came to ethno-nationalism. While party policies and manifestos decree that there is more to Northern Irish politics than ethno-nationalism, the primacy afforded to mutually exclusive ethno-religious identity saturates political thought and discourse, and thus sequesters the realm of formal political representation. Elections and formal political representation are not the most radical or revolutionary avenues of political change. In a society based on equality, surely women's right to formal political representation constitutes the most moderate and inoffensive objective. Despite being enshrined in the text of the GFA, the promise and political potential have given way to a doleful realisation that formal politics is viewed by many political parties as largely a male preserve. From a critical gender perspective, the post-Troubles political landscape is largely business as usual. While the levers of power have extended to nationalist and republican elites (mostly male), Northern Irish democracy suffers perpetually from a deficit of female representation.

Male power and control over women's bodies – through various forms of violence or the prohibition or restriction of access to full reproductive rights – also remain prominent causes of gender inequality in Northern Ireland. The region's political parties, formal institutions, cultural norms and conservative dominant discourse are merely the manifestations and media in which they are re-enforced and reproduced. Social conservatism – particularly in relation to abortion, sexuality and divorce – remains in place despite rhetorical assurances regarding women's improving position. In sum, little has changed for women where they continue to experience high levels of physical and sexual violence, are concentrated in low-level employment, do the majority of unpaid care and continue to be the more likely to be in poverty.[110] Despite the widespread optimism among many feminists and women, what emerged in the place of the promised 'equalities and inclusions' agenda of the GFA is in fact an era of 'neo-patriarchy'.[111] While the GFA did undoubtedly provide the potential for a new era of greater equality between the sexes, more than twenty years on Northern Irish society exhibits all the trademarks and insidious characteristics of a patriarchal society that has yet to undergo a genuine transformation in gender relations.

Notes

1. Maria Deiana, 'Women's Citizenship in Northern Ireland after the 1998 Agreement', *Irish Political Studies*, 28(3) (2013), 399–412.
2. Adrian Little, 'Feminism and the Politics of Difference in Northern Ireland', *Journal of Political Ideologies*, 7(2) (2002), 163–77, p. 172.
3. Carol Cohn, *Women and Wars* (Cambridge: Polity Press, 2013).
4. Malathi De Alwis, Julie Mertus and Tazreena Sajjad, 'Women and peace processes', in Carol Cohn (ed.), *Women and Wars* (Cambridge: Polity Press, 2013), pp. 169–91.
5. Donna Pankhurst, 'The "Sex War" and Other Wars: Towards a Feminist Approach to Peace Building', *Development in Practice*, 13(2/3) (2003), 154–77.
6. De Alwis et al., 'Women and peace processes'.
7. Judy El-Bushra, 'Feminism, Gender, and Women's Peace Activism', *Development and Change*, 38(1) (2007), 131–47.
8. Sanam Naraghi Anderlini, *Women Building Peace: What They Do, Why It Matters* (Boulder, CO: Lynne Rienner, 2007); Tsjeard Bouta, Georg Frerks and Ian Bannon, *Gender, Conflict, and Development* (Washington, DC: World Bank, 2005); Cynthia Cockburn, *The Space Between Us: Negotiating Gender and National Identities in Conflict* (London: Zed Books, 1998); Fionnuala Ní Aoláin, Dina Francesca Haynes and Naomi R. Cahn, *On the Frontlines: Gender, War, and the Post-Conflict Process* (Oxford: Oxford University Press, 2011).
9. Cockburn, *Space Between Us*; Marie Mulholland, 'The challenge to inequality: women, discrimination and decision-making in Northern Ireland', in Caroline Moser and Fiona Clark (eds), *Victims, Perpetrators or Actors: Gender, Armed Conflict and Political Violence* (New York: Zed Books, 2001), pp. 164–77.
10. Claire Hackett, 'The Republican Feminist Agenda', *Feminist Review*, 50 (1995), 111–16; Theresa O'Keefe, *Feminist Identity Development and Activism in Revolutionary Movements* (Basingstoke: Palgrave Macmillan, 2013); Rosemary Sales, *Women Divided: Gender, Religion and Politics in Northern Ireland* (London: Routledge, 1997); Margaret Ward, 'Times of transition: republican women, feminism and political representation', in Louise Ryan and Margaret Ward (eds), *Irish Women and Nationalism: Soldiers, New Women and Wicked Hags* (Dublin: Irish Academic Press, 2004), pp. 184–200.

11 O'Keefe, *Feminist Identity Development and Activism in Revolutionary Movements*.
12 Fidelma Ashe, 'From Paramilitaries to Peacemakers: The Gender Dynamics of Community-Based Restorative Justice in Northern Ireland', *British Journal of Politics and International Relations*, 11 (2009), 298–314.
13 Kate Fearon and Monica McWilliams, 'Swimming against the mainstream: the Northern Ireland Women's Coalition', in Carmel Roulston and Celia Davies (eds), *Gender, Democracy and Inclusion in Northern Ireland* (London: Palgrave, 2000), pp. 117–38.
14 El-Bushra, 'Feminism, Gender, and Women's Peace Activism'.
15 Katherine Side, 'Women's Civil and Political Citizenship in the Post-Good Friday Agreement Period in Northern Ireland', *Irish Political Studies*, 24(1) (2009), 67–87.
16 Fearon and McWilliams, 'Swimming against the mainstream'; Mulholland, 'Challenge to inequality'; Cera Murtagh, 'A Transient Transition: The Cultural and Institutional Obstacles Impeding the Northern Ireland Women's Coalition in its Progression from Informal to Formal Politics', *Irish Political Studies*, 23(1) (2008), 21–40.
17 Cynthia Cockburn, 'A Movement Stalled: Outcomes of Women's Campaign for Equalities and Inclusion in the Northern Ireland Peace Process', *Interface: a journal for and about social movements*, 5(1) (2014), 151–82; Mulholland, 'Challenge to inequality'.
18 For example, see O'Keefe, *Feminist Identity Development and Activism in Revolutionary Movements*; Eilish Rooney, 'Women's Equality in Northern Ireland's Transition: Intersectionality in Theory and Place', *Feminist Legal Studies*, 14 (2006), 353–75.
19 Deiana, 'Women's Citizenship in Northern Ireland after the 1998 Agreement'.
20 Ibid.; Yvonne Galligan, 'Gender and Politics in Northern Ireland: The Representation Gap Revisited', *Irish Political Studies*, 28(3) (2013), 413–33; Ward, 'Times of transition'.
21 Drude Dahlerup and Lenita Freidenvall, 'Quotas as a "Fast Track" to Equal Representation for Women', *International Feminist Journal of Politics*, 7(1) (2005), 26–48.
22 Marie Braniff and Sophie Whiting, '"There's Just No Point Having a Token Woman": Gender and Representation in the Democratic Unionist Party in Post-Agreement Northern Ireland', *Parliamentary Affairs*, 69(1) (2016), 93–114; Kimberly Cowell-Meyers, 'Women in Northern Ireland Politics: Gender and the Politics of Peace-Building in the New Legislative Assembly', *Irish Political Studies*, 18 (2003), 72–96; Bernadette Hayes and Ian McAllister, 'Gender and Consociational Power-Sharing in Northern Ireland', *International Political Science Review*, 34(2) (2013), 123–39.
23 Galligan, 'Gender and Politics in Northern Ireland'.
24 Neil Matthews, 'Gendered Candidate Selection and the Representation of Women in Northern Ireland', *Parliamentary Affairs*, 67(3) (2014), 617–46.
25 Eileen Connolly, 'Parliaments as Gendered Institutions: The Irish Oireachtas',

26 Ward, 'Times of transition'.
27 Anne Phillips, *The Politics of Presence* (Oxford: Oxford University Press, 1995).
28 Paul Chaney, 'Devolved Governance and the Substantive Representation of Women: The Second Term of the National Assembly for Wales, 2003–2007', *Parliamentary Affairs*, 61(2) (2008), 272–90.
29 Kimberly Cowell-Meyers, 'Gender, Power and Peace: A Preliminary Look at Women in the Northern Ireland Assembly', *Women and Politics*, 23(3) (2001), 55–88.
30 Ward, 'Times of transition'.
31 O'Keefe, *Feminist Identity Development and Activism in Revolutionary Movements*.
32 Niall Gilmartin, *Female Combatants after Armed Struggle: Lost in Transition?* (New York: Routledge, 2019); O'Keefe, *Feminist Identity Development and Activism in Revolutionary Movements*.
33 Fiona Buckley, 'Women and Politics in Ireland: The Road to Sex Quotas', *Irish Political Studies*, 28(3) (2013), 341–97; Galligan, 'Gender and Politics in Northern Ireland'.
34 Rachel Ward, *Women, Unionism and Loyalism in Northern Ireland: From 'Tea-Makers' to Political Actors* (Dublin: Irish Academic Press, 2006).
35 Miranda Alison, 'Women as Agents of Political Violence: Gendering Security', *Security Dialogue*, 35(4) (2004), 447–63.
36 Michael Potter, 'Loyalism, Women and Standpoint Theory', *Irish Political Studies*, 29(2) (2014), 258–74.
37 Ward, 'Times of transition'.
38 Dawn Purvis resigned from the PUP in June 2010 over the killing of Bobby Moffett on Belfast's Shankill Road. Although on ceasefire at the time, the killing was widely linked to the Ulster Volunteer Force (UVF). Dawn continued as an Independent MLA until she lost her seat in the 2011 Assembly elections. She remained a prominent activist and was the first director of Marie Stopes in Belfast from 2012 to 2015.
39 Aaron Edwards, 'The Progressive Unionist Party of Northern Ireland: A Left-Wing Voice in an Ethnically Divided Society', *British Journal of Politics and International Relations*, 2(4) (2010), 590–614.
40 Yvonne Galligan and Rick Wilford, 'Women's political representation in Ireland', in Yvonne Galligan, Eilis Ward and Rick Wilford (eds), *Contesting Politics: Women in Ireland, North and South* (Boulder, CO: Westview Press, 1999), pp. 130–48; Elizabeth Porter, 'Women, Political Decision-Making and Peace-Building in Conflict Regions', *Global Change, Peace and Security*, 15(3) (2003), 245–62.
41 Matthews, 'Gendered Candidate Selection and the Representation of Women in Northern Ireland'.
42 Braniff and Whiting, '"There's Just No Point Having a Token Woman"'.

43 Galligan, 'Gender and Politics in Northern Ireland'.
44 Tahnya Barnett Donaghy, 'The Impact of Devolution on Women's Political Representation Levels in Northern Ireland', *Politics*, 24(1) (2004), 26–34.
45 Matthews, 'Gendered Candidate Selection and the Representation of Women in Northern Ireland'.
46 Ibid.
47 Ward, 'Times of transition'.
48 Jonathan Tonge, Máire Braniff, Thomas Hennessey, James W. McAuley and Sophie A. Whiting, *The Democratic Unionist Party: From Protest to Power* (Oxford: Oxford University Press, 2014); Brian Walker, *Past and Present: History, Identity and Politics in Ireland* (Belfast: Institute of Irish Studies, Queen's University Belfast, 2000); Ward, 'Times of transition'.
49 Matthews, 'Gendered Candidate Selection and the Representation of Women in Northern Ireland'.
50 Niall Gilmartin, 'Feminism, Nationalism and the Re-Ordering of Post-War Political Strategies: The Case of the Sinn Féin Women's Department', *Irish Political Studies*, 32(2) (2017), 268–92.
51 Braniff and Whiting, '"There's Just No Point Having a Token Woman"'.
52 Yvonne Galligan and Lizanne Dowds, 'Women's Hour?', *ARK Northern Ireland: Social and Political Archive* (Belfast, 2004).
53 Joane Nagel, 'Nation', *Ethnic and Racial Studies*, 21(2) (1998), 242–69.
54 Fidelma Ashe and Ken Harland, 'Troubling Masculinities: Changing Patterns of Violent Masculinities in a Society Emerging from Political Conflict', *Studies in Conflict & Terrorism*, 37(9) (2014), 747–62; Cowell-Meyers, 'Women in Northern Ireland Politics'; Kate Fearon, *Women's Work: The Story of the Northern Ireland Women's Coalition* (Belfast: Blackstaff Press, 1999).
55 Cowell-Meyers, 'Women in Northern Ireland Politics'; Gilmartin, 'Feminism, Nationalism and the Re-Ordering of Post-War Political Strategies'.
56 Ian O'Flynn, 'Democratic Autonomy, Women's Interests and Institutional Context', *Irish Political Studies*, 22(4) (2007), 455–71.
57 Matthews, 'Gendered Candidate Selection and the Representation of Women in Northern Ireland'.
58 Nancy Naples, *Grassroots Warriors: Activist Mothering, Community Work, and the War on Poverty: Perspectives on Gender* (London: Routledge, 1998).
59 Robert L. Miller, Rick Wilford and Freda Donoghue, *Women and Political Participation in Northern Ireland* (Aldershot: Avebury, 1996); Sales, *Women Divided*.
60 Carmel Roulston, 'Democracy and the challenge of gender: new visions, new processes', in Carmel Roulston and Celia Davies (eds), *Gender, Democracy and Inclusion in Northern Ireland* (London: Palgrave, 2000), pp. 24–46).
61 Gráinne McCoy, 'Women, community and politics in Northern Ireland', in Carmel Roulston and Celia Davis (eds), *Gender, Democracy and Inclusion in Northern Ireland* (London: Palgrave, 2000), pp. 3–23.

62 Naples, *Grassroots Warriors*; Helen Safa, 'Women's Social Movements in Latin America', *Gender and Society*, 4(3) (1990), 354–69.
63 Srilatha Batliwala and David Brown, *Transnational Civil Society: An Introduction* (Boulder, CO: Kumarian Press, 2006).
64 Valerie Bryson, *Feminist Political Theory*, 3rd edn (Basingstoke: Palgrave Macmillan, 2016); Iris Marion Young, *Inclusion and Democracy* (Oxford: Oxford University Press, 2000).
65 McCoy, 'Women, community and politics in Northern Ireland'; Sales, *Women Divided*.
66 Elizabeth Porter, 'The challenge of dialogue across difference', in Carmel Roulston and Celia Davies (eds), *Gender, Democracy and Inclusion in Northern Ireland* (London: Palgrave, 2000), pp. 141–62.
67 Nira Yuval-Davis, *The Politics of Belonging: Intersectional Contestations* (London: Sage, 2011).
68 Cockburn, *The Space Between Us*; Murtagh, 'A Transient Transition'.
69 Rooney, 'Women's Equality in Northern Ireland's Transition'.
70 Fidelma Ashe, 'The Virgin Mary Connection: Reflecting on Feminism and Northern Irish Politics', *Critical Review of International Social and Political Philosophy*, 9(4) (2006), 573–88.
71 Hackett, 'The Republican Feminist Agenda'; O'Keefe, *Feminist Identity Development and Activism in Revolutionary Movements*.
72 McCoy, 'Women, community and politics in Northern Ireland'.
73 Cynthia Cockburn, 'A Movement Stalled: Outcomes of Women's Campaign for Equalities and Inclusion in the Northern Ireland Peace Process', *Interface: a journal for and about social movements*, 5(1) (2014), 151–82.
74 Galligan and Wilford, 'Women's Political Representation in Ireland'.
75 Deiana, 'Women's Citizenship in Northern Ireland after the 1998 Agreement'.
76 Adopted in October 2000, SCR 1325 'reaffirms the important role of women in the prevention and resolution of conflicts, peace negotiations, peace-building, peacekeeping, humanitarian response and in post-conflict reconstruction and stresses the importance of their equal participation and full involvement in all efforts for the maintenance and promotion of peace and security. Resolution 1325 urges all actors to increase the participation of women and incorporate gender perspectives in all United Nations peace and security efforts.' The full text of the resolution is available at: www.un.org/womenwatch/osagi/wps/. Accessed 7 January 2021.
77 Melanie Hoewer, 'UN Resolution 1325 in Ireland: Limitations and Opportunities of the International Framework on Women, Peace and Security', *Irish Political Studies*, 28(3) (2013), 450–68.
78 Avila Kilmurray, *UN Resolution 1325: The Experience within Local Communities*, Working Papers in British-Irish Studies, Institute for British-Irish Studies (Dublin: University College Dublin, 2013).
79 Cockburn, 'A Movement Stalled'.
80 Ibid.
81 Deiana, 'Women's Citizenship in Northern Ireland after the 1998 Agreement'.

82 Ronan Kennedy, Claire Pierson and Jennifer Thomson, 'Challenging Identity Hierarchies: Gender and Consociational Power-Sharing', *British Journal of Politics and International Relations*, 18(3) (2016), 618–33.

83 Ann J. Tickner, *Gender in International Relations: Feminist Perspectives on Achieving Global Security* (New York: Columbia University Press, 1992).

84 Laura Sjoberg, *Gender and International Security: Feminist Perspectives* (New York: Routledge, 2009).

85 Mary Caprioli, 'Gendered Conflict', *Journal of Peace Research*, 37(1) (2000), 51–68; Cynthia Enloe, *Bananas, Beaches and Bases: Making Feminist Sense of International Politics*, 2nd edn (Berkeley: University of California Press, 2014).

86 Anderlini, *Women Building Peace*.

87 Anu Pillay, 'Violence against women in the aftermath', in Sheila Meintjes, Anu Pillay and Meredeth Turshen (eds), *The Aftermath: Women in Post-Conflict Transformation* (New York: Zed Books, 2001), pp. 35–45; Lori Handrahan, 'Conflict, Gender, Ethnicity and Post-Conflict Reconstruction', *Security Dialogue*, 35(4) (2004), 429–45.

88 Azza Karam, 'Women in War and Peace-Building', *International Journal of Feminist Politics*, 3(1) (2001), 2–25; Laura McLeod, 'Configurations of Post-Conflict: Impacts of Representations of Conflict and Post-Conflict Upon the (Political) Translations of Gender Security within UNSCR 1325', *International Feminist Journal of Politics*, 13(4) (2011), 594–611.

89 Cockburn, 'A Movement Stalled'.

90 Women's Aid Federation Northern Ireland, Annual Report 2018–19. Available at: www.womensaidni.org/assets/uploads/2020/01/A4-Womens-Aid-Annual-Report-2018-19.pdf. Accessed 11 March 2020.

91 PSNI, Domestic Abuse Incidents and Crimes Recorded by the Police in Northern Ireland. Available at: www.psni.police.uk/globalassets/inside-the-psni/our-statistics/domestic-abuse-statistics/2019–20/q3/domestic-abuse_-bulletin-dec-19.pdf. Accessed 11 March 2020.

92 Notwithstanding the shocking levels indicated here, it is also important to bear in mind that the increases of reported incidents may be linked to the Sinn Féin acceptance of the PSNI in 2007. Since the foundation of the provisional republican movement in 1970, its members refused to recognise the legitimacy of the Northern Ireland state, including its police force, the Royal Ulster Constabulary (RUC). As part of the GFA, the RUC was reformed and renamed the Police Service of Northern Ireland (PSNI) in 2001. While initially rejecting this new force, republicans signed up to accept and recognise the legitimacy of the PSNI in 2007. The move paved the way for the wider nationalist and republican community to engage with and use the police. Undoubtedly, this increased the numbers recorded in statistics.

93 Police Service of Northern Ireland, *Trends in Domestic Abuse Incidents and Crimes Recorded by the Police in Northern Ireland, 2004/05 to 2018/19* (Belfast: PSNI, 2019), p. 5; Police Service of Northern Ireland, *Domestic Abuse Incidents and Crimes Recorded by the Police in Northern Ireland: Update to 30 June 2020* (Belfast: PSNI, 2020).

94 Police Service of Northern Ireland, *Trends in Hate Motivated Incidents and Crimes Recorded by the Police in Northern Ireland 2004/05 to 2018/19* (Belfast: PSNI, 2019), p. 6: Police Service of Northern Ireland, *Incidents and Crimes with a Hate Motivation Recorded by the Police in Northern Ireland Update to 30 June 2020* (Belfast: PSNI, 2020), p. 4.
95 Ashe and Harland, 'Troubling Masculinities'.
96 Sara Davies and Jacqui True, 'Reframing Conflict-Related Sexual and Gender-Based Violence: Bringing Gender Analysis Back In', *Security Dialogue*, 46(6) (2015), 495–512.
97 Ban Ki-Moon, 'Conflict-Related Sexual Violence: Report of the Secretary-General. S/2012/33' (New York: United Nations, 2012).
98 Melanie Hoewer, 'Women, Violence, and Social Change in Northern Ireland and Chiapas: Societies between Tradition and Transition', *International Journal of Conflict and Violence*, 7 (2013), 216–31.
99 John D. Brewer, *Peace Processes: A Sociological Approach* (Cambridge: Polity Press, 2010).
100 Eileen Fegan and Rachel Rebouche, 'Northern Ireland's Abortion Law: The Morality of Silence and the Censure of Agency', *Feminist Legal Studies*, 11 (2003), 221–54; Sales, *Women Divided*.
101 The Eighth Amendment to the Republic of Ireland's constitution, ratified by referendum in 1983, acknowledged the 'right to life of the unborn' as 'equal to the right of the mother'. The Eighth Amendment meant that abortion was prohibited other than for extreme instances such as the immediate threat to the life of the woman. The repeal referendum took place on 25 May 2018 and was passed with a significant 2:1 majority in favour of repealing the Eighth Amendment.
102 Fiona Bloomer and Kellie O'Dowd, 'Restricted Access to Abortion in the Republic of Ireland and Northern Ireland: Exploring Abortion Tourism and Barriers to Legal Reform', *Culture, Health & Sexuality*, 16(4) (2014), 366–80.
103 Goretti Horgan and Julia O'Connor, 'Abortion and Citizenship Rights in a Devolved Region of the UK', *Social Policy & Society*, 13(1) (2014), 39–49.
104 Rob Kitchin and Karen Lysaght, 'Sexual Citizenship in Belfast, Northern Ireland', *Gender, Place & Culture*, 11(1) (2013), 83–103.
105 Ann Rossiter, *Ireland's Hidden Diaspora: The 'Abortion Trail' and the Making of a London-Irish Underground, 1980–2000* (London: IASC, 2009).
106 Although the SDLP sat in the assembly for the proceedings, they refused to take part in electing a speaker, an essential constitutional element in reconvening the Assembly.
107 Fegan and Rebouche, 'Northern Ireland's Abortion Law'.
108 Fiona Bloomer, Sylvia Estrada-Claudio and Claire Pierson, *Reimagining Global Abortion Politics: A Social Justice Perspective* (Bristol: Policy Press, 2019); Jennifer Thomson and Claire. Pierson, 'Can Abortion Rights Be Integrated into the Women, Peace and Security Agenda?', *International Feminist Journal of Politics*, 20(3) (2018), 350–65.
109 Galligan, 'Gender and Politics in Northern Ireland'.

110 Cockburn, 'A Movement Stalled'; Fegan and Rebouche, 'Northern Ireland's Abortion Law'; Theresa O'Keefe, 'Sometimes it would be nice to be a man: negotiating gender identities after the Good Friday Agreement', in Cillian McGratton and Elizabeth Meehan (eds), *Everyday Life after the Irish Conflict* (Manchester: Manchester University Press, 2012), pp. 83–97.
111 Campbell, cited in Cockburn, 'A Movement Stalled', p. 165.

7

The political economy of peace in Northern Ireland: social class in an age of boom and bust

Introduction

In mainstream reflections on the Northern Irish conflict it has long since become commonplace to depict the violence that overtook the region as so widespread as to have been more or less universal. In his autobiography, for instance, doyen of the mid-morning chat show and native of north Belfast Eamonn Holmes observes that the carnage of the Troubles 'affected everyone'.[1] And in her sublime eulogy for those murdered during the conflict, *Bear in Mind These Dead*, Derry journalist Susan McKay issues the following indelible phrase: 'But no one was really safe, and the sweat of terror could visit anyone.'[2] While these expressions of faith in the quintessentially democratic spirit of politically motivated violence continue to enjoy widespread currency, they fail to square with the distribution of fatalities that defined a quarter-century of conflict in the region. Examining the deaths that occurred over the course of the Troubles reveals a remarkably consistent and concentrated pattern. Northern Ireland has ninety-four postcodes, but more than half of the fatalities that punctuated the conflict were concentrated in just twelve of them.[3] What these dozen neighbourhoods shared in common was that they were – as they remain – sites of grinding, multigenerational poverty. Indeed, if we were to draw maps of material deprivation and fatal incidents during the Troubles the two images would be more or less interchangeable.[4] The coincidence of poverty and violence during the Northern Irish conflict becomes especially apparent when we consider patterns of political violence in the region's capital. Of the 3,700 deaths that occurred during the Troubles, almost two out of every five happened in north and west Belfast alone.[5] These neighbourhoods were the most deprived in Northern Ireland during the conflict and they have retained that wretched status throughout the peace process. According to Devlin et al.,[6] no fewer than eighteen of the twenty poorest areas in the region today are to be found in these two parliamentary constituencies. Examining the specific patterns of political violence that marked the

Troubles suggests, then, an important qualification to that familiar refrain that the traumas of the period were essentially universal in their impact.[7] While the conflict might well perhaps have affected *everyone*, it most certainly did not affect *everyone equally*.

The intimate association between political violence and material deprivation that defined the Troubles would have an important bearing on the forms of discourse that framed the Northern Irish peace process. Those who designed and championed the Good Friday Agreement (hereafter GFA) were keenly aware that ending the conflict would require a dramatic change in the fortunes of Northern Ireland's long-ailing economy.[8] If those communities that had been at the very heart of the Troubles were to move away from violence for good they would require economic opportunities denied to them previously. Influential figures in London, Washington and Dublin were, accordingly, at pains from the outset to underline that the end of the conflict would usher in an era of sustained prosperity. This discursive connection between political and economic progress was given a characteristically evangelical tone by the British prime minister who presided over the signing of Northern Ireland's celebrated peace deal. In May 1998, Tony Blair arrived in Belfast in an attempt to coax wavering voters into lending their support in the forthcoming referendum on the centrepiece of the Northern Irish peace process. Among the places the British premier chose to visit was the annual Royal Agricultural Show, allowing him to address an important section of a unionist community that was evidently deeply divided on the GFA. Those who cast a vote in favour of the new deal struck between all but one of the main local parties would in effect, Blair insisted, be saying 'yes to hope, to peace, to stability, and to prosperity'. A ringing endorsement of the new political dispensation would, he went on, signal a 'peaceful and stable future' in which Northern Ireland would come to enjoy the favour and regenerative power of multinational capital:

> I have no doubt that there is a well of economic goodwill and potential inward investment out there just waiting for the right opportunity and the right conditions. Let us turn that prospect into a reality.[9]

The at times evangelical faith that influential figures routinely expressed in the potential of the GFA to pave the way to economic prosperity has over time appeared more and more misguided. The much vaunted 'peace dividend' that was promised to those poor communities that endured the worst of the Troubles has simply failed to materialise in any meaningful sense.[10] That failure is the origin of perhaps the most crucial of the multiple forms of stasis that continue to afflict Northern Ireland. For all the changes that have occurred since the advent of the GFA, the region has managed largely to retain its distinctive and iniquitous social class profile. In that baleful period when it became synonymous with bitter internecine conflict, Northern Ireland existed as a society blighted by deep and durable material inequalities. More than two decades after the signing of the celebrated peace deal, little has occurred to alter that abject state of affairs. Indeed, if anything, the era of austerity has meant that the already iniquitous class divisions that blight Northern Ireland have in fact become even starker still.[11]

Northern Ireland in the age of the 'new economy'

It is important to remember that the Northern Irish peace process unfolded in a wider geopolitical context that for some time appeared ideally suited to the cause of economic progress in the region. After all, those important moments of conflict resolution that culminated in the GFA took place against the backdrop of a sustained global economic boom.[12] The end of the Cold War sparked an historically unprecedented wave of principally US capital seeking opportunities for investment and profit overseas. This surge in foreign direct investment happened, moreover, at a moment when advances in information technology engendered the faith that it was possible to generate economic growth in ways that are ecologically sustainable. As belief in the potentially progressive synergy of capital and technology gained ground within influential circles in Washington and Silicon Valley, it would lead to claims of the emergence of 'the new economy'.[13] The frequently fevered optimism of the age was captured best in the publication that gave most explicit voice to a certain techno-utopian veneration of capitalism that was fashionable at the time. Against the backdrop of a smiley emoticon, the front page of the July 1997 edition of *Wired* instructed readers to prepare for the 'long boom' of '25 years of prosperity, freedom and a better environment for the whole world'.[14] And, for a decade or so at least, it often appeared that the editors of the magazine might well be proved right.

If ever there were a time, then, when Northern Ireland might finally experience economic prosperity it was that period in the 1990s when the peace process gathered momentum. The main specific promise of those who had promoted the prospect of a 'peace dividend' was that the end of the conflict would spark an influx of multinational capital, from the United States in particular, that would in time revive the fortunes of the Northern Irish economy. In the immediate aftermath of the 1994 paramilitary ceasefires, it appeared that this version of events might actually come to pass. During the latter half of the decade, for instance, some €1.5 billion was invested in Northern Ireland by American multinational corporations alone, accelerating an already existing downward trend in the historically chronic unemployment rate in the region.[15] This initial, promising wave of foreign direct investment would not, however, be sustained far beyond the turn of the century. The ongoing weakness of Northern Ireland when it comes to attracting foreign direct investment is illustrated vividly in the record of the state agency established in 2002 with the specific brief of luring multinational capital to the region. As Niall McCracken[16] has documented, the almost £1 billion that Invest NI spent in the first five years of its existence alone – if jobs lost, as well as those gained, in sponsored companies are factored in – led to the creation, on balance, of a mere 328 stable positions. It would seem that the 'well of economic goodwill' towards Northern Ireland that Tony Blair claimed to exist on the eve of the referendum on the GFA had all but evaporated a decade later.

While the Northern Irish economy has remained consistently unable to generate or attract a large volume of new jobs, that has not, ironically, prevented a marked decline in the region's historically high levels of joblessness. Once a notorious unemployment black spot, Northern Ireland has in recent years, remarkably, become the UK region with the lowest proportion of people officially out of work.[17] In order to explain the apparent paradox of an economy that produces relatively few jobs registering such a dramatic decline in its jobless total, we need to look more closely at the specificities of the Northern Irish labour market. The metric of unemployment used most frequently in mainstream commentary documents those who are seeking employment but excludes those who are not. As a result, the headline jobless rate provides an inaccurate profile of the labour market in a region like Northern Ireland that has the highest percentage in the UK of people of working age who are unavailable for work. The relatively high level of 'worklessness' in the six counties may be attributed primarily to a dramatically elevated incidence of physical and mental illness.[18] In recent years, one in nine people in Northern Ireland have been registered as disabled for social security purposes, compared to one in twenty in the rest of the UK.[19] The comparatively high incidence of disability in the region owes a great deal, predictably, to the enduring impact of Northern Ireland's recent violent past. A major survey conducted in 2012 revealed that over the course of the Troubles one in three Northern Irish adults had witnessed a bomb explosion, one in nine had endured the loss of a close friend and one in ten had lost a close relative.[20] This widespread experience of political violence has inevitably meant that there are a great many people in Northern Ireland who continue to suffer from physical – and, more especially, mental – illness long after the conflict drew to a close. It is estimated that 30 per cent of the population living in the six counties are suffering with mental problems and that half of these individuals are dealing with some form of psychological trauma arising out of the Troubles.[21] The relatively high incidence of such conditions in Northern Ireland is reflected in the fact that two out of every five people who have registered for disability benefits in the region over recent years have done so on grounds of mental illness.[22]

The particularities of the Northern Irish labour market ensure, then, that certain key metrics generate profiles of economic performance in the region that are misleading. As the headline rate of unemployment takes no account of those who are unavailable for work it tends to understate the true level of 'worklessness' in Northern Ireland. A rather more reliable gauge of labour trends in the region is provided by looking at levels of economic activity which estimate those in work as a proportion of the population of working age. This register provides a rather less flattering depiction of what is happening in the Northern Irish job market. While the headline unemployment rate identifies Northern Ireland as the best performing UK region, the economic activity metric suggests that the true level of 'worklessness' in the six counties runs at 5 per cent above the average in the other regions of the state.[23]

The record of the Northern Irish economy over the course of the peace process has been poor in terms not only of the volume of new jobs created but also their quality. Relatively few of the positions that have been created over the last quarter-century have been in high-wage, high value-added occupational sectors. According to Paul Nolan,[24] three in every five of the jobs that Invest NI has brought to the region have been located in 'call centres', and two-thirds of these have offered wages below the median for the private sector in general. The attraction of this particular form of multinational investment to Northern Ireland both reflects and compounds its status as a low-wage economy. While people in full-time employment in the six counties work longer hours than those in any other region of the state,[25] their gross weekly wages stand 8.6 per cent below the UK average.[26] This disparity becomes even more pronounced when we look specifically at earnings in the private sector. The universalist ethos of the public sector ensures that those employed by the state in Northern Ireland earn the same as people in equivalent positions in other UK regions, outside London at least. A rather different picture emerges when we consider those working in private enterprise. According to the latest Annual Survey of Hours and Earnings, gross weekly wages in the private sector in Northern Ireland are currently 16 per cent behind the rest of the UK.[27]

It seems reasonable, then, to conclude that the 'peace dividend' that was so central to the optimism of the early days of the peace process has never quite come to pass. Over the last two decades or more, the Northern Irish economy has been unable to generate jobs in sufficient numbers, and of sufficient quality, to alter meaningfully the material conditions of those neighbourhoods that bore the brunt of the Troubles. A combination of high levels of 'worklessness' and low levels of wages has ensured that the multigenerational poverty that consumed working-class communities in Northern Ireland during the conflict has survived into the present day.[28] The failure of the 'peace dividend' to materialise might be deemed especially dispiriting given that the GFA took form at a moment when the conditions for an economic renaissance appeared entirely optimal. If the fortunes of Northern Ireland failed to improve during that period of frenetic global economic growth that marked the turn of the century, it was even more unlikely that they would do so once that period of supposedly endless boom gave way, inexorably, to bust.

A 'rare form of consensus'

In May 2007, the devolved institutions that form the centrepiece of the GFA were restored after a five-year hiatus. The unlikely alliance formed at Stormont by erstwhile foes Ian Paisley and Martin McGuinness would face many of the same challenges at local level that had proved the undoing of previous administrations. The new coalition would also be required, however, to operate within a shifting political climate at both national and international level that was rather more demanding than that faced by previous power-sharing administrations. In the first instance, this altered context was the outcome of the critical ideological changes that had overtaken the British state a generation before finally being brought to bear on Northern Ireland. The arrival of Margaret Thatcher in Downing Street in May 1979 would of course signal a period of radical political change that would leave British society transformed and, in many quarters, traumatised.[29] While the Conservative government would pursue its neoliberal strategies ruthlessly in every other part of the UK, it would never attempt to chart the same course in Northern Ireland. That the region would remain 'a place apart' during the Thatcher revolution would owe much to its own very specific political economy.[30] Those overseeing direct rule from Westminster held to the view that the introduction to Northern Ireland of austerity measures imposed elsewhere would precipitate even greater political violence in what was then very clearly the UK's poorest region. In order to avoid that calamity, successive Conservative administrations maintained public spending and employment at the relatively generous levels more readily associated with the previous golden age of social democracy.[31] It was in this context that one of the many Conservative 'wets' sent into exile in the Northern Ireland Office, Secretary of State Jim Prior, was moved to observe: 'we are all Keynesians here'.[32]

The relative generosity of public provision in Northern Ireland would largely survive almost two decades of the Conservatives in office and it would, ironically, require the arrival in Downing Street of a government ostensibly from the Left for the transition towards neoliberal policies to begin in earnest. One of the principal achievements of the Thatcher project was to redraw much of the rest of British political life in its own image. This facility was manifested most keenly in the rebranding of the principal opposition party as *New* Labour. While Tony Blair would seek to give them a certain genial egalitarian and cosmopolitan gloss, the ideas that he advanced and the policies that he pursued bore the same distinctive neoliberal hallmark as those that had come before – hollowing out the social, demonising the poor, fetishising outlandish personal wealth, and all the rest. It would come as little surprise, then, when the ideological matriarch Margaret Thatcher identified the New Labour leader as the true heir to her political legacy.[33]

A central tenet of the Blair philosophy was, of course, that the institutions of the state would be transformed by exposure to the ethos and imperatives of private business.[34] While this conviction was pursued somewhat less vigorously in a Northern Irish context, it would over time become official policy in the region.[35] In the period between 2002 and 2007, when the devolved institutions at Stormont were suspended, New Labour set about extending in earnest to Northern Ireland the Private Finance Initiative that the party had inherited from the Conservatives but would soon make its own. In what was 'perhaps the first substantive act' after the resumption of direct rule,[36] the Strategic Investment Board was created in 2003 with the remit of involving private corporations in the funding and execution of major infrastructural developments, like the building of hospitals and schools, that had once been the sole preserve of the state. In remarkably short order, this statutory agency would establish a substantial empire and transform the nature of public investment in Northern Ireland. The last annual report of the Strategic Investment Board to appear prior to the restoration of devolution in May 2007, for instance, records that the body had since its inception only four years earlier been responsible for the creation of 38 Public Private Partnerships (PPPs) collaborating on projects with a total value of £5.3 billion.[37]

The growing reliance on private capital to finance public infrastructure projects in Northern Ireland might be seen as emblematic of the very particular direction that public policy came to take in the decade after the signing of the GFA. Unlike its predecessors in the Conservative Party, the Blair government was quick to extend to the six counties those palpably neoliberal strategies that had been introduced throughout the rest of the UK. As a consequence, by the time the devolved institutions were restored in the early summer of 2007, the ethos and institutions required to advance a certain version of public policy were already firmly in place. While the new coalition forged between Sinn Féin and the Democratic Unionist Party

(DUP) might in principle have charted a different course, in practice they proved willing time and again to operate within the specific ideological frame that New Labour had set for them.[38] The readiness of the DUP to embrace neoliberal strategies wrapped in the language of technocratic efficiency and personal choice would of course come as little surprise. While the influence of Desmond Boal[39] ensured that the party would be founded with a commitment to being 'to the left on social policies', the Democratic Unionists would soon dispense with that avowal and come routinely to espouse the most reactionary modes of socio-economic strategy. It was always entirely predictable, then, that the DUP would embrace the neoliberal turn that preceded its coming to power in Northern Ireland.

The Democratic Unionists' partners in government, in contrast, might reasonably have been expected to adopt a rather more critical stance. Sinn Féin represents, of course, a broad church that accommodates an array of contrasting, and often contradictory, ideological positions. The current incarnation of the party emerged from those who formed the Provisional IRA in explicit rejection of the Leftist direction in which the leadership had taken the republican movement in the years immediately before the outbreak of the Troubles. Those conservative forces have remained within the Sinn Féin fold throughout the period since and would ensure, for instance, that the party would, until very recently, refuse to adopt an unequivocal position in support of a woman's right to choose.[40] Over time, however, the republican movement would become more left-wing in its orientation, with observers in the late 1970s noting 'a growing Marxist feeling' within its ranks.[41] In the aftermath of the hunger strikes, a cabal of younger, more radical activists based north of the border and long since in the ascendant would complete its takeover of Sinn Féin, ensuring that the party's rhetoric would become ever closer to that of the internationalist Left. This ideological complexion has largely remained intact, in a performative sense at least, over the last three decades. The current version of Sinn Féin seeks to style itself on either side of the Irish border as a socialist party committed to the principle that it is the state and not the market that is the principal guarantor of social justice and economic progress. In a tale familiar to many ethno-national movements with ambitions for radical social change, once in office republicans would, however, soon abandon their previously cherished political convictions. Over the initial decade that Sinn Féin shared power with the DUP, the two parties would often be at odds over the multiple sectarian concerns that have traditionally animated Northern Irish public life. The coalition partners would invariably be of one mind, however, when it came to what are often termed 'bread and butter' issues. As Brian Kelly[42] has observed, while the senior parties in the Stormont executive were 'constantly falling out' over matters of ethno-national rights and identities, in terms of social and economic policy they would become increasingly 'ecumenical' in their 'collective worship of the free market'.

This 'rare form of consensus'[43] between Sinn Féin and the DUP would be reflected in their willing embrace of the established dogma that private finance is an indispensable prerequisite of public enterprise. The initial period in which the two parties shared power at Stormont would see PPPs become a cornerstone of public policy in Northern Ireland. In 2017, as the former partners in government parted company acrimoniously, private corporations were involved in 31 major infrastructural projects in Northern Ireland with a total value of some £1.73 billion.[44] A central rationale for the introduction of the Private Finance Initiative had been the supposition that businesses are more efficient than states and hence would guarantee 'value for money' in relation to key elements of public expenditure. This ideological assumption would prove no more accurate in Northern Ireland than it had in any other UK region.[45] In the spring of 2018, it was reported that while the private loans on existing PPPs amounted to £1.44 billion, the payments on these would reach £5.8 billion over the next 25 years, an interest rate in the region of 300 per cent.[46] The uncritical introduction of the Private Finance Initiative in Northern Ireland has served, therefore, not to bring about savings and efficiencies in state spending as promised but rather, as elsewhere, to redirect vast quantities of public money into the coffers of private corporations.

The meeting of minds between Sinn Féin and the DUP suggested by their mutual enthusiasm for PPPs was illustrated even more keenly in their strategy for luring multinational corporations to Northern Ireland. A central article of faith between the two parties in government was that the performance of the local economy had been impeded by the relatively high levels of corporation tax operating in the UK. If Northern Ireland were given the opportunity to adopt the same 12.5 per cent rate as the Irish Republic, the argument went, the region would finally be able to compete successfully for transnational investment.[47] In time, it might even come to replicate the remarkable success of its neighbour, which currently hosts the overseas headquarters of nine out of the top ten multinational corporations in the areas of both pharmaceuticals and information technology.[48] The simple faith that Sinn Féin and the DUP placed in what Denis O'Hearn[49] has termed the 'magic bullet' of slashing corporation tax was of course misguided from the very outset. Those advocating this policy option chose to overlook the very real changes in the global and European context that have taken place since the Irish Republic embarked on such a path. As the Berlin Wall fell, Ireland was able to tap into an unprecedented flow of global capital by positioning itself as an economy with a highly skilled and, initially at least, relatively low-paid workforce that offered a gateway to a European Union whose boundaries had yet to expand into the former Soviet bloc. Three decades on, the global economic environment looks entirely different. It is difficult to imagine how, under current circumstances, Northern Ireland might even begin to repeat the success of its neighbour in attracting the levels of investment that were the catalyst for the Celtic Tiger boom. To take only the most pertinent illustration, the expansion of the European Union eastward requires the region to compete with countries that have rather lower wages and, in some instances, even lower rates of corporation tax than the one on which the Stormont executive had set its heart. While this proposed change in fiscal policy was unlikely to have initiated a wave of transnational investment arriving in Northern Ireland, it almost certainly would have led to major cuts in public spending in the region. One estimate suggests that cutting corporation tax to 12.5 per cent would reduce the budget available to any Stormont executive by as much as £400 million each year.[50] The most likely outcome of the *one big idea* that seemed to conjoin Sinn Féin and the DUP during their time in office would, therefore, appear to have been a period not of renewed economic opportunity in Northern Ireland, but rather one of even greater material deprivation.

'Making work pay'

When the Stormont institutions were restored in the early summer of 2007, therefore, the coalition partners faced a national context in which the policy agenda had moved palpably in a neoliberal direction. The new coalition government in Belfast would also encounter an international environment that had changed utterly since the previous, ill-starred attempts at power-sharing in Northern Ireland. As the beaming figures of Paisley and McGuinness assumed office, the crisis long since latent within global capitalism was coming to a head. Little more than a year later, Lehman Brothers would become the largest firm ever to go bankrupt in US corporate history and herald the onset of the most severe crisis in the world economy for eighty years.[51] In short order, a range of powerful political forces would seek to persuade us that the global 'credit crunch' had been caused not by deregulated financial markets but by what were deemed to be excessive levels of state spending.[52] The worst recession in several generations was, in other words, the result not of bankers having too many opportunities to behave recklessly but rather of 'Wolverhampton having too many libraries'.[53] This ideological sleight of hand would prepare the ground for austerity programmes designed to accelerate the project of hollowing out the social at the heart of the neoliberal orthodoxies that had held sway over the three previous decades.[54]

Against this backdrop of global economic recession, the Conservative Party returned to power in 2010 after thirteen years in opposition. One of the keynote policies advanced by the Conservatives and their junior coalition partners, the Liberal Democrats, gave form to the ever more ubiquitous fiction that the recession had been caused not by the $21 trillion[55] that states had given to bail out the banks, but rather by the comparatively trifling sums that governments had spent to ensure that their most vulnerable citizens might live with a little dignity. In 2012, the Westminster government unveiled what was perhaps the most radical assault on the British welfare state since its inception. The advent of the Welfare Reform Act saw six existing forms of social security and tax credit merged into a single measure named 'Universal Credit' and the Disability Living Allowance replaced by the 'Personal Independence Payment' (PIP). The explicit intention of these changes was to create greater incentives for those out of work to pursue poorly paid employment and for those already in poorly paid employment to pursue more of it. In their devotion to the ideological totem of 'making work pay',[56] the coalition partners introduced various measures and procedures designed to reduce further the already meagre incomes of those most dependent on the British welfare system. The advent of a 'benefit cap' meant that claimants now faced arbitrary upper limits on their welfare entitlements that often fell well short of the amount required to maintain a decent existence. Moreover, the implementation in 2016 of a freeze on benefits levels for the next four years ensured that the poorest sections of British society saw their incomes decline in real terms. The draconian logic of welfare 'reform' was to reduce not only the value of social security payments but also the number of people entitled to claim them. While the introduction of Universal Credit in particular was depicted as simplifying the welfare system, a wealth of anecdotal evidence soon emerged indicating that the new regime was even more complex, and even less humane, than its predecessor. The chicanery of processes and sanctions that arrived with welfare 'reform' seemed designed to weed out as many claimants as possible, and the numbers entitled to the new headline benefits went into predictable decline. In the case of the PIP, for instance, one in four of those 'migrating' to the new benefit had their applications rejected.

The introduction of a welfare regime that has resulted, as was its intention, in a smaller number of claimants who are entitled to lesser levels of benefits has inevitably had a catastrophic impact on the most disadvantaged within British society.[57] Perhaps the most dramatic index of the heightened poverty that has resulted from welfare 'reform' is the proliferation of food banks in the age of austerity.[58] While there were 29 such facilities in the entire UK at the beginning of the global financial crisis, by 2018 the total had reached 'about 2,000'.⁵⁹ The destitution that welfare 'reform' has signalled for the poorest sections of British society was captured vividly, of course, in Ken Loach's controversial film *I, Daniel Blake*. Set in Newcastle, the city where Universal Credit was 'rolled out' first, the film documents the growing desperation of an ageing former construction worker and a young single mother whose paths cross as they attempt to negotiate a byzantine and callous new welfare regime. The pivotal scene set in a food bank where the female lead, famished from having to forgo meals so that her two children can eat, abandons her dignity to devour some of the contents of her parcel on the spot is one that will remain forever in the mind of anyone who has ever seen it.

While such indelible indictments of austerity are to be expected in the agitprop of Leftist cinema, equally vehement critiques of welfare 'reform' have also come from other less predictable, more 'establishment' sources. In 2016, the same year in which Ken Loach's raw polemic opened in cinemas, the United Nations Committee on the Rights of Persons with Disabilities found evidence that the new benefits regime, and in particular its sanctions system, was engaged in 'grave and systematic violation of the rights of persons with disabilities'.⁶⁰ The following year, the High Court in London ruled that those implementing the PIP had been 'blatantly discriminatory'⁶¹ against people with mental health conditions. Perhaps the most searing indictment of social welfare in the age of austerity would, however, come in November 2018 when the United Nations Special Rapporteur on Extreme Poverty and Human Rights published the findings of his visit to the UK. Dispensing with the diplomatic equivocations that often characterise official reports, Professor Philip Alston⁶² observed that recent changes to the benefits system meant that we 'are witnessing the gradual disappearance of the post-war British welfare state'.⁶³ Warming to his task, the Australian legal scholar contested that the new order was 'punitive, mean-spirited, and often callous', bringing 'great misery' that had been 'inflicted unnecessarily'.⁶⁴ At the heart of the welfare changes was the exercise of a certain arbitrary disciplinary impulse seeking to punish for its own sake, to 'make clear that being on benefits should involve hardship'.⁶⁵ The Special Rapporteur went on to document some of the mounting evidence of the poverty that has resulted from the Welfare Reform Act. By 2022, for instance, it is estimated that two out of every five British children will be living in poverty, a proportion that rises to three out of five in the case of youngsters living in single-parent households.⁶⁶ Surveying the penury that welfare 'reform' has brought with palpable disdain, Professor Alston allowed himself the rhetorical flourish of suggesting that the new regime is 'fast falling into Universal Discredit'.⁶⁷

'A disturbingly high representation'

While the assault on the welfare state devised by the Conservatives and Liberal Democrats threatened to bring severe hardship across the UK as a whole, the provisions of welfare 'reform' had the potential to be especially catastrophic in a Northern Irish context. In their research conducted at the outset of the new welfare regime, Christina Beatty and Steve Fothergill[68] noted that there was 'a disturbingly high representation' of Northern Irish constituencies among those likely to be most badly affected by the relevant legislation. While the changes to the social security system would generate a financial loss in Great Britain equivalent to £470 for every working adult, the figure in Northern Ireland was forecast to be £650. Given that the matters of social security covered in the 2012 Welfare Reform Act are among those devolved to the Stormont parliament, it was at least possible that Northern Ireland might be spared its provisions. The London government made it clear from the start, however, that the new regime was to apply throughout the UK and that financial sanctions would, if necessary, be deployed against the Belfast Assembly to bring about that eventuality. The draconian stance adopted in Westminster would pose few problems for one of the coalition partners in the Northern Ireland Executive. As a party leaning to the right politically and working, no doubt, on the outdated assumption that the casualties of the new legislation would overwhelmingly be nationalists, it came as little surprise that the DUP would greet the prospect of massive cuts in social security with open arms. The advent of the Welfare Reform Act would, however, represent a rather greater headache for their partners in government. While the peace process has seen the republican movement secure growing middle-class support,[69] its centre of gravity remains in those impoverished nationalist districts that had experienced the worst of the Northern Irish Troubles. Given that welfare 'reform' was likely to impact most gravely on those communities that represent their electoral bedrock, it was to be anticipated that Sinn Féin would throw its energies into opposing the new legislation. And that is certainly the role in which republicans have been keen to cast themselves. The routine claims of Sinn Féin to be a resolute opponent of austerity either side of the Irish border have been readily endorsed by commentators sympathetic to the republican project.[70] If we trace the narrative of how welfare 'reform' came to Northern Ireland, however, a rather more complicated, and less flattering, picture of how the party has conducted itself while in office begins to emerge.

Although it was Sinn Féin that would ultimately bring down the Stormont institutions in January 2017, it often appeared to be the rather more enthusiastic party to Northern Ireland's latest experiment in consociational government. In the decade during which they first shared power with the DUP, there was the clear impression that republicans were becoming ever more invested in the healthy functioning of institutions they had once engaged in 'armed struggle' to destroy. This sense of investment was especially apparent in the disposition of someone widely understood to have previously been the long-standing leader of the Provisional IRA. In his time as deputy First Minister, Martin McGuinness would, as we illustrated in Chapter 1, show a genuine commitment to the peace process, prompting a sequence of reconciliatory gestures that would begin to stretch the patience even of a republican community in which he was widely revered.[71] The commitment of republicans to maintaining the Stormont institutions would inevitably require of them a series of political compromises. One of these would see Sinn Féin adopt a strategy towards welfare 'reform' that would ultimately prove deeply at odds with the party's representation of itself as a steadfast opponent of austerity.

Initial attempts to pass the 2012 Welfare Reform Act through the Stormont Assembly would once again cast light on the ideological schism dividing the two parties governing Northern Ireland. The refusal of Sinn Féin to support the relevant enabling legislation added yet another to the mounting body of issues dividing the coalition partners. As the relationship between the two parties deteriorated apace, two rounds of prolonged negotiations were initiated – one in the autumn of 2013 hosted by the US diplomatic figures Richard Haass and Meghan O'Sullivan, the other a year later overseen by the British and Irish governments – in an attempt to break the political logjam. In November 2014, it was announced that the local parties had approved a document that would, hopefully, provide the basis for stable government in Northern Ireland. In a certain sense, the signing of the Stormont House Agreement might be considered a pivotal moment in recent Northern Irish history. It was, after all, the first time that a political deal had been struck in the six counties where issues of social class were to the very fore of the agenda, albeit in an entirely reactionary way. The text of the Stormont House Agreement registered a commitment both to implement the 2012 Welfare Reform Act and to support 'public-sector reform' in the guise of job cuts. While the deal promised the release of £2 billion in additional funds from central government, that figure would almost certainly have been swiftly surpassed by the spending cuts specified in other parts of the document.[72]

Among the signatories to the neoliberal charter that was the Stormont House Agreement were of course Sinn Féin. In choosing to endorse the deal, republicans had now committed themselves in practice to policies they had long since claimed to oppose as a matter of principle. This political change of heart appeared to be confirmed at a meeting of the Northern Ireland Executive in January 2015, when Sinn Féin joined forces with the

DUP to push through a budget that would allow both for welfare cuts and redundancies in the public sector. The votes cast by republican ministers at Stormont inevitably drew criticism from various sources. In the early weeks of 2015, Sinn Féin found itself in the unaccustomed position of being outflanked by its main rival for the nationalist vote, the Social Democratic and Labour Party (SDLP), which had adopted a consistent stance of opposition to welfare 'reform'.[73] More significantly, perhaps, the prospect of changes to the social security system exacerbated certain critical strategic tensions within the republican leadership. While the pragmatist Martin McGuinness appears to have been willing to stomach welfare 'reform' in order to retain Sinn Féin's prized position at the helm of government in Northern Ireland, the rather more artful figure of Gerry Adams sought to resist such a move on the grounds that it might imperil the recent gains made by the party south of the border. The electoral success that republicans had come to enjoy in the Irish Republic was premised largely on their opposition to the painful austerity measures being introduced by successive Dublin governments. That position of principle would, of course, become increasingly difficult to sustain were Sinn Féin ministers to begin introducing similar draconian policies at Stormont. The strategic differences within the republican leadership would come to a head at the *Ard Fheis* (annual conference) held in Derry in early March 2015. It would soon become apparent that then Sinn Féin President Gerry Adams had, predictably, managed to persuade his colleagues to agree to another change of heart on the issue of welfare 'reform'. On 9 March 2015, just two days after the *Ard Fheis* concluded, business resumed at Stormont, where it was widely expected that the 2012 Welfare Reform Act would enjoy the support of both main government parties, allowing it to pass comfortably through the Assembly. When it came time to move through the lobbies, however, the Sinn Féin members in the chamber caught their coalition partners off guard by voting against the proposed legislation.[74] Amid a welter of mutual recrimination, relations between the two parties degenerated even further, requiring yet another round in Northern Ireland's seemingly endless cycle of political negotiations.

The outcome of this latest sequence of talks was a new deal struck barely a year after the Stormont House Agreement had been finalised. If anything, the text of A Fresh Start offered even greater license to the neoliberal policies that were anticipated in its predecessor. The document allowed for both the reduction of corporation tax in Northern Ireland to 12.5 per cent and the loss of almost 7,500 jobs in the public sector. In a society where even now more than one in three people work for the state,[75] the level of redundancies envisaged in A Fresh Start represented an enormous prospective loss. To give some sense of the scale here, an equivalent number of redundancies in Great Britain would see around 270,000 public-sector workers lose their jobs at a stroke. The new agreement brokered among the local parties also stipulated the introduction, once more, of the 2012 Welfare Reform Act. Various provisions were included to cushion the impact of wholesale cuts to social security in Northern Ireland. An additional £585 million was to be made available from existing funds to 'top up the UK welfare arrangements' which would ensure, *inter alia*, that the controversial 'bedroom tax' would, in effect, not operate in the six counties. These 'mitigation' measures were scheduled to last until 2020 and, while they were to be subject to review, the common assumption was that during that year the welfare system already in place in other regions of the UK would, more or less, come to operate in Northern Ireland.

While the text of the new agreement, like that of its predecessor, insisted that welfare 'reform' was to happen in Northern Ireland, it envisaged a rather different mechanism for bringing this about. Mindful no doubt of the previous failure of the assembly to ratify the 2012 Welfare Reform Act, those who framed A Fresh Start were evidently unwilling to leave matters to chance this time around. Under the terms of the new deal, Stormont was required to cede the power to introduce the relevant legislation to Westminster.[76] On 18 November 2015, the Northern Ireland Assembly agreed by a margin of 70 votes to 22 to allow the British parliament to legislate on matters of welfare 'reform' that fall within its own remit of devolved powers. While strong opposition to the move was voiced by figures from political parties ordinarily less radical on such matters, all of the Sinn Féin members present voted in favour.[77] A mere five days later, Westminster passed the relevant legislation to ensure that the writ of the 2012 Welfare Reform Act would now run throughout the entire UK.

The impact of welfare 'reform' in Northern Ireland

With the extension of the new social welfare legislation to Northern Ireland, many in the six counties would come to experience some of the dread realities already endured by people living in other regions of the UK. The introduction of the PIP would begin in June 2016, with the 'roll-out' of Universal Credit starting in September of the following year. In line with elsewhere, Northern Irish claimants have often experienced the new benefits system as complex and punitive. While the data from 2018/19 indicated that Universal Credit would provide modest increases in income for a considerable number of families (114,000 would see rises of on average £26 per week), they also suggested that a somewhat larger body of households would lose rather more substantial amounts (126,000 would see losses of on average £39 per week).[78] Furthermore, the introduction of the PIP has mirrored the experience in other UK regions, with substantial numbers of existing and prospective claimants with physical and mental disabilities excluded from the scheme. One in four of those in Northern Ireland who migrated from the Disability Living Allowance had their claims rejected, with more than half of new applicants suffering a similar fate.[79]

Although the experience of welfare 'reform' in Northern Ireland has mirrored that in other parts of the UK, it has also diverged in certain important respects. The very specific social and political circumstances that obtain in the region, as we saw earlier, prompted the Belfast Assembly to set aside £585 million to cushion the impact of the new benefits system devised by the Westminster coalition. These 'mitigation' funds have been employed to nullify the impact of several components of the new regime, namely the PIP, the benefits cap and the Social Sector Size Criteria, or 'bedroom tax'. This last reform penalises claimants who live in dwellings deemed to have more rooms than their needs require. The very specific nature of Northern Ireland's demographic and housing profiles – 45 per cent of all applicants for social housing are single, but just 18 per cent of properties in that sector are only suitable for one person[80] – means that the region is particularly vulnerable to the bedroom tax. Indeed, the proportion of dwellings in the six counties that have 'too many' rooms for the number of people living there is three times the English, and twice the British, average.[81] In this context, the provision of funds to cover the deductions associated with the bedroom tax represents an important support for some of the poorer sections of Northern Irish society. It is estimated that this form of 'mitigation' increases the incomes of around 34,000 households[82] to the tune of, on average, £12.50 per week.[83]

While the various mitigation measures that operate in Northern Ireland have certainly cushioned the blow of welfare 'reform', it is important to remember that they have only compensated for around thirty per cent of the total income losses that would otherwise have accompanied the new regime. Many of the changes to the tax and benefits system that have had the most severe impact on claimants have not in fact been subject to remedial funds from the devolved assembly.[84] The measures that fall into this category include cuts to tax credits, the benefits freeze, changes in entitlements under Universal Credit and the new child benefit regulations. The last reform mentioned here means that parents will no longer be able to claim benefits for third or subsequent children. The advent of the 'two-child rule' has a particular significance in Northern Ireland where families tend be relatively large, with 21 per cent of households having three or more children compared to the British average of 14 per cent.[85] According to research conducted jointly by two Westminster committees, recent changes in the welfare system mean that each additional child beyond the first two now entails a loss to Northern Irish families of £2,780 per year.[86]

The explicit draconian purpose of welfare 'reform' was to drive down the incomes of the poorest sections of UK society in order to 'incentivise' them to enter the labour market on even more disadvantageous terms. The deliberate objective of the project was, therefore, to widen even further the already dramatic class inequalities that define the world's sixth most productive economy. That this strategy has been an overwhelming success is borne out clearly in recent research by Howard Reed and Jonathan Portes[87] in which they modelled the effect on Northern Ireland of the various tax and social welfare changes introduced by Westminster over the last decade. In their report for the Northern Ireland Human Rights Commission, the authors illustrate that the era of welfare 'reform' has skewed even further the inequalities between rich and poor in Northern Irish society. The changes in taxes and social security benefits introduced since the global financial crash have impacted unfavourably on the bottom six deciles – the lowest 60 per cent – of income earners in the region. Those families located in deciles two and three – the poorest 11–30 per cent of the population – have been affected especially badly, having seen their incomes drop on average by around £900 a year. Households in the bottom decile have lost on average around £250 annually, a decline which is less in absolute terms than those immediately above them, but which is of course likely to have a disproportionate impact on people who are living on the lowest rungs of the social class hierarchy. While the era of welfare 'reform' has eroded the resources available to the poorest sections of Northern Irish society, those on higher incomes have had an entirely different experience. As Reed and Portes illustrate, the tax and social security changes implemented since the Conservatives returned to power have led to greater incomes for all but one of the four top deciles in Northern Ireland.[88] Those families located in decile eight, for instance, now have just under £800 more at their disposal each year. The sole exception to the rule of growing affluence among the upper echelons of Northern Irish society is found in the top decile, where households have seen their incomes drop by £100 annually. This negligible decline is unlikely, however, even to be noticed by the wealthy elite of a region whose capital has more millionaires per capita than any UK city other than London and Aberdeen.[89]

The report sponsored by the Northern Ireland Human Rights Commission provides a critical overview of a society whose already substantial inequalities are evidently becoming even more acute. Within this broad pattern of polarisation, there are a number of more specific trends that should give particular cause for alarm. The models that Reed and Portes have constructed illustrate time and again that the era of welfare 'reform' has made the most vulnerable in Northern Ireland even more so. The recent changes to the social security system have had especially grave repercussions for the disabled. For example, households with at least one disabled adult and at least one disabled child have seen their annual income decline by almost £1,800. Recent reforms of the welfare system have also proved especially harsh on single parents, more than ninety per cent of whom are women. Households headed by one adult have experienced falls in income of around £2,250 per year.[90] Finally, the era of welfare reform has proved particularly, and predictably, brutal for many children living in Northern Ireland. While there are many metrics that index the mass poverty deliberately and needlessly manufactured since the Conservatives returned to power, few capture it more starkly than the fact that by 2022 one in three Northern Irish children are expected to be living in absolute poverty, a proportion that rises to more than one in two in the case of those youngsters living in single-parent households.[91]

The politics of social class

The current dismantling of the British welfare state has, therefore, clearly had a devastating impact on the social fabric of Northern Ireland. These draconian changes may also, however, have the potential to signal a progressive turn in the political life of the region. In order to understand this apparent paradox, we need to retrace our steps a little and recall the role that republicans played in bringing welfare 'reform' – albeit in modified form – to Northern Ireland. As with many nationalist social movements before them, the professed radicalism of Sinn Féin has been compromised by the pursuit of power in Northern Ireland. Although adopting an explicitly anti-austerity stance, the party nonetheless signed up to two different political agreements that entail the erosion of essential forms of social security, and was even prepared to suspend the authority of the government in which it sat in order to secure that eventuality. We are faced, then, with two remarkable ironies. Not only is Sinn Féin the 'socialist' party that endorsed the introduction of welfare cuts in Northern Ireland, but it is also the Irish 'republican' party that ceded power to the British parliament in order to ensure they would come into being. This all-too familiar drift to the right on the part of a once radical ethno-nationalist movement has at times promised to create the conditions of the possibility of a different, more progressive mode of politics in Northern Ireland.

The acquiescence of Sinn Féin in the face of Westminster demands for welfare 'reform' added the final component to the neoliberal consensus that came to define the decade in which they previously shared power with the DUP at Stormont. While the coalition partners would continue to bicker endlessly over the dog-eared demands of ethno-national competition, they would time and again find common cause in seeking to slash corporation tax, privatising public services, eliminating state jobs and imposing ever greater misery on the poorest sections of Northern Irish society. As the austerity measures facilitated by the Stormont Executive took hold, it was possible that growing public resentment might give rise to new forms of political opposition. The long-avowed 'socialism' of the republican movement made Sinn Féin especially vulnerable, of course, to any prospective public backlash.

In the weeks that followed the decision to extend the new welfare regime to Northern Ireland, there existed in the six counties an historically unparalleled set of political circumstances. For the first time, the region was experiencing sustained and perhaps even sustainable devolved government that entailed representatives of *both* ethno-national traditions preparing to implement austerity measures whose impact would be felt on *both* sides of the sectarian divide.[92] As the likely impact of the neoliberal consensus at Stormont became ever more painfully apparent, conditions in Northern Ireland became altogether more conducive to the emergence of dissenting political voices seeking to privilege issues of social class over those of ethno-national affiliation. The kindling of a socialist alternative would become evident in the elections to the Northern Ireland assembly held on 5 May 2016, a mere six months after the legislation was passed preparing the ground for the new draconian welfare regime in the region. In the Foyle constituency, veteran campaigner Eamonn McCann finally broke an electoral duck stretching back over half a century to secure a seat for the People Before Profit Alliance (PBPA). The grouping would taste further success, more significantly, in the republican heartland of west Belfast. Building on a previous sequence of promising performances, the young activist Gerry Carroll would astonish most political commentators by securing 8,299 first preferences and topping the poll ahead of an evidently disgruntled Sinn Féin. This widely unanticipated electoral success for the Left marked a development in Northern Irish political life that has no little historical significance. It meant that when the Stormont assembly resumed a week later, Northern Ireland would, for the first time since the start of the Troubles, be run by a devolved legislature that included individuals prepared to identify themselves as 'socialists' without feeling the need to add the prefix 'republican'.

It is often tempting to amplify the importance of those political developments we might deem progressive, and the 2016 Northern Ireland assembly election represents perhaps a case in point. Socialist candidates standing for office, after all, ran in only three constituencies and received a total of fewer than 14,000 votes. While the return of two socialists to the Stormont assembly certainly did not break the mould of Northern Irish politics, it did perhaps illustrate that the field of political possibility in the six counties was beginning to broaden. Had the coalition of parties that resumed government in the early summer of 2016 served out its full term, there was every prospect that the ground might have become more fertile still for the Left. In particular, the ever more injurious impact of the welfare 'reform' measures facilitated and then implemented by Sinn Féin and the DUP would have given greater resonance to the argument that it is social class and not sectarian background that represents the principal arbiter of the manifest inequalities blighting Northern Ireland. In this shifting ideological context, space might well have opened up for a more substantial and sustainable challenge from the Left. A herculean task, admittedly, but one that was perhaps not entirely beyond the realm of political possibility.

Such speculation about the possibility of progressive politics in Northern Ireland would soon appear to have been rendered moot by the actuality of regressive politics elsewhere in the UK. A mere seven weeks after two socialists took their places on the benches of the Stormont assembly, a slim majority of the British electorate voted to leave the European Union. The advent of the Brexit vote would, predictably, see the already narrow ground of Northern Irish political life become even more circumscribed. Ongoing speculation about what will happen to the Irish border after the UK leaves the European Union has prompted a debate over the future of Northern Ireland that has at times reached an historically unparalleled pitch.[93] Amid all the sound and fury surrounding the 'constitutional question', those voices seeking to draw attention to crucial issues of social class were increasingly drowned out. As the space that opened up in response to the neoliberal turn at Stormont began to narrow again, socialists would see their already limited electoral appeal begin to evaporate. In the March 2017 assembly elections, held in an attempt to revive the devolved institutions that collapsed two months before, the PBPA was unable to repeat its success in Foyle, a victim of the reduction of assembly seats in each constituency from six to five. Gerry Carroll would retain his seat in west Belfast but, on this occasion, he was forced into fifth place. Buoyed by their strong performance in the previous assembly election, the PBPA had added a running mate to the ticket in the republican citadel. The combined vote of the two candidates would, however, fall some 2,300 votes short of the total Carroll received when running unaccompanied the year before. Worse was to come in the snap Westminster election held three months later. On this occasion, Carroll polled 4,312 first preferences, a creditable return but one that was only half of the number of votes the PBPA candidate had secured in the assembly election barely a year before. As with many others previously, this talented young activist had run up against the stark reality that when the sap of ethno-national feeling rises in Northern Ireland, among the first casualties is the space available to socialist politics.

While the febrile atmosphere that marked the immediate aftermath of the collapse of the Stormont Executive reasserted the dominance of the 'constitutional question' in Northern Irish politics, over time the ground available for alternative perspectives has begun to emerge once more. As the suspension of the Assembly began to take on the appearance of permanence, disaffection with the intransigence of unionist and nationalist politicians alike saw the rise of political forces striving to transcend the conventional ethno-national binaries of local political life. One of the minor beneficiaries of this shift in the popular mood was the PBPA. In the May 2019 local government elections, the group took five seats, drawing support primarily in working-class nationalist districts in Belfast and Derry. Moreover, in the general election seven months later, Gerry Carroll polled 6,200 votes in west Belfast, suggesting that he has every chance of retaining his seat in the next assembly elections. The modest success enjoyed by socialist candidates in recent polls has hinged crucially on their ability to carve out a space to the left of the republican movement by underlining the latter's involvement in the introduction of welfare 'reform'. One eye-catching PBPA poster that has appeared in recent elections has sought to remind republican voters of a certain inconvenient truth: 'PIP & Universal Credit brought to you by Sinn Féin, the DUP and the Tories'. While the critiques issued by socialist candidates have yet to have a widespread electoral impact on Sinn Féin, they have nonetheless begun to make the normally very assured leadership of the party appear rather discomfited on their record on welfare 'reform'.

Over the course of 2019, with the Stormont institutions still in cold storage, a coalition of voluntary associations sought to highlight that in March the following year the measures introduced to cushion the impact of the new welfare regime were due to come to an end. If these 'mitigations' were not extended, the network warned, many of the most vulnerable members of Northern Irish society would be plunged over a 'cliff edge'. When the Stormont assembly was revived finally in January 2020, it would appear that, for once at least, the parties of government had been listening to those advocating for the poorest sections of Northern Irish society. The signatories to the political deal that broke the deadlock – *New Decade, New Approach* – agreed that the measures introduced to ease the burden of welfare 'reform' would be extended beyond the existing March 2020 deadline. The anxiety of the republican movement to be seen to be taking a progressive approach on these matters became apparent when, barely three weeks after the resumption of the assembly, the Sinn Féin Minister for Communities Deirdre Hargey announced that funds were being made available to extend the 'mitigation' of what is legally known as the 'social sector size criteria'.[94] Press releases announcing the admittedly welcome news made no reference, of course, to the supporting role that the minister's party had played in the introduction of the dreaded 'bedroom tax' to Northern Ireland in the first place.

The optimistic talk about the 'mitigation' of welfare 'reform' emerging from the recently restored Stormont Executive might be said to be misleading in at least two further senses. First, the measures to soften the blow of the new social security apparatus that are being extended, while certainly important, are nonetheless merely partial. Even if all the existing 'mitigation' provisions were to continue beyond the 'cliff edge' at the end of March 2020, then the poorest sections of Northern Irish society would still be exposed to the welfare changes responsible for the greatest impact on their already meagre incomes. Second, those measures that have been adopted to ease the burden of the new social security system were originally conceived as provisional, and that is how they are likely to remain. In his relentless critique of the dismantling of the British welfare state, Professor Philip Alston acknowledged the importance of measures to protect citizens from aspects of the new order but went on to observe that 'mitigation comes at a price and is not sustainable'. This astute observation reminds us that once the current assembly term comes to an end in 2022, it is entirely possible that Northern Ireland will become subject to the full force of welfare 'reform'. The even more profound hardship that would arise from such an eventuality might create conditions rather more conducive to those currently marginal forces seeking to advance class interests over ethno-national affiliation. In large measure, the success of this project will hinge on the facility of republicans to cover their own tracks and dissociate themselves from the introduction of welfare 'reform'. If Sinn Féin can be successfully outed as having been in league with the DUP to bring Universal Credit and the PIP to Northern Ireland, as indeed they were, it is just possible perhaps that the Left might yet gain ground at a time when sections of the Northern Irish electorate appear to be looking beyond the ethno-national binaries that are the traditional fare of local political life. While historical experience would not of course encourage unbridled optimism about such a development, there remains at least the prospect that the ongoing Conservative assault on the welfare state may well prepare the ground for the emergence of a politics of social class in Northern Ireland.

Conclusion

In the early years of the peace process, a sequence of international political figures made solemn pledges that a permanent end to the conflict would prepare the ground for a dramatic economic upturn in Northern Ireland. Those promises of prosperity that were issued routinely from London,

Dublin and Washington have indeed come to fruition for certain sections of Northern Irish society. The very specific political economy that emerged during the Troubles ensured that those middle-class communities that were largely insulated from the violence saw their standards of living soar.[95] In particular, the inflated state spending that accompanied the conflict provided the middle classes with generously paid positions in the public sector and allowed their children to attend some of the best schools on 'these islands' free of charge. The persistence of the generous Westminster 'subvention' during the peace process – currently running at almost £11 billion a year, or around £5,750 for every man, woman and child in the six counties[96] – has meant that the 'contented classes' in Northern Ireland now enjoy lifestyles that are, if anything, even more comfortable than before. The widespread affluence that exists in neighbourhoods that were essentially untouched by the Troubles has become ever more apparent as the 'post-conflict' era has facilitated the 'normalisation' of Northern Irish society. Over time, the local middle classes have come increasingly to indulge in modes of breathless consumption exalted endlessly in all those glossy advertisements promoting the 'new Northern Ireland' to an audience at home and abroad.[97] One telling index of the very considerable, and indeed long-standing, wealth that exists in parts of Northern Irish society is that in 2019, as the immiseration of the austerity era continued apace, the sales of luxury cars such as the Jaguar, Porsche and Aston Martin reached record highs in the region.[98]

The experience of those living in poor neighbourhoods that were at the epicentre of the Troubles has, predictably, proved rather less fortunate. That period of global economic expansion which attended the end of the conflict would never prove sufficient to bestow a 'peace dividend' on those working-class communities that had borne the brunt of the violence.[99] Moreover, the subsequent worldwide financial crisis would provide the Conservative Party with the opportunity to impose austerity measures that would dramatically compound the poverty already endemic in such districts. It should come as little surprise, then, to discover that those sections of Northern Irish society that were poor when Tony Blair counselled that the GFA would herald an era of prosperity are, if anything, even more so almost a quarter-century down the line.[100] The statistics documenting the level of deprivation in contemporary Northern Irish society make for genuinely harrowing reading. In a region of one of the wealthiest states on the face of the planet, some 110,000 children are living in poverty,[101] women located in the poorest quintile of the population can expect to live fourteen years less than their counterparts in the richest,[102] and there are as many as 37 food banks[103] in operation, providing an annual total of around 45,000 three-day parcels to the ever-growing band of people in Northern Ireland who would not otherwise have enough to eat.[104] The economic fallout from the UK's departure from the EU, coupled with the global recession widely expected to come on foot of the coronavirus pandemic, will, of course, merely serve to heighten further these already baleful levels of destitution.

What is striking about the poverty that exists in Northern Ireland is not merely its scale but also the infrequency with which it makes any real impression on mainstream political debate.[105] Politicians in the region typically appear rather more focused on the immaterial needs of the tribe than the material needs of the poor, more preoccupied with the fate of the dead than with that of the living. As we observe on several other occasions in this book, the particular mould into which the Good Friday Agreement sought to cast Northern Irish political life increasingly feels like a constraint that fails to acknowledge or nurture the diversity and complexity that increasingly define the region. More specifically, the sectarian binary that defines the prevailing political settlement in Northern Ireland seems an increasingly poor fit for a society in which the inequalities and injustices associated with ethno-national affiliation have long since been eclipsed by those that arise out of social class.

Notes

1 Eamonn Holmes, *This is My Life: The Autobiography* (London: Orion, 2007), p. 49.
2 Susan McKay, *Bear in Mind These Dead* (London: Faber & Faber, 2008).
3 Marie-Therese Fay, Mike Morrissey and Marie Smyth, *Northern Ireland's Troubles: The Human Costs* (London: Pluto Press, 1999), p. 150.
4 Victor Mesev, Peter Shirlow and Joni Downs, 'The Geography of Conflict and Death in Belfast, Northern Ireland', *Annals of the Association of American Geographers*, 99(5) (2009), 893–903, pp. 900–1.
5 Colin Coulter, *Contemporary Northern Irish Society: An Introduction* (London: Pluto Press, 1999), p. 73.
6 Anne Devlin, Keara McKay and Raymond Russell, *Multiple Deprivation in Northern Ireland* (Belfast: Northern Ireland Assembly Research and Information Service, 2018), p. 11.
7 Gabi Kent, 'Shattering the Silence: The Power of *Purposeful Storytelling* in Challenging Social Security Policy Discourses of "Blame and Shame" in Northern Ireland', *Critical Social Policy*, 36(1) (2016), 124–41, p. 130.
8 Colin Coulter, 'Under Which Constitutional Arrangement Would You Still Prefer to be Unemployed? Neoliberalism, the Peace Process, and the Politics of Class in Northern Ireland', *Studies in Conflict & Terrorism*, 37(9) (2014), 763–76, pp. 746–7.

9 Tony Blair, *Speech at the Royal Agricultural Show*, Belfast, 14 May 1998. Available at: http://cain.ulst.ac.uk/events/peace/docs/tb14598.htm. Accessed 1 September 2020.
10 Colin Knox, 'Northern Ireland: where is the peace dividend?', *Policy & Politics*, 44(3) (2016), 485–503.
11 David Herbert, 'Legacies of 1998: what kind of social peace has developed in Northern Ireland? Social attitudes, inequalities, and territorialities', in Charles I. Armstrong, David Herbert and Jan Erik Mustad (eds), *The Legacy of the Good Friday Agreement: Northern Irish Politics, Culture and Art after 1998* (Cham, Switzerland: Springer, 2019), pp. 249–70.
12 Conor McCabe, *The Double Transition: The Economic and Political Transition of Peace* (Dublin: Irish Congress of Trade Unions, 2013).
13 Doug Henwood, *After the New Economy: The Binge ... And the Hangover That Won't Go Away* (New York: The New Press, 2005).
14 Peter Schwartz and Peter Leyden, 'The Long Boom: A History of the Future, 1980–2020', *Wired*, 5(7) (July 1997). Available at: www.wired.com/1997/07/longboom/. Accessed 11 January 2021.
15 Portland Trust, *Economics in Peacemaking: Lessons from Northern Ireland* (London: Portland Trust, 2007), p. 23.
16 Niall NcCracken, 'Going to plan? How Invest NI's strategy is really working out', *The Detail*, 5 October (2012). Available at: www.thedetail.tv/issues/128/invest-ni/going-to-plan-how-invest-nis-strategy-is-really-working-out. Accessed 1 September 2020.
17 Office for National Statistics, *Regional labour market statistics in the UK: September 2020* (London: ONS, 2020), pp. 2–3.
18 Joseph Rowntree Foundation, *Poverty in Northern Ireland 2018* (York: Joseph Rowntree Foundation, 2018), p. 1.
19 Northern Ireland Audit Office, *Welfare Reforms in Northern Ireland* (Belfast: NIAO), p. 1.
20 Herbert, 'Legacies of 1998', p. 254.
21 Siobhan Fenton, *The Good Friday Agreement* (London: Biteback Publishing, 2018), p. 144; Northern Ireland Audit Office, *Welfare Reforms*, p. 8.
22 Northern Ireland Audit Office, *Welfare Reforms*, p. 61; Mike Tomlinson, 'Risking peace in the "war against the poor"? Social exclusion and the legacies of the Northern Ireland conflict', *Critical Social Policy*, 36(1) (2016), 104–23, p. 117.
23 Office for National Statistics, *Regional labour market*, p. 3.
24 Paul Nolan, *Northern Ireland Peace Monitoring Report Number Two* (Belfast: Community Relations Council, 2013), p. 25.
25 Office for National Statistics, *Regional labour market*, p. 8.
26 Northern Ireland Statistics and Research Agency, *Northern Ireland Labour Market Report*, August (Belfast: NISRA, 2020), p. 30.
27 Northern Ireland Statistics and Research Agency, *Northern Ireland Annual Survey of Hours and Earnings* (Belfast: NISRA, 2019), p. 2.
28 Joseph Rowntree Foundation, *Poverty in Northern Ireland 2018*.

29 Andrew Gamble, *The Free Economy and the Strong State: The Politics of Thatcherism* (Basingstoke: Palgrave Macmillan, 1994).
30 Richard Rose, 'Is the United Kingdom a state? Northern Ireland as a test case', in Peter Madgwick and Richard Rose (eds), *The Territorial Dimension in United Kingdom Politics* (London: Palgrave Macmillan, 1982), pp. 100–36.
31 Derek Birrell, *Direct Rule and the Governance of Northern Ireland* (Manchester: Manchester University Press, 2009), p. 155; Sean Byrne, *Economic Assistance and Conflict Transformation* (London: Routledge, 2010), pp. 63–4.
32 Frank Gaffikin and Mike Morrissey, *Northern Ireland: The Thatcher Years* (London: Zed Books, 1990), p. 87.
33 Michael Temple and Jo Campling, 'Thatcher's legacy to Blair', in Michael Temple (ed.), *How Britain Works: From Ideology to Output Politics* (Palgrave Macmillan, London, 2000), pp. 1–12.
34 George Monbiot, *Captive State: The Corporate Takeover of Britain* (London: Pan Books, 2001).
35 John Nagle, 'Potemkin Village: Neo-liberalism and Peace-building in Northern Ireland?', *Ethnopolitics*, 8(2) (2009), 173–90, p. 177.
36 Mark Hellowell, David Price and Allyson Pollock (2008), *The Use of Private Finance Initiative (PFI) Public Private Partnerships (PPPs) in Northern Ireland* (Belfast: Northern Ireland Public Service Alliance, 2008), p. 9.
37 Strategic Investment Board, *Annual Review and Financial Statements* (Belfast: SIB, 2007), pp. 8–9.
38 Ciaran Hughes, 'Resisting or Enabling? The Roll-out of Neoliberal Values through the Voluntary and Community Sector in Northern Ireland', *Critical Policy Studies*, 13(1) (2019), 61–80.
39 Christopher Farrington, *Ulster Unionism and the Peace Process in Northern Ireland* (Basingstoke: Palgrave, 2006), p. 92.
40 Daniel Finn, *One Man's Terrorist: A Political History of the IRA* (London: Verso, 2019), pp. 179, 223.
41 Ibid., p. 136.
42 Brian Kelly, 'Neoliberal Belfast: Disaster Ahead?', *Irish Marxist Review*, 1(2) (2012), 44–59, p. 45.
43 John Nagle, 'Between Conflict and Peace: An Analysis of the Complex Consequences of the Good Friday Agreement', *Parliamentary Affairs*, 71(2) (2018), 395–416, p. 404.
44 Her Majesty's Treasury, *Private Finance Initiative and Private Finance 2 projects: 2017 summary data* (London: Her Majesty's Treasury, 2017).
45 Monbiot, *Captive State*.
46 Andrew Madden, 'PFI has left Northern Ireland paying £4.4bn over the odds', *Belfast Telegraph*, 3 April 2018. Available at: www.belfasttelegraph.co.uk/news/northern-ireland/pfi-has-left-northern-ireland-paying-44bn-over-the-odds-36767956.html. Accessed 1 September 2020.
47 Brendan Murtagh, 'Contested Space, Peacebuilding and the Post-conflict City', *Parliamentary Affairs*, 71(2) (2018), 438–60, p. 444.

48 Colin Coulter and Francisco Arqueros-Fernández, 'The Distortions of the Irish "Recovery"', *Critical Social Policy*, 40(1) (2020), 89–107.
49 Denis O'Hearn, 'How has Peace Changed the Northern Irish Political Economy?', *Ethnopolitics*, 7(1) (2008), 101–18, p. 112.
50 Goretti Horgan and Ann-Marie Gray, 'Devolution in Northern Ireland: A Lost Opportunity?', *Critical Social Policy*, 32(2) (2012), 467–78, p. 475.
51 Pierre Dardot and Christian Laval, *Never-Ending Nightmare: The Neoliberal Assault on Democracy* (London: Verso, 2019), pp. 14–27.
52 Mark Blyth, *Austerity: The History of a Dangerous Idea* (Oxford: Oxford University Press, 2013).
53 The phrase is that of comedian Alexei Sayle. See interview in the *Metro*, 27 September 2019. Available at: www.metro.news/weekend-comic-alexei-sayle-is-still-angry-after-all-these-years-but-he-says-hes-mellowing/1733061/. Accessed 4 September 2020.
54 Colin Coulter, Francisco Arqueros-Fernández and Angela Nagle, 'Austerity's model pupil: the ideological uses of Ireland during the Eurozone crisis', *Critical Sociology*, 45(4–5) (2019), 697–711.
55 David McNally, *Global Slump: The Economics and Politics of Crisis and Resistance* (Oakland, CA: PM Press, 2012), pp. 2–3.
56 Northern Ireland Audit Office, *Welfare Reform in Northern Ireland*, p. 17.
57 Lisa McKenzie, *Getting By: Class and Culture in Austerity Britain* (Bristol: Policy Press, 2015); Darren McGarvey, *Poverty Safari: Understanding the Anger of Britain's Underclass* (London: Picador, 2018).
58 Aaron Bastani, *Fully Automated Luxury Communism: A Manifesto* (London: Verso, 2019), pp. 24–5.
59 Philip Alston, 'Statement on Visit to the United Kingdom, United Nations Special Rapporteur on extreme poverty and human rights', London, 16 November 2018. Available at: https://www.ohchr.org/en/NewsEvents/Pages/DisplayNews.aspx?NewsID=23881. Accessed 15 September 2020.
60 Antonia Jones, Wendy Wilson, Tim Jarett, Steven Kennedy and Andrew Powell, *The UN Inquiry into the Rights of Persons with Disabilities in the UK*, House of Commons Briefing Paper Number 07367 (London: House of Commons, 2017), p. 3.
61 Howard Reed and Jonathan Portes, *Cumulative Impact Assessment of Tax and Social Security Reforms in Northern Ireland* (Belfast: Northern Ireland Human Rights Commission, 2019), p. 78.
62 Alston, 'Statement on Visit to the United Kingdom'.
63 Ibid., p. 9.
64 Ibid., pp. 2–3.
65 Ibid., p. 5.
66 Ibid., pp. 18–19.
67 Ibid., p. 4.
68 Christina Beatty and Steve Fothergill, *The Impact of Welfare Reform on Northern Ireland* (Belfast: Northern Ireland Council for Voluntary Action, 2013), p. 20.

69 Nagle, 'Between Conflict and Peace', p. 402.
70 B. O'Leary, 'The Twilight of the United Kingdom & *Tiocfaidh ár lá*: Twenty Years after the Good Friday Agreement', *Ethnopolitics*, 17(3) (2018), 223–42, p. 228; Tomlinson, 'Risking peace', p. 105.
71 Nagle, 'Between Conflict and Peace', p. 405.
72 Ibid., p. 407.
73 Chris Gilligan, 'Austerity and Consociational Government in Northern Ireland', *Irish Studies Review*, 24(1) (2016), 35–48.
74 Ibid.
75 Eoin Flaherty and Martina McAuley, 'Class and inequality in Northern Ireland', in Gerard Boucher and Iarfhlaith Watson (eds), *Contemporary Ireland and Northern Ireland* (Dublin: UCD Press, forthcoming).
76 Robin Wilson, *Northern Ireland Peace Monitoring Report Number Four* (Belfast: Community Relations Council, 2016), p. 103.
77 Northern Ireland Assembly, *Minutes of Proceedings*, 18 November 2015. Available at: http://www.niassembly.gov.uk/assembly-business/minutes-of-proceedings/archive-minutes/session-2015-2016/wednesday-18-november-2015/. Accessed 1 September 2020.
78 Northern Ireland Audit Office, *Welfare Reform in Northern Ireland*, p. 47.
79 Ibid., p. 12.
80 Work and Pensions and Northern Ireland Affairs Committees, *Welfare Policy in Northern Ireland* (London: House of Commons, 2019), p. 11.
81 Joseph Rowntree Foundation, Ruth Patrick and Mark Simpson, *Joint Submission to the Northern Ireland Affairs Committee and Work and Pensions Committee* (York: Joseph Rowntree Foundation, 2019), p. 5.
82 Work and Pensions and Northern Ireland Affairs Committees, *Welfare Policy in Northern Ireland*, p. 4.
83 Joseph Rowntree Foundation, Patrick and Simpson, *Joint Submission*, p. 27.
84 Ibid., p. 5.
85 Work and Pensions and Northern Ireland Affairs Committees, *Welfare Policy in Northern Ireland*, p. 6.
86 Cliff Edge Coalition NI, *Submission to the Joint Inquiry into Welfare policy in Northern Ireland* (2019), p. 7. Available at: www.nicva.org/article/cliff-edge-ni-coalition-submission-to-the-joint-inquiry-into-welfare-policy-what-are-the. Accessed 15 September 2020.
87 Reed and Portes, *Cumulative Impact Assessment*, pp. 46–7.
88 Ibid., p. 47.
89 John Burn-Murdoch, 'UK multi-millionaires mapped: where do the wealthy live?', *Guardian*, 13 September 2012. Available at: www.guardian.co.uk/news/datablog/interactive/2012/sep/13/money-uk-multi-millionaires-regional-breakdown. Accessed 25 August 2020.
90 Reed and Portes, *Cumulative Impact Assessment*, p. 55.
91 Ibid., pp. 91–3.
92 Coulter, 'Under Which Constitutional Arrangement Would You Still Prefer to be Unemployed?'

93 Mary P. Murphy, *Europe and Northern Ireland's Future: Negotiating Brexit's Unique Case* (Newcastle: Agenda Publishing, 2018).

94 Rebecca Black, 'Bedroom tax welfare mitigation to be extended', *Belfast Telegraph*, 3 February 2020. Available at: www.belfasttelegraph.co.uk/news/northern-ireland/bedroom-tax-welfare-mitigation-to-be-extended-38921359.html. Accessed 5 September 2020.

95 Colin Coulter, 'Direct rule and the unionist middle classes', in Richard English and Graham Walker (eds), *Unionism in Modern Ireland: New Perspectives on Politics and Culture* (Dublin: Gill & Macmillan, 1996), pp. 169–91: Colin Coulter, 'The culture of contentment: the political beliefs and practice of the unionist middle classes', in Peter Shirlow and Mark McGovern (eds), *Who Are 'the People'? Unionism, Protestantism and Loyalism in Northern Ireland* (London: Pluto Press, 1997), pp. 114–39.

96 Paul Gillespie, 'Post-Brexit Britain may not want to pay for Northern Ireland', *Irish Times*, 8 December 2018. Available at: www.irishtimes.com/opinion/post-brexit-britain-may-not-want-to-pay-for-northern-ireland-1.3723855. Accessed 5 September 2020.

97 Stephen Baker, 'Tribeca Belfast and the on-screen regeneration of Northern Ireland', *International Journal of Media & Cultural Politics*, 16(1) (2020), 11–26.

98 Margaret Canning and Laura Kelly, 'Northern Ireland Porsche sales hit record high despite economic downturn', *Belfast Telegraph*, 3 February 2020. Available at: www.belfasttelegraph.co.uk/business/northern-ireland/northern-ireland-porsche-sales-hit-record-high-despite-economic-downturn-38923649.html. Accessed 5 September 2020.

99 John Bradley, 'The Agreement's Impact on Economic and Business Cooperation', *Irish Political Studies*, 33(3) (2018), 311–30, p. 327.

100 Herbert, 'Legacies of 1998', p. 260.

101 Joseph Rowntree Foundation, *Poverty in Northern Ireland 2018* (York: Joseph Rowntree Foundation, 2018).

102 Wilson, *Northern Ireland Peace Monitoring Report Number Four*, p. 126.

103 Ibid., p. 94.

104 Trussell Trust, 'End of year stats', April 2020. Available at: www.trusselltrust.org/news-and-blog/latest-stats/end-year-stats/. Accessed 5 September 2020. It is worth noting that in 2014/15, the last year before the changes to the welfare system were extended to Northern Ireland, the number of food parcels distributed in the region was 17,425. Within five years of the introduction of the new regime, that total had soared to 45,008.

105 Coulter, 'Under Which Constitutional Arrangement Would You Still Prefer to be Unemployed?'

8

Changed utterly? Northern Ireland's paralysis in a world of uncertainty

'This virus knows no borders, no nationality'[1]

It was unusual to see her walk alone across the Great Hall in Stormont towards the waiting press. Without any other Executive ministers or Sinn Féin party colleagues beside her, Michelle O'Neill approached the cameras and made a short statement. As a tour group of nonplussed students looked on, the deputy First Minister called on schools and universities in Northern Ireland to close in an effort to stop the spread of the coronavirus. A 'global health pandemic' had been declared by the World Health Organisation, she noted. The European Centre for Disease Prevention and Control had advised early and coordinated action from governments. O'Neill observed that 'many European countries have taken decisive action, robust action', including in 'the south of Ireland', where schools had been closed and large gatherings cancelled. She said that she had spoken over the course of the night 'to many people out there who are just very fearful about what is a very unclear situation across this island'. And, in response, she stated her belief 'that now is the time to take action; now is the time to ensure that all schools are closed ... and that needs to happen immediately'.[2] In other places, a statement from such a senior political figure would be taken as a collective decision of the Executive. But in Northern Ireland, in the middle of a burgeoning international crisis, this statement was an indication of quite the opposite. There was no collective agreement among those in charge. Indeed, in the space of just under two minutes, the deputy First Minister had declared open conflict with the position of the Northern Ireland Executive which she herself had publicly announced and endorsed the previous evening. A global pandemic had been added to the already substantial pile of irreconcilable differences between the two largest parties in Northern Ireland.

The deputy First Minister's statement was one of personal preference, not one of ministerial decision; but despite her expressed wish to address the 'angst that is there among the wider public', it only underlined the broader context of confusion. While commentators speculated about the hidden powers in Sinn Féin which placed pressure on the party vice-president to push for an all-island approach, the Northern Ireland parties were placed in an invidious position.[3] The guidance of the chief medical officer to the Stormont Executive matched that of his counterpart in the UK government; it thus differed from that being given by the chief medical officer to the government of Ireland. Northern Ireland's ministers were caught by the fact that the scientific advice was conflicting. And as Sinn Féin and the Social Democratic and Union Party (SDLP) pointed south and called for a common approach on the island,[4] the Alliance Party, Ulster Unionist Party (UUP) and Democratic Unionist Party (DUP) did not want to move against the medical advice the NI Executive was receiving. Thus, without anyone particularly wishing it to be so, the reaction to the most indiscriminate and transnational threat of our time increasingly became a matter for community-level decision-making. The Catholic Archbishop of Armagh wrote to the Minister for Education, the DUP's Peter Weir, urging that he consider closing all schools.[5] Soon the decisions of individual parents became those of principals and boards of governors, and schools began to take unilateral decisions to stay closed after the St Patrick's Day holiday.[6] Pressure was particularly acute on all-island organisations. The Gaelic Athletic Association (GAA) announced the suspension of all its club and county activity, across Ireland and Britain.[7] The Irish Football Association (Northern Ireland), 'having listened to partners throughout the football family', decided to suspend the season.[8] The Church of Ireland Archbishop of Armagh-elect and Archbishop of Dublin issued a press release to all parishes which began: 'Follow all public health guidance provided by state authorities'.[9] The fact that the guidance could be quite different from one part of a diocese to another was a problem that was left for the community to manage as diplomatically as possible.

As confusion began to give way to political tension, the news that the leaders, health ministers and chief medical officers of the Irish government and NI Executive were to meet in an emergency session on Saturday, 14 March 2020 to discuss Covid-19 was broadly welcomed. The meeting took place against a backdrop of quite extraordinary strain on relations among those around the table. When announcing the (as it turned out, very short-lived) common position of the NI Executive two days beforehand,[10] First Minister Arlene Foster had not hidden her irritation at Taoiseach Leo Varadkar's failure to inform her in advance of his announcement earlier that day (12 March) of strict measures to tackle Covid-19.[11] 'Acting together, as one nation,' he had exhorted, 'we can save many lives.' If such measures caused confusion among border communities unsure of which guidance to follow, language like this only compounded the irritation of nationalist parties at the inability of the north to simply follow suit. The solo run of the deputy First Minister was shown to be a marathon, not a sprint, as O'Neill doubled down in the accompanying press conference on the need for a 'joined-up approach'.[12] The First and deputy First Ministers made little effort to hide the divergence of their views. And political tensions were only exacerbated by the fact that the Irish government ministers were acting purely in a 'caretaker capacity', Fine Gael having been knocked into third place by the success of Sinn Féin in the Irish general election held the previous month. The coronavirus crisis was coming at a time of extreme inconvenience for politicians across the island of Ireland. The release of the long-anticipated Renewable Heating Incentive (RHI) Report amid it all, on 13 March, went virtually unnoticed.[13]

The best efforts of the leaders from both jurisdictions could only get them so far as to emphasise that they shared a common goal, i.e. to minimise the deaths caused by Covid-19, and differed only in regard to 'timing'.[14] The notion that the differences in the policies between north and south were temporal rather than substantial was clever but offered little comfort, given that 'timing' is everything when it comes to avoiding an epidemiological catastrophe. And with each day that passed, the UK's insistence on taking an approach that was viewed by the Irish government as irresponsible had the effect of deepening the strain on north/south relations. Despite attempting to show that the UK was inching towards the same position as the Irish government on coronavirus measures, Tánaiste Simon Coveney admitted in response to a question about the openness of the Irish border: 'In truth I am concerned.'[15] It was to be a week before the policies, north and south, became more closely aligned. If a week is a long time in politics, it felt an agonising aeon for society, although organisations and institutions slowly began making their own decisions. St Patrick's Day parades were cancelled. Church buildings were closed. Belfast International Airport suspended passenger flights, while Belfast City Airport and Derry City Airport were down to just a few flights a day. The universities announced the suspension of all classes. Small businesses and cafés began shutting of their own accord. In an extraordinary way, this showed a sense of community in action – even, as one social media user from west Belfast put it in a Facebook video, 'love in action': 'What you are seeing in those empty spaces', he said, 'is how much we do care for each other.'[16] Social interaction, civic freedoms, public spaces, communal activities and shared rituals were being closed down, with people told to 'stay at home' in 'lockdown'. But in so doing, a sense of a Northern Ireland 'demos' appeared, tentatively, to emerge – an embryonic sense of what it is to be a people with common interests, values and cares. The growing sense of solidarity and common cause comes only in a negative context, however, in which freedoms are constrained and in which fear is the overriding emotion.

The inching towards a sense of 'public' and the slow weaving of bonds of common cause among the people of Northern Ireland was never quite matched by the building of trust among the politicians responsible for protecting them. This was in part because of the very nature of the Executive itself. Five parties are seated around the table, but their effectiveness is determined by the relationship of the two largest parties – each of whom are essentially driven by a desire to see the failure of all that the other one stands for. Whereas Taoiseach Varadkar, Prime Minister Johnson and Scottish First Minister Nicola Sturgeon could go on television to give 'state of the nation' speeches announcing the most dramatic curtailment of freedoms and economic contractions known in peacetime, Arlene Foster and Michelle O'Neill were forced to deliver policy announcements and press briefings together. And if one stepped beyond the carefully agreed script, the other could feel entitled (or obliged) to disagree. In a press conference on 27 March 2020, for example, the Irish and British sign-language interpreters appeared side by side, reflecting the fact that both languages are used in Northern Ireland. As the First Minister and deputy First Minister answered questions from journalists, the sign-language interpreters had to simultaneously interpret almost contradictory statements from the two leaders, as they disagreed over the definition of 'non-essential' businesses and whether they should be closed.[17] But the tension was higher than party-level and far greater than personality differences. The pressure on the NI Executive came from outside, specifically from the fact that the UK and Irish governments had such different approaches to the pandemic. Coming after three years of worsening strain on the intergovernmental relationship, the sense of fragility was acute. Perhaps recognising the double whammy of tension on the NI Executive, the two governments began to move. At the very end of March, the Secretary of State for Northern Ireland, Brandon Lewis, the Tánaiste, the First and deputy First Ministers and the two ministers for health began having conference calls.[18] In issuing a joint statement afterwards, the ministers promised

> cooperation for the practical and mutual benefit of the people living in both jurisdictions on the island of Ireland will be taken forward. [And] agreed that all cooperation will be based on the need to be agile, open and consistent and that close and ongoing contact will be maintained North-South and East-West.

The challenge of cooperation across all three strands of the 1998 Agreement was both more urgent and more difficult than ever before.

A British–Irish problem with no British–Irish solution

The challenge of finding common ground between the UK and Ireland even in the middle of a global crisis was particularly significant because the peace process in Northern Ireland has been built on a close British–Irish relationship. This process has been carefully honed and fostered through diplomatic savvy and courage on both sides during years of violent conflict and political distrust.[19] It has pivoted on a sharing of sovereignty, on an acceptance of multiple identities, on collaboration, and on joint British–Irish commitments to Northern Ireland. This was embodied in the Good Friday Agreement (hereafter GFA) but only made conceivable by the common membership of the European Union (EU), which offered both context and model.[20] The principles of the sharing of sovereignty, multilevel governance, deepening integration and cross-border cooperation are at the heart of the European Union project – and no doubt are qualities most loathed by Eurosceptics. But at the very least, EU membership meant that both the UK and Ireland were heading in the same direction, couched in the same broad legal, economic, regulatory and – just as important – values regime. Crucially, as partners in the EU, the British and Irish governments could manage the Irish border in a way that emphasises practical benefit and common interest, without prejudice to the legitimacy of both unionism and nationalism. The very logic of Brexit threatened all these things. It has put the UK and Ireland on different trajectories, and as a result Northern Ireland risks being stretched in between. And the nature of the 1998 Agreement means that this pressure comes not only in terms of governance, or the economy; it also reaches down to the level of the individual. Just as governance is multilayered, so too is citizenship and so too is identity.

On the eve of the UK leaving the EU, the EU's chief negotiator, Michel Barnier, visited Belfast and delivered a speech outlining what he saw as the key consequences of Brexit for UK–EU relations, and Northern Ireland's particular position within it. When he discussed the 1998 Agreement, he was careful to mention the 'multitude of identities' which he described as 'a distinctive aspect of Northern Ireland'. He continued:

> The Good Friday (Belfast) Agreement cannot be celebrated enough. It was, and still is, indispensable for progress. The Good Friday Agreement allowed, and still allows, the people of Northern Ireland to identify themselves as British, or Irish, or both – and be accepted as such. You can choose to be British, Irish, very British with a bit of Irish, more Irish than British, Irish and European, British and European. Others might think of themselves as Northern Irish, or Northern Irish and European. Or, indeed, Northern Irish and anti-European.[21]

Such arrangements functioned steadily, unremarkably within the safety harness of joint EU membership. Now Northern Ireland is outside the EU, such dualities and complexities are harder to accommodate. Fundamentally, Brexit has meant a very practical distinction between British and Irish citizenship; now an Irish passport is a means of retaining EU citizenship, and with associated benefits and rights that are no longer held by British citizens. As a consequence, in the first instance, there has been a tremendous growth in the demand for Irish passports in Northern Ireland (as well as from those eligible in Britain). There was plenty of anecdotal evidence in the weeks and months following the June 2016 referendum on UK withdrawal that suggested that even those places in Northern Ireland which may have liked to have been viewed as being, to recall a once-familiar phrase, 'as British as Finchley', were experiencing a surge in active Irish identification. Indeed, one of the most striking reactions to the Brexit referendum result on social media in Northern Ireland were the posts and comments about which post offices had run out of the forms for Irish passport applications – the more unlikely the constituency, the greater the indication that Brexit really had upset the apple cart. Even Ian Paisley Jr, the DUP MP, went so far as to advise his constituents to get an Irish passport.[22] They were clearly not alone. In the decade up to 2015 there were around 150,000 new applications for Irish passports from residents in Northern Ireland. The increase in applications from Northern Ireland in 2016 was up 26.5 per cent to almost 68,000,[23] and in 2017 it rose another 20 per cent to nearly 82,000.[24] These were new applications. By 2019, this surge had settled somewhat to around 19,000 applications for Irish passports from Northern Ireland.[25] Needless to say, as Paisley Jr would no doubt attest, exercising your right to Irish citizenship does not necessarily make you identify as, or consider yourself to be, 'Irish'.

In many ways, the post-Brexit growth in demand for Irish passports actually highlights the importance of choice rather than any essentialist conception of national identity in Northern Ireland. What it shows is that the ability to be 'both' British and Irish in Northern Ireland has functional and pragmatic consequences. The matter of choice means that people born in Northern Ireland can take on many of the benefits of Irish citizenship without either the sentiment or the duties of such citizenship. On the other hand, however, Brexit has also revealed the elective nature of the dual nationality to have negative consequences too. UK law was never changed in such a way that would adjust the default nationality that people born in Northern Ireland are assumed to have from being that of British. In a fundamental way, the political rights given by the 1998 Agreement had not been matched by the necessary legal adjustments in the UK. This was revealed by the case of Emma DeSouza against the Home Office, which began in 2016 following an application for an European Economic Area (EEA) residence card for her US-born husband. She made the application on the grounds of her Irish (therefore EEA) citizenship, but the application was denied on the grounds that, having been born in Northern Ireland, she is automatically considered a British citizen by the British government and not an EEA citizen. She was advised to either reapply identifying herself as British or renounce British citizenship and reapply as an Irish citizen.[26] DeSouza appealed on the grounds that she has only ever held Irish citizenship and cited the birthright provisions of the GFA.[27] What the case revealed is the distinction between a right of identification and a right of citizenship. Although people can choose to be British, Irish or both, when it comes to the legal effect of that right the matter is rather more murky. The assumption of 'British by default' has growing significance in light of the increased difference between the rights of British and Irish citizens (as EU citizens) that has arisen as a result of Brexit. Such distinctions are exacerbated by a sense of insecurity that has escalated more broadly in Northern Ireland since the UK left the EU. This is felt in part simply because Northern Ireland has been taken out of the EU despite a 56 per cent vote to Remain (a figure which would, studies suggest, have only risen if there were to have been a second referendum).[28] Such insecurities are felt by pro-Remain voters of all backgrounds, as well as those who identify as Irish. But a sense of threat and vulnerability is also felt in new ways by pro-Leave voters and by many unionists in Northern Ireland. What they all have in common is that this sense of insecurity centres on what the British government decided to do when it secured the withdrawal agreement from the EU.

Brexit and the invidious choice (that wasn't Northern Ireland's to make)

It is no exaggeration to say that thirteen pages (minus preamble and annexes) of an international treaty (in which none of Northern Ireland's elected representatives had any hand or part in negotiating) will to a large extent determine the shape and stability of Northern Ireland as it enters its second century of existence. The Protocol on Ireland/Northern Ireland annexed to the UK–EU Withdrawal Agreement was so important that its revision was the reason for the fact that the UK left the EU on 31 January 2020 rather than the original date of 29 March 2019.[29] Despite its length, it is not a simple document. The 'constructive ambiguity' in the 1998 Agreement is renowned; it enabled the GFA to get across the line with support from parties from both the unionist and nationalist traditions. The

Protocol also contains elements of ambiguity. However, there is a serious danger that these ambiguities risk being more destructive than constructive. This is because unionists and nationalists, and those who were pro-Leave and those who were pro-Remain within Northern Ireland, were led to see directly oppositional outcomes in the revised Protocol. At the centre of this potentially destructive ambiguity is the potential for pressure on the integrity of the UK internal market for the movement of goods. The risk of political fears building on economic ones was only exacerbated by the fact that the UK approach to Brexit consistently failed to acknowledge existing levels of differentiation within the UK. This was, no doubt, in part encouraged by the fact that, for the course of the withdrawal negotiations, the Conservative Party was in a confidence and supply agreement with the DUP. As the only large party in Northern Ireland that campaigned for Brexit, the DUP entered this arrangement determined to ensure that the Union would not suffer any weakening as a result of the UK's exit from the EU. This was made more difficult as an ambition by the fact that the type of Brexit that Prime Minister Theresa May had promised her party was of the 'hard' variety. And a hard Brexit – leaving the single market, outside any customs union – by definition meant harder borders between the UK and the EU. May soon found herself caught between a commitment to the Brexiteers and a commitment to unionists, and her emphasis upon 'protecting the integrity of the United Kingdom' was vague enough to assuage fears from both sides as the hard work of negotiation continued.

These negotiations focused on three priorities: settling the UK's financial obligations to the EU, protecting the rights of EU citizens in the UK and UK citizens in the EU, and protecting the 1998 Agreement and avoiding a hard border on the island of Ireland. The Joint Report issued by the UK and EU as an update on negotiations at the end of 2017 set out three possibilities for achieving the latter objective. First, there could be a 'soft' Brexit, with minimal divergence between the UK and EU, and thus minimal change in requirements for what happened at the Irish border, as the UK/EU land boundary. Second, there could be 'specific solutions' for Northern Ireland. The implicit understanding in that scenario is that these solutions would entail bespoke arrangements for Northern Ireland and thus further differentiation within the UK. Finally, if there were no agreement found, the UK could commit to maintaining alignment with the EU indefinitely until such a time as mutually agreeable arrangements for avoiding a hard border were found. This latter scenario was the least unpalatable to the UK. It set off looking for such arrangements, focusing almost exclusively on the question of how to avoid physical infrastructure and checks and controls at a 'hard' border between the UK and EU. The EU, for its part, interpreted it in quite a different way, namely aspiring to the type of UK–EU relationship that would avoid the need for those border checks and controls in the first place. In the end, the 'backstop' came into being, in the form of a Protocol to the UK–EU Withdrawal Agreement that would see the UK continue to commit to alignment with the EU on rules relating to the movement of goods until such a time a 'alternative arrangements' could be found for avoiding a hard Irish border.

Announced in November 2018, the 'backstop' soon became a byword in the British press for national humiliation.[30] Unionists didn't like it because it was a special arrangement for Northern Ireland and they feared the UK might be tempted to drop those commitments to align as soon as it was convenient. Those in the Leave camp hated it because of that very commitment to align to EU rules indefinitely. And Remainers rejected it because it would see the UK leave the EU. After three humiliating defeats in parliamentary votes in 2019, Theresa May was sent back to the negotiating table to 'get rid of the backstop'. Despite vowing that the Withdrawal Agreement was closed, the EU could see that May had no hope of getting it passed without amendments. In avoiding the worst-case scenario of the UK leaving with 'No Deal' – all of which had sucked energy and money into government departments preparing for imminent crisis – the EU eventually extended the deadline to leave to the end of October 2019. May's premiership had suffered a critical blow. After surviving several threatened leadership coups, she lost what remained of the confidence of her party and was forced to resign. Boris Johnson came into power with the promise of getting the UK out of the EU by the deadline. In so doing, he had to decide where to compromise; a poster boy for the Leave campaign, he was never going to opt for an indefinitely close and soft relationship with the EU. Despite having been a popular speaker at the DUP party conference at the end of 2018, Johnson's red, white and blue colours were more of a 'miniature union flag on a stick' style than a 'the Union at all costs' one. The backstop was out; 'special arrangements' for Northern Ireland took its place.

The decision of the UK government to have separate post-Brexit arrangements for Northern Ireland compared to the rest of the UK was, unsurprisingly, interpreted in Northern Ireland as symbolically and politically (as well as economically) significant. Johnson abandoned the commitment to a customs union with the EU and to continued regulatory alignment in relevant areas of EU law, but the new Protocol leaves Northern Ireland precisely in that place. While the Protocol meets the common UK and EU objective of largely maintaining the status quo with the land border on the island of Ireland (particularly as regards avoiding the need for new checks and controls or infrastructure), significant concerns were raised about it, from businesses as well as from unionists. Indeed, these same concerns were picked up by the UK government towards the end of the 'transition period' in 2020, when it made the decision to seek to put in domestic law the powers to breach certain parts of the Protocol. This move came as part of a negotiating tactic (in an effort to strengthen the hand of the British negotiators regarding a UK–EU deal), but the ramifications were enormous in political as much as legal terms. The fact that it was the Secretary of State for Northern Ireland who confirmed at the dispatch box that 'yes, this will break international law' was a particularly direct blow for confidence in the stability of the arrangements negotiated to meet Northern Ireland's unique circumstances post-Brexit.[31] It was inevitable that the effect would be destabilising within Northern Ireland, regardless of whether that 'tactic' proved effective with Brussels.

Right from the beginning, very different interpretations were placed on the Protocol by groups on either side of the constitutional debate in Northern Ireland, although nobody was happy with it. And the distrust from Northern Ireland towards the British government in the post-Brexit world arises in part from the fact that the Protocol was 'sold' to various quarters on very different grounds. To supporters of a hard Brexit in Britain, the Protocol was presented as a means of minimising constraints on the UK's pursuit of free-trade deals with international partners by ensuring that any customs and regulatory obligations necessary to avoid a hard border on the island of Ireland are limited in their application to Northern Ireland. It was presented to Irish nationalists (and, indeed, to supporters of a 'hard Brexit') as providing a 'front-stop', not a backstop, and so essentially establishing a permanent status, with Northern Ireland being treated differently from the rest of the UK indefinitely. As such, the revised Protocol was presented as placing the avoidance of a hard border on a permanent footing. What this effectively means is that a permanent outcome for Northern Ireland is established in a static Withdrawal Agreement rather than as part of a dynamic, negotiable future UK–EU relationship.

Conversely, the revised Protocol was presented to unionists as an arrangement with a built-in self-destruct button. This promise focused on the new article in the Protocol that allows the future dis-application of the part of it that sees Northern Ireland to be *de facto* in the EU's customs union and single market for goods (Articles 5–10). What would trigger this exit would be if there were no democratic consent forthcoming from a majority of Northern Ireland's MLAs for the continued application of the Protocol in this way. This would be judged by a vote to be held no later than four years after the end of the transition period, when Northern Ireland MLAs would be able to pass judgement on whether Northern Ireland should continue to align with the EU or should shift to align with the UK. If the vote was for the latter, it would trigger a two-year period in which, unless alternative arrangements were agreed and implemented, the default location of customs and regulatory checks and controls would revert to the Irish land border, which would thus become what the Protocol was intended to avoid, i.e. rendering the external boundary of the EU customs union and single market *de facto* as well as *de jure*. Johnson's government had made much of the need for unionist consent to the future post-Brexit arrangements for Northern Ireland. This is addressed by the provision for giving greater weight to cross-community consent over a simple majority in this vote. Cross-community consent could be determined by the terms of either parallel consent or weighted majority, as per an Assembly vote; if these conditions were to be reached, then that vote will not need to be held again for eight years. If there is only a simple majority in favour, then the vote will be taken again four years later after a process of public consultation. Why is this significant? Because it seeks to reassure communities across Northern Ireland that their consent for the new arrangements is sought (albeit not to the extent of giving either side a veto). As such, what this does is bring the unionist/nationalist divide directly into the heart of a decision that is fundamentally about product regulations and customs procedures.

The persistent potential for polarisation

The fundamental challenge posed by Brexit was that it proved impossible to frame the consequences of all efforts to protect the 1998 Agreement in anything other than binary terms. That is to say, the choice when it came down to it was of Northern Ireland being 'closer' to Ireland (or, now, the EU) (as nationalists wish) or to Britain (as unionists wish). Of course, the real difficulty was that this choice was not Northern Ireland's to make but, ultimately, Westminster's. And the vast majority of MPs – especially after the December 2019 election which gave Johnson such a decisive majority – made this choice for Northern Ireland with barely a second thought being given to the region; for them it was really about the type of Brexit they most wished to see England have. But having framed the debate in this way – a border across the island of Ireland or a border down the Irish Sea – the old conflictual tensions in the region were inevitably exacerbated. Such tensions can be readily exploited by those who never fully accepted the compromises of the 1998 Agreement to begin with. It is unsurprising, therefore, to find that unionists and nationalists within Northern Ireland are increasingly polarised by the subject of Brexit. NI Life and Times Survey data from 2016 (the year of the Brexit referendum) and 2019 show some interesting trends.[32] There has been an increase in respondents from all communities who believe that Brexit is having an impact both on the likelihood and the desirability of a united Ireland. People in Northern Ireland increasingly think Brexit is having an impact when it comes to the prospects for Irish unification. This is the case regardless of constitutional preference. Unsurprisingly, there has been a steady and consistent increase in the proportion of nationalists who believe that Brexit makes a united Ireland more likely (from 37 per cent in 2016 to 77 per cent in 2019).[33] In 2016, 62 per cent of unionists said that Brexit made no difference to the likelihood of a united Ireland; but this had dropped to 50 per cent three years later. Correspondingly, in 2019, a fifth of unionists (22 per cent) thought that Brexit has made a united Ireland more likely. Those who identify as 'neither' unionist nor nationalist appeared to be increasingly of the view that Brexit makes a united Ireland more likely, but do not necessarily feel more positive or negative about that prospect, and may in fact be quite ambivalent towards it. All this suggests that there is increasingly broad agreement across Northern Irish society that Brexit will have some effect on the future constitutional status of Northern Ireland, even if there remains disagreement over what that change should be and whether it should occur at all.

Indeed, expecting something to happen is not the same as wanting it to happen. NILT data also indicate that there is a deepening entrenchment in oppositional positions regarding the future of Northern Ireland. A quite predictable finding from NILT data is that Brexit has made those who hold a stronger Irish identity more likely to be in favour of a united Ireland, while those holding a stronger British identity are increasingly against it. Nationalists are increasingly in favour of Irish unity; unionists, who have traditionally been overwhelmingly against such an eventuality, are now even more opposed. By the time it came to 2019, 94 per cent of nationalists were saying that Brexit had confirmed or increased the desirability of Irish unity for them. This trend is particularly evident among nationalist party supporters. In 2016, 38 per cent of Sinn Féin supporters said that Brexit made them even more strongly in favour of Irish unity, and this had risen to 77 per cent by 2019. At the same time, 86 per cent of unionists said it had made no difference to their view or had actually increased their opposition to it.[34] Although the clear majority of people across all backgrounds in Northern Ireland were opposed to any new frictions in movements across its borders, it was inevitable that Brexit would bring such change and that it would reach right to the heart of political and national identities.[35]

All in all, regardless of whether Brexit is viewed as a positive or a negative move for the UK, few disagree that Northern Ireland's position is more precarious as a consequence of it.[36] For nationalists, there is a deep concern that the fact the Irish border now marks the external boundary of the EU. This means that Northern Ireland is no longer in a common legal milieu with Ireland, and this will inevitably give rise to creeping differences over time – even between the experiences of Irish citizens on either side of the border. Even though the Protocol is intended to 'maintain the necessary conditions for continued North–South cooperation' on the island of Ireland, the monitoring of this objective now becomes the ultimate responsibility of the UK–EU Joint Committee – a high-level body in which neither Irish nor Northern Irish ministers have an automatic right to be present. And for unionists, there is a growing sense that the threat to the union of the UK may well come from within. The Scottish referendum on independence in 2014 was not so decisive a defeat for Scottish nationalists that a win is inconceivable for them. This was before the increasing tensions evident in intergovernmental relations within the UK, and the tremendous success of the Scottish Nationalist Party in the same 2019 election that gave the Conservatives such a large pro-Brexit majority.[37] In the debates about the future UK–EU relationship and the future of the UK itself, Northern Ireland feels increasingly marginal. The high profile given to Northern Ireland in the Brexit process – a region, lest we forget, that constitutes 3 per cent of the population and 2 per cent of the economy of the UK – appears to have reminded many in the English political classes of why they had been so glad not to have had to have given much thought to the place since 1998 or so. Northern Ireland is only associated with a politics of awkwardness in the minds of many in Britain. Making a 'positive case' for the Union is difficult for unionists, whose efforts to do so within Northern Ireland are all too easily undermined by public opinion polls in Britain which show, at best, a lacklustre passion to keep Northern Ireland.[38] Nationalists may have the benefit of broad public sentiment in favour of a united Ireland (something that has grown as the Brexit process has unfurled, including with its stark exposure of anti-Irish sentiment in England);[39] however, the resistance of the Irish political class to discussing Irish unification stands in contrast to British politicians' easy advocacy of the Union. It is less controversial to support the status quo than to advocate for radical constitutional change – especially knowing that it is something that will be opposed by so many directly affected by it. Of course, just as the 2019 UK General Election result proved a shock to the pro-Remain left, so the 2020 Irish General Election result (which saw Sinn Féin emerge with the greatest proportion of votes) showed that the shift in tectonic plates beneath Northern Ireland could come from outside as well as from within.

A civic voice

Amid all this flux, with mutual wariness in the British–Irish intergovernmental relationship and competing interests in intergovernmental relations within the UK itself, where might stability be found? Related to this, how might the decisions that are made about Northern Ireland's future be ones that reflect the interests of the people that actually live there? Peace was agreed between the British and Irish governments and political parties of Northern Ireland after a long and difficult negotiating process. However, it was only embedded by the mundane, everyday actions of ordinary men and women. These small decisions that build bridges and trust are crucial to deep transformation. The scope for civic action is crucial. One positive consequence of the Brexit process has been the emergence of new efforts at civic or social dialogue. This has been occurring in a way not seen since the 1998 referendum on the GFA, after which time politicians began to occupy the roles previously taken by civic actors who had attempted to generate new debate and ideas about the future of the region.[40] There are two shocks which have prompted renewed or fresh engagement from civic actors in Northern Ireland as it approached its centenary. The first was Brexit; the second was the collapse of the Stormont Executive and Assembly in January 2017. Both events created a sense both of a vacuum in representation and a sense of urgency to have the interests of Northern Ireland heard. There are two types of civic engagement that we might distinguish. The first is around the 'constitutional question'; the second is – most conscientiously – not. We will consider the first of these types to begin with.

We know from recent referendums in both the UK and Ireland that social media and grassroots campaigns can play a huge (perhaps even decisive) part in the outcome of any such poll. As such, it is worth recognising the role played by grassroots movements in advocating both for and against such a vote, including those that have their primary activity online. It is notable that these groups, from different perspectives, have all become active since the Brexit referendum. On the pro-union side, the Castlereagh Foundation is mentioned in the *New Decade, New Approach* document as a fund to 'support academic research through universities and other partners to explore identity and the shifting patterns of social identity in Northern Ireland'. Although there are few details about this, it is seen as 'a unionist push to create a civic voice for Britishness through research and educational material', and apart from occasional mentions by DUP politicians, its existence remains out of the public eye.[41] A more publicly visible pro-union movement is *These Islands*, which describes itself as a 'forum for debate' which 'stands unabashedly for the view that more unites the three nations of Great Britain than divides them, and that good relations between the various communities of Northern Ireland, Great Britain, and Ireland are all the more important to work for in the wake of Brexit'.[42]

Also responding to Brexit, but with an opposite objective, in January 2019, a conference called 'Beyond Brexit' held at the Waterfront Hall was primarily organised by the grouping Ireland's Future. This body also organised open letters, including one to 400 of the candidates in the Irish general election of February 2020, asking them to support the formation of a citizens' assembly on Irish unity. The letter argues that 'it is only right and prudent that a government plans for the future', and that 'we must debate and discuss, plan and prepare for constitutional change on our island'.[43] It is worth acknowledging that such civic action in even putting the term 'Irish unity' into public discourse, both north and south, was a remarkable step. In the years leading up to and after the GFA, the term 'united Ireland' became less common in policy and statements from Irish political parties, including Sinn Féin. Other terms with similar meaning but greater ambiguity were preferred instead, such as 'an agreed Ireland', 'a new Ireland', or 'an Ireland of Equals'.[44] While keen to stress the GFA as a staging post to a united Ireland, most republicans and nationalists accepted that the idea of a united Ireland lay some distance ahead in the future. A united Ireland became considered, at least in official nationalist discourse, more as an 'aspiration' than as a likelihood or even a very strong possibility. The term 'united Ireland' became increasingly the preserve of hardline or dissident republican parties and groups. The prospect of Brexit changed this dramatically. This is seen in the fact that Fine Gael Taoiseach Enda Kenny negotiated a statement from the European Council acknowledging that 'the entire territory of such a united Ireland would … be part of the EU' if there were a majority voting in favour of Irish unification in concurrent referendums on the two jurisdictions on the island.[45] Brexit reignited a phrase and an objective that even Sinn Féin had more or less moulded into an 'Ireland of Equals'. Brexit managed to reignite the very issue at the heart of both the conflict and the GFA. We can be reasonably sure that had Brexit not occurred, discussions regarding a united Ireland would be nonexistent, save in dissident rhetoric. Not only has dissident rhetoric received a boost with Brexit and the prospect of a hard border,[46] but the very presence of a 'united Ireland' as a 'live' concept in political and civic discourse across the island is an indication of the broader socio-political consequences of Brexit on the island.

Another example of the increasingly common use of the notion of Irish unity and a 32-county Ireland is seen in Think32, who describe themselves as a 'grassroots, cross-community, non-party political movement to promote and encourage debate on the reunification of Ireland'. Think32 have no dedicated website and are primarily active on Twitter, but in October 2019 there was a public separation among the members of Think32, with some members setting up a second account. Also using social media is Shared Island Podcast, a 'team who are promoting a new & shared Ireland', but which also have a dedicated website.[47] A more traditional grouping is Trade Unionists for a New and United Ireland, originally launched in early 2018, although its website has not been maintained.[48] Similarly from the left wing is Yes for Unity. This group is different from the other three nationalist groupings in that it is Eurosceptic. It describes itself as a 'socialist broad front campaign for Irish unity', founded in 2016 by activists with the goal of achieving a 'Socialist Republic'. Also gathering attention through means other than online tactics, the 'March for Irish unity' saw around a thousand participants in its first outing. Walking across the border down the River Foyle, from Lifford to Strabane, the march incorporated republican political organisations (such as Sinn Féin and the 32 County Sovereignty Movement), but it was carefully presented as 'non-party, non-political, non-sectarian, peaceful'. Although their motivations go to the very heart of the political divide that has been institutionalised in Northern Ireland, many groups see being 'apolitical' as key to their success.

The same is true of those groups that were initiated specifically to address Brexit and its fallout. 'Border Communities against Brexit' was one of the most high-profile groupings, and it made much use of props like old customs officers' uniforms and fake brick walls for photo opportunities along the Irish border. Other campaigns centred less on the ground and more in the digital sphere. Unsurprisingly, this included those initiatives that were specifically intended to represent young people, such as the Our Future, Our Choice campaign for a second referendum on EU membership. A different approach, and one that has not been either pro-Leave or pro-Remain but very much centred upon Brexit, has been taken by the business community. There has been a proliferation of cross-sectoral initiatives in its wake, sometimes gathered under the informal title of the 'NI Business Brexit Working Group'. This is an ad hoc group of fourteen umbrella business organisations that was mobilised first by 10 Downing Street in support of Prime Minister May's doomed backstop. Collaboration and communication within the group continued to gather momentum as Johnson's new Protocol was drawn up and the Withdrawal Agreement Act passed the House of Commons. Through lobbying and quiet conversations, the common concerns from the business community that were articulated by the group made their way into the shared objections raised by Northern Ireland's MPs to the Withdrawal Agreement Bill.[49] Such efforts were to no avail against Johnson's overbearing majority following the December 2019 landslide; nonetheless, the initiative was a significant development in Northern Ireland. It suggested that it is possible for businesses to create space for politicians to find common cause and make difficult decisions. A number of the key concerns that the business community raised about the Withdrawal Agreement were reflected in the *New Decade, New Approach* document. This shows the impact that such cooperation can have. It also shows the value of stakeholder input and engagement. And, of course, this is not confined to business, although the involvement of business organisations in cross-sectoral letters was once rare but is now a commonly used tactic. It is quite usual to see open letters signed by business groups, trade unions, human rights organisations, community organisations, chambers of commerce and professional associations. Letters of thanks to Speaker Nancy Pelosi for her support for the 1998 Agreement,[50] letters warning against a No Deal Brexit,[51] letters demanding the restoration of Stormont[52] ... all these reflect a growing trust among, and confidence in, cross-sectoral cooperation. Indeed, the principles of consultation, civic engagement and consensus-building that are contained in the *New Decade, New Approach* document hold some potential. Seeing these in light of the truly multilevel nature of the governance of Northern Ireland would be a crucial way of making sure that Northern Ireland is ready for the Brexit-related challenges and potential opportunities of the new decade.

No conclusion

The Church of Ireland Bishop of Clogher (later Archbishop of Armagh), the Rt Revd John McDowell, wrote an open letter to the recently installed Prime Minister Boris Johnson in July 2019. His diocese included most of the central Irish border region of Ireland, i.e. parishes which now lie divided by the external EU border. McDowell described the sense of fear in the region very well:

> the molten lava of the past flows hot and dangerous under the thin crust of the present. The ground on which people build and grow in the Border region feels particularly fragile today. It is almost possible to feel the heat of the past burning the soles of our feet.[53]

The greatest fear of those in Northern Ireland is that the future will mean a return to the distrust, polarisation and violence of the past.

The peace we have come to assume in Northern Ireland is far from a perfect peace. It is ragged at the edges and torn in the middle. It allows flags celebrating paramilitary organisations to fly from lampposts in front of shops and playgrounds. It expects mothers to bring their sons to be crippled by the shots of masked vigilante gunmen to their teenage knees and elbows. It accommodates the high walls topped by barbed wire that serve to shield neighbour from neighbour in the capital city of the new Northern Ireland. It sees families lose all their sons to suicide because they see no other way out. It advises women to numb the psychological pain of conflict trauma with prescription medication, and for their daughters to do the same. It scrawls racist graffiti on the homes of refugee families. It sweeps up the ashes from yet another sectarian arson attack, in the full knowledge that the flames will soon be lit again.

All these conditions can persist and yet we may still call this 'peace'; the Troubles are behind us, but conflict remains both a sullen presence and an insidious threat as Northern Ireland enters its second century.

Notes

1 Quotation from Taoiseach Leo Varadkar, press conference, Armagh, 14 March 2020. 'Coronavirus: Varadkar says his Government and NI Executive share same goal', *Belfast Telegraph*, 14 March 2020. Available at: www.belfasttelegraph.co.uk/news/northern-ireland/coronavirus-varadkar-says-his-government-and-ni-executive-share-same-goal-39044607.html. Accessed 10 April 2020.
2 'Michelle O'Neill calls for Northern Ireland schools to close over coronavirus', *Belfast Telegraph*, 13 March 2020. Available at: www.belfasttelegraph.co.uk/news/northern-ireland/michelle-oneill-calls-for-northern-ireland-schools-to-close-over-coronavirus-39042109.html. Accessed 10 April 2020.
3 Alex Kane, 'Michelle O'Neill and John O'Dowd have just made greater cross-border cooperation on coronavirus more, not less, difficult to achieve', *Belfast Telegraph*, 16 March 2020. Available at: www.belfasttelegraph.co.uk/opinion/comment/michelle-oneill-and-john-odowd-have-just-made-greater-cross-border-co-operation-on-coronavirus-more-not-less-difficult-to-achieve-39049083.html. Accessed 15 April 2020.
4 'Eastwood: Coordination required on coronavirus response', SDLP news, 13 March 2020. Available at: www.sdlp.ie/news/2020/eastwood-coordination-required-on-coronavirus-response/. Accessed 10 April 2020.
5 'Coronavirus: Close NI schools, urges Archbishop Eamon Martin', *BBC News*, 13 March 2020. Available at: www.bbc.co.uk/news/uk-northern-ireland-51868557. Accessed 10 April 2020.
6 'Schools closures spread as Stormont stalls on lockdown amid Coronavirus fears', *Irish News*, 16 March 2020. Available at: www.irishnews.com/news/northernirelandnews/2020/03/16/news/schools-to-voluntary-shut-down-amid-coronavirus-fears-1868507/. Accessed 10 April 2020.
7 'Coronavirus (Covid-19) Guidance Document for GAA Clubs', 13 March 2020. Available at: ulster.gaa.ie/wp-content/uploads/2020/03/Coronavirus-Note-for-Clubs.pdf. Accessed 10 April 2020.
8 'Irish Football Association statement: Coronavirus', 13 March 2020. Available at: www.irishfa.com/news/2020/march/irish-fa-statement-coronavirus. Accessed 10 April 2020.
9 'Update: Church of Ireland Guidance in relation to Novel Coronavirus (Covid-19)', Church of Ireland press release, 13 March 2020. Available at: www.ireland.anglican.org/news/9445/update-church-of-ireland-guidance. Accessed 10 April 2020.

10 It is only fair to note that some members of Varadkar's own cabinet were also taken by surprise by his statement from Washington, DC. 'Foster not briefed about Republic's coronavirus delay measures', RTÉ News, 12 March 2020. Available at: www.rte.ie/news/coronavirus/2020/0312/1121934-foster-northern-ireland-covid-19/. Accessed 15 December 2020.

11 'Statement by An Taoiseach Leo Varadkar On measures to tackle Covid-19 Washington', 12 March 2020. Available at: https://merrionstreet.ie/en/News-Room/News/Statement_by_An_Taoiseach_Leo_Varadkar_On_measures_to_tackle_Covid-19_Washington_12_March_2020.html. Accessed 10 April 2020.

12 'Political leaders and officials meet in Armagh to discuss Coronavirus strategy', UTV News, 14 March 2020. Available at: www.itv.com/news/utv/2020-03-14/political-leaders-and-officials-meet-in-armagh-to-discuss-coronavirus-strategy/. Accessed 10 April 2020.

13 The report of the public inquiry into the Renewable Heating Initiative scheme, which had a projected overspend of £700 million and triggered the collapse of the Executive in 2017. The report highlighted the limits of policy and administrative capacity in Northern Ireland and recommended a change to the ministerial code to enhance accountable decision-making.

14 'Coronavirus: Varadkar says his Government and NI Executive share same goal', *Belfast Telegraph*, 14 March 2020. Available at: www.belfasttelegraph.co.uk/news/northern-ireland/coronavirus-varadkar-says-his-government-and-ni-executive-share-same-goal-39044607.html. Accessed 10 April 2020.

15 Available at: https://twitter.com/ShonaMurray_/status/1239892821978513408?s=20. Accessed 10 April 2020.

16 Available at: https://m.facebook.com/story.php?story_fbid=2423098651123633&id=100002705648744?sfnsn=scwspwa&d=w&vh=i&extid=r52GSUIj3mayD1kX&d=w&vh=i. Accessed 10 April 2020.

17 'Covid-19 press conference', NI Executive, 27 March 2020. Available at: www.executiveoffice-ni.gov.uk/news/covid-19-press-conference-27-march-2020. Accessed 10 April 2020.

18 'A Joint statement following a COVID-19 call chaired by Secretary of State and Tanaiste', 31 March 2020. Available at: www.gov.uk/government/news/secretary-of-state-participates-in-joint-ministerial-covid-19-conference-call. Accessed 10 April 2020.

19 Mary E. Daly, *Brokering the Good Friday Agreement: The Untold Story* (Dublin: Royal Irish Academy, 2019); John Coakley and Jennifer Todd, *Negotiating a Settlement in Northern Ireland, 1969–2019* (Oxford: Oxford University Press, 2020).

20 Mary C. Murphy, *Northern Ireland and the European Union: The Dynamics of a Changing Relationship* (Manchester: Manchester University Press, 2014); Katy Hayward and Mary C. Murphy, 'The EU's Influence on the Peace Process and Agreement in Northern Ireland in Light of Brexit', *Ethnopolitics*, 17(3) (2018), 271–96.

21 Michel Barnier, 'Speech by Michel Barnier at the William J. Clinton Leadership Institute', Queen's University Belfast, 27 January 2020. Available at: https://

ec.europa.eu/commission/presscorner/detail/en/SPEECH_20_133. Accessed 10 April 2020.
22 'Apply for Irish passport if you can, advises DUP MP Ian Paisley', *Belfast Telegraph*, 27 June 2016. Available at: www.belfasttelegraph.co.uk/news/northern-ireland/apply-for-irish-passport-if-you-can-advises-dup-mp-ian-paisley-34835231.html. Accessed 10 April 2020.
23 '733,060 Irish passports issued in 2016 – Minister Flanagan', Department of Foreign Affairs press release, 5 January 2017. Available at: www.dfa.ie/news-and-media/press-releases/press-release-archive/2017/january/passport-numbers-2016/. Accessed 10 April 2020.
24 'Record number of Irish passports issued to NI residents in 2017', Belfast Live, 2 January 2018. Available at: www.belfastlive.co.uk/news/record-number-irish-passports-issued-14100462. Accessed 10 April 2020.
25 'Record 900,000 passport applications in 2019 – 94,000 from UK', *Irish Times*, 27 December 2019. Available at: www.irishtimes.com/news/ireland/irish-news/record-900–000-passport-applications-in-2019–94–000-from-uk-1.4124946. Accessed 10 April 2020.
26 The matter was temporarily addressed by the UK Home Office with a time-limited change to the process known as the 'EU settlement scheme', allowing family members of British or dual British–Irish citizens from Northern Ireland to apply for post-Brexit residency.
27 Feargal Cochrane, *Breaking Peace: Brexit and Northern Ireland* (Manchester: Manchester University Press, 2020), pp. 59–61.
28 The results of the University of Liverpool NI General Election Survey 2019 indicated that, in December 2019, 62.8 per cent would vote to remain in the EU in a second referendum. Available at: www.liverpool.ac.uk/media/livacuk/research/heroimages/The-University-of-Liverpool-NI-General-Election-Survey-2019-March-20.pdf. Accessed 10 April 2020.
29 *Revised Protocol on Ireland and Northern Ireland included in the Withdrawal Agreement*, 17 October 2019. Available at: https://ec.europa.eu/commission/publications/revised-protocol-ireland-and-northern-ireland-included-withdrawal-agreement_en. Accessed 10 April 2020.
30 For example, Boris Johnson stated in a debate in the House of Commons on 12 February 2019: 'We must extricate this country from the humiliation of the backstop'; he also tweeted the same comment. Available at: https://twitter.com/BorisJohnson/status/1095319443469676545?s=20. Accessed 15 April 2020.
31 Jon Stone, 'Minister admits Boris Johnson Brexit plan breaks international law', *Independent*, 8 September 2020. Available at: www.independent.co.uk/politics/brexit-deal-northern-ireland-brandon-lewis-boris-johnson-international-law-b417624.html. Accessed 19 September 2020.
32 All data taken from *Northern Ireland Life and Times Surveys*, 2016, 2017 and 2018. Available at: www.ark.ac.uk/nilt/. Accessed 10 April 2020.
33 *Northern Ireland Life and Times Survey*, 2019. Available at: www.ark.ac.uk/nilt/2019/Political_Attitudes/UNIRLIKL.html. Accessed 19 September 2020.

34 *Northern Ireland Life and Times Survey*, 2019. Available at: www.ark.ac.uk/nilt/2019/Political_Attitudes/UNIRFAV.html. Accessed 19 September 2020.
35 John Garry, Kevin McNicholl, Brendan O'Leary and James Pow, *Northern Ireland and the UK's Exit from the EU: What Do People Think?* (London: The UK in a Changing Europe, 2018). Available at: www.qub.ac.uk/sites/brexitni/BrexitandtheBorder/Report/Filetoupload%2C820734%2Cen.pdf. Accessed 15 April 2020.
36 Even those who advocated Leave and who see opportunities for Northern Ireland after Brexit note that its prospects are far from secure, with much depending on 'local businesses' ability to trade globally by taking advantage of new free trade deals' amid the 'transformational change' generated by Brexit (see Owen Polley and David Hoey, *An Agenda for Northern Ireland after Brexit: How to Build a Secure, Peaceful and Prosperous Future* (London: Global Britain, 2018). Available at: https://globalbritain.co.uk/wp-content/uploads/2017/03/NIs-future-after-Brexit-Final.pdf. Accessed 15 April 2020).
37 'Scotland election results 2019: SNP wins election landslide in Scotland', *BBC News*, 13 December 2019. Available at: www.bbc.co.uk/news/election-2019-50766014. Accessed 15 April 2020.
38 The 2019 Future of England Survey revealed that half of all those polled in Wales and England and almost two-thirds in Scotland thought that Brexit would be likely to lead to the break-up of the UK. It also found that majorities on both sides of the Brexit divide are willing to see substantial change to the union to get their own way on Brexit. Three-quarters of Leave voters in England and Wales believed the break-up of the UK would be worth it to take back control via Brexit; similar proportions of Remain voters stated their belief that staying in the EU is more important than holding the UK union together. See 'Future of England Survey reveals public attitudes towards Brexit and the union', 24 October 2019. Available at: www.cardiff.ac.uk/news/view/1709008-future-of-england-survey-reveals-public-attitudes-towards-brexit-and-the-union. Accessed 15 April 2020.
39 'Two-thirds of Irish would vote for united Ireland, poll says', Politico, 29 May 2019. Available at: www.politico.eu/article/election-two-thirds-of-irish-would-vote-for-united-ireland/. Accessed 15 April 2020.
40 A good example of this type of debate is the Cultural Traditions Group series of conferences and books based on conference proceedings published by the Institute of Irish Studies, Queen's University Belfast, beginning in 1989 and continuing into the late 1990s. See, for example, Maurna Crozier and Roy F. Foster (eds), *Cultural Traditions in Northern Ireland* (Belfast: Institute of Irish Studies, 1989).
41 Agenda NI, 'New Decade, New Approach', March 2020. Available at: www.agendani.com/new-decade-new-approach-2/. Accessed 10 April 2020.
42 Available at: www.these-islands.co.uk/. Accessed 10 April 2020.
43 Available at: https://irelandsfuture.com/letter-to-party-leaders/. Accessed 11 January 2021.

44 Katy Hayward, *Irish Nationalism and European Integration: The Official Redefinition of the Island of Ireland* (Manchester: Manchester University Press, 2009).
45 European Parliament, 'Outcome of the special European Council (Article 50) meeting of 29 April 2017', Post European Council Briefing, May 2017. Available at: www.europarl.europa.eu/RegData/etudes/ATAG/2017/603226/EPRS_ATA(2017)603226_EN.pdf. Accessed 30 April 2020.
46 'Brexit is a "huge help" to Irish republicanism, says dissident leader', *Guardian*, 6 March 2019. Available at: www.theguardian.com/world/2019/mar/06/brexit-is-a-huge-help-to-irish-republicanism-says-dissident-leader. Accessed 30 April 2020.
47 Available at: https://sharedireland.com/. Accessed 10 April 2020.
48 Available at: https://tu4ui.com/. Accessed 10 April 2020.
49 'Brexit: DUP, SDLP and Alliance suggest amendments to legislation', *BBC News*, 6 January 2020. Available at: www.bbc.co.uk/news/uk-northern-ireland-51000560. Accessed 15 April 2020.
50 Available at: www.belfasttelegraph.co.uk/news/northern-ireland/nancy-pelosi-urged-to-only-back-us-uk-trade-efforts-that-protect-peace-deal-38463828.html. Accessed 10 April 2020.
51 Available at: www.nicva.org/article/northern-ireland-civic-society-calls-for-a-no-deal-brexit-to-be-prevented. Accessed 10 April 2020.
52 Available at: www.londonderrychamber.co.uk/chamber-news/business-groups-call-for-restored-assembly/. Accessed 10 April 2020.
53 'Dear Prime Minister, please tread carefully in your handling of the Irish border', The Telegraph, 29 July 2019. Available at: https://www.telegraph.co.uk/politics/2019/07/26/dear-prime-minister-please-tread-carefully-handling-irish-border/. Accessed 23 March 2021.

Index

abortion 51–2, 213–14, 228–35
  in the Irish Republic 234
abstention at elections 197
abuse
  domestic 225–6
  sexual 149–50, 212, 226
accountability 83
activism 220–2
Adams, Gerry 47, 83, 139, 141, 259
affluence 268
'Agreement generation' 14, 194
Ahern, Bertie 1
Alderdice, Lord 115
Alliance Party 16, 19, 38, 52, 55–6, 180, 189, 213–15, 233
Allister, Jim 32
Alston, Philip 256, 267
amnesties 87–90, 93–4, 107, 111, 125
Amnesty International 231
Anderson, Gillian 151
Anderson, Martina 52–3
Anglo-Irish identity 179
apologising 83–5, 109
Ardoyne Commemoration Project (ACP) 80–1
Argentina 87
'armed struggle' process 5, 24, 46, 130–1, 258
artistic talents 16
austerity measures 254–9, 263–4, 268
  opposition to 258–9

'backstop' issue 283
Baka, Aphrodite 191
Baker, Stephen 130, 148, 157
Barnier, Michel 19, 279
Beatty, Christina 257
'bedroom tax' 260–1, 267
Belfast 10, 129–31, 146–8, 151–3, 245
Belfast Agreement (1998) 70; *see also* Good Friday Agreement
Belfast City Council 38, 52
Belfast City Hall 22, 38–9

Belfast Telegraph 24
Belfast Women's Collective 206
'benefit cap' 255, 261
Berardi, Franco 133
Blair, Tony 1, 37, 81, 92, 233, 246, 248, 251, 268
Bloody Sunday (1972) 84, 87–8, 132
Bloody Sunday Justice Campaign 81
Bloomfield Report (1998) 78, 80
Boal, Desmond 252
Border Communities against Brexit group 290
border poll 172–5, 189
Bourne, Alec 229
Breen-Smyth, Marie 86, 90
Brewer, John 86, 228
Brexit 17, 19, 23, 46–7, 54–6, 62–3, 176–7, 194, 197, 223, 234, 268, 279–91
  overall effect on Northern Ireland 184
  referendum on 265, 280
  'soft' form of 282
British Household Panel Survey 171
British Social Attitude Surveys 171
Britishness 181, 288
Brunsdon, Charlotte 146
Business Network of Northern Ireland 290

Cahill, Máiría 226
Cameron, David 84, 132
candidate selection 214–15
Carroll, Gerry 264–6
Carson, Jan 6
Castlereagh Foundation 288
Catholic Church and Catholic identity 170–1, 175, 181
ceasefires and 'ceasefire babies' 6, 71, 79, 94, 156–7, 247
Celtic Tiger boom 254
census of population (2021) 61
Chaney, Paul 211
Chiapas 228
child benefit 261
Chile 87

Chinese community 187
church attendance 170–1
church influence 196
citizenship 176
  full and *secondary* 108, 110
civic culture 164
Civic Forum and Civic Advisory Panel 17, 220, 223
civil society 16, 78, 85, 218, 221–2
Clár na mBan 206
Clinton, Bill 1
Coakley, John 165–6, 173–5
Cockburn, Cynthia 222
Coghlin, Sir Patrick (and Coghlin Report, 2020) 45, 53
collective amnesia 70
Commission for Historical Clarification (CEH) 77
Common Travel Area 176
community cohesion 168
community-led initiatives 71, 77
community sector 218–23
Confederation of British Industry (CBI) 184
'confidence and supply' arrangements 60, 282
conflict, 'hardening' of 166
conflict resolution 3–8, 11–14, 20, 70, 205, 223
  centrality of gender to 233
  liberal approaches to 72
conflict transformation 72, 79, 117
conflict transition 104, 205–8, 228
Connolly, Paul 193
'consent' principle 89, 164, 189
Conservative Party 250, 254–7, 266–8
consociational models of governance 1, 13–14, 17–18, 34, 166, 208, 221, 257
constitutional status of Northern Ireland 63, 190, 194, 265, 286–9
'constructive ambiguity' 61, 180, 281
  limits of 33–7
corporation tax 253–4, 259
corruption 53
Cory, Peter 82
councillors, mayors and chairs in local government 210
Coveney, Simon 19, 57, 277
covert operations 145–6
Covid-19 pandemic 14–15, 60–1, 268, 275–7
An Crann 79
Creasy, Stella 51–2
criminal prosecution 75–6, 82, 89
criminalisation 104–13, 125
criminality 5, 8, 194

'critical mass' of female political representation 210–11
cultural memory 167

Davie, Grace 167
Davison, Gerard ('Jock') 42
Dawson, Graham 132
deaths in the Troubles, pattern of 245
de Chastelain, John 115
decommissioning of weaponry 34–6, 104–5, 115, 207
Demange, Yann 142
demilitarisation 115
demobilisation 104, 115
Democratic Unionist Party (DUP) 18, 35–57, 90, 92, 132–3, 180, 190, 208, 212–16, 221, 232–4, 251–4, 257–9, 263–7, 276, 282
denial of suffering 83
deprivation 12, 194, 245–6, 254, 268
Derrida, Jacques 133–4
Derry Girls (tv series) 6, 154–7
DeSouza, Emma 280–1
Devlin, Anne 245
devolution 37, 156, 190, 192, 208, 251, 257, 260, 264
D'Hondt mechanism 13
Dickson, Anne 213
direct rule from Westminster 190, 250
disability 248–9, 262, 269
Disarmament, Demobilisation and Reintegration (DDR) mechanisms 104, 113–19
discrimination 81, 213, 217–18, 227
disillusionment with and disengagement from politics 23, 35, 196–7
diversity and division in Northern Ireland 195–6
divided societies 73, 80, 164–6, 189, 195–6
division of labour, gendered 216–17
Donnelly, Tom 83
Downey, John 92
drugs trade 5
Drumm, Maire 139

Eames–Bradley Report 7, 77, 88
Eastwood, Colum 55
Edwards, Sharni 52
election results 59, 210, 233, 287; *see also* Northern Ireland General Election Survey
Elff, Martin 193
El Salvador 87, 89
empathy 73
employment 247–8
equality of opportunity 207

ethnic differences and ethnic identity 168, 182–8
ethno-nationalism 10, 17–22, 41, 44, 50, 60, 152, 181, 217–19, 228–31, 234, 236, 252, 263–9
   and masculine traits 217
Eurobarometer surveys 168
Europa Hotel, Belfast 32
European Union (EU) 176, 182–4, 253–4, 279, 282–3
   funding from 107, 223
   see also Brexit
Euroscepticism 290
An Everlasting Piece 130
Extinction Rebellion movement 16, 195

fair employment legislation 11
Fair Employment and Treatment Order (FETO) 112, 118–19
The Fall 146–51
Families Acting for Innocent Relatives (FAIR) 82
Families Against Intimidation and Terror (FAIT) 82
Farry, Stephen 55
Father Ted 154
feminism 204, 206, 211–12, 218–24, 236
Fenton, Siobhán 3
Fifty Dead Men Walking 145–6
financial compensation for those injured in the Troubles 7
Finucane, John 82
Finucane, Pat 54–5, 82
The Firestarters 6
Fisher, Mark 133–5, 151
'flag' protests 10, 38–9, 179
Flanagan, Charlie 41
food banks and food parcels 40, 255–6, 268
foreign direct investment 247–8
forgiveness 83–4
Foster, Arlene 19, 44–9, 58, 61, 93, 213, 276, 278
Fothergill, Steve 257
400 Blows 137
Fresh Start Agreement (2015) (FSA) 6–8, 43, 57, 91–2, 133, 223, 259–60
Freud, Sigmund 133–4
Fulton, John 168

Galtung, Johan 8, 11, 72
Garry, John 179, 181
'gay marriage' 51
gender equality 207–8, 211–15, 235–7
gender identity 22
gender relations 205–8, 212, 216, 227–8

generational differences 193–6, 232
genocide 34
Ghost Box record label 134
Givan, Paul 48, 232
global financial crash (2008) 254, 262
Gomez, Raul 179
Good Friday Agreement (GFA) 1–4, 13–14, 18–20, 23, 32–4, 41, 43, 70, 74–5, 95, 97, 104, 107–9, 113–14, 118–19, 125, 130–2, 157–8, 164, 176, 188–9, 194, 204–9, 225, 235–7, 246, 250, 268–9, 279–82, 285, 289
   achievements of 1–2, 74
   alterations to 23
   arduous process since 2
   hegemonic status of 19–20
   ideological assumptions of 20
   meaning different things to different people 34
Good Vibrations 151–4
governance
   failures of 58
   structures of 17
Graff-McRae, Rebecca 138–9
Gramsci, Antonio 11, 20
grassroots truths 79
Grey, Chris 62
Guatemala 77, 86–7

Haass, Richard 39–40, 48, 258
Haass–Sullivan talks (2013) 88
Hackett, Claire 79–80
Hägglund, Martin 134
Halapannavar, Savita 229
Hamber, Brandon 73
Hamill, Robert 82
Hamilton, George 76
'hard border' issue 62–3, 234, 282, 289
Hargey, Deirdre 266
Harrison, Rory 226
hate crime 186–8
'hauntology' 133–5, 158
Hayward, Katy (co-author) 191–2
Healing Through Remembering (HTR) 77, 80–1, 96
Hermon, Lady Sylvia 55–6, 210
Hewitt, John 129
Hewitt, Michael 158
High Court (Belfast) 95
High Court (London) 256
Hill, John 147
Historical Enquiries Team (HET) 74–6, 91
Historical Investigations Unit (HIU) 91, 94
Hoewer, Melanie 228
holistic approach 71

hollowing out
  of the social system 254
  of the women's sector 223
Holmes, Eamonn 245
Hughes, Francis 139
human rights 235
humour, sense of 254
Hunger 132, 135–41
hunger strikes 139–41
Huyse, Luc 73

I, Daniel Blake 256
identity
  formation of 165–6
  inherited and *chosen* aspects of 166
  mixed 171–2
  see also national identity; political identity
'identity innovation' 166
illness, physical and mental 248; *see also* mental illness
immigration 10, 12, 182–8
imprisonment 75; *see also* prisoners, conflict-related
incumbency effects 215
Independent Commission on Information Retrieval (ICIR) 91
inequality 11–12, 247, 261–2, 265
infrastructure projects 251, 253
in-group identity 174
inquiries into the past 71, 74
intergenerational effects 4–5, 96–7, 108, 113, 168
Internal Market Bill 62–3
international law, breaking of 284
international relations 12
  realist and *liberal* schools of 4, 8
Invest NI 248–9
Irish language question 48–9, 58–9
Irish Republican Army (IRA) 83–4, 156
Irish unification 62

Jackson, Paddy 226
Jewish community 187
Johnson, Boris 54, 62–3, 94, 278, 283, 285, 290–1
Johnson, Donald C. 115
judiciary, the 11
justice 72

Kelly, Brian 252
Kelly, Gráinne 73
Kenny, Enda 289
key decisions needing cross-community support 190

killings, unsolved 7, 75–6
Kincora Boys' Home 149–50

Labour Force Survey 169, 182
Labour Party 233, 251–2
languages other than English 183
Lavery, Diarmuid 158
Lederach, John-Paul 8, 72–3, 96
legacy of the Troubles 4–8, 20, 70–1, 74, 94–8, 129, 132–3, 193, 227
  complexities in dealing with 71
Legg, George 140
Lehman Brothers 254
Leonard, Madeleine 193–4
Lewis, Brandon 62, 94, 278
LGBT+ rights 233
liberal attitudes 14, 190, 194, 233
Liberal Democrats 254–7
Lijphart, Arend 13
Lisburn Partnership Strategy 114
Lo, Anna 11, 187–8
Loach, Ken 256
Long, Declan 22
Long, Naomi 53
'long peace' 23, 33
Lost Lives 80, 158
Lundy, Patricia 76

McAlinden, Justice 7
McBride, Sam 53
McCallion, Elisha 55
McCann, Eamonn 264
McConnell, James 10
McCoy, Gráinne 219–20
McCracken, Niall 248
McDowell, John 291
McEvoy, Kieran 114
McGartland, Martin 146
McGee, Lisa 154
McGinn, Conor 52
MacGinty, Roger 12
McGrattan, Cillian 79, 138, 141
McGuigan, Kevin 42
McGuinness, Martin 2, 36–7, 44–7, 132, 250, 254, 257–9
McIlroy, Blane 226
McKay, Susan 245
McKee, Lyra 6, 49–50, 157
McKeown, Shelley 180
McKiernan, Joan 9
McLaughlin, Greg 130, 157
McLoone, Martin 142
McManus, Cathal 191–2
McNicholl, Kevin 179–81
McQueen, Steve 135–8
McWilliams, Monica 9
Magill, Martin 50

Maguire, Michael 94–5
majoritarianism 189
Making Women Seen and Heard initiative 220
making work pay 254–6
male dominance 205–10, 216–18, 221, 224, 229, 236
March for Irish unity 290
marching season 39
masculinity 217
  and violence 227
Maskey, Alex 32
May, Peter 93
May, Theresa 49, 54, 282–3, 290
media coverage 3
Members of the Legislative Assembly (MLAs) 18, 33, 189, 209, 284
Members of Parliament (MPs) 208
mental illness 4, 8, 248–9
Merchant Hotel 153
middle classes 268
The Mighty Celt 130–1
migration *see* immigration
Military Reconnaissance Force (MRF) 142–5
millionaires, number of 262
minorities, society of 165
misogyny 226
Mitchell, Claire 168
Mitchell, George 1
  principles set out by 43
mitigation measures 261, 266–7
Morgan, Sir Declan 92–3
Morris, Allison 226
Morris, Martin 226
Morrow, Duncan 196
The Most Fertile Man in Ireland 130
multiculturalism 10, 22
multinational corporations 253
murders, unsolved 7

Nagel, Joane 217
Nagle, John 18
national identity 171
  British, Irish or both 175–81
  neither one nor the other 190–4
nationalism 174, 179, 189–93
  comparison with unionism 213–14
Nelson, Brian 82
Nelson, Rosemary 82
'neoliberal peace' 12
neoliberalism 37–42, 250–4, 259, 263–5
neo-patriarchy 237
New Decade, New Approach document (2020) 7, 57–8, 71, 93–4, 223, 266, 288–91
New Labour *see* Labour Party

'new' Northern Ireland 131, 187, 258, 291
Ní Aoláin, Fionnuala 108
Nieminen, Tauno 115
Nolan, Paul 165, 249
Northern Ireland
  changes in 13, 16–17, 21–3
  continuity in 23
  future prospects for 196, 265
  moving on from its violent past 4, 129–31
  sparking of conflict in 11
  unease felt in 164
Northern Ireland Assembly 32, 36, 51, 57, 93–4, 189–90, 194, 234–5, 260–1, 266, 288
Northern Ireland Executive 2, 41–2, 47–8, 95, 234, 265–6, 275–8, 288
Northern Ireland General Election Survey 185, 193, 195, 231
Northern Ireland Life and Times (NILT) survey 50, 105, 165, 168–76, 185–91, 195, 285–6
Northern Ireland Women's Coalition (NIWC) 206–9, 217, 220
Northern Ireland Women's European Platform (NIWEP) 222
Northern Ireland Women's Rights Movement 206
'Northern Irish' as an identity 179–82
nostalgia 5–6, 14, 134–5, 151, 154, 157
nurses' strike 53–4

O'Dowd, Liam 13, 18
Offences Against the Person Act (1861) 229
O'Flynn, Ian 217
Ogle, Ian 6
O'Hearn, Denis 253
O'Kane, Eamonn 33
Olding, Stuart 226
O'Leary, Brendan 14
Ó Muilleoir, Máirtín 45
O'Neill, Michelle 45, 60–1, 275–8
'Operation Banner' 144
opinion makers, myopia of 3
opinion polls 232, 287
optimism in Northern Ireland 24
oral history 80
Oral History Archive (OHA) 92
Orange Order 39
O'Sullivan, Meghan 39–40, 258
O'Toole, Fintan 137–8, 141
Our Future, Our Choice campaign 290

Paisley, Ian 34–7, 132, 250, 254
Paisley, Ian Jr 280
Parades Commission 39
paramilitaries 5–9, 43, 75, 227
  cinematic portrayal of 130

parity of esteem and of treatment 13
The Passion 137
passport applications 280
Pat Finucane Centre 81
patriarchy 216, 218, 235; *see also* neo-patriarchy
Patterson, Glenn 23, 157
peace, 'negative' and 'positive' 72
peace-building 20–1, 72, 104–5
   formal or *informal* 205
peace dividend 12, 246–50, 268
'peace generation' 14, 194
'peace lines' 22, 148
peace-making
   liberal and *neoliberal* models of 11
   women's role in 206
peace process 23, 42, 46, 74, 88–9, 106, 156, 158, 205, 207, 235–6, 246, 257–8, 279
   high-level and *local* 2
   'messiness' of 33
   role of women in 204–6
   rosy image of 3
   starting point for 71
Pelosi, Nancy 291
People Before Profit Alliance (PBPA) 44, 52, 264–6
Peoples, Robyn 52
perpetuation of conflict 109
Personal Independence Payment (PIP) 255–6, 260, 266–7
'petition of concern' procedure 58
Phillips, Anne 211
Poland 186
polarisation 173, 262
   potential for 285–7
policing and the Police Service of Northern Ireland (PSNI) 5, 9–10, 36–9, 76, 85, 92–3, 148, 186–7, 225–6, 236
political 'deals' 13–14
political identity 165, 174, 178, 188–93
political prisoners 7
politicians, disenchantment with 17
pop music 133–5
population figures 182–3
Porter, Elizabeth 219
Portes, Jonathan 262
post-conflict society 9, 72, 110, 113, 117, 204, 228, 268
post-traumatic stress disorder 4
poverty 12, 42, 245, 249, 255–7, 262, 266, 268
power-sharing 1–2, 13–14, 34–6, 44–5, 48–9, 58–62, 74, 89, 93, 97, 132–3, 190, 207–8, 218, 220, 250
   threats to 59–62
prejudice 186–8, 193–5

PriceWaterhouseCoopers 38
Pride parade 16
Prior, Jim 250
prisoners, conflict-related 104–19, 126
Private Finance Initiative (PFI) 37–8, 251, 253
Progressive Unionist Party (PUP) 213
proportional representation (PR) 209
prosperity, economic 246–7, 267
Protestantism and Protestant identity 167, 170–1, 175, 181
Provisional IRA 34–7, 42, 130, 252, 257–8
public life, dysfunctionality of 18–19
public–private partnerships (PPPs) 251, 253
punishment attacks 5
punk rock 152–3
Purvis, Dawn 213

the Queen 46–7
Queen's University gathering (April 2018) 1–2
quotas by gender 222

racial prejudice 10
racism 186–8
recidivism 114
reconciliation 71–4, 83, 96, 98
   often ill-defined 73
   political and *societal* 74
   three steps towards 73
   and transitional justice 72–4
redundancies 258–9
Reed, Howard 262
refugees 185
reintegration of prisoners 104–10, 114–19, 125
relatives by marriage 186, 195–6
Relatives for Justice group 81
release of prisoners 104–5, 111
relevance of the party-political system 196
religious affiliation 169–75
   communal 173–4
   reporting of 'no religion' 171–5
religious identity 167–75
   changes in 168–71
   ratio of Protestants to Catholics 169
religious observance 167–71
   church attendance 170–1
   intensity of 168–9
Renewable Heating Incentive (RHI) 18, 44–6, 53, 58, 277
reproductive rights 51, 204, 224, 228–36
Resurgam organisation 106
Review Panel for conflict-related convictions 115–24
rights of *individuals* and of *groups* 111
Robinson, Gavin 55

Robinson, Iris 51
Robinson, Peter 10–11, 37, 44–5
Rolston, Bill 79–80
Rooney, Eilish 219
Royal Ulster Constabulary (RUC) 76

St Andrews Agreement (2006) 36, 74, 119, 190, 207, 220–1, 235
saliency of social and political arrangements 193
same-sex marriage 229, 234
Sands, Bobby 136–41
Saville Report (2010) 7, 84, 87, 132
Scappaticci, Freddie 145–6
scepticism 24
Scottish Assembly 211
Scottish independence 287
sectarianism 2, 9–10, 17–19, 22, 44, 47, 106, 188, 269, 291–2
　'banal' 194
secularisation 168
security checks (SCs) 113
security threats 225–7, 235
segregation 194, 216
　physical and *cultural* 22
Sens, Andrew D. 115
'71 (film) 142–4
Sex Discrimination Act (2002) 215
sexism 217, 226
sexual abuse of children in care 149–50
Shadow Dancer 145
Shankill bombing (1993) 83
Shared Island (podcast) 289
Shelley, Pete 135
Shirlow, Peter (co-author) 96, 109, 114
Simpson, Kirk 79
Sinn Féin 2, 18–19, 34–60, 83, 88, 91–2, 95, 106–7, 118, 125, 132–3, 139–42, 180, 190, 208, 212, 214, 221, 232–4, 251–4, 257–60, 263–7, 276, 287, 289
　in the Irish Republic 59, 259
Smith, Julian 7, 57
social bonding 168
social class 246–7, 258, 263–9
　politics of 263–7
social conservatism 236
Social Democratic and Labour Party (SDLP) 19, 34–6, 42, 88, 91, 180, 189–90, 214, 233, 258–9, 276
social exclusion 108
social learning 73
social movements 218
social sector size criteria 266
social structures 167
socialisation 167
socialism 264–6

'soft' Catholic support for the Union and for Irish unity 173
South Africa 85–9
special advisers 53, 58, 120–1
Spence, Gusty 84
Starmer, Sir Keir 226
stereotyping 218
stigmatic shaming 109, 119
Storey, Bobby 60–1
Stormont House Agreement (2014) (SHA) 40–3, 71, 91–4, 133, 258
Stormont institutions, suspension of 2–3, 23, 33–7, 56–9, 94, 190, 207, 220, 229, 234, 250–1, 257, 265–6
storytelling 78–80, 85
Strategic Investment Board 37, 251
Sturgeon, Nicola 278
subvention from Westminster 268
suicide 5, 291

Tar Isteach group 106
Taylor, Rupert 17
Teenage Kicks 152
terrorism, definition of 112
Thatcher, Margaret 250–1
These Islands movement 288
Think32 movement 289
Thompson, Judith 95
Todd, Jennifer 166, 180
tokenism 214
Tonge, Jonathan 179
Tookey, Chris 137
tourism 32, 129
Trade Unionists for a New and United Ireland 289–90
trans people 195
transitional justice 71–3, 81, 97, 195
　recent broadening of concept 72–3
transnational perspectives 195
transversalism 219
trauma and traumatisation 4–5, 8, 74, 76, 80, 94–7, 132, 248, 291
truth, subjective forms of 79
truth commissions
　problems with 86–7
　proposals for 71, 82, 85–90, 125
'truth and reconciliation' process 7, 132
truth recovery 70–1, 76–8, 81, 86–90, 96–7
turnout at elections 17, 44
'two-child rule' 261
'two communities' thesis 165, 177, 181, 189, 196

UK–EU Joint Committee 287
'Ulster' identity 179
Ulster Unionist Party (UUP) 34–8, 56, 189–90, 213–16, 233, 276

unemployment rate 249
unification of Ireland 172–5, 190, 285–90
unionism 212–14, 174, 179, 189–93, 196–7
  comparison with nationalism 213–14
United Kingdom, fractious relations between countries of 63
United Nations (UN) 87, 222–4, 227, 256
Universal Credit 256, 260–1, 266–7
upbringing, religious 169

Van Deth, Jan 193
Varadkar, Leo 49, 276, 278
vetting of ex-prisoners 110–13, 116–25
  case studies of 120–5
victims' groups 81–2
victims of violence 21
  definition of 95
  hierarchies of 8–13
vigilantes 5
Villiers, Theresa 41–2
violence
  agents of 21
  domestic 9, 224, 227
  ethno-sectarian 225–6
  forms of 9, 21
  gender-based 204, 226–8
  political 1–2, 5, 12, 22, 42, 95, 149, 153, 193, 204, 245–8
  racially-motivated 10
  sexual 226
  see also women, violence against
voting, weighted 13

Walsh, Enda 136
war and peace, nature of 4–5, 8–12, 20–1, 72
Ward, Margaret 211
Ward, Peter 84
WAVE Trauma (group) 77, 80–1
Weir, Peter 276
welfare reform 40–4, 91, 107, 255–67
  impact of 260–3
  opposition to 259

welfare state provision 256, 267
Wells, Jim 231–2
Welsh National Assembly 211
West Tyrone Voice 82
Whyte, John 167
Widgery Inquiry 81–2
Wild About Harry 130–1
Wilson, Marie and Gordon 83
Wired magazine 247
With or Without You 130
women 204–37
  'back-room' work of 216
  candidate selection 214–15
  in decision-making 213, 220–3
  inequality faced by 204, 212–18
  'innate' peacefulness of 205–6
  representation in electoral politics 208–13, 218
  role in the peace process 204–6
  status of 235–6
  violence against 9–12, 20, 151, 224–5, 228, 236
Women Into Politics 220
Women's Aid 225–7
Women's Centres Regional Partnership 226–7
women's interests and issues 211, 219, 222
women's organisations, groups and centres 220–1
women's rights 204–7, 212, 235–6
Women's Support Network (WSN) 219–20
work–life balance 216
working-class communities 268
worklessness 248–9
world-views 167
Wright, Billy 82

Yes for Unity group 290
Young, Iris 11
young people 4–6, 14, 16, 22, 51–2, 106, 171, 175–81, 193–5, 290
Yuval-Davis, Nira 219

CPSIA information can be obtained
at www.ICGtesting.com
Printed in the USA
JSHW032140240921
19011JS00004B/152